THE LEGACIES (

MW01254073

This is the first collection to exa... ....on.
It considers the extent to which ... .temporary laws, policies and practices
affecting people with disabilities are moving towards the promised end point
of enhanced social and political participation in the community, while others
may instead reinstate, continue or legitimate historical practices associated with
this population's institutionalisation. Bringing together 20 contributors from
the UK, Canada, Australia, Spain and Indonesia, the book speaks to overarching themes of segregation and inequality, interlocking forms of oppression and
rights-based advancements in law, policy and practice. Ultimately this collection
brings forth the possibilities, limits and contradictions in the roles of law and
policy in processes of institutionalisation and deinstitutionalisation, and directs
us towards a more nuanced and sustained scholarly and political engagement
with these issues.

Oñati International Series in Law and Society

A SERIES PUBLISHED FOR THE OÑATI INSTITUTE
FOR THE SOCIOLOGY OF LAW

General Editors
Rosemary Hunter   David Nelken

Founding Editors
William L F Felstiner   Eve Darian-Smith

Board of General Editors
Carlos Lugo, Hostos Law School, Puerto Rico
Jacek Kurczewski, Warsaw University, Poland
Marie-Claire Foblets, Leuven University, Belgium
Ulrike Schultz, Fern Universität, Germany

Recent titles in this series

**For the complete list of titles in this series, see
'Oñati International Series in Law and Society' link at
www.bloomsburyprofessional.com/uk/series/
onati-international-series-in-law-and-society**

The Legacies of Institutionalisation

Disability, Law and Policy in the 'Deinstitutionalised' Community

Edited by
Claire Spivakovsky
Linda Steele
and
Penelope Weller

Oñati International Series in Law and Society

A SERIES PUBLISHED FOR THE OÑATI
INSTITUTE FOR THE SOCIOLOGY OF LAW

•HART•
OXFORD • LONDON • NEW YORK • NEW DELHI • SYDNEY

HART PUBLISHING

Bloomsbury Publishing Plc

Kemp House, Chawley Park, Cumnor Hill, Oxford, OX2 9PH, UK

1385 Broadway, New York, NY 10018, USA

29 Earlsfort Terrace, Dublin 2, Ireland

HART PUBLISHING, the Hart/Stag logo, BLOOMSBURY and the Diana logo are
trademarks of Bloomsbury Publishing Plc

First published in Great Britain 2020

First published in hardback, 2020
Paperback edition, 2022

A catalogue record for this book is available from the British Library.

Library of Congress Cataloging-in-Publication Data

Names: Disability and (Virtual) Institutions?: Interventions, Integration and Inclusion (Conference)
(2018 : (Oñate, Spain) | Spivakovsky, Claire, editor. | Steele, Linda, 1981- editor. |
Weller, Penelope, editor. | Oñati International Institute for the Sociology of Law, organizer.

Title: The legacies of institutionalism : disability, law and policy in the 'deinstitutionalised'
community / edited by Claire Spivakovsky, Linda Steele and Penelope Weller.

Description: Oxford ; New York : Hart, 2020. | Series: Oñati international series in law and society |
"This manuscript emerged from a workshop that was held in June 2018 at the Oñati International
Institute for the Sociology of Law in the Basque Country."—ECIP acknowledgements. |
Includes bibliographical references and index.

Identifiers: LCCN 2020009657 (print) | LCCN 2020009658 (ebook) |
ISBN 9781509930739 (hardcover) | ISBN 9781509930746 (epub)

Subjects: LCSH: People with disabilities—Legal status, laws, etc.—Congresses. | Inmates of institutions
—Legal status, laws, etc.—Congresses. | People with disabilities—Institutional care—Congresses.

Classification: LCC K1970.A6 D57 2018 (print) | LCC K1970.A6 (ebook) | DDC 344.03/240485—dc23

LC record available at https://lccn.loc.gov/2020009657

LC ebook record available at https://lccn.loc.gov/2020009658

ISBN: HB: 978-1-50993-073-9
PB: 978-1-50994-431-6
ePDF: 978-1-50993-075-3
ePub: 978-1-50993-074-6

Typeset by Compuscript Ltd, Shannon

To find out more about our authors and books visit www.hartpublishing.co.uk. Here you will find
extracts, author information, details of forthcoming events and the option to sign up for our newsletters.

Acknowledgements

THIS MANUSCRIPT EMERGED from a workshop that was held in June 2018 at the Oñati International Institute for the Sociology of Law in the Basque Country. Claire Spivakovsky, Linda Steele and Penelope Weller would like to thank the Institute for choosing to support our workshop and for enabling us to run it at the Institute's beautiful premises. In particular, we would like to thank Malen Gordoa for her outstanding work in supporting and organising our group during our workshop and Leire Kortabarria for her guidance in the development of this edited collection.

Our workshop at the Institute would not have been possible without the excellent contributions to the initial application by both Fleur Beaupert and Melania Moscoso Pérez, including Melania's willingness to connect us with other scholars located in Spain. We are also grateful to all of those who contributed papers to the workshop, both in person and by skype. Your enthusiasm enlivened our discussion and enabled us to develop a shared vision for this collection. Thank you. The workshop attendees were: Katie Aubrecht (skype), Roxanne Mykitiuk, Eduardo Díaz Velázquez, Ameil Joseph, Leanne Dowse, Sheila Wildeman, Claire Spivakovsky, Elvira Pértega Andía, Linda Steele, Shelley Bielefeld and Fleur Beaupert (skype), Melania Moscoso Pérez and R. Lucas Platero, Salvador Cayuela Sánchez, Isabel Karpin and Karen O'Connell, Dio Ashar Wicaksana, Peter Bartlett, Liz Brosnan, Lucy Series, Jill Stavert and Penelope Weller.

Linda Steele and Penelope Weller would like to thank Claire Spivakovsky for leading the development of the book, including supporting the copy-editing process.

Finally, we would like to thank Hart Publishing, in particular, Rosamund Jubber and Rosemarie Mearns for their support and guidance bringing this edited collection project to fruition.

Contents

PART ONE
POWER DYNAMICS THAT SHAPE THE
CONDITIONS AND POSSIBILITIES OF PEOPLE WITH
DISABILITIES WITHIN AND BEYOND SITES
OF PHYSICAL CONFINEMENT

Notes on Contributors

Peter Barlett is the Nottinghamshire Healthcare NHS Trust Professor of Mental Health Law at the School of Law and Institute of Mental Health, University of Nottingham, England.

Fleur Beaupert is an independent scholar in Australia.

Shelley Bielefeld is an ARC DECRA Fellow and Senior Lecturer at Griffith Law School at Griffith University, Australia.

Liz Brosnan is a Research Associate on the Wellcome funded EURIKHA Project based at the Service User Research Enterprise at the Institute of Psychiatry, Psychology and Neuroscience, Kings College London, England.

Salvador Cayuela Sánchez is an Associate Professor in the Faculty of Medicine of Albacete, University of Castilla-La Mancha, Spain.

Eduardo Díaz Velázquez is the Director of the Centro Español de Documentación sobre Discapacidad (CEDD), SIIS Centro de Documentación y Estudios, Spain.

Leanne Dowse is Professor and Chair in Intellectual Disability and Behaviour Support at the University of New South Wales, Australia.

Ameil Joseph is an Associate Professor in the School of Social Work at McMaster University, Canada.

Isabel Karpin is a Distinguished Professor in the Faculty of Law at the University of Technology, Australia.

Melania Moscoso Pérez is a Tenured Researcher at the Instituto de Filosofía, at the Centre for Human and Social Sciences of the Spanish National Research Council, Spain.

Roxanne Mykitiuk is a Professor of law at Osgoode Hall Law School, York University, Canada.

Karen O'Connell is an Associate Professor in the Faculty of Law at the University of Technology, Australia.

Elvira Pértega Andía is a PhD candidate in law at the University of Technology Sydney.

R Lucas Platero is a Juan de La Cierva Researcher at the University of Barcelona, Spain.

Lucy Series is a Wellcome Research Fellow and Lecturer in Law at the Cardiff School of Law and Politics, Cardiff University, Wales.

Karen Soldatic is an Associate Professor at the Institute for Culture and Society, Western Sydney University, Australia.

Claire Spivakovsky is a Senior Lecturer in Criminology in the School of Social and Political Sciences at the University of Melbourne, Australia.

Jill Stavert is a Professor of Law and Director of the Centre for Mental Health and Capacity Law, Edinburgh Napier University, Scotland.

Linda Steele is a Senior Lecturer in the Faculty of Law at the University of Technology, Australia.

Penelope Weller is a Professor in Law at the Graduate School of Business and Law, RMIT University, Australia.

Dio Ashar Wicaksana is the Executive Director of Indonesian Judicial Monitoring Society, Faculty of Law, University of Indonesia, Indonesia.

Sheila Wildeman is an Associate Professor of Law at the Schulich School of Law at Dalhousie University, Canada.

Introduction: The Lasting Legacies of Institutionalisation

Questioning Law's Roles in the Emancipation of People with Disabilities

CLAIRE SPIVAKOVSKY, LINDA STEELE AND PENELOPE WELLER

F ROM THE 1970s onward, governments in several Western jurisdictions began to close large institutional settings, such as mental asylums and move people with disabilities[1] into the community. This process is what is commonly referred to as 'deinstitutionalisation'. While deinstitutionalisation has been lauded as one of the most significant and positive developments in the history of people with disabilities, questions have been raised about the extent to which it has achieved its aims of enhancing the social and political participation of people with disabilities within the community. Not only does research suggest that, in the 'post-deinstitutionalisation' era, people with disabilities have been left with insufficient social, economic and health care support within the community, including poor access to appropriate housing and voluntary community-based mental health treatment,[2] but some critical scholars have begun to argue that these well-known failures of deinstitutionalisation provide new opportunities for control, confinement and segregation in the post-deinstitutionalisation context. Ben-Moshe, for example, argues that presenting the 'failure' of deinstitutionalisation in terms of unmet individual housing,

---

[1] The United Nations Convention on the Rights of Persons with Disabilities (CRPD) defines 'persons with disabilities' as including 'those who have long-term physical, mental, intellectual or sensory impairments which in interaction with various barriers may hinder their full and effective participation in society on an equal basis with others' (Article 1). The CRPD moves beyond a purely medical and diagnostic approach to disability, stating in the Preamble that 'disability is an evolving concept and that disability results from the interaction between persons with impairments and attitudinal and environmental barriers that hinders their full and effective participation in society on an equal basis with others'.

[2] M Dear and J Wolch, *Landscapes of Despair: From Deinstitutionalization to Homelessness* (Princeton, Princeton University Press, 1987).

financial and medical needs can be used to justify an eventual and 'inevitable' return to the asylum, with the certainty the asylum provides emerging as the only way to manage people with disabilities.[3] In the meantime, however, we have already moved down the path of relocating people with disabilities to other institutional settings such as group homes, nursing homes and prisons.[4] We have also subjected people with disabilities to other institution-like forms of control and restraint within the community – such as chemical restraints[5] – which can amount to less visible, or 'virtual' forms of institutionalisation. And we have dragged our feet: some people with disabilities have only very recently been released from the large-scale, locked institutional settings that were supposedly 'dismantled' decades ago.[6]

Recently, the United Nations Convention on the Rights of Persons with Disabilities (CRPD) demanded completion of the unfinished business of deinstitutionalisation. Article 19 of the CRPD provides for 'the equal right of all persons with disabilities to live in the community'. The UN Disability Committee has stated that to realise this right:

> States parties must adopt a strategy and a concrete plan of action for deinstitutionalization. It should include the duty to implement structural reforms, to improve accessibility for persons with disabilities within the community and to raise awareness among all persons in society about inclusion of persons with disabilities within the community.

> Deinstitutionalization also requires a systemic transformation, which includes the closure of institutions and the elimination of institutionalizing regulations as part of a comprehensive strategy, along with the establishment of a range of individualized support services, including individualized plans for transition with budgets and time frames as well as inclusive support services.[7]

---

[3] L Ben-Moshe, 'Why Prisons are not "the New Asylums"' (2017) 19(3) *Punishment & Society* 272.

[4] B Harcourt, 'From the Asylum to the Prison: Rethinking the Incarceration Revolution' (2006) 84 *Texas Law Review* 1751. Available at: www.law.uchicago.edu/files/file/harcourt_institutionalization_final.pdf; A Hatch, *Silent Cells: The Secret Drugging of Captive America* (Minneapolis, University of Minnesota Press, 2019); AR Hatch, M Xavier-Brier, B Attell and E Viscarra, 'Soldier, Elder, Prisoner, Ward: Psychotropics in the Era of Transinstitutionalization' in BL Perry (ed), *50 Years After Deinstitutionalization: Mental Illness in Contemporary Communities* (Emerald Publishing, Bingley, 2015); N Spagnuolo, 'Building Back Wards in a "Post" Institutional Era: Hospital Confinement, Group Home Eviction, and Ontario's Treatment of People Labelled with Intellectual Disabilities' (2016) 36(4) *Disability Studies Quarterly*. Available at: www.dsq-sds.org/article/view/5279/4480.

[5] E Fabris, *Tranquil Prisons: Chemical Incarceration Under Community Treatment Orders* (University of Toronto Press, Toronto, 2011); E Fabris and K Aubrecht, 'Chemical Constraint: Experiences of Psychiatric Coercion, Restraint, and Detention as Carceratory Techniques' in L Ben-Moshe, C Chapman and AC Carey (eds), *Disability Incarcerated: Imprisonment and Disability in the United States and Canada* (New York, Palgrave Macmillan, 2014) 185.

[6] Ben-Moshe, 'Why Prisons are not "the New Asylums"' (2017) 272.

[7] UN Committee on the Rights of Persons with Disabilities. *General Comment No 5 (2017) on Living Independently and Being Included in the Community*. CRPD/C/GC/5 paras 57–58. Available at: www.tbinternet.ohchr.org/_layouts/15/treatybodyexternal/Download.aspx?symbolno=CRPD/C/GC/5&Lang=en.

Lawson identifies Article 19 as the first time in international human rights law that such a right has been recognised.[8]

More broadly, the CRPD has put a spotlight on the inequality, discrimination, impoverishment and social and political marginalisation of people with disabilities in contemporary society and provided instruments for their redress. The CRPD provides for the protection and fulfilment of people with disabilities' human rights, including self-determination with respect to accommodation and living arrangements (Article 19a), relationships (Article 23) and health care (Article 25) and that – on an equal basis with others – people with disabilities have the right to life (Article 10) and an adequate standard of living (Article 28). The CRPD also provides that people with disabilities should not be subject to restraint or deprivation of liberty on a basis related to their disability (Article 14) and that measures must be taken to prevent all forms of exploitation, violence and abuse experienced by this group both within and outside the home (Article 16). In these ways, the CRPD offers significant promise for changing the current circumstances of people with disabilities in society. It provides tools to challenge institutionalisation itself, as well as inequitable and discriminatory treatment of people with disabilities across a range of fronts.

Yet, questions have been raised about the pace and extent to which the CRPD effects change at a domestic level. Socio-legal scholars point to contemporary laws, policies and practices that continue to limit and sometimes breach the rights of people with disabilities to flourish within the 'deinstitutionalised' community.[9] It is a timely moment, therefore, to reflect on law's role in the lives of people with disabilities and the complex contributions law makes to contemporary policies and practices affecting people with disabilities' participation in the community. In this collection, we and our contributors consider the extent to which contemporary laws, policies and practices in the post-deinstitutionalisation era continue or legitimate historical practices associated with this population's institutionalisation. The collection brings together contributors from across the world and speaks to overarching themes of segregation and inequality, interlocking forms of oppression and rights-based advancements in law, policy and practice. Some necessary foundations for engaging with these themes are offered below.

THE LASTING LEGACIES OF INSTITUTIONALISATION

Institutionalisation has a long history in western jurisdictions. 'Madmen' and 'lunatics' were placed in shrines, monasteries and 'madmen's towers' in the thirteenth century and later in specialised 'hospitals' such as the infamous 'Bedlam'

---

[8] A Lawson, 'People with Psychosocial Impairments or Conditions, Reasonable Accommodation and the Convention on the Rights of Persons with Disabilities' (2008) 26(2) *Law in Context: A Socio-Legal Journal* 62, 62–63.

[9] In relation to institutionalisation, see R Stanev and S Wildeman, 'Freedom: A Work in Progress' in E Flynn, A Arstein-Kerslake, C de Bhalis and ML Serra (eds), *Global Perspectives on Legal*

hospital in London and the Hotel Dieu in Paris.[10] In the 'great confinement' of the seventeenth century, large hospitals and workhouses provided compulsory 'refuge' to abandoned children, the poor, the indigent, prostitutes, petty thieves, beggars and the 'incurable'.[11] In the nineteenth century 'new', 'humane' asylums emerged to replace the brutality of these 'old' institutional practices and were characterised by figures such as Philippe Pinel as 'casting off the chains'.[12] During these centuries, imperial nations brought institutionalisation to colonies and, along with criminal justice and child welfare institutions, these disability institutions were central to the establishment of colonial authority and colonial nation building and, in turn, to enacting and legitimating Indigenous land dispossession and genocide.[13]

It was not until the second half of the twentieth century that the use of mass institutionalisation as an important tool for managing people with disabilities as a population began to fall out of favour. Multiple factors and conditions contributed to this shift in popularity, notably the emergence of rights-based logics from within the Scandinavian scholarship of the late 1960s and early 1970s. For example, Bank-Mikkelsen[14] and Nirje[15] both promoted the

---

Capacity Reform: Our Voices, Our Stories, Routledge, Abingdon & New York, 2018); L Steele, K Swaffer, L Phillipson and R Fleming, 'Questioning Segregation of People Living with Dementia in Australia: An International Human Rights Approach to Care Homes' (2019) 8(3) *Laws* 18. Available at: www.doi.org/10.3390/laws8030018. In relation to mental health treatment, see F Beaupert, 'Silencing Prote(x)t: Disrupting the Scripts of Mental Health Law' (2018) 41(3) *UNSW Law Journal* 746. Available at: www.unswlawjournal.unsw.edu.au/wp-content/uploads/2018/09/Beaupert.pdf; P Weller, 'Mental Capacity and States of Exception: Revisiting Disability Law with Giorgio Agamben' (2017) 31(3) *Continuum* 400. In relation to sterilisation, see L Steele, 'Court-authorised Sterilisation and Human Rights: Inequality, Discrimination and Violence Against Women and Girls with Disability?' (2016) 39(3) *UNSW Law Journal* 1002. Available at: www.classic.austlii.edu.au/au/journals/UTSLRS/2016/32.html. In relation to criminal justice, see E Baldry, 'Rights of Persons with Disabilities not to be Criminalised' in E Stanley (ed), *Human Rights and Incarceration: Critical Explorations* (Cham, Palgrave Macmillan, 2018) 53; C Spivakovsky, 'From Punishment to Protection: Containing and Controlling the Lives of People with Disabilities in Human Rights' (2014) 16(5) *Punishment & Society* 560, doi: 10.1177/1462474514548805. In relation to aged care, see Steele, Swaffer, Phillipson and Fleming, 'Questioning Segregation' (2019).

[10] R Porter, *The Greatest Benefit to Mankind: A Medical History of Humanity from Antiquity to the Present* (London, Fontana Press, 1992) 127.

[11] M Foucault, *Madness and Civilisation* (London, Tavistock, 1961).

[12] J Crosby, D Harper and P Reavey, *Psychology, Mental Health and Distress* (New York, Palgrave Macmillan, 2013) 30.

[13] S Avery, *Culture is Inclusion: A Narrative of Aboriginal and Torres Strait Islander People with Disability* (First People's Disability Network (Australia), Sydney, 2018); C Chapman, 'Five Centuries' Material Reforms and Ethical Reformulations of Social Elimination' in Ben-Moshe, Chapman and Carey (eds), *Disability Incarcerated* (2014) 25; C Coleborne and D MacKinnon, 'Psychiatry and its Institutions in Australia and New Zealand: An Overview' (2006) 18(4) *International Review of Psychiatry* 371; C Cunneen, E Baldry, D Brown, M Schwartz and A Steel, *Penal Culture and Hyperincarceration: the Revival of the Prison* (Routledge, Abingdon, 2013).

[14] N Bank-Mikkelsen, 'A Metropolitan Area in Denmark: Copenhagen' in R Kugel and W Wolfensberger (eds), *Changing Patterns in Residential Services for the Mentally Retarded* (Washington DC, President's Committee on Mental Retardation, 1969).

[15] B Nirje, 'The Normalisation Principle and its Human Management Implications' in Kugel and Wolfensberger (eds), *Changing Patterns* (1969).

rights-based principle of 'normalisation', arguing that people with disabilities share the same rights as other citizens and that all citizens are entitled to live a normal life within the community. Indeed, Wolfensberger proposed that it was this rights-based logic which ultimately 'broke the back of the institutional movement'.[16] There were, however, other factors and conditions at play. There was growing disquiet among the general public about the operation of large-scale institutions, especially after a series of exposés documented the human rights abuses taking place within them.[17] The rising costs of institutions, at a time when many countries were experiencing fiscal crises, became politically problematic.[18] There were also broader shifts taking place at that time in the nature of social control and welfare capitalism.[19] In combination, these factors appear to have eroded faith in the practices and processes of institutionalisation and, from the 1970s onwards, a process of deinstitutionalisation began in many countries.

Despite the trend outlined above, versions of institutionalisation persist. Large institutional settings such as mental asylums have – for the most part – closed down, but the legacies of institutionalisation – that is, the logics of segregation, of coercive 'care' and eugenics that underpinned the practice of institutionalisation – continue to be far more difficult to dismantle. This is why it is common within disability studies to speak not of deinstitutionalisation but of *trans*-institutionalisation.[20] Indeed, research from the decade immediately following the onset of deinstitutionalisation of people with disabilities shows that many were moved from mental asylums into smaller institutions like group homes,[21] nursing homes,[22] or the other key form of large-scale institution for population management in society: prisons.[23]

Additionally, even in circumstances where people with disabilities have returned to the community unfettered, many are yet to experience the full promise of 'normalisation' that was made at the time of deinstitutionalisation. Some people with disabilities are still prevented from or limited in their equal and effective participation in the political and public life of their country, for example

---

[16] W Wolfensberger, 'A Contribution to the History of Normalization with Primary Emphasis on the Establishment of Normalization in North America between ca. 1967–75' in R Flynn and R Lemay (eds), *A Quarter Century of Normalization and Social Role Valorization Evolution and Impact* (Ottawa, University of Ottawa Press, 1994) 60.

[17] C Chapman, A Carey and L Ben-Mosche, 'Reconsidering Confinement: Interlocking Locations and Logics of Incarceration', in Ben-Moshe, Chapman and Carey (eds), *Disability Incarcerated* (2014).

[18] M Oliver, *The Politics of Disablement* (Basingstoke, Macmillan and St Martin's Press, 1990).

[19] A Scull, *Decarceration: Community Treatment and the Deviant: A Radical View* (New Jersey, Prentice-Hall Inc, 1977).

[20] Oliver, *The Politics of Disablement* (1990).

[21] S Taylor, R Bogdan and J Racino (eds), *Life in the Community: Case Studies of Organizations Supporting People with Disabilities* (Baltimore, Paul Brookes, 1991).

[22] Dear and Wolch, *Landscapes of Despair* (1987); B Hudson, 'Deinstitutionalisation: What Went Wrong?' (1991) 6 *Disability, Handicap and Society* 21.

[23] M Oliver, *The Politics of Disablement* (1990).

by being excluded from voting or participating on juries.[24] Furthermore, the vast majority of people with disabilities living in the community face significant barriers to equal access to work[25] and education[26] (with many having only provisional access to this right through segregated 'special' schools and 'supported' employment). These barriers lead to significantly poorer outcomes for people with disabilities in both these key fields of attainment.[27]

Advocates and scholars have also drawn attention to the lower life expectancy of people with intellectual disabilities and their higher incidences of sexual and other violence (particularly women with intellectual disabilities).[28] Moreover, ongoing settler–colonialism and racism has meant that First Nations disabled people experience significant levels of incarceration, premature death and social deprivation,[29] leading First Nations scholar and advocate Avery to suggest that contemporary practices of exclusion and segregation are more specifically a Western or settler–colonial phenomenon, with First Nations communities having strong cultures of inclusion and acceptance of diversity.[30]

Finally, as critical disability scholars and scholars of ableism remind us, there are also far more subtle ways in which the legacies of institutionalisation and, in particular, its eugenic logics, continue to live on within the deinstitutionalised community. As Robert McRuer aptly puts it, there is a 'system of compulsory able-bodiedness [in society, which] repeatedly demands that people with disabilities embody for others an affirmative answer to the unspoken question, "Yes, but in the end, wouldn't you rather be more like me?"'[31] As such, as Fiona Kumari Campbell explains, 'disabled people have not yet established their entitlement to exist unconditionally as disabled people' and are often expected to welcome all forms of intervention in their everyday lives, even if they are no longer confined behind specific institutional walls.[32]

---

[24] UN OHCHR, *Thematic Study by the Office of the United Nations High Commissioner for Human Rights on participation in political and public life by persons with disabilities*, 21 December 2011, A/HRC/19/36.
[25] See eg OECD, *Sickness, Disability and Work: Breaking the Barriers: A Synthesis of Findings across OECD Countries* (Paris, OECD Publishing, 2010).
[26] See eg UNICEF, *The Right of Children with Disabilities to Education: A Rights-Based Approach to Inclusive Education* (Geneva, UNICEF Regional Office for Central and Eastern Europe and the Commonwealth of Independent States, 2012).
[27] World Health Organization and World Bank, *World Report on Disability* (Paris, UNESCO, 2011).
[28] Disabled Peoples Organisations Australia, *Disability Rights Now 2019: Australian Civil Society Shadow Report to the United Nations Committee on the Rights of Persons with Disabilities: UN CRPD Review 2019*. Available at: www.dpoa.org.au/rights-of-people-with-disability-routinely-ignored-new-report/.
[29] Avery, *Culture is Inclusion* (2018).
[30] Ibid.
[31] R McRuer, *Crip Theory: Cultural Signs of Queerness and Disability* (New York, New York University Press, 2006) 9.
[32] FK Campbell, 'Stalking Ableism: Using Disability to Expose "Abled" Narcissism' in D Goodley, B Hughes and L Davis (eds), *Disability and Social Theory* (New York, Palgrave, 2012) 215. See also A Kafer, *Feminist, Queer, Crip* (Indiana, Indiana University Press, 2013); E Kim, *Curative Violence:*

Placed together in this way, the various bodies of scholarship suggest that while we have largely moved away from the practice of sending people with disabilities to the specific large-scale institution of the mental asylum for the purposes of segregation and confinement, we have, in reality, taken far fewer steps away from the various logics that underpinned this practice for centuries. The question therefore becomes: What enables the logics and various other legacies of institutionalisation to live on within the deinstitutionalised community? For us, a key but often overlooked, part of the answer to this question can be found by looking to the role of law in relation to the lives of people with disabilities.

LEGITIMATING INSTITUTIONALISATION'S LEGACIES: CONSIDERING LAW'S LONGSTANDING VIOLENCE

Law has always played a significant role in the lives of people with disabilities. While 'lunacy', 'mental hygiene' and 'mental treatment' legislation all worked in the era of institutionalisation to segregate and contain people with disabilities, in the post-deinstitutionalisation era, legislation rebranded 'mental health' and 'disability' has emerged to govern the ways people with disabilities can participate in the community. These modern-day laws are often positioned as 'progressive' in comparison to their predecessors. At face value, post-deinstitutionalisation mental health and disability legislation work to limit the scope of non-consensual coercive interventions through clear legal criteria and legal processes. They also provide rights-based safeguards for people with disabilities receiving government and private services, including complaints commissions and other independent oversight bodies.[33] At the same time, however, this legislation usually contains provisions which limit the rights of people with disabilities in various ways. Indeed, nestled within most modern mental health and disability acts are compulsory treatment and/or involuntary detention orders which run against the very core of what we understand to be the rights of 'liberal individuals': autonomy, liberty and so on. It is the persistent presence of provisions like these, we argue, which enable the logics and various other legacies of institutionalisation to live on within the deinstitutionalised community.

We are not alone in advancing this line of argument. Rather, the premise of this collection is based upon work that has been emerging from various pockets within critical socio-legal, disability and Mad studies scholarship over the past few years. It is based upon the scholarship of Spivakovsky, for example, who explored how modern-day disability group homes assume a coercive quality for

Rehabilitating Disability, Gender, and Sexuality in Modern Korea (Durham, Duke University Press, 2017).

[33] B McSherry and P Weller, *Re-thinking Rights-Based Mental Health Laws* (Oxford, Hart, 2010).

a specific subset of residents through diverse laws including supervised treatment orders, restrictive practice provisions made under the Disability Act (Vic) 2006 and work health and safety laws.[34] Or Fabris, who argues that community treatment orders work to 'detain' people in the community through the use of psycho-pharmaceuticals which act as 'chemical restraints', confining individuals from within their bodies.[35] Or Steele, who argues that a variety of legal orders made pursuant to guardianship, forensic mental health and civil mental health laws enable the heightened carceral (ie, prison-like) control of certain individuals with disability in the 'free' community outside conventional institutional settings; that these controls travel with these disabled individuals through space and time and make otherwise 'free' spaces carceral.[36]

The premise of this collection is also informed by the small collection of work attending to legal epistemologies and ontologies of disability. For example, Beaupert,[37] Spivakovsky[38] and Wildeman's[39] separate works, which allow us to see how contemporary law continues to facilitate the segregation, coercion and control of disabled people post-deinstitutionalisation by maintaining age-old, paternalistic and protectionist legal epistemologies which privilege assumed connections between disability and 'risk' or 'vulnerability'. As scholars such as Steele[40] and Weller[41] have noted, this relationship between legal epistemologies and ontologies of disability is especially apparent in the foundational legal division of (in)capacity which grounds legal authority in many areas of law (eg, criminal law, tort law, contract law) and is premised on psychological understandings of mental capacity. Pursuant to this division, people without mental capacity are seen as incapable of having their choices recognised in law, thus enabling others (eg, judiciary, government officials, family members) to make decisions about their bodies and their lives.

[34] C Spivakovsky, 'From Punishment to Protection: Containing and Controlling the Lives of People with Disabilities in Human Rights' (2014) 16 *Punishment & Society* 560; C Spivakovsky, 'Making Dangerousness Intelligible in Intellectual Disability' (2014) 23 *Griffith Law Review* 389; C Spivakovsky, 'Governing Freedom Through Risk: Locating the Group Home in the Archipelago of Confinement and Control' (2017) 19 *Punishment & Society* 366.

[35] Fabris, *Tranquil Prisons* (2011); Fabris and Aubrecht, 'Chemical Constraint' in L Ben-Moshe, C Chapman and A Carey (eds), *Disability Incarcerated: Imprisonment and Disability in the United States and Canada* (New York, Palgrave Macmillan, 2014).

[36] L Steele, 'Disabling Forensic Mental Health Detention: The Carcerality of the Disabled Body' (2017) 19 *Punishment & Society* 327; L Steele 'Troubling Law's Indefinite Detention: Disability, the Carceral Body and Institutional Injustice' (2018) *Social & Legal Studies*. Available at: www.doi.org/10.1177/0964663918769478.

[37] Beaupert, 'Silencing Prote(x)t' (2018) 746.

[38] Spivakovsky, 'From Punishment to Protection'; C Spivakovsky, 'Making Dangerousness Intelligible in Intellectual Disability'; C Spivakovsky and K Seear, 'Making the Abject: Problem Solving Courts, Addiction, Mental Illness and Impairment' (2017) 31 *Continuum* 458; L Steele, 'Temporality, Disability and Institutional Violence: Revisiting In Re F' (2017) 26 *Griffith Law Review* 378.

[39] S Wildeman, 'Agonizing Identity in Mental Health Law and Policy (Part II): A Political Taxonomy of Psychiatric Subjectification' (2016) 39(1) *Dalhousie Law Journal* 147.

[40] L Steele, 'Disability, Abnormality and Criminal Law: Sterilisation as Lawful and Good Violence' (2014) 23 *Griffith Law Review* 467.

[41] P Weller, 'Mental Capacity and States of Exception: Revisiting Disability Law with Giorgio Agamben' (2017) 31 *Continuum* 400.

The collection is also informed by a crucial and fruitful recent turn in socio-legal scholarship which explores the particular implications of law's role in legacies of institutionalisation in the specific context of Indigenous and racialised populations. This work is premised on the entanglement of disability with ableism as well as settler–colonialism, racism, sexism and other forces of oppression such that understandings of disability are always bound up in dynamics of abjection that sustain white privilege. Scholars such as Chapman[42] and Joseph[43] have proposed that legal and regulatory frameworks of control and intervention which apply on the basis of disability carry on racialised practices of segregation, control and violence, but that these practices are often hidden under the guise of medicalised, individualised notions of disability and through interventions purportedly associated with 'therapy' and 'care'.[44] This scholarship resonates with Avery's exploration of intersectionality and oppression in relation to First Nations people with disabilities,[45] as well as ongoing resistance by First Nations people to settler–colonial legally sanctioned interventions in their bodies, families, communities and Country, including through the very medical and welfare services positioned as empowering in a post-deinstitutionalisation context and support for their self-determination and Indigenous nation building.[46]

Placed together like this, these various emergent pockets of critical socio-legal, disability and Mad studies scholarship and longstanding activism by disability communities sketch out some of the features of modern law and legal practice which enable the logics and various other legacies of institutionalisation to live on within the deinstitutionalised community. Yet this is only one side of the picture. Increasingly, socio-legal scholars, activists and practitioners are turning to the legal instrument of the CRPD as a promising way to remedy these situations.

CONSIDERING THE PROMISE OF THE CONVENTION ON THE RIGHTS OF PERSONS WITH DISABILITIES

The United Nations CRPD brings the possibility of a radical revision in law as it applies to people with disabilities. The CRPD demands that people with disabilities be afforded full and effective participation in all aspects of life and

---

[42] C Chapman, 'Five Centuries' Material Reforms and Ethical Reformulations of Social Elimination' in Ben-Moshe, Chapman and Carey (eds), *Disability Incarcerated* (2014).

[43] A Joseph, 'Beyond Intersectionalities of Identity or Interlocking Analyses of Difference: Confluence and the Problematic of "Anti"-Oppression' (2015) 4 *Intersectionalities: A Global Journal of Social Work Analysis, Research, Polity, and Practice* 15; A Joseph, *Deportation and the Confluence of Violence within Forensic Mental Health and Immigration Systems* (Basingstoke, Palgrave-Macmillan, 2015).

[44] See also Steele, 'Troubling Law's Indefinite Detention' (2018); D Wadiwel, 'Disability and Torture: Exception, Epistemology and "Black Sites"' (2017) 31 *Continuum* 388.

[45] Avery, *Culture is Inclusion* (2018).

[46] See, eg, Referendum Council, *Uluru Statement from the Heart* (2017). Available at: www.referendumcouncil.org.au/sites/default/files/2017-05/Uluru_Statement_From_The_Heart_0.PDF.

that they receive recognition before the law on an equal basis with non-disabled people.[47] The CRPD addresses participation in decision-making by asserting the right to legal capacity. This is expressed in the CRPD as the right to 'equal recognition before the law' (Article 12(1)) and the right to enjoy 'legal capacity on an equal basis with others in all aspects of life' (Article 12(2)). Here, legal capacity is defined as 'the ability to hold rights and duties (legal standing) and the ability to exercise those rights and duties (legal agency)'.[48] With these words, the CRPD rejects the nexus between legal and mental capacity. In law, a determination that a person lacks mental capacity triggers the use of alternative mechanisms (such as guardianship or substitute decision-making) to make 'lawful' decisions for that person. Instead, the CRPD requires that the decisions and wishes of people with disabilities are always recognised in law and always given credence.

Importantly, rather than merely asserting the right to make decisions, the CRPD demands that people with disabilities receive support for decision-making (Article 12(3)). Support for decision-making includes the full range of strategies, mechanisms, interactions and relationships that will enable people with disabilities to formulate, express and assert decisions.[49] Tied with the obligation to provide support is the requirement of reasonable accommodation.

> 'Reasonable accommodation' means necessary and appropriate modifications and adjustments not imposing disproportionate or undue burden, when needed in a particular case, to ensure to persons with disabilities the enjoyment or exercise on an equal basis with others of all human rights and fundamental freedoms.[50]

'Reasonable accommodation' requires the differential treatment of people with disabilities in order to allow for their different needs and abilities in mainstream systems.[51] Exactly what is required depends on the needs of the person with respect to, for example, support for decision-making and exercise of legal capacity. Respect for legal capacity and support for decision-making similarly require a radical revision of all decision-making laws, policies and arrangements and universal access to the provision of support mechanisms.

Moreover, in its guidance on Article 19 (discussed above), the UN Disability Committee emphasises the important interrelationship between legal capacity and independent living: individuals should have support in making their choice as to where they live and then support to live in that place.[52] Of course, ending the institutionalisation of specific individuals via supported decision-making

---

[47] A Dhanda, 'Legal Capacity in the Disability Rights Convention: Stranglehold of the Past or Lodestar for the Future' (2006) 34 *Syracuse Journal of International Law and Commerce* 429.

[48] B McSherry, 'Legal Capacity under the Convention on the Rights of Persons with Disabilities' (2012) 20 *Journal of Law and Medicine* 22.

[49] CRPD Committee, (2014).

[50] CRPD Article 2 – Definitions.

[51] A Lawson, 'Disability Equality, Reasonable Accommodation and the Avoidance of Ill-Treatment in Places of Detention: The Role of Supranational Monitoring and Inspection Bodies' (2012) 16 *The International Journal of Human Rights* 845.

[52] UN Committee on the Rights of Persons with Disabilities, *General Comment No 5* (2017).

needs to be situated in the context of the CRPD's structural implications that institutions should not even exist and thus not even be available as a choice.[53] In a similar vein, the CRPD demands the reform of laws in order to abolish legislation for discriminatory medical interventions. In short, the CRPD provides individual rights to choose and thus resist oppressive and violent interventions in a context of transformation of our legal systems as a whole.

While the promise of the CRPD is apparent, in many ways the full potential of this radical instrument of international human rights law is yet to be realised. Primarily, this discrepancy occurs because, as an international law instrument, the CRPD provides an international standard but, in most countries, it is not directly incorporated into law. While most state parties to the CRPD have developed some response to the treaty, including legal responses, there is little evidence that there is an engagement with the CRPD at the scale and intensity necessary to achieve the goal of full participation. Instead, under-resourced and misplaced service provision continues, prompting new questions about the role and limits of law in dismantling, legitimating or propagating the logics and legacies of institutionalisation. It is the purpose of this collection to engage with these new questions about the role and limits of law and offer new insights.

AIM AND STRUCTURE OF THE COLLECTION

The aim of this edited collection is to consider the extent to which some contemporary laws, policies and practices affecting people with disabilities are moving towards the deinstitutionalisation movement's promised end of enhanced social and political participation in the community, while other laws, policies and practices may instead reinstate, continue or legitimate historical practices associated with this population's institutionalisation. To this end, the collection focuses upon a diverse range of laws, policies and regulatory practices affecting people with disabilities around the world and is divided into three parts.

The chapters in Part One are concerned with exploring the complex legacies of institutionalisation in practice. Each of the first four chapters in this part draw attention to the ways that ostensibly positive moves towards reasonable accommodation, 'empowerment' and reducing the barriers facing people with disabilities in law, policy and practice struggle to entirely free themselves from the legacies and logics of institutionalisation. Chapter 1 by Liz Brosnan and Chapter 2 by Penelope Weller focus on purportedly progressive reforms to mental health laws. Through autoethnography, Brosnan reflects on the tensions and contradictions she observes as a person of lived experience of the civil mental health system who is working alongside lawyers and psychiatrists as

---

[53] Steele, Swaffer, Phillipson and Fleming, 'Questioning Segregation' (2019).

a lay member of interdisciplinary decision-making teams of Mental Health Review Tribunals. Weller reflects on the goal of 'recovery' in community and inpatient mental health treatment. In different ways they argue that ostensibly positive moves to empower certain people with disabilities in their relationship with law and policy may still work, at the same time, to reinforce the interests of the state in relation to these populations. Ultimately these laws still reinforce relations of disempowerment and ultimately facilitate continuation of forced treatment.

Chapter 3 by Salvador Cayuela Sánchez and Chapter 4 by Eduardo Díaz Velázquez engage with concerns about complex legacies of institutions in the Spanish context. Cayuela Sánchez focuses on a consideration of the biopolitics of disability during Late-Francoism and the beginning of the Spanish Democratic Transition. Here, Cayuela Sánchez shows how the Franco regime's reforms at the end of the Spanish Civil War (1936–39) included measures aimed at repressive institutional settings, but these were coupled with increased control of people with disabilities through their explicit inclusion in 'disciplinary' institutions (such as education and medicine). Moving further along the timeline in Spain, Díaz Velázquez draws attention to contemporary tensions and contradictions in legislation and public policies relating to education, employment and disability support. A shift to viewing disability through the lens of the social model is undercut by the neoliberal context in which the laws and policies are situated and the lack of attention to socioeconomic inequalities experienced by some people with disabilities. Díaz Velázquez argues these laws and policies perpetuate exclusion, segregation and inequality and ultimately prevent people with disabilities from realising full citizenship.

The final two chapters in this part, by Roxanne Mykitiuk and Sheila Wildeman, focus on anti-discrimination and human rights laws, which are conventionally viewed as progressive legal developments for people with disabilities. Chapter 5 by Roxanne Mykitiuk reflects, through the method of autoethnography, on the embodied consequences for and impacts on people with disabilities of the disjuncture between ostensibly supportive and empowering laws and policies and the problematic practices that they produce. Her chapter focuses on the regime of accommodation and inclusion for a particular subset of Canadian university faculty members with disability: those with episodic disability that are characterised by unpredictable or intermittent, fluctuating periods of impairment and wellness. Access to the positive institution of the university becomes at best fraught or at worst impossible, as academics with episodic disabilities must negotiate neoliberal and ableist performance demands and contend with human resource policies and procedures that are premised on narrow conceptions of disability. In Chapter 6, Wildeman then considers the extent that recent Canadian human rights litigation challenging solitary confinement disrupts broader practices and patterns of control of people with disabilities that occurs through mental health. Wildeman highlights the risks in seeing mental health diagnosis, treatment and detention as humane and therapeutic alternatives to the mainstream prison system because they are themselves controlling and sustain (and mask) dynamics and forces of oppression such as colonialism, ableism and racism. She instead posits 'anti-carceral' lawyering as an alternative strategy which can potentially disrupt institutionalisation.

In light of the legacies of institutionalisation drawn out in Part One of the collection, Part Two brings attention to the ways these legacies often form complicated alliances with other longstanding practices of oppression and segregation. Indeed, Chapter 7 by Ameil Joseph on anti-immigration discourses in the context of Brexit and Trump's politics and Chapter 8 by Karen Soldatic on contemporary poverty management regimes in Australia draw out the often obscured and historic confluence of and alliances between, ableist, sanist, gendered, classed and racialised logics within law, policy and practice.

Chapters 9 by Isabel Karpin and Karen O'Connell and 10 by Leanne Dowse then consider the role of law and the institutions charged with its enforcement and administration in the legitimation of ableist, sanist, gendered, classed and racialised social norms. In the case of Karpin and O'Connell, this exploration focuses on women with personality disorder who have turned to workers compensation and family law to facilitate or remediate their interactions with the social institutions of work and family. In the case of Dowse, the focus is on people with cognitive disability experiencing corrosive social disadvantage who are subject to systematic and patterned regimes of incapacitation through institutions charged with law's enforcement and administration (ie, the prison).

Part Two concludes with a chapter by Fleur Beaupert and Shelley Bielefeld which analyses the emergence and operation of fixated persons units alongside counter-terrorism initiatives, that is, joint policing–mental health units developed to respond to persons who have allegedly become 'fixated' on public figures or social causes and are presumed to pose a risk of harm to the community. Through this chapter, Beaupert and Bielefeld remind us of the ease with which dissenting responses to political marginalisation and structural injustice by those existing at the interstices of raced, ableist and classed oppression can be both silenced and subverted through law, policy and practice.

In an attempt to find ways and means to move beyond some of the current tensions in law and policy identified in Parts One and Two, the final part of the collection considers the role of the CRPD in the emancipation of people with disabilities from the legacies of institutionalisation. In Chapter 12, Peter Bartlett considers the international debate about strong or weak readings of the CRPD. In Chapter 13, Lucy Series questions and analyses cases of equality, legal capacity and deprivation of liberty in the United Kingdom. Moving beyond Anglo-western perspectives, Chapters 14 and 15 by Melania Moscoso Pérez and R Lucas Platero and Elvira Pértega Andía respectively consider how the introduction of CRPD-based laws intersect with local laws and practices in Spain, causing contradiction and tension for both legal and medical practitioners, care workers and those with disabilities. Finally, in Chapters 16 and 17, Jill Stavert explicitly considers the value of the CRPD as a basis for mental health and capacity law reform while Dio Ashar Wicaksana points to the critical importance of civil society advocacy in the implementation of CRPD-based laws.

Ultimately, this collection brings forth the possibilities, limits and contradictions in the roles of law and policy in the institutionalisation and deinstitutionalisation of people with disabilities and their alternatives and directs us towards a more nuanced and sustained scholarly and political engagement with these issues.

Part One

Power Dynamics that Shape the Conditions and Possibilities of People With Disabilities Within and Beyond Sites of Physical Confinement

CONVENTIONALLY, THE INJUSTICES of disability institutionalisation are associated with the aesthetic, architectural and material forms of specific sites of physical confinement – large buildings, high fences, locked doors and physical restraints. Such an approach encourages us to assume that the political and social status of people with disabilities (PWD) can be transformed through deinstitutionalisation strategies of closing, opening up or downsizing their physical sites of confinement.

Yet, as we discussed in the Introduction, a body of scholarship spanning early work by Goffman and Foucault to current scholarship by critical disability studies and Mad studies scholars unsettles these assumptions. This scholarship invites us to shift our focus to less visible and tangible dynamics of power that shape the conditions and possibilities of PWD within and beyond sites of physical confinement, through attention to power relations, individual identity and subjectivity, and the defining and sorting of populations. For the chapters in this Part, that scholarship is particularly significant in three respects. The first is that it draws our attention to continuities in logics and practices across a range of coercive interventions ranging from physical confinement to interventions that emerged in the light of deinstitutionalisation such as community mental health treatment, disability case management and supported living in group homes. Second, the scholarship suggests that we should not concentrate only on the repressive dynamics of power – coercion and restraint – but be attentive to productive and positive dynamics of power in terms of how the conditions and possibilities for PWD come to be shaped and limited through freedom, choice and empowerment (the very ideals we might think of as the antithesis of those driving institutionalisation). Third, this scholarship draws attention to the centrality to the continued oppression of PWD of epistemic and ontological injustices: they continue to be positioned as incapable of knowing and articulating their own experiences and needs, thus creating a lacuna that can be conveniently filled by professional experts who are assumed to know best when they recommend, support or enact confinement and coercive interventions.

The chapters in Part One contribute to this scholarship through exploring how, in the deinstitutionalised community, laws and policies give rise to possibilities for injustice including segregation, control, violence and epistemic negation to ultimately denying full citizenship and indeed full humanness to PWD. Particular attention is paid to laws and policies that are premised on enhancing the liberty, rights, inclusion and wellbeing of PWD.

This Part opens with Liz Brosnan's autoethnographic exploration of the inclusion on Irish mental health tribunals (MHTs) of lay persons (i.e. individuals with an 'interest in mental health' which covers social workers, journalists, and possibly family members). These lay persons work as part of interdisciplinary decision-making teams alongside lawyers and psychiatrists, and form part of a larger set of reforms to the legal procedures for coercive mental health interventions. Brosnan reflects on her experiences as a member of a lay panel. She highlights the profound limitations and contradictions of being a lay person who has lived experience of the civil mental health system by reason of the continued privileging of legal and medical authority in the structure of the tribunal and in the overarching discourses of the legislation. Through her reflections on the hearing of one woman, 'Margaret', Brosnan illuminates how the pervasive epistemic invalidation of those who appear before the MHTs facilitates their confinement and coercive intervention. While Brosnan is ambivalent about her ability, as a 'peer', to challenge these dynamics, the autoethnographic methods employed in her chapter represent one strategy for disrupting the epistemic injustices of contemporary mental health law.

Continuing the focus on contemporary mental health laws, in Chapter 2 Penelope Weller takes a closer look at how ostensibly positive moves to 'empower' certain PWD in their relationship with law and policy may still work, simultaneously, to reinforce the interests of the state in relation to these populations. Weller's analysis of Australian civil mental health law highlights that ideas of freedom that emerge against specific sites of physical confinement provide openings for the emergence of virtual institutions that are legitimated and sustained through what she refers to as 'coercive freedom' – the harnessing of ideas of choice, recovery and community for very specific ends. Drawing on the writings of US political philosopher Barbara Cruikshank, Weller contends that the empowerment and recovery movement in mental health is an example of a technology of personal governance tailored toward PWD which, through the reification of the neoliberal ideal of choice, limits the recognition of the substantively restricted options available to PWD beyond submission to mental health treatment, notably when their recovery and empowerment in legal terms manifests in coercive mental health treatment.

In Chapter 3, Salvador Cayuela Sánchez shifts from a specific focus on mental health law to consider a broader set of policy sectors that are conventionally understood as key sites of political and social transformation for PWD after deinstitutionalisation. Cayuela Sánchez argues that in the wake of deinstitutionalisation in Spain, new forms of control emerged through the re-organisation of populations within the community into segregated systems of education, health and employment that were intrinsically linked to legitimating nation building and democratic transformation, and thus ultimately limited the extent to which PWD could access full citizenship. Cayuela Sánchez makes these arguments through a case study of Late Francoism and the beginning of the Spanish Democratic Transition. Here, Cayuela Sánchez shows how at the end of the Spanish Civil War (1936–39), the Franco regime had to activate a huge number of biopolitical mechanisms to garner the legitimacy necessary to uphold the recently established political order, and how these mechanisms saw the regulation of PWD become a specific objective for this new governmentality.

In Chapter 4, Eduardo Díaz Velázquez draws attention to tensions and contradictions in legislation and public policies on disability in contemporary Spain. Díaz Velázquez shows how individual enjoyment of citizenship rights provided in laws and policies relies on access to supports in a context where such access is not guaranteed and instead depends on one's socioeconomic circumstances. On a related note, he highlights the persistence of institutionalisation (or segregation) through laws and policies ostensibly focused on inclusion in the community, with individuals' relative exposure to institutionalisation in part depending on their socioeconomic circumstances and financial capacity to avoid requiring state-funded services. Díaz Velázquez argues that Spanish legislation and public policies do not include enough regulatory or economic guarantees to actually achieve material and political equality between people with and without disability, resulting in the perpetuation of limitations in inclusive education, access to employment, and independent living.

In Chapter 5, Roxanne Mykitiuk also explores the contradictions of empowering 'reform' in employment and education sectors through an analysis of the operation of equality and anti-discrimination law for academics. She focuses on a particular subset of Canadian university faculty members with disability, those with episodic disability that are characterised by unpredictable or intermittent, fluctuating periods of impairment and wellness. Utilising autoethnographic methods, Mykitiuk discusses how processes for seeking reasonable accommodations available to her through university policies premised on equality and anti-discrimination laws ultimately served to enable and legitimate the university as a site of control and exclusion. She suggests that equality and anti-discrimination laws purportedly directed towards enhancing representation and participation of PWD in the workforce do not unsettle ableist neoliberal frameworks driving universities, forcing academics with disabilities to 'normalise' themselves to accommodate the unrealistic, unjust and disabling expectations of the academy.

In Chapter 6, Sheila Wildeman turns our attention to the criminal justice context. She raises concerns about what she refers to as the increasing 'mental-healthification' of prison justice. By this she is referring to the reliance on mental health diagnosis, treatment and detention as a purported humane and therapeutic set of responses to problems with the mainstream incarceration of people with disabilities. Wildeman sees this focus on mental health as individu-alising and pathologising injustice and distracting attention from addressing socio-structural dynamics of criminalisation and incarceration. She develops this argument through an analysis of recent Canadian human rights litigation challenging solitary confinement. Wildeman highlights the perhaps unexpected complicity of Canadian Charter of Rights and Freedoms jurisprudence which draws on progressive legal concepts such as procedural justice and non-discrimination, in legitimating the confinement and coercive intervention of prisoners with disabilities. Her chapter encourages us to consider the ways in which institutionalisation is sustained through judicial decision making and domestic human rights law and suggests 'anti-carceral' lawyering as one way that the legal profession can challenge the ongoing legacies in law of institutionalisation.

1

Navigating Mental Health Tribunals as a Mad-identified Layperson

An Autoethnographical Account of Liminality

LIZ BROSNAN

T HIS CHAPTER PRESENTS autoethnographical reflections upon the socio-medico-legal operation of Irish mental health law; specifically, mental health tribunal (MHT) reviews of involuntary detention under the Mental Health Act 2001/2006. In the context of examining how contemporary law, policy and practices can inadvertently legitimate legacies of institutionalisation practices, I offer my personal experiences and perspectives as a layperson member of approximately 40 MHTs over the course of seven years (2006–13). As someone with insider experience of several involuntary detentions in the 1990s, I seek to illustrate the institutionalised ethos within spaces purported to uphold safeguards against arbitrary detention, a lingering remnant of the old asylum regimes. I argue that what occurs within these regulated spaces reinforces the institutions of psychiatry (aided by law) to exert absolute control over the lives of people subject to mental health legislation. One particular instance evidences how the epistemic violence of institutions of law and psychiatry play out in intimate, micro-scale enactments of institutional power, invalidating individuals' experiences and worldviews through the privileging of expert authority.

Mental health tribunals are a ubiquitous feature of modern mental health legislation. They were introduced to provide oversight of medico-legal decisions and protect people who are detained and treated involuntarily against arbitrary detention and treatment.[1] Irish mental health law does not permit compulsory

---

[1] See D Whelan, 'Mental Health Tribunals: A Significant Medico-Legal Change' (2004) 10 *Medico-Legal Journal of Ireland* 84. See also F Beaupert and L Brosnan, 'The CRPD and Weaponizing Absent Knowledges: Countering the Violence of Mental Health Law' in J Russo, P Beresford

treatment orders in the community,[2] so MHTs regulate compulsory inpatient detention in designated acute psychiatric units. The functions, procedures and powers of MHTs differ somewhat across legislative contexts, but they always have three members: a chairperson who is a legal expert, a psychiatrist and a 'lay person'. Lay members were introduced to contribute a perspective that complements and balances the medical and legal expertise. The lay member holds an ill-defined role, characterised as someone from the general public with an 'interest in mental health' but ineligible to be a legal or medical member. There is no requirement or expectation that a lay member has personal experience of services. Indeed, the legislation and associated MHT policy guidance are silent about recruiting lay members who are Mad-identified or have 'lived experience' of involuntary detention and treatment, despite recent initiatives in the mental health services more generally.

I was a national activist with the peer advocacy movement when MHTs were being established in Ireland; becoming a lay member on MHTs appeared to offer an opportunity to influence change from within and to participate in the biggest legislative shift since 1945 (the prior Mental Health Act). As a lay member I operated as a statutory officer and was not formally 'out' about my prior experience of detention, because this was officially discouraged by the Mental Health Commission. All personal dimensions and interests were to be concealed behind the mask of professionalism, abiding by pre-determined operational procedures. My experiences and subsequent emotions required frequent processing and, in the absence of any debriefing opportunities for lay members lacking pre-existing medical and legal professional networks, I had few outlets except writing down my personal reflections. My writings from this period illustrate the inherent tensions within the assumed separateness between different subjectivities: an ex-detainee under mental health legislation, an officer of MHTs, and latterly a researcher. My reflections at the time were concerned with the liminality of my position and troubled by the institutionalised power dynamics I observed but failed to overcome. Autoethnography offers a framework to problematise the unexamined institutional ethos and epistemic politics of tribunal decision-making by writing myself into the account (all others being carefully anonymised, necessitating strategic omissions).

Autoethnography offers a way to disrupt taboos, break silences and reclaim lost and disregarded voices.[3] It refuses and disrupts canonical narratives, writes against hegemonic beliefs and practices, and describes

and K Boxhall (eds), *Routledge Handbook of Mad Studies* (Abingdon, UK and New York, USA, Routledge, in press).

[2] L Brosnan, 'Who's Talking About Us Without Us? A Survivor Research Interjection into an Academic Psychiatry Debate on Compulsory Community Treatment Orders in Ireland' (2018) 7 *Laws* 33.

[3] T Adams, S Jones and C Ellis, *Autoethnography: Understanding Qualitative Research* (Oxford, Oxford University Press, 2016), 41.

particular – rather than general – experience.[4] By centring the writer as an embodied relational being, autoethnography seeks to create textual space for talking back to neglected cultural experiences and offer accounts which give others a chance to 'bear witness'. Autoethnographers seek to bridge the gap between the heart and the head by telling stories that challenge our understanding of the world as it is.[5] In the tradition of autoethnography, I connect my personal, insider institutional knowledge with larger cultural and political conversations, contexts and understandings operating in the psy-complex.[6] As Brenda LeFrançois demonstrates, by foregrounding the writer's vulnerabilities and uncertainties in relation to oppressive social structures such as professional collusion with coercive and disempowering practice, autoethnography offers possibilities to problematise hegemonic narratives. It leaves room for 'interpretation, for misunderstandings, for not knowing … to leave things unfinished and unanswered'.[7] Likewise, I risk exposing myself as someone who fell into collusion with an oppressive and violent system in the naive belief my collaboration would make a difference. Autoethnographical writing is particularly significant (and rarely done) in the context of socio-legal scholarship. Autoethnography of institutional decision-making by someone previously 'sectioned' also challenges the fundamental denial of epistemic authority operating in mental health law. Therefore, this work in itself offers a technique for undermining the logics of institutionalisation that live on in contemporary mental health law.

The story I tell of my experience as a lay member is fragmentary, incomplete, and disturbing from many perspectives. I relate one instance among many – an MHT review of the detention of one woman, who remains an elusive character. I do not conclude her story, leaving this to the imagination of the reader. While this story is about a woman appearing before an MHT, the two principal characters are two MHT professional members. These individuals play a more central role than the woman, because they performed, alongside myself, a statutory review of the decision to uphold the order to detain her, always referred to as the 'patient' in MHT decisions. I shall call her Margaret. The story as presented is based on notes written afterwards and interjected with theoretical reflections based on my subsequent critiques as a Mad scholar.

[4] H Reid and L West, *Constructing Narratives of Continuity and Change: A Transdisciplinary Approach to Researching Lives* (Abingdon, UK and New York, USA, Routledge, 2014).

[5] C Ellis, 'Heartful Autoethnography' (1999) 9 *Qualitative Health Research* 669.

[6] BA LeFrancois, 'The Psychiatrization of Our Children, or, an Autoethnographic Narrative of Perpetuating First Nations Genocide through "Benevolent" Institutions' (2013) 2 *Decolonization: Indigeneity, Education & Society* 108. The term 'psy-complex' originated in N Rose, *The Psychological Complex: Psychology, Politics and Society in England 1869–1939* (Abingdon, UK and New York, USA, Routledge and Paul, 1985).

[7] TJ Adams and SH Jones (2011) 109 cited in LeFrancois, 'The Psychiatrization of Our Children' (2013) 119.

SETTING THE SCENE: DIARY ENTRY, 10 JUNE 2010

I had a very disturbing experience at a tribunal recently. The other two members were, as always, crucial in the way the session unfolded. The chair ('Robert') was someone I felt could be relied on to be fair in his assessments, but the tribunal psychiatrist ('Dr Byrne') was a particularly arrogant, implacable opponent. My heart sank, because I always felt very intimidated by his demeanour.

As usual, we reviewed and discussed the paperwork before the tribunal: the medical records, the independent psychiatrist's report, and the official forms created to record the journey of the patient through the system. In these situations, the person is always called a patient, in the text of the Mental Health Act and the paperwork. We agreed how we would proceed – who would ask what questions – and began. Margaret arrived, accompanied by her legal representative, and the treating psychiatrist. Writing this at a few weeks remove, I cannot even recall her legal representative, what he looked like, what he said; he made no impression on me at all.

The treating psychiatrist explained how Margaret had presented when admitted and the order invoked to detain her. Her general practitioner had requested admission. The treating psychiatrist gave her diagnosis, bipolar disorder, and said she had been 'floridly psychotic' in a 'manic phase' and 'posing a risk to herself and to her children.' He reported she had improved with medication since admission 15 days previously, was almost in remission, but not ready to leave now, because she lacked insight into her need (in his opinion) to continue taking her medication. He maintained she should remain detained under the Act, because treatment was working and she remained a risk to others – namely her children.

Among the many layers of power unfolding in this scene, the gender dynamics are evident. Margaret is cast as lacking insight, an 'irrational' woman, a mother, in danger of being categorised as 'a risk' to her children by the all-male professionals.[8] Fortunately, this potential pathway – with all of the additional trauma – was not pursued on this occasion, most likely because Margaret was an educated middle-class woman with resources. Thus, I will not pursue an analysis of these obvious power imbalances and will instead focus on how psychiatric discourse peppers the language of MHTs to uphold the legitimacy of what unfolds.

---

[8] See eg how epistemic violence plays out in the imposition of diagnosis-related risk on pregnant women and mothers: TL Haley, 'The (Un)Writing of Risk on my Mad Pregnant Body: A Mad Feminist Political Economy Analysis of Social Reproduction and Epistemic Violence Under Neoliberalism' 184; Anonymous 'A Personal Account of Mental Distress in Motherhood' 34 in A Daley, L Costa and P Beresford (eds), *Madness Violence and Power, A Critical Collection* (Toronto, University of Toronto Press, 2019).

Medico-legal terminology acts as a code that permits psychiatrists, and latterly lawyers, to understand each other, but it sets the tone and frames the context for how the MHT operates. It also may – depending on the individual concerned – be a code the 'patient' might understand but which they rarely replicate in speaking of their experience. Medico-legal terminology packages and slices up experience into cold clinical language that bears no relation to how the person herself understands her situation.

Those who use mental health services or experience psychosocial distress are, by definition, positioned as the irrational, the emotional, the 'other';[9] clinical language replicates the symbolic violence of disregarding people's subjective experiences. This discourse masks the unpalatable facts of how law operates to underpin coercive psychiatry. Cath Roper identifies mental health laws as the political structures that dehumanise psychiatrised people and eloquently explains the alienation experienced by people subjected to mental health law.[10] She outlines the essential experience of forced psychiatry as follows.

> 'People subject to mental health laws can be detained against their will.
>
> 1. Needles, pills, electro-convulsive therapy and other psychiatric treatment can be given without the consent of the person.
> 2. In the face of refusal, treatment will be administered with violence.
> 3. That violence will not be seen for what it is, rather it will be re-interpreted as 'necessary' for health and wellbeing.
> 4. All of these are little known facts 'out there'.
> 5. These facts matter.'

These facts matter because they constitute the knowledge and experience of people on the receiving end of involuntary psychiatry. They underpin the invisible power of psychiatric hegemony and haunt the boundaries of the liminal spaces occupied by (ex)users/survivors – such as myself, when acting as a lay member – who seek to reform services on behalf of those still trapped within the coercive web of psychiatry. Those captive folk may be dealing with extreme states of distress, interpreted by psychiatry as requiring treatment with their violent methods. Such responses to distress are frequently experienced as further traumatising on a personal level and, at a macro level, result in symbolic violence, epistemic injustice and silencing.[11] I have written

---

[9] S LeBlanc and EA Kinsella, 'Toward Epistemic Justice: A Critically Reflexive Examination of "Sanism" and Implications for Knowledge Generation' (2016) 10 *Studies in Social Justice* 59, and J Voronka, 'Turning Mad Knowledge into Affective Labor: The Case of the Peer Support Worker' (2017) 69 *American Quarterly* 333.

[10] C Roper in C Roper and P Gooding, 'This is Not a Story: From Ethical Loneliness to Respect for Diverse Ways of Knowing, Thinking and Being' in E Flynn, A Arstein-Kerslake, C de Bhailís and ML Serra (eds), *Global Perspectives on Legal Capacity Reform: Our Voices, Our Stories* (Abingdon, Routledge, 2018) 154.

[11] F Beaupert, 'Freedom of Opinion and Expression: From the Perspective of Psychosocial Disability and Madness' (2018) 7 *Laws* 3. See also this detailed account of how mental health law positions those subject to it: F Beaupert, 'Silencing Prote(x)t: Disrupting the Scripts of Mental Health Law' (2018) 41 *University of New South Wales Law Journal* 746.

elsewhere about the emotional labour required by those engaged in Service User Involvement, who report frequent instances of micro-aggression and denials of recognition.[12]

DIARY ENTRY, 10 JUNE 2010

In my turn I asked Margaret to tell us how she felt. How was the hospital stay, and did she believe she needed to remain? No matter how these questions are phrased, they sound awful. Can the person see I am on their side? That I want, if at all possible, to help get the order revoked, but to do so I need her to demonstrate to the other two panel members that she should not be detained any longer. This is a delicate balancing act. I need to ask questions the right way to give her space to show she can 'act' sane, and restrain her understandable anger and frustration: prove her sanity, in other words. Most detained people feel that way, and look doubtful when I have sometimes tried to tell them it is not they who are being assessed in a tribunal but actually the doctors, the services, have they acted legally in detaining the person? Cold comfort to anyone locked up against their will, but sometimes people can absorb that fact and relax somewhat. On the other hand, if my questions are too general, or stimulate someone to talk about something they feel passionate about, they may display emotions deemed 'excessive' or 'uncontrolled', 'irrational' (there are clinical words for these expressions), providing 'evidence' they are still unstable, and thus the tribunal decision might swing against them. ...

So, I ask Margaret what support she has outside, and what would she do if she could leave today? She begins to talk about missing her children and wanting to hold them, and maybe go somewhere nice with them, to her sister's house in the countryside, to give them a nice time. From what she says, her husband is not a good supporter, rather they are on the point of splitting up. In my opinion she sounds rational. It is a natural, reasonable desire to spend time with her children, taking them on a drive, and I see no indication she is 'psychotic' or out of touch with other people's sense of the world. The Chair, Robert, asks her if she agrees to remain in hospital for another week. She replies she doesn't feel this is the best place for her to recover. Dr Byrne asks if she will continue to take the prescribed medication when she is discharged. She will, she assures us. After about 20 mins of this type of exchange, Robert asks if there is anything else either myself or Dr Byrne wants to ask. When we say no, he then asks Margaret if she wants to add

---

[12] L Brosnan, '"The Lion's Den": The Epistemic Dimensions of Invisible Emotional Labour in Service-User Involvement Spaces' (2019) *Journal of Ethics in Mental Health, Special Issue Disordering Social Inclusion* 1.

> *anything else to the proceedings. When she finishes with a plea to be allowed to go home to her children, Robert tells her the tribunal will consider every-thing and let her know the decision as soon as possible. Then she, her legal representative and treating consultant leave the room.*

There is a heavy onus on the 'patient' to present as reasonable, rational and coherent to persuade the MHT to revoke the legal order detaining them. Unless they present as no longer 'suffering from a mental disorder', offering instead a coherent, balanced account of their situation, hermeneutical injustice auto-matically prevails.[13] The weight afforded medical evidence dominates the proceedings. I saw my role to act as conduit to allow this coherent account to be heard. Yet my position was never straightforward; I was, after all, a member of the MHT.

Fleur Beaupert demonstrates the colonial and cultural oppression operation-alised through mental health laws to deny freedom of expression to psychiatrised people.[14] Deploying Bourdieu's concept of symbolic violence, she demonstrates how mental health laws constrain and silence ways of knowing, expressing, opining, and being that may be vital to a person's sense of self, a process of symbolic violence that cultivates the ontological nullification of users and survi-vors. The medico-legal discourse of mental health laws 'consecrate symbolic violence,'[15] manipulate and nullify individual ways of knowing and being, and to radically diminish opportunities for the epistemologies of users and survivors to exert influence on societal systems and structures. One such pernicious and oppressive dynamic of symbolic violence can be seen in how insight was opera-tionalised in medico-legal discourse and practice in this particular MHT.

DIARY ENTRY, 10 JUNE 2010

> *Then the closed-door decision-making kicks in. Dr Byrne and I disagree that she needs to remain, that this is the best place for her. He believes it is too soon to discharge her, that if she had another week of supervised medica-tion, she would be back to her 'pre-moribund'[16] self. I disagree, I believe she is ready to be discharged, that she can rest easier at home, that it could restore her sense of control over her own life, and that keeping her in hospital longer*

---

[13] Hermeneutical injustice is at play when the individual has no words or concepts to convey the experienced oppression because it is unrecognised as harm by those not subject to it. For a compre-hensive account, see LeBlanc and Kinsella, 'Toward Epistemic Justice' (2016).

[14] Beaupert, 'Freedom of Opinion and Expression' (2018).

[15] Ibid, 16.

[16] A common medical term, meaning in this instance how someone is before they enter the state of emotional and cognitive turmoil labelled 'mental illness' in psychiatry.

> *is unkind. In a sense, the timing of the tribunal is unfortunate; the drugs appear to have tranquilised her 'manic' episode, but Dr Byrne still detects a residual level of elevated mood. I do not believe that is a reason to keep her detained. He does, as he thinks she lacks insight into her need for the drugs.*

In this context, the framing and language used by the two psychiatrists sets them up as experts in the patient's experience and pre-determines the boundaries of the deliberations. The symbolic violence is visible in the formulation of the medico-legal discourse, in how the code of necessary treatment was established by one psychiatrist speaking to another, the treating psychiatrist speaking to the tribunal psychiatrist. Amar Shan, in asking whether MHTs can ever be fair to service users, highlights the over-reliance on medical opinion in MHTs and how both lay and legal members can be overly swayed by the authority afforded medical opinion.[17] Genevra Richardson and David Machin, in their study of 50 tribunal hearings (without a legal requirement for an independent psychiatric report), found that tribunal decisions never went against the psychiatrist MHT member's opinion.[18] In reflecting on Richardson and Machin's finding, Shan argues that affording uncontested authority to psychiatric opinion meant the other MHT members did not dispute the medical evidence. They found that no decision was made that overturned medical evidence. The presence or absence of an independent report is moot to my argument about the reliance on psychiatric opinion.

Let us turn to the role of the third member: the legal opinion presented by the lawyer member and chair of the MHT.

DIARY ENTRY, 10 JUNE 2010

> *Robert has been unusually silent throughout, listening to both of us. In the past I have thought he could be brought around to see the human rights' perspective and lean towards making decisions in favour of less restrictive decisions, and so here I am arguing that the least restrictive environment to support Margaret is at home. Dr Byrne gets stuck in the insight groove: she doesn't – he believes – have 'sufficient insight' to keep taking the medication if the tribunal revokes the order, and she is allowed home. I also doubt she sees the drugs as helpful, but argue she has the right to learn for herself whether they help. Once the 'insight' clause is used I feel I am fighting a lost*

[17] A Shah, 'Is the Mental Health Review Tribunal Inherently Unfair to Patients?' (2010) 17 *Psychiatry, Psychology and Law* 25.
[18] G Richardson and D Machin, 'Doctors on Tribunals: A Confusion of Roles' (2000) 176 *The British Journal of Psychiatry* 110.

> *cause, especially given the gravitas Dr Byrne assumes in declaring she might say she needs to take the drugs, and she might say she accepts she has bipolar disorder, but he does not believe she has real insight, the insight which would persuade him to revoke the order. She is getting the best and most appropriate treatment where she is, in his opinion.*
>
> *I argue that the acute unit is not the best place for her, there is too much overcrowding and chaotic and violent people confined in the same inadequately staffed ward. I reluctantly accept I cannot win the argument and we must disagree and look to the chair to make the casting decision. He reviews our arguments, agrees this tribunal is too early, says that in another few days in his mind there would be no doubt, but for now, he believes she is still slightly unwell and will cast his vote to uphold the order, to keep her under the MHA [Mental Health Act]. The MHT decision is not unanimous but a majority decision, 2 against 1 in favour of upholding the order to detain her.*

Breda Hamilton and Cath Roper note the deployment of insight as an act of discursive power.[19] Insight becomes a basis for enlivening legislative power to detain and treat the 'non-compliant' patient against their will under the guise of acting in their best interests. When clinicians claim the person lacks insight (and by implication will not comply with treatment), that assertion acquires medical certainty; thus, it undermines the person's credibility. Insight and lack of compliance are constantly juxtaposed in published MHT decisions. Kate Diesfeld and Stefan Sjostrom describe the circular logic: (1) lack of insight causes non-compliance; (2) non-compliance is evidence of lack of insight.[20] For a person before an MHT, it is virtually impossible to counter such circular logic.

Diesfeld and Sjostrom studied MHT decisions in Sweden, Australia and New Zealand and describe how the insight construct was used to justify continued detention.[21] In the absence of concrete evidence, claims regarding lack of insight are a convenient blanket assertion to address credibility issues. When the tribunal refers to a 'lack of insight', the person's epistemic agency regarding their internal experience is removed. Diesfeld and Sjostrom argue that concepts such as insight (and others such as, best interests, duty of care, and risk) are such loose, woolly constructs that they serve a specific function, providing sufficient flexibility to allow unanimity and agreement about decisions among legal, medical and lay MHT members. Insight provides decision-makers with 'interpretive

---

[19] B Hamilton and C Roper, 'Troubling "Insight": Power and Possibilities in Mental Health Care' (2006) 13 *Journal of Psychiatric and Mental Health Nursing* 416.

[20] K Diesfeld and S Sjöström, 'Interpretive Flexibility: Why Doesn't Insight Incite Controversy in Mental Health Law?' (2007) 25 *Behavioral Sciences & the Law* 85.

[21] For more detailed discussion of the pathologising of dissenting and unusual behaviour, see Beaupert, 'Silencing Prote(x)t' (2018) 746.

flexibility' around the philosophical minefields surrounding involuntary detention. Diesfeld and Sjostrom note how underlying assumptions about mental
illness were crucial in how MHT members interpreted individuals' behaviour
and resolved conflicting evidence about their circumstances. Problematic or
unconventional behaviour was frequently construed as bizarre, crazy or sympto-
matic. Shared opinions among MHT members about the presence and meaning
of mental illness undermined the patient's credibility; even factual statements
were likely to be disbelieved, suspected or discounted.

  In the instance I describe, Margaret stood no chance against the psychiatrists' verdict about her lack of (or at best, doubtful) insight. My inability to
dismantle this logic to highlight the inherent symbolic violence of the decision
to detain her left me troubled as an MHT participant, but the best I could do
was to have my dissenting opinion recorded in the tribunal decision.

DIARY ENTRY, 10 JUNE 2010

> *I am so disappointed and frustrated and feel I have let Margaret down.
> All my initial optimism that MHTs would make a difference has melted
> away. I also feel that the Chair has let me down on this occasion. I have
> not been able to bring him around to my point of view. I recall the initial
> enthusiasm for bringing the legal profession into the mental health field
> and conclude that it has not lived up to our expectations. There are many
> lawyers and legal educators now engaged with mental health jurisprudence
> in Ireland. However, contrary to our initial expectations, they have been
> captured by the psychiatric hegemony, and only a handful remain critical
> of the status quo.*

Acting in a statutory role in MHTs, in the context of my previous experience
of being involuntarily detained and treated under the Mental Health Act 1945,
is the essence of liminality. Vincent Turner[22] describes liminal individuals as
'neither here nor there; they are betwixt and between the positions assigned
and arrayed by law, custom, convention, and ceremony'. Being in this state is
invisible, there are: 'no status, insignia, secular clothing, rank, kinship position,
nothing to demarcate them structurally from their fellows.'[23] Liminal spaces
are challenging to negotiate as, by definition, they are ambiguous and disruptive. Incorporating my experience of being involuntarily detained (albeit never
subjected to MHT processes) and leveraging that to privilege the detainee's

---

[22] V Turner, *The Ritual Process: Structure and Anti-Structure* (London, Routledge, 1969) 95.
[23] Ibid, 98.

voice in the MHT process (with all the prescribed, statutory constraints) was emotionally challenging and exhausting. Seeking to convey the subjectivity of psychiatric violence to those who have not personally experienced put me in an invidious position. Challenging hegemony with others who wish to 'get on with the business at hand' is usually received as disruptive. Thus, my experience of navigating the pervasive risk of collusion on the one hand, and the desire to champion the individual's perspective (and challenge hegemonic practices) on the other, was complex and fraught.

Excavating 'troublesome knowledge' such as navigating between experiencing 'Madness' and sanist oppression[24] and exposing inherent epistemic injustice and symbolic violence is a core project of critical Mad Studies[25] and survivor research.[26] Survivor researchers and Mad Studies scholars are articulating marginal knowledges which trouble and disrupt medico-legal certainties.[27] One of the questions that arise from my experiences on MHTs is how (ex) service users or survivors can negotiate these liminal spaces if our knowledge remains marginalised or discredited: Can our presence make a difference?

On other occasions I had positive experiences on MHTs with psychiatrists who intently questioned their colleagues on their practices and assumptions. Sometimes it was the lawyer member and chairperson who made the difference

[24] See LeBlanc and Kinsella, 'Toward Epistemic Justice' (2016), and Poole J et al, 'Sanism, "Mental Health", and Social Work/Education: A Review and Call to Action' (2012) 1 *Intersectionalities: A Global Journal of Social Work Analysis, Research, Polity, and Practice* 20.

[25] See eg, LeBlanc and Kinsella, 'Toward Epistemic Justice' (2016); C Roper in C Roper and P Gooding, 'This is Not a Story' (2018); Diesfeld and Sjöström, 'Interpretive Flexibility' (2007); EM Nabbali, 'ID Politics: The Violence of Modernity' (2015) 4 *Intersectionalities* 1; L Costa, 'Mad Patients as Legal Intervenors in Court' in B LeFrançois, R Menzies and G Reaume (eds), *Mad Matters: A Critical Reader in Canadian Mad Studies* (Toronto, Canadian Scholars Press Inc, 2013); E Fabris and K Aubrecht, 'Chemical Constraint: Experiences of Psychiatric Coercion, Restraint, and Detention as Carceratory Techniques' in L Ben-Moshe, C Chapman and AC Carey (eds), *Disability Incarcerated: Imprisonment and Disability in the United States and Canada* (New York, Palgrave Macmillan, 2014); J Russo and A Sweeney (eds), *Searching for a Rose Garden: Challenging Psychiatry, Fostering Mad Studies* (Monmouth UK, PCCS Books, 2016) and A Daley, L Costa and P Beresford (eds), *Madness, Violence, and Power: A Critical Collection* (Toronto, University of Toronto Press, 2019).

[26] See eg, A Faulkner, 'Survivor Research and Mad Studies: The Role and Value of Experiential Knowledge in Mental Health Research' (2017) 32 *Disability & Society* 500; A Sweeney et al, 'Out of the Silence: Towards Grassroots and Trauma-Informed Support for People who have Experienced Sexual Violence and Abuse' (2019) *Epidemiology and Psychiatric Sciences* 1; D Landry, 'Survivor Research in Canada: "Talking" Recovery, Resisting Psychiatry, and Reclaiming Madness' (2017) 32 *Disability & Society* 1437; D Rose, S Carr and P Beresford, 'Widening Cross-Disciplinary Research for Mental Health': What is Missing from the Research Councils UK Mental Health Agenda?' (2018) 33 *Disability & Society* 476; Rose D, 'Service User/Survivor-Led Research in Mental Health: Epistemological Possibilities' (2017) 32 *Disability & Society* 773; A Sweeney et al, *This Is Survivor Research* (City, PCCS Books Ltd, 2009); J Russo, 'Through the Eyes of the Observed: Re-Directing Research on Psychiatric Drugs' (2018) *McPin Talking Point Papers*. Available at: www. mcpinorg/wp-content/uploads/talking-point-paper-3-final pdf.

[27] CT Sheldon and KS Spector, 'Law as a Site of Mad Resistance: User and Refuser Perspectives in Legal Challenges to Psychiatric Detention' *Journal of Ethics in Mental Health* 10 (2019) 1.

and questioned the assumption that the psychiatric professionals were doing their best for the person concerned. On those occasions, I felt empowered by the process, as I believed my arguments, as someone with experience of the consequences of attributed insanity, made a positive difference and contributed to my sense that participating in MHTs could have positive consequences for those detained. But that sense of justice prevailing occasionally dissipated over the years, and accounts such as Margaret's tribunal were distressingly common.

At this juncture, my pessimism about the perceived value of MHTs to the people caught up involuntarily in coercive treatment leaves me with uncomfortable, unanswered dilemmas. Is this the best that can be done? The premise of UNCRPD jurisprudence is that the very existence of legislation to underpin coercive treatment is unjust and discriminatory.[28] The other side of the argument is that mental health legislation will regulate such state violence and protect patient's rights by providing procedural reviews. Given my insider experiences with how epistemic injustice and symbolic violence permeate MHTs, I question whether this can be achieved. Feminist and critical legal scholars have consistently identified the inability of law to rise above a white-privileged, sanist, male-orientated conception of the world.[29] Feminist jurisprudence argues that unless the legal system considers the context of people's lives and understands the impact of accumulated disadvantages and consequent structural and symbolic violence, marginalised people will be failed. The processes and structures that give effect to justice must acknowledge the power and material relations surrounding the person at the centre of the exercise.[30]

This chapter relates one experience of attempting to challenge the inherent symbolic violence, the epistemic injustices and institutional legacies operating in MHTs from an insider position. It presents more questions than answers, and perhaps overstates the potential for change that one individual can exert within bureaucratic, procedural law. Over the course of seven years as a lay member on MHTs, occupying liminal space as an ex-detainee to contest the dominant perspective of psychiatry and legal deference to this authority was ethically

---

[28] T Minkowitz, 'Why Mental Health Laws Contravene the CRPD – An Application of Article 14 with Implications for the Obligations of States Parties' (2011). Available at: www.papers.ssrn.com/sol3/papers.cfm?abstract_id=1928600. See also Beaupert, 'Silencing Prote(x)t' (2018).

[29] F Beaupert, 'Mental Health Tribunals: From Crisis to Quality Care?' (2007) 32 *Alternative Law Journal* 219; F Beaupert, 'Mental Health Tribunal Processes and Advocacy Arrangements: "Little Wins" are No Small Feat' (2009) 16 *Psychiatry, Psychology and Law* 90; E Flynn, 'Making Human Rights Meaningful for People with Disabilities: Advocacy, Access to Justice and Equality Before the Law' (2013) 17 *The International Journal of Human Rights* 491; B McSherry, 'International Trends in Mental Health Laws: Introduction' (2008) 26 *Law in Context* 1; KW Crenshaw, 'Twenty Years of Critical Race Theory: Looking Back to Move Forward' (2010) 43 *Connecticut Law Review* 1253; P Weller, 'Taking a Reflexive Turn: Non-Adversarial Justice and Mental Health Review Tribunals' (2011) 37 *Monash University Law Review* 81; C Spivakovsky, K Seear and A Carter (eds), *Critical Perspectives on Coercive Interventions: Law, Medicine and Society* (New York, Routledge, 2018).

[30] Beaupert, 'Freedom of Opinion and Expression' (2018); Beaupert, 'Silencing Prote(x)t' (2018); Weller, 'Taking a Reflexive Turn' (2011).

troubling and emotionally exhausting. The weight of credibility is always invested in the professionals. The dynamics of epistemic injustice pervade: the patient must perform sanity yet is still likely to be discredited because they are deemed to 'suffer from a mental disorder'. It is said that justice is blind; mental health legalisation operates a procedural form of blindness to the epistemic injustice at the core of MHT processes and legitimises legacies of institutionalisation practice. This writing seeks to trouble those logics.

2

The 'Will to Empower' in Contemporary Mental Health Practice

PENELOPE WELLER

O NE OF THE challenges addressed in this volume is how to understand the features of a post-institution landscape.[1] In particular, my colleagues and I consider how the lives of people with disabilities are constituted by legal, ethical, political and practical circumstances in which they now find themselves. In this chapter, I argue that one of the effects of removing the physical structures of standalone institutions is their replacement with virtual institutions substantiated by modern forms of government. As Chris Chapman argues, modern forms of incarceration are reformulated as essential to individual improvement, assimilation and normalisation.[2] The rationale for removing institutions, for example, was explicitly expressed as a way to provide those who were incarcerated with an opportunity to live alongside others in the community and, by virtue of that placement, be recognised as participating citizens. The transposition of place raises questions about how previously incarcerated populations are governed 'in the community'. In this chapter, I explore the underlying assumptions embedded in the rationale of community participation by considering the nature of modern government.

In the late twentieth century, the work of Barbara Cruikshank provided a compelling narrative of how neo-liberal government 'worked' on populations previously thought to be ungovernable, by encouraging people to take control of their own lives, make choices and define their own future.[3] She argues that

---

[1] IB Larsen and A Topor, 'A Place for the Heart: A Journey in the Post-Asylum Landscape. Metaphors and Materiality' (2017) 45 *Health and Place* 145–51.

[2] C Chapman, 'Five Centuries of Material Reform and Ethical Reformulation of Social Elimination' in L Ben-Moshe, C Chapman and A Carey (eds), *Disability Incarcerated:Imprisonmnent and Disability in the United States and Canada* (New York, Palgrave Macmillan, 2014).

[3] B Cruikshank, *The Will to Empower: Democratic Citizens and other Subjects* (Ithaca and London, Cornell University Press, 1999).

the key feature of modern forms of government is their ability to align the aspirations of individuals with the interests of the state. While Cruikshank's substantive analysis concerns poor women in the late nineteenth century, the mechanisms of government she describes are equally applicable to other margin-alised populations. Her point is that modern forms of neo-liberal government solve problems by deploying freedom. People are governed (and limited) through empowerment and self-actualisation.

Considered in light of developments in the late twentieth and early twenty-first century, Cruikshank's analysis of neo-liberal government provides a partial explanation of the way people with disabilities are governed in a dein-stitutionalised world. However, missing from her analysis is a consideration of the regulatory force of law in the contemporary world and, specifically, of the impact of law on people with disabilities. Drawing on the recent work of Altermark, which concerns people with intellectual disability,[4] I argue that those with mental health problems who now reside in the community rather than in asylums are enjoined to pursue self-actualisation and freedom, while they are simultaneously made subject to coercive interventions, in this instance compul-sory mental health treatment. This chapter illustrates how a virtual institution for people with mental health problems is constituted by forms of legal coercion that are deployed in the name of 'freedom', 'recovery' and 'empowerment'.

The second section of this chapter underpins the argument with a brief discussion of the concept of governance and the will to empower in the govern-mentality literature. In the third section I discuss the relationship between deinstitutionalisation and rights-based mental health law. The fourth and fifth sections outline the concept of personal recovery in consumer literature and its subsequent deployment in policy, practice and law. My analysis shows how the discourse of recovery invokes a sense of rights as empowerment, but in fact reiterates clinical power and control by underpinning individuals' 'choice' and empowerment through legal coercion.

RIGHTS AND TECHNOLOGIES OF GOVERNANCE

The notion of 'technologies of governance' is a key theoretical legacy associ-ated with the work of Michel Foucault. The later period of Foucault's work is especially helpful in understanding the 'governance' of populations as an array of contradictory mechanisms and effects produced at the intersection of laws, policies and practices associated with neoliberal thought. The unique quality of neoliberal thought, according to Foucault, is that neoliberalism expands the defi-nition of economy to encompass all human conduct entailing strategic choices. Neoliberalism, therefore, is able to construct an approach that addresses the

---

[4] N Altermark, *Citizenship, Inclusion and Intellectual Disability: Biopolitics Post-Institutionalisation* (Abingdon and New York, Routledge, 2017).

totality of all human behaviour.[5] The neoliberal subject is conceived as a person who exercises the fundamental human faculty of choice and is perpetually responsive to modifications in her environment. Human capacity in neoliberalism comprises all the skills, aptitudes and competencies that constitute the self. Each individual is considered peculiarly inseparable from her capacities and is necessarily an 'enterprise of themselves'.[6] The neoliberal individual is therefore exhorted to care for herself and to practice freedom through the exercise of rational choices, guided by an 'ethic of the self'.[7] Forms of advanced neoliberal government promoting the 'ethic of the self' aim to reproduce the forms of self-mastery, self-regulation and self-control that are necessary to govern a population made up of individual subjects who care for themselves as 'free subjects'.[8] As Foucault insisted, liberal rationalities of government are concerned with deploying the agency and capacity of such individuals and populations.

Drawing on Foucault, Barbara Cruikshank understands the imperatives of neoliberalism as a demand for regimes of empowerment and self-governance, articulated as choice and citizenship.[9] According to Cruikshank, advanced liberal societies have given rise to a range of technologies that deploy the agency and capacity of individuals and populations. Cruikshank argues that multiple techniques of self-empowerment or 'technologies of citizenship' are practical techniques for the 'subjection of individuals'.[10] These technologies manifest in welfare rights struggles, community action programmes, community development and health promotion programmes,[11] making individuals in advanced liberal democracies self-governing citizens through a myriad of small-scale and everyday practices.[12] Cruikshank saw the women's 'self-help' or welfare movement of the late nineteenth century as emblematic of neoliberal government because it constituted a technique for reforming both society and the individual by indirectly harmonising the interests of both.[13] By focusing on self-help and the notion of 'a better standard of life', Cruikshank provides a useful analysis of the way techniques of government were deployed in the late nineteenth century to address the endemic social problems of poverty, charity dependence

---

[5] P O'Malley, 'Social Justice after the "Death of the Social"' (1999) 26(2) *Social Justice* 92.

[6] C Gordon, 'Governmental Rationality: An Introduction' in G Burchell, C Gordon and P Miller (eds) *The Foucault Effect* (Chicago, University of Chicago Press, 1991).

[7] G Burchell, 'Liberal Government and Techniques of the Self' (1993) 22(3) *Economy and Society* 267–81; B Cruikshank, 'Revolutions Within: Self-Government and Self-Esteem' (1993) 22(3) *Economy and Society* 327–44.

[8] N Rose, 'Government, Authority and Expertise in Advanced Liberalism' (1993) 22(3) *Economy and Society* 284–99.

[9] Cruikshank, *The Will to Empower* (1999).

[10] Cruikshank, 'Revolutions Within' (1993). See also N Altermark and H Nilsson, 'Crafting the "Well-Rounded Citizen": Empowerment and the Government of Counter-Radicalization' (2018) 12(1) *International Political Sociology* 53–69. Available at: https://doi.org/10.1093/ips/olx028.

[11] M Dean (1999) 'Risk, Calculable and Incalculable' in D Lupton (ed) Risk and Socio-cultural Theory: New Direction and Perspectives (Melbourne, Cambridge University Press) 131–59, 147.

[12] Cruikshank, *The Will to Empower* (1999), 48.

[13] Ibid.

and immorality.[14] Her account of neoliberal governance reflects the idea that the neoliberal imagination in the late twentieth century responds to deinstitutionalisation and the release of a new population of (problematic) individuals by developing and deploying new techniques of neoliberal government.

Cruikshank's analysis of empowerment and the paradox of 'freedom' describes a mode of government that assigns citizenship rights only to those who are permitted to participate in society. Writing almost 20 years later, Altermark describes the contemporary relationship between neoliberal technologies and rights as one in which there is constant reckoning and withdrawal of entitlement.[15] Altermark shows how people with intellectual disabilities in the deinstitutionalised world of the twenty-first century are recognised as citizens and (potential) subject of rights, but are simultaneously and selectively excluded from the exercise of rights.[16] Altermark argues that contemporary modes of neoliberal governance rely on a process of crafting 'free' citizens while simultaneously monitoring and correcting their conduct, sometimes through law and sometimes by brute force, whenever an appropriate 'citizen' fails to materialise. According to Altermark, neoliberal governance in the twenty-first century is an exquisite mix of coercion and freedom, or coercive freedom, characterised by the selective withdrawal or denial of rights: 'the coexistence of technologies which produce citizens and technologies that withhold their fundamentalist position rights is a defining feature of the present management of the condition.'[17] If Altermark is correct, it should be possible to identify and describe instances of governance for people with disabilities (other than those with intellectual disability) that are characterised by forms of coercive freedom. The following section describes an instance of the interplay of freedom and coercion that typically applies to individuals with mental health problems.

DEINSTITUTIONALISATION AND RIGHTS-BASED MENTAL HEALTH LAWS

The global effort to close asylums was underpinned by a compelling narrative of systematic cruelty and abuse of rights.[18] In mental health, asylums were to be replaced with community-based services where rights infringements could be avoided and better clinical outcomes achieved.[19] Adequate and appropriate

---

[14] Ibid, 54.

[15] Altermark, *Citizenship, Inclusion and Intellectual Disability* (2017).

[16] Ibid.

[17] Ibid, 2.

[18] D Kritsotaki, V Long and M Smith (eds), *Deinstitutionalisation and After: Post-War Psychiatry in the Western World* (Hampshire, Palgrave Macmillan, 2016); E Goffman, *Asylums: Essays on the Social Situation of Mental Patients and Other Inmates* (New York, First Anchor, 1961); A Ashman and L Young, 'Deinstitutionalisation in Australia Part I: Historical Perspective' (2004) 50(1) *British Journal of Developmental Disabilities* 21–28.

[19] L Young, J Sigafoos, J Suttie, A Ashman and P Grevell, 'Deinstitutionalisation of Persons with Intellectual Disabilities: A Review of Australian Studies' (1998) 23(2) *Journal of Intellectual and Developmental Disability* 155–170.

community services rarely appeared.[20] In Australia, the closing of large mental health institutions was accompanied by the introduction of mental health wards and units in large hospitals and the establishment of at least some community services.[21]

New mental health laws were an essential component of deinstitutionalisation. In Victoria, Australia, the Mental Health Act 1986 provided a rights-based framework for the regulation of mental health treatment for the acutely unwell. Rights-based mental health laws are characterised by limited civil commitment criteria focusing on the need for care and treatment, coupled with dangerousness or risk, exclusion of the requirement of informed consent and the inclusion of the legal oversight of medical decision making, usually in the form of administrative tribunal authorisation.[22] The core function of this kind of legislation was to provide clear legal authorisation for the provision of medical treatment without consent; in other words, to authorise compulsory psychiatric treatment.

A unique feature of the Victorian legislation was to permit compulsory treatment in the community in addition to compulsory detention and treatment in mental health facilities.[23] Compulsory community treament provisions in legislation require individuals to take prescribed medication in the community as a condition of discharge.[24] Non-compliance results in the person being involuntarily admitted to hospital and given treatment by force if necessary.[25] The explicit rationale for introducing laws that permit compulsory treatment in the community was to extend the reach of the new mental health facilities that replaced asylums. For example, it was argued that compulsory community treatment would prevent relapse and minimise repeated, 'revolving door' admissions.[26] Compulsory community treatment was also conceived as a way to provide support for families and carers of people with severe mental illness.[27] In other words, compulsory community treatment was seen as an adjunct to

[20] L Gostin, '"Old" and "New" Institutions for Persons with Mental Illness: Treatment, Punishment or Preventive Confinement?' (2008) 122(9) *Public Health* 906–13.

[21] Young et al, 'Deinstitutionalisation of Persons with Intellectual Disabilities' (1998); C Hobbs, C Tennant, A Rosen and L Newton, 'Deinstitutionalisation for Long-Term Mental Illness: A Two-year Clinical Evaluation' (2000) 34(3) *Australian and New Zealand Journal of Psychiatry* 476–83.

[22] P Weller, 'Lost in Translation: Human Rights and Mental Health Law' in B McSherry and P Weller (eds), *Rethinking Rights-Based Mental Health Laws* (Oxford, Hart Publishing, 2010).

[23] Mental Health Act 1986 (Victoria).

[24] L Brophy and F McDermott, 'What's Driving Involuntary Treatment in the Community? The Social, Policy, Legal and Ethical Context', 2003 11(sup1) *Australasian Psychiatry* s84–s88.

[25] D Burns, A Molodynski, J Rugkasa and T Burns, 'A Systematic Review of the Effect of Community Treatment Orders on Service Use' (2014) 49(4) *Social Psychiatry and Psychiatric Epidemiology* 651–63; E. Light, I Kerridge and C Ryan, 'Community Treatment Orders in Australia: Rates and Patterns of Use' (2012) 20(6) *Australasian Psychiatry* 478–82.

[26] J Rugkasa and J Dawson, 'Community Treatment Orders: Current Evidence and the Implications' (2013) 203(6) *British Journal of Psychiatry* 406–8; E Elbogen and A Tomkins, 'From the Psychiatric Hospital to the Community: Integrating Conditional Release and Contingency Management' (2000) 18(4) *Behavioral Sciences and the Law* 427.

[27] Power, 1999.

(and possibly a replacement for) traditional forms of community service provision. Whether compulsory community treatment has actually achieved its stated objectives is doubtful; repeated efforts to elicit 'gold standard' evidence of their clinical effectiveness have failed.[28] Victoria, Australia, has the highest rate of compulsory community treatment in the world.[29] Provision for compulsory community treatment has been adopted gradually in jurisdictions around the globe, including most recently in England and Wales, although such provisions are uncommon in European jurisdictions.[30]

Rights-based mental health laws remain the dominant model for mental health or civil commitment legislation worldwide. They include strict criteria for civil commitment and legal oversight of psychiatric decisions. This remains the case despite an active debate about the need to abandon compulsory mental health treatment in light of the United Nations Convention on the Rights of Persons with Disabilities. Rights-based mental health laws affirm the validity of compulsory treatment by claiming to provide a framework of 'safeguards' for the exercise of compulsory treatment powers, often linked to the goal of 'recovery'.[31] As is discussed in more detail below, the notion of recovery in mental health legislation is rarely defined and notoriously ambiguous. It is not clear if it refers to clinical recovery or personal recovery.

SELF-CARE, EMPOWERMENT AND RECOVERY

The consumer/survivor movement has articulated personal recovery as an alternative to institutionalisation and medical control of psychosocial distress. Leading consumer activist Pat Deegan describes personal recovery as 'a process, a way of life, an attitude, and a way of approaching the day's challenges.'[32] For Deegan, '[t]he goal of the recovery process is not to become normal. The goal is to embrace our human vocation of becoming more deeply, more fully human'.[33]

Similarly, William Anthony describes:

[A] deeply personal, unique process of changing one's attitudes, values, feelings, goals, skills and/or roles. It is a way of living a satisfying, hopeful, and contributing life even with limitations caused by the illness. Recovery involves the development of

---

[28] L Brophy, C Ryan and P Weller, 'Community Treatment Orders: The Evidence and the Ethical Implications' in C Spivakovsky, K Seear and A Carter (eds), *Critical Perspectives on Coercive Interventions* (New York, Routledge, 2018).

[29] E Light, 'Rates of Community Treatment Orders in Australia' (2019) 64 *International Journal of Law and Psychiatry* 83–87.

[30] Brophy, Ryan and Weller, 'Community Treatment Orders' (2018).

[31] Light, 'Rates of Use of Community Treatment Orders in Australia' (2019).

[32] P Deegan, 'Recovery as a Journey of the Heart' (1996) 19(3) *Psychiatric Rehabilitation Journal* 91–97.

[33] Ibid, 92.

new meaning and purpose in one's life as one grows beyond the catastrophic effects of mental illness.[34]

Personal recovery focuses on the lived experience of the individual. It is concerned with their thoughts, feelings and experiences – of 'finding a way through the illness'. Personal recovery pays attention to the whole life experience of the individual, rather than merely their symptoms and diagnosis.[35] It is 'a way of living a satisfying, hopeful, and contributing life even with limitations caused by illness.'[36]

Personal recovery stands in contrast to clinical recovery. Clinical recovery is rooted in a biomedical understanding of mental illness. It is characterised by a concern with medication compliance and the creation of 'insight' into one's diagnosis. Clinical recovery is about diagnosis, treatment and cure.[37] It is concerned with symptom remission and a 'return to normal'.[38] Personal recovery, therefore, displaces medical expertise as the primary logic through which mental illness is understood and responded to. Rather than seeing mental illness as an aberration requiring treatment and cure (clinical recovery), personal recovery calls for an understanding of mental illness as an aspect of human experience that should be recognised and responded to with empathy.

Personal recovery calls for a different relationship between the individual and their care teams. Larry Davidson, for example, argues that this shift is best described as a shift toward a person-centred approach, meaning that care must attend primarily to the person (rather than to symptoms or to diagnosis), but shift away from the traditional therapeutic stance of objectivity and neutrality.[39] According to Jan Wallcraft, it is this shift from an entanglement or passive dependency on services to an 'active stance' of selectively, thoughtfully and positively using treatment and services to support independence and self-management that characterises journeys in recovery for people with long-term conditions.[40]

This vision of self-actualisation accords with Cruikshank's analysis and the prominence of the ethic of self-care described by Foucault. Expressed in terms of rights, personal recovery in the consumer movement denotes an aspiration to define and pursue for oneself a personal version of health and wellbeing

---

[34] WA Anthony, 'Recovery from Mental Illness: The Guiding Vision of the Mental Health Service System in the 1990s' (1993) 16(4) *Psychosocial Rehabilitation Journal* 11–23.

[35] R Bland, N Renouf and A Tullgren, *Social Work Practice in Mental Health: An Introduction* (Crows Nest, Allen and Unwin, 2015).

[36] Anthony, 'Recovery from Mental Illness' (1993) 15.

[37] M Slade and G Wallace, 'Recovery and Mental Health' in M Slade, L Oades and A Jarden (eds), *Wellbeing, Recovery and Mental Health* (Cambridge, Cambridge University Press, 2017).

[38] Slade, Oades and Jarden, *Wellbeing, Recovery and Mental Health* (2017).

[39] L Davidson, 'Recovery from Psychosis: What's Love Got to do With It?' (2011) 3(2) *Psychosis* 105–14.

[40] J Wallcraft, 'Recovery from Mental Breakdown' in J Tew (ed), *Social Perspectives in Mental Health: Developing Social Models to Understand and Work with Mental Distress* (London, Jessica Kingsley Publishers, 2005).

that escapes medical definition and defies clinical expertise. Personal recovery, therefore, is inconsistent with mental health laws that rely on compulsory mental health treatment.

Recovery in Mental Health Policy

'Recovery' has appeared in mental health policy around the globe.[41] In North America, the term first appeared in the United States Surgeon General's Report of 1999 and the President's New Freedom Commission report on mental health in 2003.[42] *The National Consensus Statement on Mental Health Recovery* refers to the journey of healing as follows: 'Mental health recovery is a journey of healing and transformation enabling a person with a mental health problem to live a meaningful life in a community of the person's choice while striving to achieve his or her full potential.'[43]

The Mental Health Commission in Ireland adopted the concept in 2008:

> The recovery approach challenges the privileging of one theoretical perspective as the primary explanation for and the treatment of mental distress and the privileging of professional interpretations and expertise over expertise by experience and personal meaning. The biomedical model and medical treatments may have an important place for some people in the recovery process, but as an invited guest, rather than the overarching paradigm.[44]

In Australia, the recovery focus is reiterated in state and territory policies. In the national framework for recovery-orientated mental health services, the concept of recovery is defined as: 'conceived by, and for, people with mental health issues to describe their own experiences and journeys and to affirm personal identity beyond the constraints of diagnosis.'[45] In addition, the Australian Commission on Safety and Quality in Health Care defines recovery as:

> A deeply personal, unique process of changing one's attitudes, values, feelings, goals, skills and/or roles. It is a way of living a satisfying, hopeful and contributing life. Recovery involves the development of new meaning and purpose in one's life as one grows beyond the catastrophic effects of psychiatric disability.[46]

[41] S Ramon, W Shera, B Healy, M Lachman and N Renouf, 'The Rediscovered Concept of Recovery in Mental Illness: A Multi-Country Comparison of Policy and Practice' (2009) 38(2) *International Journal of Mental Health* 106–26.

[42] TG Kuehnel and RP Liberman, 'A Practical Guide to Recovery-Oriented Practice: Tools for Transforming Mental Health Care' (2011) 62(5) *Psychiatric Services* 567.

[43] Substance Abuse and Mental Health Services Administration, *National Consensus Statement on Mental Health Recovery* (Rockville, US Department of Health Human Services, 2006).

[44] Mental Health Commission (MHC), *A Recovery Approach Within the Irish Mental Health Services. A Framework for Development* (Dublin, MHC, 2008).

[45] Australian Health Ministers' Advisory Council, Department of Health, *National Framework for Recovery-Oriented Mental Health Services* (Canberra, AHMAC, 2013) 11.

[46] Australian Commission on Safety and Quality in Health Care (ACSQHC), Safety and Quality in Health Care (Canberra, ACSQHC, 2014) 41.

At first blush, these definitions of recovery in policy documents appear to form a positive alignment with the notion of personal recovery as expressed by the consumer movement. The apparent alignment is undermined by the ambiguity of the legislation. Personal recovery aspirations align with the objective of self-government. Clinical recovery (and compulsion) can be invoked whenever self-governance fails.

Recovery-orientated Practice

Recovery policy has been accompanied by the development of recovery practice. The articulation of recovery in mental health policy has encouraged the development of new clinical practices, referred to collectively as recovery-orientated practice. These programmes are presented as everyday practices that promote and support empowerment. What constitutes recovery-orientated practice, however, differs considerably depending on the conceptualisation of recovery that is utilised.[47] For present purposes, I define recovery-orientated practice as the influential model developed by Mike Slade and colleagues in the United Kingdom. Slade and Wallace identify the four key elements of personal recovery as:

> [A] process or continuum,
>
> that is subjectively defined by the person him- or herself
>
> or 'rated' by the person experiencing the mental health difficulties, who is considered the expert on his or her recovery, and
>
> means different things to different people, although there are aspects that many people share (emphasis added).[48]

Based on an analysis of the recovery literature, Leamy et al created a more detailed model of personal recovery.[49] They described 13 characteristics of the recovery journey and five recovery processes: connectedness, hope and optimism about the future, identity, meaning in life, and empowerment (giving the acronym CHIME).

Recovery-orientated practice models of this type rely on coaching techniques developed in positive psychology to promote the skills of self-care.

> Behavioural coaching is a structured, process driven relationship between a coach and coachee, or group which includes: assessment, examining values and motivation,

---

[47] C Le Boutillier, M Leamy, VJ Bird, L Davidson, J Williams and M Slade, 'What Does Recovery Mean in Practice? A Qualitative Analysis of International Recovery-Oriented Practice Guidance' (2011) 62(12) *Psychiatric Services* 1470–76.

[48] Slade and Wallace, 'Recovery and Mental Health' (2017).

[49] M Leamy, V Bird, C Le Boutillier, J Williams and M Slade, 'A Conceptual Framework for Personal Recovery in Mental Health: Systematic Review and Narrative Synthesis' (2011) 199 *British Journal of Psychiatry*, 526.

setting measurable goals, defining focused action plans, and using validated tools and techniques to help coachees develop competencies and remove blocks to achieve valuable and sustainable changes in their professional and personal lives.[50]

Coaching provides a road map to teach self-care and empowerment.[51] Recovery-orientated practice represents an expression of the techniques of self-actualisation and self-care identified by Cruikshank that serve to align individual aspirations for a better life with the agenda of the state.

The Critique of Recovery-orientated Practice

Recovery-orientated practice is not without its critics. Davidson, Brophy and Campbell argue, for example, that coaching models 'tend(s) to dumb down opportunities for critical practice'.[52] There is nothing in the model itself that points to a critical interpretation of one's goals or one's treatment. Indeed, they argue, treatment as recommended by clinicians appears to be enfolded in the assessment of reality and possibility. Moreover, in the context of community treatment orders requiring submission to compulsory mental health treatment, the model's acquiescence to clinical goals and a clinical notion of recovery is reinforced.

Pilgrim and McCranie have similarly pointed out that the dialogues of recovery, including those encapsulated in the coaching models, gloss over the evident contradiction between personal recovery and clinical recovery. The recovery discourse, they argue, often takes advantage of a 'working misunderstanding' about the notion of recovery.[53] Indeed, the coaching model assumes that the clinician and the patients share the same values and are working toward the same goals, but avoids explicit examination of the asymmetrical power difference between patients and clinicians. The emphasis on independence and self-determination and the different relationship with services described by Wallcraft and others is rarely a feature of the recovery-orientated practice literature.[54] As Kidd et al point out, it is critical that recovery-orientated practice includes the facilitation of dialogue about power and its implications for clinical relationships.[55] Without it, the coaching model is experienced as another clinical interaction in which the authentic consumer voice is sidelined.

[50] S Skiffington and P Zeus, *Behavioral Coaching: How to Build Sustainable Personal and Organizational Strength* (Sydney, McGraw-Hill, 2003) 6.

[51] J Passmore, 'Behavioural Coaching' in S Palmer and A Whybrow (eds), *Handbook of Coaching Psychology: A Guide for the Practitioner* (London, Routledge, 2007).

[52] G Davidson, L Brophy and J Campbell 'Risk, Recovery and Capacity: Competing or Complementary Approaches to Mental Health Social Work' (2016) 69(2) *Australian Social Work* 161.

[53] D Pilgrim and A McCranie, *Recovery and Mental Health: A Critical Sociological Account* (New York, Macmillan International, 2013) 33.

[54] Wallcraft, 'Recovery from Mental Breakdown' (2005).

[55] S Kidd, A Kenny and C Mckinstry, 'Exploring the Meaning of Recovery-Oriented Care: An Action-Research Study' (2015) 24(1) *International Journal of Mental Health Nursing* 38–48.

These critiques are forcefully reiterated in the consumer/survivor literature. Howell and Voronka, for example, observe that 'recovery' and 'resilience' have been co-opted into medical reasoning and health policy.[56] They argue that while the language of recovery appears to respond to the criticism of the 'total institution'[57] modern mental health systems in fact constitute virtual institutions, made up of a mixture of institutional and community-based services. In the virtual institution, 'psychology and psychiatry have become expert in recovery and resilience'.[58] Rather than working with a person from the person's perspective, recovery models complement, supplement and reify medical and biological explanations of psychosocial distress. Moreover, they fail to engage with structural and collective experiences and struggles.[59] The coaching programmes that are supposed to promote empowerment reify the notion of self-actualisation through choice, while ignoring the material, practical and clinical constraints that make free choice impossible for many people with mental health problems. They draw attention away from systemic deficits, and away from the real lack of choice afforded by inadequately funded mental health and social care services.

COERCION AND RECOVERY IN MENTAL HEALTH LAW

Recovery has also been included in mental health legislation. In Australia, for example, the word appears in mental health legislation in all jurisdictions except the Northern Territory. A full analysis of the use of the term 'recovery' in Australian legislation is beyond the scope of this chapter. A brief survey of its use, however, shows that 'recovery' is undefined and deployed ambiguously, eliding the concepts of personal and clinical recovery. When the term recovery is considered in context of the legislation, its statutory meaning shifts, drifting from an allusion to personal recovery on the one hand to a clear reference to a clinical concept of recovery on the other. For example, in New South Wales (NSW), the first listed object of the Act is '(a) to provide for the care and treatment of, and to promote the *recovery* of, persons who are mentally ill or mentally disordered (emphasis added)'.[60] In the absence of a definition, this statutory formulation could mean either personal or clinical recovery. In the section that sets out the principles of the act, principle (e) states that 'people with a mental illness or

[56] A Howell and J Voronka 'Introduction: The Politics of Resilience and Recovery in Mental Health Care' (2012) 6(1) *Studies in Social Justice* 1–7.
[57] See Goffman, *Asylums* (1961).
[58] Howell and Voronka, 'Introduction: The Politics of Resilience' (2012).
[59] Davidson, Brophy and Campbell, 'Risk, Recovery and Capacity' (2016) 161. See also M Jorge-Monteiro and J Ornelas, '"What's Wrong with the Seed?" A Comparative Examination of an Empowering Community-Centered Approach to Recovery in Community Mental Health' (2016) *Community Mental Health Journal* 821–33.
[60] Mental Health Act 2007 (NSW) s 3.

mental disorder should be provided with appropriate information about treatment, treatment alternatives and the effects of treatment and be supported to pursue their own recovery'.[61] This statement suggests a subjective interpretation of the idea of recovery more akin to the notion of personal recovery. The principles also note the importance of assisting people to make 'treatment plans' and 'recovery plans'. Here the definition of recovery becomes more ambiguous, but seems to point to a distinction between a treatment plan which sets out clinical matters and a recovery plan which sets out personal matters.[62] Finally, the provisions relating to the NSW Mental Health Tribunal require the Tribunal to consider, among other things, whether:

> (d) care and treatment following involuntary admission resulted, or could have resulted, in an amelioration of, or *recovery* from, the debilitating symptoms of a <u>mental illness</u> or the short-term prevention of deterioration in the mental or physical condition of the affected person (emphasis added).[63]

In this instance, it seems that recovery is clearly intended to refer to clinical recovery, thereby undermining the possibility that personal recovery will be pertinent to the considerations of the Tribunal. Similar ambiguity can be identified in other mental health acts in Australia, although interpretations in Victoria and the Australian Capital Territory are clearly influenced by the presence of human rights legislation in those jurisdictions.[64]

The point to be made for the purpose of the present discussion is that laws permitting compulsory psychiatric treatment, which in Altermark's analysis, constitutes a clear withdrawal of the rights that are enjoyed by others, is couched in the language of recovery. It is assumed that recovery can sit alongside coercion. If people fail to adhere to the correct model of recovery represented in the legislative text, they can be forced to accept treatment. The elision or ambiguity provides example of the tensions identified by both Cruikshank and Altermark. The effect is especially acute for those 'in recovery', that is those who are past the acute phase of their illness and are or will soon be in the community, perhaps subject to a compulsory treatment order. The effect is the same for those who are deemed to be voluntary patients, because their position is equally precarious. The statutory juxtaposition of recovery and coercion combines clinical imperatives with an enforceable obligation to practice care of the self.

CONCLUSION

In contemporary mental health care, recovery-orientated practice crystallises into formulaic programmes that create and substantiate behaviours consistent

---

[61] Ibid
[62] Ibid, s 68 (h)(h1).
[63] Ibid, s 53.
[64] See *PBU & NJE v Mental Health Tribunal* [2018] VSC 564 (1 November 2018). Available at: www.austlii.edu.au/cgi-bin/viewdoc/au/cases/vic/VSC/2018/564.html.

with preferred clinical outcomes which are then reinforced by laws permitting compulsory mental health treatment. Altermark's analysis of coercion therefore adds a critical dimension to Cruikshank's understanding of the demand for self-governance, articulated through the rhetoric of empowerment, choice and citizenship.[65] The objective of neoliberal technologies such as these is to reform society and the individual by harmonising the interests of both.[66] Recovery-orientated practice, like the self-help movement, purports to transform the relationship between consumers of mental health services and the state by reconciling clinical goals and personal recovery goals. Like the self-help programme of the nineteenth century, recovery enhances the subjectivity of people with disabilities through day-to-day practices of empowerment, self-help and participation, which are simultaneously techniques of subjectification. The analysis of recovery in mental health policy and its juxtaposition with compulsory treatment in law shows how practices of freedom are reinforced by coercion. In this case, coercion is in the form of a legal framework that permits compulsory mental health treatment within mental health facilities and beyond in the community. Coercion and recovery are rendered compatible. The virtual institution identified by this analysis comprises recovery, community and coercion – indeed a modern form of coercive freedom.

[65] Cruikshank, *The Will to Empower* (1999).
[66] Ibid, 48.

3

The Biopolitics of Disability in Late Francoism and the Spanish Democratic Transition (1959–81)

SALVADOR CAYUELA SÁNCHEZ

THE AIM OF this chapter is to show the functioning of the biopolitics of disability during Late Francoism and the Spanish Democratic Transition. In order to this, I first introduce the theoretical and method-ological framework. Secondly, I analyse both the discourses and the dynamics of the 'disability dispositive' by studying three areas and their specific institutions: the economic field, the social and medical area, and pedagogical practices. The main objective of this analysis is to expose the specificities of the biopolitics of disability during 1959–81 and the functioning of the institutions involved.

At the end of the Spanish Civil War (1936–39), the Franco regime tried to govern many spheres of Spanish people's lives, creating a wide range of mech-anisms and institutions to do so.[1] Children and young people, women and industrial workers, prisoners and farmers were all subjected to comprehensive sets of government practices and standardising discourses aimed, essentially, at laying down the framework for the new political system. Amongst these mecha-nisms and institutions, the education system, the *Frente de Juventudes* (Youth Movement), the Women's Section of the Falange Party, the regime's propaganda facilities, economic policies and medical and psychiatric discourses stand out. All these manifested as biopolitical devices – disciplinary mechanisms, aimed at governing individuals, and regulating mechanisms, aimed at governing the population[2] – which were capable of creating certain attitudes and behaviours among a large part of the Spanish people. These attitudes were characteristic

---

[1] S Cayuela, 'Governing Goods, Bodies and Minds: The Biopolitics of Spain during the Francoism (1939–1959)' (2019) 26 *Foucault Studies* 21; S Cayuela, *Por la Grandeza de la Patria: La Biopolítica en la España Franquista (1939–1975)* (Madrid, Fondo de Cultura Económica, 2014).

[2] M Foucault, *'Il faut défendre la société'. Cours au Collège de France. 1976* (Paris, Gallimard, 1997) 213–35; M Foucault, *Histoire de la Sexualité I. La Volonté de Savoir* (Paris, Gallimard, 2003) 177–211.

of a specific subjectivity, that of the *homo patiens*, which worked as one of the regime's true keystones.[3] In fact, these were subjects who were expected to be resigned to their circumstances, apolitical and apathetic regarding public life, whose main aim in life was to enhance the homeland through selfless, hard work. Given this, if in Franco's 'New Spain' work had become the true religion of the State, what was the role assigned to those who could not work according to the criteria established at the time? More specifically, what place was occupied in society by people with physical disabilities, who had difficulty performing activities considered by the regime as most beneficial for the nation's prosperity?

Taking these questions and theoretical approaches as a starting point, in this chapter I will show how a certain 'governing of physical disability' began to take shape within the framework of Franco's biopolitics.[4] Reducing my analysis to the period between 1959 and 1981 — that is to say, so called Late Francoism and the Spanish Democratic Transition – I will distinguish between three areas of study that are nonetheless interconnected: economics, medical–social and pedagogy. With respect to each, I will analyse the policies and active mechanisms within the disability framework, which will allow me to understand, on the one hand, the institutionalisation – in the sense of establishing a shared set of norms and practices – of people with physical disabilities and, on the other hand, the evolution from a 'medical' understanding of disability to the first steps of the so-called 'empowerment' of this social group. From this perspective, it is inside the institutions and laws involved in the government of physical disability during Late Francoism where we can find (paradoxically) the starting point of the deinstitutionalisation of people with physical disabilities and their struggle against segregation and urban and social barriers.

To understand this process, it is necessary to address the concept of 'institution' in a double sense: as a framework of total control executed in concrete spaces (as per Goffman[5] or Foucault) but also as a set of norms spread through discourses and practices produced by specific cognitive strategies (as used by Mary Douglas[6]). This double sense of the concept of 'institution' allows us to understand how the process of institutionalisation of people with physical disabilities – in different 'disciplinary institutions' – was a previous and necessary step for the deinstitutionalisation which followed. In this regard, the disciplinarisation of the bodies and minds of these people in these new institutions initiated – as non-desirable consequence but assimilated by the system for its own benefit – a more subtle and self-regulated government. Thus, a new rhetoric of inclusion and biopolitical strategies created new spaces of economic and

[3] Cayuela, 'Governing Goods, Bodies and Minds' (2019) 36–38.

[4] Cayuela, *Por la Grandeza de la Patria* (2014) 351.

[5] E Goffman, *Asylums: Essays on the Social Situation of Mental Patients and Other Inmates* (New York, Doubleday, 1961).

[6] M Douglas, *How Institutions Think* (Syracuse, Syracuse UP, 1986).

political action, as well as new ways for people with disabilities to understand themselves, others and the world.

Effectively, the shaping of these policies and institutions, their lines of inter-pretation and influence, as well as the operation of the incorporated mechanism, shows the transformations in the governing of disability in Spain – from disci-plinary institutions to regulatory strategies. If we understand 'govern' in a Foucauldian way as a productive 'conduct of conducts',[7] it is clear that these laws, policies and practices introduced by the regime in the studied spheres some-how permitted the emergence of this collective and its new demands. Of course, it was an unwanted consequence, but was assimilated by the system in terms of legitimacy. On the other hand, we cannot forget the pressure and progres-sive importance of nascent associations for the rights of people with disabilities since the 1960s.[8] But these practices and discourses, strategies and 'resistance' from people with disabilities undoubtedly marked the future of the government of disability in Spain, progressively assimilated into the rest of Europe and the West under the emerging conditions of neoliberalism.[9]

A NEW NEED FOR LABOUR: THE ECONOMIC SPHERE

Since the nineteenth century, labour was considered the privileged strategy of social inclusion for people with disability.[10] The fact is that industrialised nations needed to maintain their workers in good physical and moral condi-tions for their development[11] and, in the case of an occupational accident or congenital or acquired disability, the incorporation or reincorporation of the individual to the productive system could be potentially crucial for the country's economy.[12] These discourses also permeated Spain, where they led to the materi-alisation of mechanisms such as the *Asilo para Inválidos del Trabajo* (Asylum for

---

[7] M Foucault, 'La Gouvernamentalité' in D Defert and F Ewald (eds), *Michel Foucault, Dits et Écrits II. 1976–1988* (Paris, Gallimard, 2001) 635–57; M Foucault, *Sécurité, Territoire, Population. Cours au Collège de France. 1977–1978* (Paris, Gallimard/Suil, 2004) 10–12.

[8] M Del Cura and J Martínez-Pérez, 'From Resignation to Non-Conformism: Association Move-ment, Family and Intellectual Disability in Franco's Spain' (1957–1975) (2016) 68(2) *Asclepio: Revista de Historia de la Medicina y de la Ciencia* 149.

[9] DT Mitchell and SL Snyder, *The Biopolitics of Disability. Neoliberalism, Ablenationalism, and Peripheral Embodiment* (Ann Arbor, University of Michigan Press, 2015); JK Puar, *The Right to Maim: Debility, Capacity, Disability* (Durham, Duke University Press, 2017); S Tremain (ed), *Foucault and the Government of Disability* (Ann Arbor, University of Michigan Press, 2005).

[10] P Abberley, 'Work, Utopia and Impairment' in L Barton (ed), *Disability and Society: Emerging Issues and Insights* (Harlow, Longman, 1996), 61–79; C Barnes and G Mercer, 'Disability, Work and Welfare: Challenging the Social Exclusion of Disabled People' (2005) 19(3) *Work, Employment and Society* 527.

[11] A Labish, 'Doctors, Workers and the Scientific Cosmology of the Industrial World: The Social Construction of Health and the "Homo Hygienicus"' (1985) 20 *Journal of Contemporary History* 599.

[12] G Eghigian, *Making Security Social: Disability, Insurance, and the Birth of the Social Entitle-ment State in Germany* (Ann Arbor, Michigan University Press, 2000).

Work Invalids) (1887), the passing of the *Ley de Accidentes del Trabajo* (Law on Accidents at Work) (1900) and the creation of the *Instituto para la Reeducación Profesional* (Institute for Professional Retraining) (1922).[13] The introduction of these laws and the building of the associated institutions or training schools can be considered points of reference in the national government of disability, even if their completed development became impossible when the Spanish Civil War broke out and with the establishment of Franco's dictatorship. Moreover, in spite of the fact that, as the *Fuero del Trabajo* (Labour Law) of 1938 (the first of the *Cartas Fundamentales* (Fundamental Charters) of the Franco regime) stated on its title II, labour had become an obligation for all Spaniards, since 'the right to work is a result of the duty imposed on Mankind by God, to fulfil his individual purposes and the prosperity and greatness of the Homeland'.[14]

In fact, it was a 'national and patriotic' conception of labour that reserved a significant place for disability within the Francoist ideology: on the one hand, due to its potential negative effect on productivity and therefore, on the nation's prosperity; and on the other hand, given that it could mean a disregard concerning the individual's supreme duty towards the homeland.[15] All of this meant positioning the loss or decrease in the productive capacity of people as an essential criterion for their categorisation and classification in comparison with others, essential vectors in the official discourse about the 'problem of disability'.[16]

This philosophy however, lacked a coordinated programme regarding disability, as was acknowledged by Dr Piga in the *First Social Medical Symposium by the National Welfare Institute*, held in 1958, entitled 'Rehabilitation of the Alleged Disabled Person and Social Security'.[17] The pressure to change this came from various sources at the end of the 1950s: firstly, the same experts that participated in this symposium; secondly, the international organisations and the fieldwork of their experts;[18] and finally, the creation of a national rehabilitation programme – the *Patronato de Rehabilitación y Reeducación de Inválidos* (Patronage of Rehabilitation and Retraining of Invalids).[19] However, the text of

---

[13] J Martínez-Pérez and M Del Cura González, 'Work Injuries, Scientific Management and the Production of Disabled Bodies in Spain, 1920–1936' in S Barsch, A Klein and P Verstraete (eds), *The Imperfect Historian: Disability Histories in Europe* (Frankfurt am Main, Peter Lang, 2013) 191–211.

[14] OSG (Official Spanish Gazette/Boletín Oficial del Estado, BOE), 10 March 1938.

[15] J Martínez-Pérez (2017), 'Work, Disability and Social Control: Occupational Medicine and Political Intervention in Franco's Spain (1938–1965)' (2017) 37(4) *Disability Studies Quarterly* 1–21.

[16] J Martínez-Pérez and M Del Cura González, 'Bolstering the Greatness of the Homeland: Productivity, Disability and Medicine in Franco's Spain, 1938–1966' (2015) 28(4) *Social History of Medicine* 805.

[17] A Piga, 'Bases y Proyecto de un Servicio de Rehabilitación y Valoración de Lesionados en el Instituto Nacional de Medicina y Seguridad del Trabajo' in A Piga et al., *I Symposium Médico-Social en el INP. Tema de Estudio: Rehabilitación del Presunto Inválido y Seguridad Social* (Madrid, Instituto Nacional de Previsión, 1959) 317–24.

[18] FJ Safford and K Jansson, *Programa Nacional de Rehabilitación de Niños Físicamente Disminuidos (Informe de una Misión en España)* (Madrid, Ministerio de la Gobernación-Dirección General de Sanidad, 1957).

[19] OSG, *Boletín Oficial del Estado*, 13 July 1957.

the decree establishing the programme explicitly indicated the need to promote the 'organisation of study centres for the social problems set forth by disability and training for social care personnel'.[20] In this way, it is possible to detect a growing concern about the group's social integration: namely, 'the retraining and placement of the physically disabled'.

These steps must be understood to be closely linked to the gestation period of the so-called 'economic developmentalism' that occurred in Spain in the 1960s and 1970s. The time of extreme poverty in the 1940s and 1950s was over[21] and the economic situation permitted the creation of a new social security system more capable to attend to the demands of people with disabilities (as I will show in the following section of this chapter). However, the progressive implementation of the scientific organisation of labour was then presented as an essential requirement for the consolidation of growth: setting work rates, the determination of optimum and normal yields and the necessary professional qualifications were, at that point, priority strategies.[22] In this new economic and labour model, destined to prepare for the arrival of neoliberalism in Spain, people with disabilities also had to play their part. This meant moulding their bodies – just like everyone else – to the demands of the new labour market, with its attitudes far removed from the traditional charity models, 'fleeing from charity, simplistic solutions of the system of benefits, pensions, etc'.[23]

As I will show, rehabilitation was going to become the privileged biopolitical strategy to ensure the reincorporation into work of people with physical injuries under the rise of neoliberalism.[24] Concepts such as 'inclusion', 'participation' and 'equality' became possible, particularly after the death of Franco in 1975, when the rehabilitation process was not exclusively framed in terms of the benefit of the nation, but also in rights-based, individualised and empowerment discourses. The bodies of people with physical disability remained one of the battlefields where corrective techniques of modern scientific medicine and the economic demands of the new capitalism came together. But it was inside the walls of some total institutions such as the Centros de Recuperación

---

[20] Ibid.

[21] R Moreno, 'Pobreza y Supervivencia en un País en Reconstrucción' in C Mir, C Agustí and J Gelonch (eds), *Pobreza, Marginación, Delincuencia y Políticas Sociales Bajo el Franquismo* (Lleida, Espai/Temps, 2005), 139–64; M Richards, *A Time of Silence: Civil War and the Culture of Repression in Franco's Spain, 1936–1945* (Cambridge, Cambridge University Press, 2006).

[22] S Cayuela, *Por la Grandeza de la Patria* (2014), 164; J Mª Vegara, *La Organización Científica del Trabajo, ¿Ciencia o Ideología?* (Barcelona, Fontanella, 1971).

[23] A López Fernández and J Bataller Sallé, 'Importancia de la Rehabilitación en los Planes de la Seguridad Social' in Vv.Aa., *I Symposium Médico-Social en el INP. Tema de Estudio: Rehabilitación del Presunto Inválido y Seguridad Social* (Madrid, Instituto Nacional de Previsión, 1959) 305–9.

[24] J Martínez-Pérez and M Del Cura, 'El "Llamamiento del Deber": Influencia Exterior, Interés del Estado y Modernización de las Estrategias de Gestión de la Discapacidad en España (1956–1970)' in D González, AM Ortiz and JS Pérez (eds), *La Historia, Lost in Translation: Actas del XIII Congreso de la Asociación de Historia Contemporánea* (Albacete, Universidad de Castilla La-Mancha, 2017) 1775–86; MJ Sullivan, *Paraplegic Bodies: Self and Society* (PhD Thesis, University of Auckland, 1996).

de Minusválidos Físicos (Recovery Centres for the Physically Handicapped), or boarding schools for children with physical disabilities created at the beginning of the 1970s[25] – in which medicine and pedagogy worked together – where the claims for deinstitutionalisation and equality reached a new peak.[26]

CORRECTING BODIES: THE MEDICAL SPHERE

Since the end of the 1950s, the World Health Organization (WHO) has been defining rehabilitation policies to guide the social and labour participation of people with disabilities. In 1958, the WHO[27] emphasised the need to coordinate social rehabilitation programmes, which, in an integrated way, allowed these objectives to be achieved. Furthermore, it underlined new possibilities opened up by therapeutic and rehabilitation techniques.[28] This meant reserving a central position for medical professionals in the treatment of disabilities, granting them maximum authority over the rehabilitation process. In turn, this reinforced medical professionals' traditional function of social control agents in charge of the institutional assignment of the condition of 'invalid', always suspiciously coupled with the possibility of fraud.

In this new context, Spanish doctors took advantage of the Franco regime's general demand for greater openness, incorporating the WHO guidelines into national policies while, at the same time, redefining their social position. In this way, the 'medical body' was not only going to play a main role in the government of the working situation regarding people with disabilities (as we have just seen), but its attributions were always going to go way beyond it.

The changes in the discourses and governing strategies for disability incorporated into Spain over those years encouraged the promotion and social position of certain medical specialities and their professional groups. For instance, foreign experts who visited the country during the 1950s criticised the lack of staff training and the generally pitiful situation of Spanish healthcare and welfare centres; this prompted the development of the medical speciality of rehabilitation and of its professionals.[29] It was a time of economic and institutional opening up, which was completely necessary for the regime, and it is in this context that Spanish progress in the governing of disability, and of the actual socio-healthcare model itself in general, should be understood.

[25] S Cayuela and J Martínez-Pérez, 'El Dispositivo de la Discapacidad en la España del TardoFranquismo (1959–1975): Una Propuesta de Análisis (2018) 70(2) *Asclepio: Revista de Historia de la Medicina y de la Ciencia* 232.
[26] N Altermark, *Citizenship, Inclusion and Intellectual Disability: Biopolitics Post-Institutionalisation* (Abingdon, Routledge, 2018).
[27] WHO, *Technical Report Series* (1958) Geneva, nº 158.
[28] R Ballester, 'Los Organismos Sanitarios Internacionales y la Rehabilitación de los Niños con Discapacidades Físicas (1948–1975)' (2012) 12 *Revista de Estudios do Seculo XX* 89.
[29] Martínez-Pérez and Del Cura, 'El "Llamamiento del Deber"' (2017), 1783–84.

In the 1960s, two new laws brought about a revitalisation of Spain's public socio-healthcare system: the *Ley de Bases de la Seguridad Social* (Social Security Act) in 1963[30] and the *Ley General de la Seguridad Social* (General Social Security Act) in 1966.[31] This new legislative framework on the subject of social welfare meant the introduction of important changes in the care of disability and the 're-training and rehabilitation of invalids', a true common denominator with regard to invalidity.[32] Accordingly, and as was indicated in the fourth section of Chapter V of the 1963 Law – regarding the General Rules of the Social Security System – the granting of aid for the retraining and rehabilitation of invalids was explicitly contemplated, consisting of: 'Treatments of physiological and functional recovery, re-adaptation processes, special courses of professional instruction adapted to the needs and aptitudes of the invalid, as well as, if such is the case, additional steps of selective employment.'[33] Moreover, within title II, General Regime of the Social Security, Chapter VI was devoted to invalidity, breaking down the actual concept and the types of invalidity from a legal point of view, and establishing a recovery plan that had to attend to the 'aptitudes and faculties, age, sex and residence of the invalid, as well as their previous occupation and their reasonable wish for social promotion, always within the technical and professional demands'.[34]

All of this meant programmatic acceptance of the principles of rehabilitation and retraining of invalids sustained and fostered by the WHO itself, amongst which the restoring of the patient's physical condition using all the necessary medical, surgical and physiotherapeutic methods stood out. The conception of the individual therefore held a specific place, with the reintegration of all their functions being the ultimate aim of the rehabilitation. The Social Security Act therefore allowed an increase and considerable improvement in the care of people with disabilities, increasing the number of centres that provided rehabilitative care throughout the country and forcing the development of specific programmes.

These changes in the government of disability allow us to understand how health professionals continued to impose their standardisation practices on disabled bodies generating, at the same time, specific 'forms of subjectivity'. Furthermore, in this process we can see the development in Spain of the so-called 'medical model', not understood as a normative phenomenon, but as a prism through which one can understand the politics of disability (ie the way in which the medical system spread its discourses and views about people with disabilities, focusing on impairments and possible corrections, while neglecting

[30] OSG, 30 December 1963.
[31] OSG, 21 April 1966.
[32] AM Águila, *El Debate Médico en Torno a la Rehabilitación en España (1949–1969)* (PhD Thesis, Universidad Complutense de Madrid, 2007).
[33] OSG, 21 April 1966.
[34] AM Águila, *El Debate Médico* (2007) 153.

the individuals themselves). Accordingly, people who were considered 'invalid' remained in a particularly uncomfortable position:

> On the one hand, they had to consider the opportunity of subjecting themselves to a protocol of actions on their bodies which, even when successful, often led to the frustration of seeing how they could not reach the reward of finding work. On the other hand, in the case of deciding to not undertake the rehabilitating process, they were exposed to being contemplated as people who preferred to enjoy a pension instead of fulfilling their obligation to use their work to contribute to the increase in production.[35]

This was, in fact, the great dilemma for people with disabilities in a developing Spain: either subjecting themselves to the hard and painful rehabilitation process, or facing up to the more than likely loss of their 'official condition of invalid' and the subsequent withdrawal of the (possible) associated benefits. On this point, the legislation passed by way of Decree 792/1961 of the 13 April was transparently clear:

> Any injured or sick worker who refuses to subject his or herself to rehabilitation, as well as those who do not follow the medical prescriptions, may have the economic perception they had been enjoying as compensation for temporary or permanent incapacity suspended, or decreased, by resolution of the General Directorate for Welfare, at the proposal of the insurance entities, the compensating Fund of the Insurance for Accidents at Work and Occupational Illnesses or the employer who had been authorised to directly assume the risk of work incapacity.[36]

EDUCATING DISABILITY: THE EDUCATIONAL SPHERE

Despite all its problems, the Social Security Act meant the implementation of a new socio-healthcare system in Spain, partially devoted to calming increasingly determined protests by workers and students.[37] It was not just an important step, but rather a new trial in the American strategy of the global fight against communism,[38] promoted in Europe from the end of the Second World War, which at that time, had to accompany economic development and the free market. Nonetheless, one area of action had to be revitalised to drive the process: education. World Bank experts had warned in a report in 1962 that major investment in education was needed:

> The Spanish Government expected to devote large amounts to fixed investment. However, these hopes would not produce the desired results unless the necessary

[35] Martínez-Pérez and M Del Cura, 'El "Llamamiento del Deber"' (2017) 1784.
[36] OSG, 30 May 1961.
[37] C Molinero and P Ysàs, *Productores Disciplinados y Minorías Subversivas: Clase Obrera y Conflictividad Laboral en la España Franquista* (Madrid, Siglo XXI, 1998).
[38] S Cayuela, '¿Biopolítica o Tanatopolítica? Una Defensa de la Discontinuidad Histórica' (2008) 43(33) *Daimon: Revista Internacional de Filosofía* 44–46.

attention was paid to investment in human resources, given the fact that the skilled labour offer was an important factor when determining the economic growth rate ... An increase in production with modern techniques would increase the demand for specialised labour at all levels, a demand that would only be able to be met if the performance of the teaching system was planned correctly ... A good general education is essential for all of this.[39]

These declarations, and others along the same lines, were aimed at convincing the Francoist government to face up to the necessary but continuously postponed reform of the education system and finally bore fruit in the passing of the Ley General de Educación (General Education Law) in 1970.[40] This Law was used to design a new education system, with a clear universalist vocation, as indicated in its Preamble:

The national education system currently takes on tasks and responsibilities of an unprecedented magnitude. Now it must provide educational opportunities for the entire population, thus making fully effective the right of any human to education and it must attend to the specialised preparation of the large number and diversity of professions that modern society requires.

The universalisation of education brought a large number of children into classrooms from which they had previously been excluded. Among these were many children affected by physical and intellectual impairments. In fact, Article 12.2 of the Law referred explicitly to these children, affirming that 'the modalities that are demanded by the peculiarities of the students, the methods and the subjects will also be included in the education system'.[41] Further, Chapter VII of Title I, Article 49.1 stated:

Special education will be aimed at preparing, by way of adequate educational treatment, all the impaired children and misfits for incorporation into social life, as fully as possible in each case, according to their conditions and resulting from the education system; and to a work system whenever possible, which allows them to look after themselves and to be useful to society.

This new Law seemed to want to introduce innovative methodologies and strategies regarding the education of disabled students, incorporating a 'pedagogical approach' to the new problems.[42] In fact, the extension of schooling in many cases allowed the detection of mental and sensorial problems. Moreover, the creation of two educational modalities for disabled children – 'slight' and 'profound' – is worth mentioning. Whilst the former were educated in ordinary

[39] Vv.Aa., *Informe del Banco Internacional de Reconstrucción y Fomento: El Desarrollo Económico en España* (Madrid, Oficina de Coordinación y Programación Económica, 1962) 543–44.
[40] Law 14/1970, OSG, 6August 1970.
[41] Ibid.
[42] T González, 'Itinerario de la Educación Especial en el Sistema Educativo. De la Ley Moyano a la Ley General de Educación' in M Reyes Berruezo and María y S Conejero (eds), *El Largo Camino Hacia la Educación Inclusiva: La Educación Especial y Social del Siglo XIX a Nuestros Días: XV Coloquio de Historia de la Educación* (Pamplona-Iruñea, 2009) 261–70.

schools which catered to their specific requirements, based on an integrated education model, the latter were taken to special centres. Despite the obvious educational improvement that the new General Education Law introduced for disabled people – including them in the national education system for the very first time – the truth is that the construction of these special education centres and the creation of special education classrooms in ordinary centres for slightly disabled pupils, was at the very least insufficient, due to deficient economic support.[43] In fact, the private initiatives and efforts of parents continued to play a crucial role in the education of disabled children, as had been occurring since at least the beginning of the 1960s.[44]

Moreover, since the end of the 1950s, the top priorities of associations such as the *Asociación Pro Niños Anormales* (Association for Abnormal Children), created in 1959, and the *Federación Española de Asociaciones Protectoras de Subnormales* (Spanish Federation of Associations for the Protection of Subnormal Patients), founded in 1963, were to become recognised by the public authorities and be instruments for solidarity amongst the affected families. Their goals could be summarised as making the State and society aware of the problem of disability; analysing the difficulties faced by both disabled people and their families; challenging the State and its institutions to take the necessary steps and study the problems related to disability; promoting the creation of centres for care, training, residential homes, etc.; and finally, encouraging the training of specialised personnel.[45]

To conclude, the educational framework developed by the Francoist regime contributed to raising the profile of the problem of children with disabilities. However, its strategies were too close to the old disciplinary model and operated through institutions in which notions such as inclusion and opportunity remained in the background. Nevertheless, the residential institutions created in this period contributed, in many cases, to the creation of 'communities', permitting people with disabilities to leave the closed spaces of their homes and meet others similar to them. As I noted in my introduction, this 'golden age' of institutionalisation in Spain created, without any plan, the process of deinstitutionalisation and a new biopolitical governance of disability which followed.

FINAL REMARKS

In an article published in 1976, Michel Foucault stated that in Europe since the 1950s there was:

the forming of a new right wing, a new moral, a new economy, a new political ideology of the body [...] Since then, an individual's body had become one of the main

[43] Ibid, 256–58.
[44] Del Cura and Martínez-Pérez, 'From Resignation to Non-Conformism' (2016).
[45] E Puerto, 'Función de las Asociaciones de Padres y Familias de Subnormales', in *El Problema de los Niños Subnormales* (Madrid, Servicio Nacional de Asociaciones Familiares, 1970) 293–320.

objectives of State intervention, one of the great goals of which the State itself had to take charge.[46]

This new model, which had accompanied the establishment of the so-called 'Welfare State' in the old world, also without any doubt influenced the biopolitical measures adopted by Francoist Spain, which was particularly susceptible to international dynamics from the mid-1950s. With its own undercurrents, Franco's Spain progressively adapted its strategies and life-governing mechanisms to those deployed in its European neighbours, partially as political and social legitimation mechanisms, and partially due to the demands of the new production system. And precisely in this new context, as had happened on an international scale, a specific method for governing disability in Spain was shaped. Effectively, as we have just seen, in this period the old strategies of segregation and control of people with disabilities, articulated through several laws, twisted into a new stage of post-institutionalisation and biopolitical control of a new community.

In fact, although always connected to previous dynamics, a new conception of disability started to emerge in Spain from the end of the 1950s, full of new meanings and attended to by new mechanisms and institutions. From a broad range of areas – the economy, education, the associative movement, medical discourses and practices, etc. – a new disability mechanism was shaped that went beyond the standardisation and regularisation practices that would end with the arrival of democracy in the 1970s and 1980s. Within this new context, the bodies and minds of people with physical disabilities were obliged to subject themselves to certain standardisation practices. Jorge Gallardo claims:

> The standardising disciplines, claiming to incorporate the aspirations of those who wish to be integrated [...] are no more than a reproduction and violence that is not only symbolic, but rather pertaining to class, as this depoliticises the origin of disabilities. [And the fact is that] the supposed overcoming of the individual and biological model operates surreptitiously, depoliticising, removing from history and 'making social' something that has a structural origin and that is emanated by the State and its economy.[47]

With the death of General Franco in 1975, these practices and discourses regarding disability became more widespread, and their mechanisms of action more significant. Accordingly, for example, the Social Security Act (1963) remained in effect until the enactment of the *Ley General de Sanidad* (General Healthcare Act) in 1986,[48] a socialist law strongly inspired by the British National Health Service. In this Law, which stipulated the protection of health and healthcare for all Spaniards, the care of disabled people was covered in great depth, specifically

---

[46] M Foucault, 'Crise de la médicine ou crise de l'antimedicine?' in D Defert and F Ewald (eds), *Michel Foucault, Dits et Écrits II. 1976–1988* (Paris, Gallimard, 2001) 40–58, 42.

[47] J Gallardo, Discapacidad y Producción: Ideología de la Normalidad Neoliberal' in *Seminario Cuerpos y subjetividades: Estrategias de Disciplinamiento y Control Social en Chile*, 24–25 April (Santiago de Chile, Universidad de Arte y Ciencias Sociales de Chile, 2013).

[48] OSG, 24 April 1986.

under heading 5 of Article 18, which specified the creation of 'care programs for population groups at greatest risk and specific protection programs against risk factors, as well as deficiency prevention programs, both congenital and acquired'.[49] This also occurred with the General Education Law of 1970, which remained in effect, as mentioned previously, until 1990, including the provisions relative to care for disabled people.

In this chapter I have shown how, in the Spain of Late Francoism and the Spanish Democratic Transition, a new government of disability emerged which, in many ways, translated global dynamics into a national setting. A new dispositive was born in the convergence of expert knowledge about disability, manifesting in social, medical and economic discourses, institutions and physical fields. As I underlined at the beginning of the chapter, this dispositive can be understood within the general framework of Francoist biopolitics, and its idiosyncratic way of governing the population of Spain.[50]

---

[49] Ibid.
[50] Cayuela, 'Governing Goods, Bodies and Minds' (2019).

4

Disability Law in Spain
Moving Forward Towards Full Citizenship and Inclusion?

EDUARDO DÍAZ VELÁZQUEZ

THIS CHAPTER ANALYSES the extent to which Spanish legislation guarantees the access to the condition of citizenship of persons with disabilities on an equal footing with the rest of the population in education, employment or the supply of supports for personal autonomy. In Spain, disability law has progressively evolved incorporate new social views that consider disability a result of the interaction of a person's impairments and environmental barriers. This new conception emanates from the 2006 United Nations Convention on the Rights of Persons with Disabilities, among other sources, and aims, fundamentally, for the inclusion of persons with disabilities on an equal footing with the rest of the population, with support as needed. However, a more detailed analysis of the regulations brings up continuing relevant contradictions between their inspiring principles of equality and inclusion and rules promoting institutionalisation and segregation in some citizenship spaces, such as employment, education, and daily life support. Moreover, this legislation does not include sufficient regulatory and economic guarantees for the effective exercise of the citizenship rights of persons with disabilities. Thus, social inclusion ultimately depends on the person's economic situation – sufficient financial capacity allows for the acquisition of the necessary resources and support through the market.

The sociological analysis of disability has frequently been linked explicitly[1] or implicitly to the study of the citizenship of persons with disabilities.

---

[1] See J Morris, 'Citizenship, Self-Determination and Political Action: The Forging of a Political Movement', *Conference on Citizenship and Disability* (Sydney, 1998); J Morris, *Citizenship and Disabled People: A Scoping Paper Prepared for the Disability Rights Commission* (Leeds, Disability Archive UK, 2005); D Marks, 'Disability and Cultural Citizenship: Exclusion, Integration and Resistance' in N Stevenson (ed), *Culture and Citizenship* (London, Sage, 2001).

Citizenship is a 'status bestowed on all those who are full members of a community. Its beneficiaries are equal in terms of the rights and obligations that citizenship implies'.[2] 'Citizenship' is composed of three main dimensions: civil, political and social rights. It is both a *formal status* (the collection of civil, political and social rights bestowed by the legal system to the members of a community) as well as a *substantive condition* (the effective practice of those rights).[3]

From a formal point of view, the legislation has tried to protect persons with disabilities from the contingencies derived from this condition. However, even though it had formerly 'protected' them through their institutional confinement (mainly of persons with intellectual disability or mental illness) and their segregation in social spaces, this legislation has evolved into the promotion of the inclusion of persons with disabilities in the community and a formal guarantee of their rights. This evolution has incorporated the ethical, technical and scientific advances of the last years and, in particular, the empirical and theoretical contributions of the social model of disability, materialised in the 2006 United Nations Convention of the Rights of Persons with Disabilities (hereafter, the Convention). Normative modifications have also been promoted by the struggles and vindications of the associative movement of persons with disabilities, which have gradually transformed some social practices and symbolic conceptions of disability, bringing them into the political and legislative agenda, and consolidating those practices as rights[4] or as guarantees for the exercise of citizenship rights.

In the same way, the development of certain subjective rights and the incorporation of some moral principles and values into the legislation intend to inspire a social change from the substantive point of view, since public policies are an '*account*: an explicit formulation, a narration, a collection of texts, a discourse, a cognitive framework that seeks to delineate, impel, catalyze, orient and legitimize the courses of action for which several agents opt or that they adopt'.[5] However, in the case of persons with disabilities, citizenship rights are not yet quite effective in the substantive sphere,[6] given that the legislation does not include any mechanisms that may sufficiently ensure the provision of necessary support and may actually reduce the social and economic inequalities that

---

[2] See TH Marshall and T Bottomore, *Ciudadanía y Clase Social* (Madrid, Alianza Editorial, 1992) 37.
[3] Ibid, 100–1.
[4] See MR Somers, 'La Ciudadanía y el Lugar de la Esfera Pública: Un Enfoque Histórico' in S García and S Lukes (eds): *Ciudadanía, Justicia Social, Identidad y Participación* (Madrid, Siglo XXI Editores, 1999) 217–34.
[5] See F Fantova, *Diseño de Políticas Sociales. Fundamentos, Estructura y Propuestas* (Madrid, Editorial CCS, 2014) 41.
[6] See E Díaz Velázquez, *El Acceso a la Condición de Ciudadanía de las Personas con Discapacidad en España. Un Estudio Sobre la Desigualdad por Razón de Discapacidad.* (Madrid, Ediciones Cinca, 2017).

derive from disability, which would enable persons with disabilities to exercise their rights on an equal footing with the rest of the population.[7] The gradual consolidation of a neoliberal social and economic model has permeated both legislation and public policies, resulting in the debilitation of the social rights sustained by the principle of social justice.[8] This has heightened economic and social inequalities based on disability, since sufficient economic, personal or technical supports for the development of personal autonomy and, ultimately, for the exercise of full citizenship rights, are not guaranteed. Whether or not a person has the necessary support would depend on a previous socioeconomic condition or on the class trajectory[9] of the person with disability and her/his purchasing power,[10] given that the provision of those personal or technical supports is mediated by the marketand its supposed ideal of freedom of election.[11]

In addition, some tensions and contradictions between institutionalisation (or segregation) and inclusion in the community persist in the legislation. In some instances, the legislation favours the institutionalisation of persons with disabilities and their confinement in segregated centres and thus hinders their participation in the community. This segregation is directly connected to other forms of social segregation (economic, ethnic or by gender) in the historical context of the privatisation of social resources and dismantlement of the welfare state. These varied modalities of segregation are justified in our neoliberal societies under the mantra of freedom of choice, even though, as mentioned before, this choice is subordinated to the person's economic capacity to acquire specific services in the market.

Nevertheless, although other forms of social segregation or inequality answer to social, economic or cultural dynamics, which are more or less complex, what is genuine about segregation in terms of disability is that it is, in many cases, socially and, overall, legally legitimated or justified because people with disabilities supposedly require different treatment. Segregated institutionalisation in special education, protected employment, residences, legal incapacitation and so on are considered acceptable measures for the segregated wellbeing of the person with disability, without considering that this contradicts the principles of inclusion and equality.

---

[7] See J Martínez de Pisón, *Políticas de Bienestar. Un estudio Sobre los Derechos Sociales* (Madrid, Editorial Tecnos, 1998).

[8] See especially A Sen, *Nuevo Examen de la Desigualdad* (Madrid, Alianza Editorial, 2003); M Nussbaum, *Las Fronteras de la Justicia. Consideraciones Sobre la Exclusión* (Barcelona, Editorial Paidós, 2007); and J Rawls, *La Justicia Como Equidad. Una Reformulación* (Barcelona, Paidós, 2002).

[9] See C Ferrante and MAV Ferreira, 'Cuerpo y Habitus: El Marco Estructural de la Experiencia de la Discapacidad' (2011) 5(2) *Intersticios* 85–101.

[10] See DT Mitchell and S Snyder, *The Biopolitics of Disability: Neoliberalism, Ablenationalism, and Peripheral Embodiment* (Ann Arbor, University of Michigan Press, 2015).

[11] See E Díaz Velázquez, 'Ciudadanía, Identidad y Exclusión Social de las Personas con Discapacidad' (2010) 4(1) *Política y Sociedad* 115–35.

In the next sections I analyse the extent to which Spanish legislation, while promoting inclusion in the community as an aspirational principle and objective, does not establish formal guarantees (in the shape of social rights) to make the inclusion of persons with disabilities as citizens effective. Moreover, I will suggest that this legislation even allows several forms of institutionalisation and social segregation within domains such as education, employment or the provision of supports for personal autonomy. In order to achieve this, I analyse the content and discourse of Spanish legislation on disability, identifying the tensions and contradictions that are reproduced between inclusion in the community and segregation and institutionalisation. I will concentrate on two main laws, the General Law on Rights of Persons with Disabilities and their Social Inclusion (hereafter, General Law), which was passed in 2013 and that, though not sufficiently, tries to adapt Spanish legislation to the Convention, and Law 39/2006, of 14 December, for the Promotion of Personal Autonomy and the Attention of Persons in Dependency Situations, commonly and hereafter called the *Dependency Act*, which was passed in the same year as the Convention and that, therefore, does not incorporate its philosophy regarding the guarantee of personal supports needed by persons with disabilities in their daily lives.

A SEGREGATED EDUCATION SYSTEM

The first barrier that prevents the access of persons with disabilities to the condition of citizenship on an equal footing with the rest of the population can be found in the education system. Barriers and inequalities in access to the education define the life opportunities of students with disabilities and, thus, condition their social and economic position in adulthood. A public and free education system favours access to education under equal conditions. However, the Spanish education system is far from guaranteeing equal access to all students.

During the Franco dictatorship (1939–75), the Spanish education system was mainly controlled by Catholic institutions, with public schools being a residual option. In the case of students with disabilities, the segregated educational institutions that existed at the time also belonged to the Catholic Church. In the 1980s, after Spain's return to democracy, a public and free education system began to emerge, but budget shortfalls hindered its initial developments. This led to the establishment of charters with the existing private (mainly Catholic) schools, which received public funding in return for providing supposedly free education for the students whom the State was as yet unable to place in the public system. These charters were intended to be provisional measures, meant to last only during the creation of new public schools. During that period the process of integrating students with disabilities into ordinary schools started to be carried out while, at the same time, new special education centres were created, many of them by specialist disability associations. Currently, charter schools, understood as tax-funded private schools established by a charter between the State or by regional governments, have considerable weight in the Spanish education system, while public education lacks funding in the majority of Spain's regions. This fact, and the growing privatisation and elitisation within the Spanish education system, has favoured social and territorial segregation according to the socioeconomic or ethnic origin of the students and, in the case of some private elite schools, goes as far as to segregate by sex.[12] In completely private elite schools (iethose with neither acharter with the State nor public funding) the social and class distinction of the students is higher than in chartered private schools. Tuition fees are also higher, and students with disabilities make up barely 0.5 per cent of the student body.

In the same way, segregation of students according to disability exists. For the school year 2016–17, 2.67 per cent of students had special needs and 16.5 per cent of them were schooled in special education centres. Students with a higher degree of disability or with specific types (such as intellectual disability) are more likely to be segregated in special education schools, where they receive specific attention and are separated from other students. While 94.4 per cent of students with hearing impairments, 96.0 per cent of students with vision disability or 85.3 per cent of students with physical disability are schooled in ordinary centres, only 77.6 per cent of students with intellectual disability and 41.7 per cent of students with multiple disabilities study in ordinary schools. Students with special needs who are schooled in ordinary centres are considerably more abundant in public schools than in charter or private ordinary schools. Thus, 74.5 per cent of students with disabilities schooled in ordinary centres study in public schools and 23.8 per cent of them are schooled in charter schools (1.6 per cent in private schools). In special education, 40.2 per cent of students are schooled in charter centres.[13] However, these are not elite schools, but special education schools run by Catholic organisations or disability associations and funded by the State, which has turned special education into business.

This type of segregated education, which contradicts Article 24 of the Convention, is sanctioned by Article 18.3 of the General Law, as well as by the 2/2006 Organic Law of Education. Although Article 18.1 of the General Law establishes that 'PWD have the right to inclusive, quality and free education, on an equal footing with the rest of the population', the abovementioned Article 18.3 opens the way for segregation, which in practice has become frequent. Article 18.3 states:

> schooling of students in special education centres or in their substitute education units will only take place when the needs of these students cannot be looked

---

[12] See E J Díez Gutiérrez, 'Una Amenaza para la Escuela Pública: Laicidad, Privatización y Segregación', (2014) 81(28.3) *Revista Interuniversitaria de Formación del Profesorado* 105–17.

[13] See Estadística de las Enseñanzas no Universitarias. Subdirección General de Estadística y Estudios del Ministerio de Educación y Formación Profesional: www.estadisticas.mecd.gob.es.

after in ordinary schools, taking the opinion of parents or legal tutors into consideration.[14]

However, some judgments of the Spanish Constitutional Court have endorsed the schooling of students in special education centres, even against the will of their families.[15] This has happened despite the fact that the law itself indicates that educational administrations must:

> ensure an inclusive education system at all educational levels, as well as lifelong education, and guarantee the schooling of students with disability in basic education, taking care of their educational needs through the regulation of supports and reasonable adjustments for the attention of those of them who need special learning or inclusion needs.[16]

Some additional guarantees, which theoretically would make the right to inclusive education possible, are developed in Article 20. Among them is the passage from special to inclusive education: 'Special education centres will create whatever conditions necessary in order to make the connection between them and between ordinary centres easier, and the inclusion of their students in the ordinary education system.'[17] However, the law does not define how this process should take place (itineraries, procedures, compliance mechanisms), nor is there a prospect for the achievement of future goals or for the gradual dismantlement of special education.

The Spanish education system has gone through continuous normative change insofar as it is a domain in ideological dispute between two antagonist visions and models: the model of excellency and the model of equity. So, the *8/2013 Organic Law of December 9, for the improvement of the quality of education*, establishes a classist and ableist education system which hinders inclusive education. This model, in which centres will be allowed to select a part of the student body according to academic achievements, toughens the conditions of permanence in the education system by establishing a set of evaluations or examinations (*reválidas*) that imply the discrimination of students according to their cognitive capacities from the earliest learning stages and that harden the conditions to pass from one stage to the next. Notwithstanding, the law vaguely points out that these examinations must be adapted in the case of special needs

[14] See Art 18, *Real Decreto Legislativo 1/2013, de 29 de Noviembre, por el que se Aprueba el Texto Refundido de la Ley General de Derechos de las Personas con Discapacidad y de su Inclusión Social.* Available at: www.boe.es/eli/es/rdlg/2013/11/29/1/con.

[15] See the sentence of the Constitutional Court which denies the right of special needs students to be schooled with supports in an ordinary centre (see www.boe.es/diario_boe/txt.php?id=BOE-A-2014-2058), a ruling which was issued after the promulgation of the General Law. The matter received plenty of media attention (eg www.elperiodico.com/es/noticias/sociedad/avala-que-estado-decida-nino-debe-ser-escolarizado-educacion-especial-3077569).

[16] See Art 18.2, *Real Decreto Legislativo 1/2013, de 29 de Noviembre, por el que se Aprueba el Texto Refundido de la Ley General de Derechos de las Personas con Discapacidad y de su Inclusión Social.* Available at: www.boe.es/eli/es/rdlg/2013/11/29/1/con.

[17] Ibid, Art 20.

students ('adequate measures will be set up so that the conditions in which the examinations will be carried out can be adapted to special needs students'). This discrimination, as we have seen, can also be spatial, since it is possible that education centres can be separated into high- and low-achievement centres mediated by socioeconomic conditions), on the basis of the neoliberal ideal of *excellence*. In regard to inclusive education and the development of the special education system, this law modifies the *Organic Law of Education* by means of Article 79 (bis) *of Measures for schooling and attention*, which establishes that 'educational administrations are in charge of adopting those measures necessary to identify students with specific learning difficulties and to evaluate their needs at an early stage' and that 'schooling of students with learning difficulties will be carried out following the principles of normalisation and inclusion and will guarantee their non-discrimination and effective equality in the access and permanence in the education system'.[18] It does so without explicitly mentioning what role special education will have in the schooling process, if it will be a priority or a negligible option, or if the right to inclusive education will prevail over special education, especially if the student's parents or legal tutors opt for ordinary schools.

The new Project of Organic Law which modifies the 2/2006 of 3 March Organic Law of Education,[19] as designed by the current interim Spanish Government, provides in its fourth additional disposition that:

> the government, in collaboration with the educational administrations, will develop a plan, in accordance with Article 24.2.e) of the United Nations Convention for the Rights of Persons with Disabilities and in compliance with the Fourth Goal of the 2030 United Nations Agenda for Sustainable Development, so that ordinary centres may have the resources necessary in order to be able to take care of students with disabilities in the best possible conditions, within a ten-year period. Educational administrations will continue to give support to special education centres, so that they may be reference and support centres for ordinary schools, besides schooling those students that require very specialised attention.[20]

This bill and other legislative initiatives have provoked the reaction of the Catholic Schools, the employers' organisation, as well as the constitution of the platform 'Inclusive, Special too' ('Inclusiva sí, Especial también'), opposed to the (supposed) closure of special education centres. This platform's discourse focuses on the advantages of special education in segregated centres in comparison with ordinary undersupplied schools. In this sense, it is not only a collision between two views as to how students with disabilities must be taken care of

---

[18] See *Ley Orgánica 8/2013, de 9 de Diciembre, para la Mejora de la Calidad Educativa*. Available at: www.boe.es/eli/es/lo/2013/12/09/8/con.

[19] See *Proyecto de Ley Orgánica por la que se Modifica la Ley Orgánica 2/2006, de 3 de Mayo, de Educación*. www.educacionyfp.gob.es/dam/jcr:4aa926b3-4dc6-4ef0-8458-3e02589cdd99/1-proyecto-ley-20190215.pdf.

[20] Ibid.

in the education system, but between corporatist and business interests which define the positions of the different actors in it.

To be schooled in the ordinary education system is a necessary but not sufficient condition for inclusion, since sufficient support staff and resources need to be available at ordinary centres to respond to the needs of students with disabilities. Inclusive education would therefore be a first step towards an inclusive society in which PWD could be considered equal citizens. Inequalities in access to the ordinary education system or segregation of education will condition the life opportunities of students and, thus, produce employment and economic inequalities in adulthood.

TWO TYPES OF ACCESS TO EMPLOYMENT

Access to employment and its quality define the social and economic position of persons with disabilities in society and, therefore, the exercise (or lack of) their citizenship rights on an equal footing with the rest of the population. But, as with education, some precepts of Spanish legislation do not guarantee inclusion and access to ordinary employment. The General Law establishes two types of integration: ordinary and protected employment (through special employment centres). The now abrogated Law 13/1982, of 22 April, for the Social Integration of the Disabled conceived this second type as a minor option for those groups of persons with disabilities with greater difficulties in employment inclusion, and as a bridge in order to obtain inclusion in the ordinary work system. However, this goal has disappeared in the General Law, because of the lobbying power of the corporations in the protected employment sector.[21]

From 1982, successive laws have been issued with the common goal of softening the access conditions and requirements for persons with disabilities to enter the ordinary work system. Hence, Article 38.1 of Law 13/1982, incorporated in Article 42 of the General Law, establishes that companies with over 50 workers must meet the 2 per cent reserve quota of workers with disabilities in their overall staff. However, companies often argue they have considerable difficulties in meeting this quota, caused by the supposed imbalance between their productivity needs and demands and the employment profiles and the qualifications of PWD. As such, the requirements for hiring workers with disabilities were progressively loosened in ordinary companies through the development of alternative measures to the reserve quota. These measures were gradually introduced in the legal system from the 1990s and have been combined in the General Law. As a result, it is possible to record workers from temporary recruitment agencies as part of the reserve quota, as well as to be exempted from it by the means of collective bargaining agreements and by the voluntary adoption of alternative

---

[21] See R Esteban and D Gutiérrez, 'La Incentivación del Empleo de las Personas con Discapacidad en el Medio Ordinario de Trabajo' (2014) 2(1) *Revista Española de Discapacidad* 7–32.

measures, as established by the Law 50/98 in its eleventh additional disposition, or by the Royal Decree 27/2000, of 14 January, of alternative measures. These measures changed focus from the acquisition of goods or services from special employment centres (that is, protected employment) to the donation to bodies concerned with the creation of employment for persons with disabilities. Later, the Royal Decree 364/2005, of 8 April, that regulates the exceptional alternative compliance with the reserve quota for people with disabilities, simplified the request procedures for the declaration of exceptionality in the compliance with the reserve quota and added new productive, organisational, technical and economic exception criteria.[22] Currently, employment statistics show that many companies with over 50 workers do not comply with the reserve quota through direct hiring.[23]

These alternative measures reinforced the role of protected employment as against employment inclusion in ordinary companies. Together with this, special taxation conditions and advantages in the social security fees of special employment centres have encouraged the creation of this type of centre by large corporations, which aim to maximise their profit by hiring workers with disabilities without employment inclusion difficulties in the ordinary work place, often under precarious working and wage conditions. Today, around one of five workers with disabilities works in a special employment centre, although only 25.9 per cent of persons with disabilities of working age had a job in 2017.[24] Generally, the wages of persons with disabilities who work in special employment centres are lower than for non-disabled workers in similar jobs. In 2008, the average gross pay for persons without disabilities was €57.6/day, persons with disabilities working in ordinary companies received €46.1/day, and the average gross pay for those of them working in special employment centres was €38.1/day.[25] However, in the collective bargaining agreements of special employment centres, the wages of professional groups occupied by persons with disabilities (as operators) are usually below the minimum wage (currently €900/month).[26]

Due to the high inactivity rates among persons with disabilities, employment policies must be coordinated with those of income guarantees and of social and economic protection,[27] which, in the case of persons with disabilities, ensure

[22] See M Paloma, *Empleo Protegido en España. Análisis de la Normativa Legal y Logros Alcanzados* (Madrid, Ediciones Cinca, 2007).

[23] See Instituto Nacional de Estadística (INE), *El Empleo de las Personas con Discapacidad* (Madrid, INE, 2017).

[24] Ibid.

[25] See V Rodríguez, *Discapacidad y Mercado de Trabajo: Tres Análisis Empíricos con la Muestra Continua de Vidas Laborales* (Madrid, Fundación de las Cajas de Ahorros, 2013).

[26] See XV Convenio Colectivo General de Centros y Servicios de Atención a Personas con Discapacidad (BOE, 2019) www.boe.es/eli/es/res/2019/06/27/(2).

[27] See F Fantova, *Diseño de Políticas Sociales. Fundamentos, Estructura y Propuestas* (Madrid, Editorial CCS, 2014) 233–36.

sufficient economic resources in periods of inactivity. This is particularly the case for inactivity due to permanent incapacity caused by illness or accident, whether this illness or accident is due to work or not. These economic benefits on the basis of disability (permanent incapacity or invalidity), regulated by the *General Social Security Law*, considerably scarce and incompatible to work (which disincentivise work search), are closer to an assistance-based perspective than to a redistributive logic which may guarantee decent living conditions. Moreover, the effectiveness of these measures is reduced for persons with disabilities of lower socioeconomic conditions, especially those who have not worked previously, and who would have the right to a non-contributory benefit. These persons often have congenital disabilities, which by their type and scope make employment inclusion and self-income creation harder.

The situation creates an important disability gap in the access to employment, especially in access to high-quality employment. Employment policies for persons with disabilities have displayed greater concern for the interests of companies than guaranteeingaccess to quality employment. Thus, dualism between persons with disabilities included and excluded from employment, typical of current neoliberal societies, also implies inequality in the exercise of citizenship rights, so far closely related to employment. Those who do not access employment or who do so in precarious conditions make up an infraclass or a second-class citizenry.[28]

A SYSTEM FOR THE PROVISION OF SUPPORTS AND CARE THAT FAVOURS INSTITUTIONALISATION

Law 39/2006, of December 14, for the Promotion of Personal Autonomy and the Attention of Persons in Dependency Situations, commonly called the Dependency Act (with the great symbolism that this word implies in the social conception of disability), was created more out of a gerontological perspective than one of rights, as it is conceived in the domain of disability, in reproduction of the assistance-based logic of the rehabilitation paradigm. This norm is mainly concerned with responding to the new social needs of ageing populations, often accompanied by disabilities that imply functional dependency, and not so much with the needs of persons whose disabilities were acquired earlier in their lives. This law's background includes the development of actions orientated toward the promotion of personal autonomy, independent life and inclusion in the community, since it limits the attention of the System for the Autonomy and Attention to Dependency (SAAD) to the basic activities of daily life. In this sense, it is a missed opportunity to guarantee, at least formally, the provision of necessary support for the full development of the personal autonomy of persons with disabilities. This is caused, in part, by the economic

[28] See E Díaz Velázquez, 'Ciudadanía, Identidad y Exclusión' (2010).

interests which were at stake in the creation of the system, in particular, those of long-term care companies, who tried to develop a business model based on the creation of taxpayer-funded private residential infrastructure. In turn, Article 3 of the Dependency Act consecrated the participation of private business in the management of services and benefits.

In this context, companies in the dependency sector built residential institutions chartered by the administration to take care of the needs of new users. These new infrastructures were also funded through the Spanish state-owned industrial holding company Sociedad Estatal de Participaciones Industriales which, in 2009, created a Support Fund for the Promotion and Development of Infrastructures and Services of the System of Autonomy and Dependency Attention for companies in this sector, recently extended to associations in the disability domain.[29] This has been denounced by, among others, the United Nations Committee for the Rights of Persons with Disabilities, which –in its 2019 Report, issued after its evaluation of Spain's compliance with the Convention –indicated that these residential institutions should stop receiving public funding.[30]

Thus, residential lodging services have been growing alongside this system and now have considerable weight in it: 12.29 per cent of the services in September 2019, which means 169,723 institutionalised persons. In contrast, economic benefits for personal assistance have been granted to only 7,657 persons, 0.55 per cent of the total.[31] Moreover, the maximum amount of personal assistance economic benefit is €833.96/month, which would not allow more than three hours of personal assistance per day, which is just not enough time in the majority of the cases. Hence, only those with sufficient economic resources of their own would have access to an independent life with full community inclusion, as they could supplement the economic benefits provided by the SAAD. Personal assistance services are most often received by persons with disabilities with higher economic and education status, whereas institutionalisation is much more common among persons with disabilities from the lower social classes (excepting luxury residential institutions, which only house persons with disabilities from the upper-middle and upper social classes). Other housing models for persons with disabilities, such as supported or sheltered homes, are designed mainly for persons with intellectual disabilities.

In this context of neoliberal capitalism, the conditioning factor in the configuration of the dependency attention system is economic and is orientated to the provision of support for persons with disabilities or in dependent situations.

---

[29] See www.boe.es/diario_boe/txt.php?id=BOE-A-2019-11237.

[30] See Committee for the Rights of Persons with Disabilities, *Concluding Observations on the Combined Second and Third Periodic Reports of Spain*, CRPD/C/ESP/CO/2-3 (New York NY, United Nations, 2019).

[31] See Imserso, *Información Estadística del Sistema para la Autonomía y Atención a la Dependencia (30 de septiembre de 2019)*. Available at: www.imserso.es/InterPresent2/groups/imserso/documents/binario/estsisaad20190930.pdf.

These economic interests have also ideologically influenced the attention model, arguing for institutionalisation and that residential services are more professional than those than can be supplied at home or in the community, in contradiction to Article 19 of the Convention.

CONCLUSIONS

The translation into the Spanish legal system of some guarantees for compliance with the fundamental rights of persons with disabilities as manifested in the Convention has contributed to a greater recognition of their condition of formal citizenship, which should have eased its exercise on an equal footing with the rest of the population. However, for the reasons mentioned above, formal condition should not be considered as having been fulfilled. Although positive measures that reinforce the social rights of persons with disabilities exist, they are currently insufficient and often do not respond effectively to the goal of inclusion promoted in the legislation. In this sense, a substantive analysis allows us to confirm a 'disability gap' between persons with disabilities in comparison to people without regarding access to education, employment, and social and political participation.

These social rights are intended to guarantee the development of persons with disabilities' full autonomy as citizens, including their participation in public life, their employment and educational inclusion, their access to public spaces of citizenship, as well as their right to enjoy their private sphere. Thus, the consolidation of these specific social rights for persons with disabilities should allow the exercise of their civil and political rights and their inclusion in the community, although their reach is uneven, especially for those with intellectual disabilities or mental illness.[32]

As we have seen, the contradictions that exist in the legislation regarding the inclusion and segregation of persons with disabilities hinder their exercise of full citizenship. In this sense, the insufficient development of the Dependency Act is a missed opportunity to ensure some of these social rights, limiting the provision of support for the basic activities of daily life. Moreover, the services provided by the dependency system have experienced dramatic budget cuts during the period of economic crisis and internment in residential institutions has been increasingly favoured over the provision of support at home or in the community.

In the same way, disability employment regulations have consolidated a parallel, protected job market (mostly for specific types of disabilities), leaving positive action measures for inclusion in ordinary companies, such as the reserve quota, in the background. These measures, originally conceived as a way for

---

[32] See X Etxeberria, *La Condición de Ciudadanía de las Personas con Discapacidad Intelectual* (Bilbao, Universidad de Deusto, (2008).

subsequent inclusion in the ordinary job market, may have a harmful effect, as happens in the domain of education with special education centres, which may create participation spaces segregated from the rest of society.

As shown in this chapter, resistance to inclusion and promotion of segregation and institutionalisation in these spaces respond to the economic interests of the companies in the sector.[33] They own residential institutions, special employment and special education centres, and have considerable capacity to influence the legislative and political decisions made in the configuration of social policies of disability in the domains of social services, education or employment. Thus, economic benefits based on disability should be substantially restructured, according to their desired role, from the point of view of redistributive and universal social justice. Especially in the case of non-contributory benefits, they should be increased in value, while discarding incompatibilities with work, so they can stop being mere charity subsidies and can start to improve the social conditions of persons with disabilities as a fundamental guarantee for their inclusion.

In this sense, the socioeconomic protection of persons with disabilities has not always been well thought of by some of the defenders of the models which belong in the paradigm of personal autonomy or independent living. Conceptions of autonomy from neoliberal or individualist socioeconomic models are incompatible with the principles of redistributive social justice, and provoke, in my opinion, a mistaken rejection of economic benefits and State intervention in the reduction of inequalities, that would, according to their view, favour passiveness, conformism or dependency. Dependency, autonomy, protection and assistance, among others, are polysemic words, which, mediated by the ideological views of whomever pronounces them, can have a pernicious use when it comes to tackling the discourse of the defence of the rights of persons with disabilities. The discourse of autonomy and independent living, if it is not combined with the discourse of social justice, with an appreciation of the State's predistributive and redistributive capacity in order to reduce social inequalities, may entail important dangers when determining the conditions set out by society as ideal for persons with disabilities. Assistance-based or charity policies do not favour persons with disabilities, but social protection policies (against inequalities) do not necessarily imply the creation of dependency. Quite the opposite, the disappearance of social protection policies would mean acceptance that inequalities are not a social product, thereby individualising and personalising social problems. However, as long as the economic value of benefits is insufficient or decaying, as long as barriers are set up against combining economic benefits and access to work and no guarantees exist for this access, we will not

---

[33] They are united in an employers' association with the euphemistic name of the Spanish Council for the Defense of Disability and Dependency (Consejo Español para la Defensa de la Discapacidad y la Dependencia – CEDDD). Available at: www.ceddd.org.

be able to affirm either that the legal system guarantees formal equality or that social justice is at its heart.

In conclusion, although the discourse in the Spanish legal system has been partly modified, several evident contradictions, persist regarding segregation and institutionalization of persons with disabilities. Moreover, the system lacks sufficient regulation (compliance obligations, sanctions regimes) and economic guarantees to carry out the measures that would make the rights of persons with disabilities effective.

5

Accommodation in the Academy
Working with Episodic Disabilities and Living In Between

ROXANNE MYKITIUK

T HIS CHAPTER STEPS away from the institutions of mental health facilities, the extended care home and the prison, to enter another institutional setting within which disability as a concept is constructed and
materialises, but where, until recently, its lived experience has generally been
excluded: the university. Unlike the institutional settings from which people with
disabilities have conventionally wished to flee, the university is one into which
many people, including those with disabilities, have sought entry. Historically,
and even now, universities are regarded as elite institutions that restrict entry
based on achievement and performance. As both an educational setting and
a workplace, the university creates and enforces norms about who properly
belongs within its sphere. Examining whether people with disabilities are permitted entry into the hallowed halls of the university and the conditions of
their inclusion if and when they arrive exposes the dynamic interplay between
the complex institutional logics of belonging and the inadequacy of the legal
and policy regime of accommodation to dismantle the barriers to fully include
people with disabilities.

While the rights of students with disabilities in higher education have
received much attention in recent years,[1] attention to the accommodation of
faculty members with disabilities has been more limited.[2] In Canada, federal

---

[1] M Price, *Mad at School: Rhetorics of Mental Disability and Academic Life* (Ann Arbor, University of Michigan Press, 2011); E Reynolds Weatherup, *Disability and Academic Exclusion: Voicing
the Student Body* (Lanham, Lexington Books, 2017); EB Keefe, VM Moore and FR Duff (eds),
Listening to the Experts: Students with Disabilities Speak Out (Baltimore, Paul H Brookes Pub Co,
2006); OECD, Centre for Educational Research and Innovation Staff, Organisation for Economic
Co-operation and Development et al, *Inclusive Education at Work: Students with Disabilities in
Mainstream Schools* (Paris, Organisation for Economic Co-operation and Development, 1999).

[2] AH Franke, MF Bérubé, RM O'Neil and JE Kurland, 'Accommodating Faculty Members Who
Have Disabilities' (2012) 98(4) *Academe* 30.

and provincial human rights laws protect persons with disabilities from discrimination in the employment context.[3] However, the representation of faculty members with disabilities on campuses is disproportionately low in relation to the general population.[4] While universities are required by law to implement policies and procedures to accommodate faculty members with disabilities, the experience of faculty members on the ground is often one of misfit[5] between the able-bodied norms governing the university worker and the body/mind of the faculty member. Required to meet medicalised and individualised conceptions of disability, live up to neoliberal performance indicators and navigate a convoluted bureaucratic system, faculty members who seek accommodations do not encounter an institution aimed at ensuring equitable and inclusive conditions and a fit between body/mind and environment. Rather, universities remain sites of stigma and discrimination whereby '[d]isabled people are expected to be recipients of professional attention, not professionals themselves'.[6]

In this chapter I consider one example of the interaction between the institutional logics of the university and the system of accommodation in achieving inclusion for people with disabilities. I focus on the inclusion and accommodation of faculty members with episodic disabilities – shifting experiences of moving in and out of health and illness, disability and non-disability – in the university. The chapter utilises my own experience of requesting support for two separate episodic disabilities in 2011 and 2012, and builds on qualitative and autoethnographic studies undertaken in Canada and the United Kingdom[7] to explore how supportive and inclusive the university is for faculty members with episodic disabilities, and the inadequacies of the law of reasonable

---

[3] Note that when the first provincial *Human Rights Code* came into force in 1962 in Ontario, it did not protect disability as a ground of discrimination. In response to widespread social criticisms of the original Code being too narrow in scope, disability (narrowly conceived as 'handicap' at the time, along with race, ancestry, sex, age, etc.) was added as a Code-protected ground in 1981. See generally RB Howe, 'The Evolution of Human Rights Policy in Ontario' (1991) 24(4) *Canadian Journal of Political Science* 783.

[4] In 2012/13, 3.9 per cent of faculty in universities declared they had an impairment or health condition compared to 16 per cent of working age adults. N Brown and J Leigh, 'Ableism in Academia: Where Are the Disabled and Ill Academics?' (2018) 33(6) *Disability & Society* 985. Statistical data from Canada is difficult to obtain due to a lack of reporting and collection.

[5] The concept of misfit is developed by Rosemarie Garland-Thomson in 'Misfits: A Feminist Materialist Disability Concept' (2011) 26(3) *Hypatia* 591.

[6] B Waterfield, BB Beagan and M Weinberg, 'Disabled Academics: A Case Study in Canadian Universities' (2018) 33(3) *Disability & Society* 332.

[7] See eg, S Kerschbaum, A O'Shea, M Price and M Salzer, 'Accommodations and Disclosure for Faculty Members with Mental Disability' in S Kerschbaum, L Eisenman and J Jones (eds), *Negotiating Disability: Disclosure and Higher Education* (Ann Arbour, University of Michigan Press, 2017); S Bassler, '"But You Don't Look Sick": A Survey of Scholars with Chronic, Invisible Illnesses and their Advice on How to Live and Work in Academia' (2009) 15(3–4) *Music Theory Online* doi: 10.30535/mto.15.3.3; P Moss, 'Not Quite Abled and Not Quite Disabled: Experiences of Being "In Between" ME and the Academy' (2000) 20(3) *Disability Studies Quarterly* 287; B Waterfield, BB Beagan and M Weinberg, 'Disabled Academics: A Case Study in Canadian Universities' (2018) 33(3) *Disability & Society* 332.

accommodation to effectively include the bodies/minds of persons who live between ability and disability. The duty to accommodate is the cornerstone of the law of anti-discrimination and is held out as providing the mechanism by which adaptations inclusive of people with disabilities will occur. However, the implementation of the duty in the university continues to shore up the foundational exclusionary nature of the institution and operates to exclude minds/bodies that cannot be made (even with accommodations) to approximate the preferred institutional subject.

The chapter begins by situating the university as a valued institution, but one in which disability is generally excluded and unwelcome. I then describe the concept of episodic disability and introduce the idea of living 'in between' as a way of illustrating how people who live with episodic disabilities exist between states of health and illness and between the legal and policy categories within which accommodations are regulated in the university. In the third section I discuss my own experiences of trying to access support and accommodation at a Canadian university as a way of contextualising and illustrating one example of an attempt to achieve workplace inclusion while living in between. Elaborating on this discussion, section four highlights ways in which the institutional logics of the university, and the requirements of the duty to accommodate, operate to be unwelcoming of those living with episodic disabilities.

THE UNIVERSITY AS AN INSTITUTION

Jay Dolmage ponders whether the 'university is in fact exactly the same as the almshouse or asylum, organizationally and even architecturally'.[8] Like those institutions, the university is characterised as one removed from the rest of society, the site of hard work and isolation where its members labour in similar work alongside each other and in which defined routines are upheld. However, the subjects of one institution are restrained while those in the other are respected. Those who enter the university as professors self-select their participation and inclusion in the institution. Their admission is voluntary and competitive due to an increasingly high demand for coveted positions and the strict requirements regulating their entry and employment. Unlike extended care homes, mental health facilities and prisons, which focus (allegedly) on care, treatment and rehabilitation, the telos of the university is different: knowledge creation and dissemination and the education and training of the next generation of professionals[9] and citizens. This combination of characteristics of the university

---

[8] JT Dolmage, *Academic Ableism – Disability and Higher Education* (Ann Arbour, University of Michigan Press, 2017) 4.

[9] DT Mitchell, 'Disability, Diversity, and Diversion: Normalization and Avoidance in Higher Education' in D Bolt and C Penketh, *Disability, Avoidance and the Academy* (New York, Routledge, 2016) 12.

sustains an intellectualism that has historically excluded persons with disabilities from this elite institution. Indeed, people with disabilities were and are the objects of research in the university, and not often its subjects.

In addition to its defining characteristics as an institution, the normative subject of the university is identified by the traits of rationality, presence, participation, productivity, collegiality and independence.[10] A faculty member is expected to have mental agility, including the capacity for analysis and evaluation; mastery of a complex subject; initiative, creativity and strong communication skills.[11] But qualities of mind are not all that are valued and expected of university faculty. In a work culture that prizes long hours, high productivity, competitiveness and individualism, bodies who do not conform to the normative ideal and exhibit stamina, high energy, unchanging health status and reliability are problematic in failing to live up to the expected standards of functioning.[12] Thus, while we don't typically think of the university as an institution that operates through control, restraint and coercion, it is, in part, through the surveillance and disciplining of the activities, purpose and membership of the institution that it retains its narrow and fixed character.

Unlike other institutions considered in this collection, many of which have undergone transformative processes of deinstitutionalisation as a move towards social and political participation in the community for people with disabilities, the university remains a site where policies and practices continue to legitimate many of the historical systems and beliefs associated with this institution's exclusion of people with disabilities. While it might make little sense to speak of a deinstitutionalised university, some barriers to contemporary academia have been somewhat eroded to include a more diversified embodied subject concomitant with our now largely deinstitutionalised society. Current inclusion policies consistent with human rights and anti-discrimination laws are examples. However, this formal inclusion of people with disabilities can have the effect of carving out spaces for 'special' or 'separate' inclusion. Moreover, Allison Carey argues that laws and policies can grant formal rights and simultaneously legitimise their retraction.[13] Likewise, as Niklas Altermark notes, policies related to ideals of citizenship can empower and formally include people with disabilities while at the same time setting a public threshold for them to live up to idealised expectations of citizen[14] or employee. Within the university, policies that are designed to protect faculty members can also have this binding effect: on the one hand,

---

[10] M Price, *Mad at School Rhetorics of Mental Disability and Academic Life* (Ann Arbour, University of Michigan Press, 2011) 5.

[11] Franke et al, 'Accommodating Faculty Members Who Have Disabilities' (2012). This list of capacities is adapted from AAUP's list of 'Essential elements common to all faculty positions'.

[12] A Vick, 'Living and Working Precariously with an Episodic Disability: Barriers in the Canadian Context' (2014) 3(3) *Canadian Journal of Disability Studies* 8–9.

[13] AC Carey, *On the Margins of Citizenship: Intellectual Disability and Civil Rights in Twentieth-century America* (Philadelphia, Temple University Press, 2009).

[14] N Altermark, *Citizenship, Inclusion and Intellectual Disability* (Abingdon, Routledge, 2018).

reasonable accommodation is the means through which employees are protected through anti-discrimination law; on the other hand, universities retain the power and authority to recognise what does and does not count as disability and the extent to which accommodations sought are reasonable. Mitchell and Snyder argue that inclusionist strategies (practices and policies) in present-day universities operating in conditions of neoliberalism fail to achieve meaningful inclusion for people with disabilities: 'Inclusionism requires that disability be tolerated as long as it does not demand an excessive degree of change from relatively inflexible institutions, environments, and norms of belonging.'[15] According to them, universities continue to be institutions that produce professionals of normalisation and reinforce norms of normalisation.

For some in the university context, flexible work schedules, strategies to conserve energy and adjusting expectations about promotion and advancement are measures taken to self-accommodate.[16] However, when employees with episodic disabilities self-accommodate, or do not disclose their need for accommodation, qualities of atomistic self-sufficiency and non-reliance that are valorised within the academy are perpetuated. Moreover, some employees with episodic disabilities, having internalised the responsibilisation of self-governance, work to meet able-bodied norms that in some cases 'intensify bodily symptoms that become increasingly difficult to manage'.[17] Thus, when the disabled subject remains hidden from view, they reify the neoliberal ideal subject who flexibly, independently and successfully navigates the university workplace. By providing an opportunity to engage in critical reflection, the experiences of those living with episodic disabilities offer rich case studies from which to meaningfully complicate our understanding of disability inclusion and its relationship to the meaning of reasonable accommodation in the university setting.

EPISODIC DISABILITIES AND THE 'IN BETWEEN'

Episodic disabilities are characterised by unpredictable or intermittent, shifting periods of impairment and wellness. People with episodic disabilities often experience a 'fluctuating reality of pain, fatigue ... functional capacities, and side effects of medications'.[18] Episodes of impairment may affect a person's ability to work in their usual manner for a brief or extended time. Many episodic disabilities are invisible and will often not be evident to others

---

[15] Mitchell, 'Disability, Diversity, and Diversion' (2016) 12; DT Mitchell and SL Snyder, *The Biopolitics of Disability – Neoliberalism, Ablenationalism, and Peripheral Embodiment* (Ann Arbour, University of Michigan Press, 2015), 14.

[16] S-D Stone, VA Crooks and M Owen, 'Going Through the Back Door: Chronically Ill Academics' Experiences as "Unexpected Workers"' (2013) 11(2) *Social Theory & Health* 151.

[17] Vick, 'Living and Working Precariously with an Episodic Disability' (2014).

[18] Ibid.

without disclosure. Examples of diagnoses that may result in episodic disability include multiple sclerosis, lupus, HIV/AIDS, Crohn's disease, chronic fatigue syndrome, migraine, chronic pain syndromes, some forms of cancer and some mental health conditions, including bipolar mood conditions and depression.[19] It is estimated that 82.4 per cent of adult Canadians who report a disability can be classified as having an episodic disability,[20] while 77 per cent who report having an episodic disability state that it affects their ability to do their job.[21] In 2012, among those Canadians between the ages of 18 and 64 with episodic disabilities, just over half were in the labour force, while about 24 per cent were of the view that they would be able to work with the appropriate accommodations and flexibility. Of those who were employed, 77 per cent were full time, 21.2 per cent were professionals or managers, 59.2 per cent had a post-secondary credential and 46.3 per cent had been in their job for 12 years or more.[22] There is no cure for episodic disabilities, and some individuals experiencing an episode may appear healthy, evoking suspicion and experiencing marginalisation from others.[23]

As people with episodic disabilities move between periods of health and illness, ability and impairment, they do not fit into the institutionally recognised and rigid categories of able/disabled that are often used to determine eligibility for sick leave benefits, return to work and accommodation plans. Indeed, as Lightman et al contend, people with episodic disabilities challenge homogenised constructions of ability, disability, health and illness. They 'threaten the logic of classificatory systems by straddling ... boundaries ... they are between the statuses of sick and well'.[24]

Several scholars have invoked the concepts of 'between', 'in between' and 'living in between'[25] to draw attention to 'the constitutive permeability of moving back and forth between embodied states and identities'.[26] Living in

[19] House of Commons Canada, Standing Committee on Human Resources, Skills and Social Development and the Status of Persons with Disabilities, *Taking Action: Improving the Lives of Canadians Living with Episodic Disabilities* (Ottawa: House of Commons March 2019) 35.

[20] A Furrie et al, *Episodic Disabilities in Canada* (Ottawa, Adele Furrie Consulting Inc, 2016) 8. Available at: www.adelefurrie.ca/PDF//episodic_disabilities_in_canada --_october_4_final.pdf. These statistics are based on data from Statistics Canada's 2012 Canadian Survey of Disability.

[21] Ibid, 22.

[22] A Furrie, *People with Episodic Health Conditions Speak About ...* Final Report for Employment and Social Development Canada (Ottawa, Adele Furrie Consulting Inc, 2017). Available at: www.adelefurrie.ca/PDF//People_with_episodic_health_conditions_speak_out-about.pdf, 22. These statistics are based on data from Statistics Canada's 2012 Canadian Survey of Disability.

[23] E Lightman, A Vick, D Herd and and A Mitchell, '"Not Disabled Enough": Episodic Disabilities and the Ontario Disability Support Program' (2009) 29(3) *Disability Studies Quarterly*. doi: dx.doi.org/10.18061/dsq.v29i3.932.

[24] Ibid, citing RA Hilbert, 'The Acultural Dimensions of Chronic Pain: Flawed Reality Construction and the Problem of Meaning' (1984) 31(4) *Social Problems*, 365.

[25] Ibid; Kerschbaum et al, 'Accommodations and Disclosure' (2017); Bassler, '"But You Don't Look Sick"' (2009); Moss, 'Not Quite Abled and Not Quite Disabled' (2000); Waterfield et al, 'Disabled Academics' (2018); Vick, 'Living and Working Precariously with an Episodic Disability' (2014) 9.

[26] Lightman et al, '"Not Disabled Enough"' 4.

between is 'not a merging of opposite states of being or an oscillation between polarities, but an inhabiting of permeable borders that are fused, fleeting, and held in tension'.[27] Given the variability and unpredictability with which impairments are experienced, the concept of living in between embraces the elasticity and fluidity of what becomes possible given the inconsistency of body/mind states in relation to the variation in work projects, responsibilities and expectations persons with disabilities encounter.

Moss describes how faculty members with episodic disabilities live in between the institutional categories available in university policies and procedures for disability accommodation.[28] The university system discounts the complex reality of people whose bodies or minds resist permanent constructions as neither fully able nor completely disabled but shift between these spaces.[29] This embodiment is deemed experientially impossible within the realm of university policy. Faculty members with episodic disabilities are expected to recover in a set time period or not recover at all, to work full time or not work at all, to be fully abled or fully disabled. The categories of institutional ordering, and the policies and programmes that implement them, do not recognise those who live in between – who are both able and disabled, ill and healthy, or 'in between the distinguishable spaces of ability and disability'.[30] University policies and procedures regarding accommodation, accessibility, short and long-term disability or sick leave are not designed around the experiences of episodic disabilities. Thus, there is a misfit[31] between existing university policies and procedures and the experiences and needs of faculty members with episodic disabilities.

Telling Tales in and of School – My Experiences/Accommodating the In-Between

In late autumn 2010, I received notice that two large and well-funded research grants on which I was a co-principal investigator had been successful. While this was good news for me and my university, the grants did not provide funding to relieve any teaching or administrative responsibilities. In anticipation of the increased workload and in the knowledge that my Dean and I could arrange teaching release in the event of successful national grant funding, I made an appointment with him. I sought a reduced course load as a preventive measure to avoid migraines, which for me are triggered principally by lack of sleep but are subject to and compounded by other factors. It is essential that I get enough

---

[27] Ibid, 4.

[28] Moss, 'Not Quite Abled and Not Quite Disabled' (2000) 288.

[29] P Moss and I Dyck, 'Body, Corporeal Space, and Legitimizing Chronic Illness: Women Diagnosed with M.E.' (1999) 31(4) *Antipode* 372.

[30] Moss, 'Not Quite Abled and Not Quite Disabled' (2000) 288.

[31] Garland-Thomson, 'Misfits' (2011) 591.

sleep, thus restricting my ability to pull 'all-nighters' and fit research and writing into the late night and early morning hours as is often the case with many academics.

Like many who experience episodic disabilities, my flare-ups and symptoms can result in physical, psychological, cognitive and social limitations that hinder my work, but 'may or may not reappear with the same symptoms, intensity, duration, or within the same contexts with each flare-up'.[32] The body/mind experience of having an episodic disability is unpredictable: some days, or even parts of a day, you feel well – able to organise thoughts, speak intelligently and cogently, run from meeting to meeting, concentrate for hours and 'be on'. But this can be quickly supplanted by unsubsiding fatigue, loss of bodily sensation and coordination, unrelenting brain fog, dizziness, excruciating pain, vision and hearing loss and crashing change of mood. Unlike more apparent and familiar disabilities such as blindness, a missing limb or a spinal cord injury, whose embodiments are quite static and permanent, episodic disabilities fluctuate between periods of disability and ability.[33]

My Dean assured me at our meeting that 'something would be done' to adjust the workload issue. It was a surprise, then, when in late April 2011 I was informed that I was assigned to teach three courses in the 2011–12 academic year, two of which I had never taught before. Additionally, I was assigned to three committees, including the most onerous Senate committee and to the only Faculty committee required to meet and do a substantial amount of work over the summer. My summer now needed to include work on two new research grants, previous research commitments, preparation for two new courses, and an active committee. While I had been given a teaching release of two out of 12 teaching credits, the fact that I was assigned two new courses seemed punitive and intended to eliminate any benefit from the small course release that I was granted.

This two-credit teaching release was characterised as a special favour from the Dean. However, my faculty had a policy that faculty members who had research grants worth at least $100,000 were eligible for a course release. My grants were worth more than $200,000, satisfying the condition for two course releases under the policy. Nonetheless, I was informed by the Associate Dean that I did not 'meet the threshold' and there were concerns about my 'characterisation of entitlement to teaching release'. I was denied the two releases to which I should have been eligible under this policy, and no reasons were provided.

The correspondence I received from the Associate Dean in late April 2011 accompanying the 2011–12 course assignment stated further that: 'I am mindful that this is not the result for which you were hoping, but it is the best we can do in the circumstances – really better than best, absent documented medical advice

---

[32] Lightman et al, '"Not Disabled Enough"' 7.
[33] A Vick, 'Living and Working Precariously with an Episodic Disability' (2014).

that stipulates a reduced teaching load.'[34] The same memo stipulates that my teaching load for the following year – 2012–13 – when I would be under the same intensive research obligations – would be a full load.

In the midst of these discussions, the one issue about which there was almost silence was my migraine. Having raised the issue once with the Dean in late autumn 2010 and being assured that it would be 'dealt with', I assumed that the research grant policy would accommodate my needs. When discussions about a course reduction became particularly problematic in late April 2011, I asked to meet with the two of them about my situation and the problematic application of law school policy. At that meeting my migraines were again raised and the Dean replied, in passing, that 'we may need to pursue accommodations if the time comes'. At that time I was not in favour of pursuing a course release as a form of accommodation, first, because the application of the law school research grant policy should have entitled me to a course release and, second, because I had been informed that there would be a proportionate loss of income in relation to the reduction of teaching hours. This seemed tremendously unfair, especially in a situation where my research responsibilities were increasing correspondingly such that my time commitment to the academic position would not be reduced.

I did not see what I was asking for as an accommodation. I wanted a redistribution among the essential duties of my position: research, teaching and administration to keep the number of hours of sleep more or less constant to prevent migraine flares. The message I received was that disability prevention could not be negotiated; however, for some episodic disabilities it is precisely this kind of accommodation that is required. Just as preventive health strategies in the workplace such as providing ergonomic chairs, safety equipment, proper ventilation, lighting and rest breaks make sense in protecting the health of the worker and preventing injury, preventive accommodations save resources by reducing the need to take time off if there is a flare-up, thereby reducing the unpredictability of episodic conditions if and where possible.

At the end of the spring of 2011, I questioned whether I should have had a proactive conversation with the Dean about my migraines and the need to rearrange the allocation of some of my work hours. It seemed to me that administrative suspicion about my disability status was used to influence a decision about the application of the research grant policy, a policy which was silent about disability and determined eligibility for teaching release on the basis of the amount of grant funding brought in by the faculty member. (Note that the course release policy and $100,000 threshold for a course release was announced just prior to the time I was requesting one, which is why I did not refer to it in my conversations with the Dean five months earlier.) Had I not raised the issue

---

[34] Memo from the Associate Dean – Teaching and Committee Assignment in 2011–12, 25 April 2011. On file with the author.

of migraine as a reason for requiring teaching release previously, in my view it is highly unlikely that the Associate Dean would have referred to 'documented medical advice' in her memo to me. After all, at that point I was seeking course releases based on the value of my research grants. I argue that a kind of disability-suspicion overreach informed the decision-making of the Association Dean, one so capricious as to infuse the application of a policy which – in relation to non-disabled faculty members – would normally be valourised. My experience of negotiating an adjusted allocation of work responsibilities suggests how disability can become a basis of further debilitation, associated with suspicion, dishonesty and denial, rather than a basis of capacity building or recognition connected with legitimacy, rights and support.[35]

Over the next three months I worked tirelessly under strenuous pressure of deadlines, amidst a lack of institutional support, and growing feelings of alienation and unfairness. I had significant periods of migraine that I self-accommodated and then the deep root of depression surfaced. I could no longer function and my physician determined that I should take a leave of absence.

I discovered that navigating the accommodation and disability support system of the university is onerous. It was difficult to determine the proper office to which a request for accommodation should be directed: human resources (HR), the Dean, or a disability services office. Such difficulties are exacerbated when one's health is impaired, depriving one of the energy to make inquiries. Eventually I was directed to the euphemistically titled Employee Well-Being Office of the HR department, where I was informed that my university provided 15 weeks of 'sick leave' at full pay for short-term absences with medical validation and after that, the possibility of long-term disability leave for up to a maximum of three years, paid at up to a maximum of $6,000 a month. After that time my employment would be terminated.

I was sent a Practitioner's Report on Abilities and Limitations for my treating physician to complete in determining my eligibility for short-term sick leave. This is the same form used to determine accommodation needs. It provides tick boxes to indicate physical ability and limitations regarding specific body parts and functional abilities and asks whether ergonomic or assistive devices are required due to the condition and whether the employee is undergoing any treatment that would affect their ability to perform their essential duties. Fearful of disclosing depression, I asked my physician to state something more generic. She wrote that I had been 'struggling with many occupational demands which would seem impossible to manage in a work week that has led to excessive hours of work and burnout'. In response, I was sent a letter from the Employee Well-Being Office stating that this information was insufficient to 'constitute the basis for a medical leave and further accommodations on medical grounds'.

---

[35] I am grateful to Linda Steele for these insightful reflections. For a discussion and theorisation of debility and capacity, see JK Puar, 'Prognosis Time: Towards a Geopolitics of Affect, Debility and Capacity' (2009) 19(2) *Women & Performance: A Journal of Feminist Theory*, 161.

Contrary to the form's clear privacy protection provision, a copy of the letter was sent, without my authorisation, to two university administrators, including the Dean of my law school. When I called the HR office to inquire about the protection of my privacy and why it had been breached, I was told that confidentiality is only protected for those whose applications are successful.

Despite eventually being granted sick leave, I was pressured by my Associate Dean to return to work earlier than my health permitted. Seven months later I had a relapse, even more serious than the first, and was required to take subsequent leave. It was only with a change in Associate Dean (one with a close family member who experienced depression) that my need for a reduced teaching load was understood and implemented. However, the letter regarding that plan clearly stated that this was a one-time-only arrangement – counter to any understanding of the flexible, fluid nature of episodic disabilities.

BARRIERS TO ACCOMMODATION

Accommodation practices, while ostensibly aimed at equity, often reinforce individualised normative standards of functioning by making personal adjustments in relation to the person with the impairment rather than systemic changes to the environment in which the person is situated. Despite provincial laws and policies regarding workplace accommodation and accessibility in Canada, there are several reasons why people with episodic disabilities choose not to pursue accommodations or are blocked by barriers to accommodation, such as navigation and gatekeeping, disclosure, and inadequate workplace accommodation policies.

Navigation and Gatekeeping

Navigating the accommodation and disability support systems of many universities is onerous. As noted earlier, it is often difficult to determine the proper office to which a request for accommodation or leave should be directed, especially when one's health is impaired.

HR personnel are often unhelpful in processing and implementing requests for faculty sick leave and accommodation, playing the role of gatekeeper rather than facilitating the equitable working conditions of the faculty member. This is especially true for faculty members with episodic disabilities, about whose condition HR personnel and other administrators have little or no knowledge, and about which much stigma exists.

Given the lack of institutional support for and knowledge about episodic disabilities, in some instances requests for accommodation are met with refusal[36]

---

[36] Bassler, '"But You Don't Look Sick"' (2009) 4.

(especially if they interfere with an essential work duty) and in others the kind of accommodation that would be appropriate for the episodic disability is not agreed to by HR. Recall that, in my case, in order to qualify for medical leave, not only was medical certification required, but the level of disclosure and the details provided needed to correspond to a predetermined standard of illness or disability. Consequently, I had to instruct my physician to provide a diagnosis of depression to comply with the university's requirements. Privacy with respect to this disclosure was not an option.

Moreover, university administrations lack policies and publicly available precedents to initiate systemic policy changes for episodic disabilities. As a result, faculty with episodic disabilities are left to negotiate individual leave, workloads and accommodations not as systemic issues but as isolated, individualistic occurrences in the face of institutional policies that fail to recognise those who live in between.

Disclosure

The politics of disclosure are complex. Some regard disclosure as a political act, whereby failing to disclose reinforces the invisibility of episodic disabilities and the status quo that episodic disabilities are not a legitimate form of disability. Further, not being open about disability creates its own harm to employees, who are forced to work in a timeframe consistent with 'healthy' scholars.[37] By not disclosing, those who make university policy remain unaware of the numbers of disabled faculty and the kinds of accommodations that would be useful.[38]

However, disclosure – a necessary pre-condition of accommodation – can put one's job at risk by raising suspicion and soliciting scrutiny from administrators and colleagues who doubt the 'existence, seriousness, and impact' of the episodic disability.[39] Stigma may make the very disclosure required for accommodation fraught. Disclosure may also place one in a burdensome position of having to continually represent oneself institutionally and interpersonally as ill or disabled and needing accommodation, to make visible to others what is, in fact, invisible, so as to be believed.[40]

Some faculty find ways of identifying disabilities for which accommodation appears more acceptable upon which to base their requests,[41] or they avoid disclosure altogether by self-accommodating – for example, by adopting flexible work schedules, employing strategies to conserve energy, or adjusting

[37] Ibid, 8.

[38] S-D Stone, VA Crooks and M Owen, 'Going Through the Back Door: Chronically Ill Academics' Experiences as "Unexpected Workers"' (2013) 11(2) *Social Theory & Health* 168.

[39] K Teghtsoonian and P Moss, 'Signaling Invisibility, Risking Careers? Caucusing as an SOS' in D Driedger and M Owen (eds) *Dissonant Disabilities* (Toronto, Canadian Scholars Press, 2008) 199.

[40] Ibid.

[41] Kerschbaum et al, 'Accommodations and Disclosure' (2017) 320.

expectations about promotion and advancement. However, self-accommodation may not be an adequate way to comprehensively address one's disability needs – especially in a teaching context, as well as with grading, office hours, and site-specific research, such as labs.

Other people with episodic disabilities internalise the responsibilisation of self-governance and work to meet able-bodied norms that in some cases 'intensify bodily symptoms that become increasingly difficult to manage'.

Inadequate Accommodation Policies

For faculty members with episodic disabilities, the procedures for accessing accommodations tend to be ineffective. Models of accommodation and leave embedded in university policies and procedures assume that disability is a static, individual condition that can be fixed with simple accommodation. However, episodic disabilities that are intermittent and unpredictable often make it 'impossible to predict exactly when accommodations need to be in place or even which accommodations would be helpful at which times'.[42] University policies regarding short-term disability apply only to illnesses with short and predictable recovery periods and reserve long-term disability for conditions that can go on for extended periods of time, leaving no room for episodic disabilities.[43]

The objective of short-term leave and return-to-work arrangements is always to have a faculty member resume full-time work. This is often impossible for faculty members who live in between. Indeed, at my university, full-time work means full-time teaching, plus research and administration. Any accommodation that reduces one's teaching load results in a loss of salary, notwithstanding that for faculty with episodic disabilities, increased admin and research responsibilities and less teaching might be a more flexible way of accommodating episodic disabilities. This further demonstrates the misfit between the model of accommodation and the disability and a misfit between the way the job is conceived and the way impairments play out in the job. Moreover, consistent with Mitchell and Snyder's critique of inclusionism,[44] only accommodations that align with norms of able-bodiedness are permitted, allowing the deeper structures, values and practices of the institution to go largely unchanged.

CHALLENGING ACADEMIA'S LOGICS AND LEGACIES: REIMAGINING ACCOMMODATIONS

The twenty-first century university aims to be more inclusive and diverse, opening its programmes and its employment opportunities to members of groups

[42] Ibid.
[43] Moss, 'Not Quite Abled and Not Quite Disabled' (2000) 283.
[44] Mitchell, 'Disability, Diversity, and Diversion' (2016) 12.

who have traditionally been denied entry. This form of desired institutional inclusion is often facilitated and circumscribed by the requirements of the legal duty to accommodate, which structure and regulate the terms of belonging. For example, having to meet and prove a particular definition of disability, perform essential requirements of a job, rigidly construed, or disclose one's disability are integral to the legal concept of accommodation. However, as this chapter has illustrated, implementing the duty to accommodate within the university, an institution, which at the administrative/executive level, remains committed to neoliberal values aligned with able-bodied norms, has not led to the easy inclusion of people with episodic disabilities.

Faculty members who live in between embody different ways of being in the world and alternate ways of being a scholar. It is therefore imperative that universities develop systemic, policy-based approaches to accommodating faculty members with episodic disabilities to avoid reliance on the empathy or capriciousness of individual university administrators. Academic institutions need to understand episodic disabilities in ways that incorporate the experience and requirements of those who live in-between, rather than reinforcing dichotomies of disabled/abled and failing to make adjustments to the workload balance and conditions of academic workers.

Ultimately, university accommodation policies, practices and procedures need to recognise a different model of bodies and disability whereby decisions about a faculty member's work arrangements arise out of a set of principles that seek to create a barrier-free working environment for all disabilities. Discussions between the employer and the employee should focus on adjusting working conditions, both socially and materially, to ensure that a faculty member with an episodic disability has what they need to accomplish essential service, teaching, and research duties. Limitations that constrain the working lives of those with episodic disabilities are determined by those who make choices about workplace design and implement policies and expectations based on discriminatory notions of who university faculty ought to be. As long as we continue to separate the material body of the individual faculty member from the financial and structural forces that facilitate the operation of the university as an institution, there will be little or nothing done to accommodate those living with episodic disabilities other than to attempt to retrofit them so they fit within the tidy conceptual boxes that define the boundaries of the legal concept of reasonable accommodation.

6

Disabling Solitary
An Anti-Carceral Critique of Canada's Solitary Confinement Litigation

SHEILA WILDEMAN

T HE TITLE OF this chapter signifies at least three things. The first is the
disabling effects of solitary confinement. The second is recent efforts of
prison justice advocates in Canada to use law or, specifically, litigation
to disable the logic of solitary confinement: to disrupt that logic through the
logic of human rights. The third, most oblique reference and one I develop here,
speaks to dangers presented by the path Canada's solitary confinement litigation has taken: a path of isolating disability-based prison justice claims from
the wider ambitions of intersectional substantive equality. My thesis is that this
isolation of disability (specifically, mental disorder/disability) as the organising
principle of solitary confinement's legally-cognisable harms has paradoxically
re-inscribed and reinforced disability injustice, and with it, an array of interac-
tive forms of social–structural oppression.

I situate my argument in the carceral studies tradition.[1] This means examining
the violence within prisons in light of a broader account of the social–structural
violence through which white, colonialist, patriarchal and class supremacy is
perpetuated. Recent work has brought together carceral studies with critical
disability theory to explore the manifold ways the carceral state – or 'carceral
archipelago'[2] – responds to social–structural problems through strategies of
isolation, confinement and control.[3] On this analysis, the deep function of both

---

[1] See eg M Brown and J Schept, 'New Abolition, Criminology and a Critical Carceral Studies'
(2017) 19(4) *Punishment & Society* 440.
[2] M Foucault, *Discipline and Punish: The Birth of the Prison*, trans A Sheridan (New York,
Vintage, 1979) 298.
[3] See, eg, L Ben-Moshe, C Chapman and AC Carey (eds), *Disability Incarcerated: Imprisonment and Disability in the United States and Canada* (New York, Palgrave, 2014); M Segrave,
C Spivakovsky and A Eriksson, 'The Maelstrom of Punishment, Mental Illness, Disability and
Cognitive Impairment' (2017) 19(3) *Punishment & Society* 267–71.

penal and disability-based incarceration is to make invisible the effects of gross inequality and attendant material deprivation while legitimating the power and privilege of the dominant few.[4] In other words, incarceration and other forms of carceral control reinforce the status of non-normate populations as unfit for equal social membership – dangerous, incapable, or both – while deepening their material disadvantage. My question is: Can law or, specifically, litigation, help dismantle the interlocking institutions where carceral legitimation happens: the house(s) that law built? If so, what is the role of disability in that work?

To unpack those questions, I tell a counter-story to that we keep telling about the mental health crisis in our prisons. I am not claiming that there are no crises, or mental health problems, in prisons or among prisoners. Rather, my claim is that the way we – government, corrections, also human rights litigators – keep telling that story buries the social-structural problems driving criminalisation and imprisonment: problems of ableism, poverty, colonialism, racism and patriarchy. It buries them under big clinical bags of prison/hospital fixes aimed at remedying a naturalised, individualised mental health crisis. Yet the solutions are not there – they are upstream, requiring systematic redress of social, political and economic inequality. For, I suggest (indeed, the evidence could not be clearer), the social determinants of decarceration and health are the same.[5]

The target of my critique is human rights litigation. I suggest that litigation strategies framed around the prison mental health crisis are *getting in the way* of our ability to address the social-structural determinants of criminalisation and imprisonment.[6] More specifically, I argue that Canada's recent litigation around solitary confinement has diverted legal and political analysis from engagement with these determinants – colonialism, racism, patriarchy, capitalism, ableism – while ironically enabling the return of solitary confinement, if slightly re-described. Some may suggest this to be an endemic feature of institutional authority: the 'whack-a-mole' problem whereby as soon as institutionalised violence is putatively eradicated it reappears nearby in slightly altered form.[7] I argue that there is more to it than this. That is, I argue that the litigation strategies used in the fight against solitary confinement – strategies centred on liberal-legal procedural protections and moreover on disability as

---

[4] See, eg, JR Sutton, 'The Political Economy of Imprisonment in Affluent Western Democracies' (2004) 69 *American Sociological Review* 170.

[5] World Health Organization, 'The Social Determinants of Health: Introduction'. Available at: www.who.int/social_determinants/sdh_definition/en.

[6] See S Wildeman, 'Agonizing Identity in Mental Health Law and Policy (Part II): A Political Taxonomy of Psychiatric Subjectification' (2016) 39(1) *Dalhousie Law Journal* 147; R Stanev and S Wildeman, 'Freedom: A Work in Progress' in E Flynn et al (eds), *Global Perspectives on Legal Capacity Reform* (Abingdon, Routledge, 2019).

[7] On reformist re-descriptions of solitary, see K Struthers Montford, K Hannah-Moffat and A Hunter, '"Too Wicked to Die": The Enduring Legacy of Humane Reforms to Solitary Confinement' in J Nichols and A Swiffen (eds), *Legal Violence and the Limits of the Law* (Abingdon, Routledge, 2018) 141.

the master category through which the harms of solitary are conceived – are partially responsible for these depressing results.

What this means for lawyers wishing to work in resistance to penal and disability-based incarceration is a question I address in my conclusion.

CANADA'S SOLITARY CONFINEMENT LITIGATION

The 'Mental Healthification' of Prison Justice

I begin by situating Canada's solitary confinement litigation in light of what we might call the 'mental healthification' of prison justice. By this, I mean persistent channelling of attention away from the interlocking oppressions affecting prisoner populations toward accounts focused on the mental health problems of prisoners, together with pronouncements that prisons are 'the new asylums'.[8] As Liat Ben Moshe points out, such pronouncements push to the background the racialised, class-based and other patterns of oppression marking contemporary imprisonment while legitimating reforms aimed at expanding clinically rationalised spaces of confinement and forced care.[9]

The way contemporary knowledge about prisoners is produced supports this dominant story. A 2013 Correctional Service Canada (CSC) study of federally sentenced men reported that 42.9 per cent (Ontario) to 60.1 per cent (Pacific) of those assessed met the criteria for alcohol or substance use disorders, while 36.5 per cent (Ontario) to 63.8 per cent (Pacific) met the criteria for antisocial personality disorder.[10] Over 40 per cent reportedly had other major mental health diagnoses. As for women, a 2018 study found even higher prevalence across most categories:

> Most women met criteria for a current mental disorder (79.2%); among Indigenous women the rate was 95.6% . ... The most common anxiety disorder was for Post-Traumatic Stress Disorder (PTSD) with almost one-third of the women meeting criteria.[11]

The Office of the Federal Correctional Investigator reported in 2015 that 30 per cent of federally sentenced women had previously been hospitalised for psychiatric reasons; 60 per cent were using prescribed psychotropic medications.[12]

If we press beyond these statistics, we begin to see other, social–structural forces at play. A recent study indicates that 65.7 per cent of women and

[8] L Ben Moshe, "Why Prisons are Not the New Asylums" (2017) 19 *Punishment & Society* 272.
[9] Ibid.
[10] Correctional Service Canada, *Prevalence of Mental Health Disorders Among Incoming Federal Offenders: Atlantic, Ontario, & Pacific Regions* (Ottawa, CSC, 2013).
[11] Correctional Service Canada, *National Prevalence of Mental Disorders among Federally Sentenced Women Offenders: In Custody Sample* (Ottawa, CSC, April 2018).
[12] Correctional Investigator of Canada, *Annual Report of the Office of the Correctional Investigator 2014–15* (Ottawa, Office of the Correctional Investigator, 2015) 3.

35.5 per cent of men incarcerated in Canada experienced abuse as a child and that 50 per cent of women and 22 per cent of men experienced sexual abuse.[13] Pressing deeper still, 15–20 per cent of Indigenous prisoners in the federal system attended residential schools.[14] The colonialist legacy of separating Indigenous children from their families continues in child protection systems, with Indigenous, racialised and poor children starkly overrepresented in foster care.[15] Incarcerated populations are, in turn, disproportionately comprised of persons raised in foster care.[16]

These rates of trauma and dislocation correlate with other forms of marginalisation. Canadian prisoners are disproportionately likely to have experienced poverty, homelessness, truncated education and unemployment.[17] Reflecting the complex co-incidence of social marginalisation with colonialism and status-based oppression, Indigenous persons constitute just 4.9 per cent of the population in Canada, yet 28 per cent of all federally sentenced prisoners and 40 per cent of federally sentenced women are Indigenous. While just 3 per cent of the Canadian population is Black, 8.6 per cent of federal prisoners are Black.

Constructing the problem with Canada's prisons as a problem of prisoner mental health obscures these demographics – and with them, the social–structural determinants of criminalisation and imprisonment. At the same time, construction of the prison problem as a mental health problem opens the way for further carceral responses: hyper-rationalised clinical–correctional regimes offering securitised institutional responses to social–structural problems. Yet, not only do prisons fail to rectify these problems, they intensify them – by disrupting already tenuous social support, fragmenting families and communities and subjecting those who are incarcerated to routine degradation and violence both sanctioned and unsanctioned.[18]

Litigating Solitary

Solitary confinement is defined under the Standard Minimum Rules for the treatment of prisoners (Mandela Rules) as 'confinement of prisoners for 22 hours or

[13] C Bodkin et al 'History of Childhood Abuse in Populations Incarcerated in Canada: A Systematic Review and Meta-Analysis' (2019) 109(3) *American Journal of Public Health* e1.
[14] See F Kouyoumdjian et al, 'Health Status of Prisoners in Canada: Narrative Review' (2016) 62(3) *Canadian Family Physician* 215.
[15] C Blackstock, 'Residential Schools: Did They Really Close or Just Morph into Child Welfare?' (2007) 6(1) *Indigenous Law Journal* 71.
[16] S Trevethan et al, *The Effect of Family Disruption on Aboriginal and Non-Aboriginal Inmates* (Ottawa, Correctional Service of Canada, 2001). Available at: www.csc-scc.gc.ca/research/r113-eng.shtml.
[17] Kouyoumdjian et al, 'Health Status of Prisoners in Canada' 218.
[18] C Wildeman and E Wang, 'Mass Incarceration, Public Health, and Widening Inequality in the USA' (2017) 389(10077) *The Lancet* 1464; World Health Organization, *Prisons and Health* (Copenhagen, WHO Regional Office for Europe, 2014); L Brinkley-Rubenstein, 'Incarceration as a Catalyst for Worsening Health' (2013) 1(1) *Health Justice* 3.

more a day without meaningful human contact'.[19] The Mandela Rules prohibit 'prolonged solitary confinement ('in excess of 15 consecutive days'[20]) as well as any solitary confinement of 'prisoners with mental or physical disabilities when their conditions would be exacerbated by such measures'.[21] In Canadian law, these expressions of international consensus have persuasive though not determinative force.[22]

Solitary confinement is exemplary of carceral logics: use of incarceration/ immobilisation to contain risks predictably arising within oppressive institutional and social structures.[23] My question is: Can litigation resist these logics? Or is it doomed to repeat them? To explore this, I turn to five recent Canadian cases challenging solitary confinement. Four relied on the Canadian Charter of Rights and Freedoms, while the fifth was brought (and settled) under Ontario's anti-discrimination legislation.

The most far-reaching of these cases were two public interest *Charter* challenges decided in 2017 in Ontario[24] and 2018 in British Columbia (BC)[25] and then taken on appeal. (As this chapter goes to press, both cases are on further appeal to the Supreme Court of Canada.) These decisions establish the constitutional invalidity of federal correctional law permitting 'administrative segregation': isolation of prisoners for up to 22 hours per day for indeterminate periods, on grounds of individual safety or institutional security.[26]

There were some differences in the two appellate-level judgments as to which *Charter* rights were infringed. However, there was no disagreement on the factual underpinnings of the litigation, namely that 'inmates held in prolonged administrative segregation are at risk of severe and often enduring negative health consequences',[27] including permanent harm to mental health and social functioning and increased risk of suicide and self-harm. The courts further accepted that these risks are exacerbated if the individual has a pre-existing mental health condition. However, the two appellate courts refrained from pronouncing on exactly which mental health conditions are constitutionally inconsistent with administrative segregation, leaving this to case-by-case assessment.

---

[19] UN General Assembly, *United Nations Standard Minimum Rules for the Treatment of Prisoners (Mandela Rules)*: 8 January 2016, A/RES/70/175, Rule 44.

[20] Ibid.

[21] Ibid, Rule 45.2.

[22] See CCLA [ONCA] at paras 28 and 29.

[23] D Parkes, 'Solitary Confinement, Rights Litigation and the Possibility of a Prison Abolitionist Lawyering Ethic' (2017) 32(2) *Canadian Journal of Law and Society* 179.

[24] *Corporation of the Canadian Civil Liberties Association v Her Majesty the Queen*, 2017 ONSC 7491 (CanLII) [*CCLA (ONSC)*], appeal allowed in part, *Canadian Civil Liberties Association v Canada (Attorney General)*, 2019 ONCA 243 (CanLII) [*CCLA (ONCA)*].

[25] *British Columbia Civil Liberties Association v Canada (Attorney General)* 2018 BCSC 62 (CanLII) [*BCCLA (BCSC)*] var'd in 2019 BCCA 228 (CanLII) [*BCCLA (BCCA)*].

[26] *Corrections and Conditional Release Act*, SC 1992, c 2 [*CCRA*] ss 31–33 and 37.

[27] *CCLA (ONCA)* at para 97. See also L Guenther, *Solitary Confinement: Social Death and its Afterlives* (Minneapolis, University of Minnesota Press, 2013).

The appellate courts identified two primary problems with the law: lack of independent review (contrary to principles of fundamental justice, given the liberty interests engaged) and lack of a determinate cap on the time one may be held in segregation (infringing liberty/security of the person per the court in BC and cruel and unusual treatment per the court in Ontario). On the second point, the BC Court of Appeal merely indicated that an appropriate cap must be fashioned, while the Ontario Court of Appeal looked to the Mandela Rules to establish a limit of 15 consecutive days.[28]

Discrimination was not among the rights considered in the Ontario litigation (although the rights infringements identified were anchored in evidence of harm to mental health). However, the BC trial judge declared the law discriminatory 'to the extent' that it permitted persons with 'mental illness/disability' to be segregated for any period. This was overturned at the BC Court of Appeal on the basis that the judge's concerns were with the law's application, not the law itself. The law, reasoned the Court, properly contemplated individualised assessment and accommodation. The problem was that correctional authorities had failed to meet their statutory obligation to 'give meaningful consideration to the health care needs of prisoners before placing or confirming the placement of prisoners in segregation'.[29]

A second discrimination-based ruling of the BC trial judge related to Indigeneity. He invalidated the law 'to the extent' that it authorised 'a procedure that results in discrimination against Aboriginal inmates', signalling concerns that risk assessment instruments or other correctional decision-making processes were contributing to Indigenous overrepresentation in solitary. Again, the BC appellate court disagreed, stating that while it accepted the evidence of overrepresentation, there was insufficient indication in the evidence or judgment of just what processes or instruments were to blame.

Importantly, further discrimination argumentation was raised by interveners, the Native Women's Association of Canada (NWAC) and West Coast Women's Legal Education and Action Fund (LEAF). They sought to highlight the impact of solitary confinement on federally sentenced Indigenous women through 'a robust contextual and intersectional framing of Indigeneity, of gender, and when appropriate, of disabling mental health impairments'.[30] The interveners argued that courts must recognise the unique ways solitary confinement reproduces and exacerbates interlocking oppressions affecting Indigenous women in order to remedy those harms. The BC trial judge rejected the arguments, relying on testimony that federally sentenced women have greater access to mental health treatments and Elders than do federally sentenced men.[31] The appellate court did not challenge the judge's failure to engage the interveners' argument that

[28] *United Nations Standard Minimum Rules for the Treatment of Prisoners*, Rule 45.
[29] *BCCLA* [BCCA] para 269.
[30] NWAC and LEAF Factum at iii. BCCLA (BCCA) at paras 238–39; BCCLA (BCSC) at para 458.
[31] *BCCLA* (BCSC) at paras 456–63.

solitary deepens social–structural oppressions in ways that cannot be segmented into singular or isolated 'grounds'. Instead, it adopted the still more formalistic position that intersecting grounds argumentation had not been placed directly in issue by the parties to the appeal.[32]

In Ontario, a challenge to comparable practices was brought under provincial human rights legislation. Christina Jahn had been held in segregation in a provincial jail for 210 days, during which she missed cancer treatments and was denied support for mental health conditions.[33] While a psychiatric treatment centre was available to male prisoners, women had no comparable facility. Jahn argued discrimination on combined grounds of gender and disability. The matter settled with the province committing to screen prisoners for mental health disabilities, provide access to treatment in jail, and exempt those with mental health disabilities from segregation except in cases of undue hardship. It also committed to publicly report on continuing segregation patterns and practices.[34]

In all of the above matters (notwithstanding the gender parity arguments in Jahn, and the intersectionality arguments of interveners LEAF and NWAC in the BC litigation), the damage of solitary confinement was ultimately narrowly framed as damage to mental health – whether exacerbation of pre-existing problems or creation of new ones. While the BC challenge had argued discrimination based in Indigeneity, that aspect of the claim was overshadowed and arguably undermined by an overwhelming concentration on a clinically mediated, individualised form of harm – to mental health.

Two other cases have brought mental health to the fore. One was a class action in respect of federal prisoners subject to administrative segregation while 'seriously mentally ill'.[35] In the words of the judge, these were 'the sickest of the inmates suffering from mental illness'.[36] The claimants established breach of *Charter* guarantees of liberty and security of the person as well as freedom from cruel and unusual treatment, based on lack of independent review and excessive time in segregation. Discrimination was not argued, yet pre-existing disability was clearly integral to class membership. Beyond individual damages, the court awarded $20 million for vindication and deterrence to be invested in 'additional mental health or program resources for structural changes to penal institutions'.[37] In other words, the award was earmarked for prison-based accommodation of prisoners' mental health problems.

---

[32] *BCCLA* (BCCA) at paras 238–39.

[33] Ontario Human Rights Commission, 'Segregation and Mental Health in Ontario's Prisons: Jahn v. Ministry of Community Safety and Correctional Services'. Available at: www.ohrc.on.ca/en/segregation-and-mental-health-ontario%E2%80%99s-prisons-jahn-v-ministry-community-safety-and-correctional.

[34] Ibid.

[35] *Brazeau v Attorney General (Canada)*, 2019 ONSC 1888 (CanLII) canlii.ca/t/hz9gd.

[36] Ibid, para 5.

[37] Ibid, para 459. This award was set aside on appeal on the basis that it "was not fair to either the class or Canada and it amounted to an unjustifiable assumption of judicial control over a complex public institution." (2020 ONCA 184 at para 112).

In the fifth case,[38] the claimant, Adam Capay, was an Indigenous man who had been subjected to physical and sexual violence as a child and became dependent on drugs while incarcerated. At 19, he allegedly killed another prisoner during what appears to have been a delusional episode, possibly triggered by a medication change. He was then held in continuous segregation for 1,647 days awaiting trial. For months he was kept in a plexiglass cell with the lights on 24 hours a day, with no ability to flush the toilet from inside his cell, no television and no radio.

Capay brought a *Charter* claim seeking a stay of the murder charges against him. The stay was granted. The judge found that the effects of segregation on Capay's mental health had been extreme, including worsened PTSD and attention deficit hyperactivity disorder and cognitive and memory impairment to the point of interference with his right to a fair trial. He declared that authorities had breached Capay's *Charter* rights to life, liberty and security of the person (by failing to afford him procedural protections, including independent review), his right against arbitrary detention (by failing to adhere to policy and employing continuous segregation without evidence in support) and cruel and unusual treatment (here recognising the egregious harms to Capay's psychological and physical integrity).

Capay also established discrimination based on mental health disability (ie, that segregation had exacerbated his mental health conditions, rendering him more susceptible to depression and suicide). Yet a further claim of discrimination based on Indigeneity was rejected. Like the BC appellate court, the judge was unable to connect the dots between the violence and dislocation effected by colonialism, Indigenous persons' heightened vulnerability to criminalisation, incarceration, and overrepresentation in solitary and the claimant's individual circumstances. Specifically, the judge reasoned that the evidence had not established anything peculiar to Indigenous persons that would make their experiences of segregation markedly worse than others'.[39]

THREE WORRIES (CARCERAL RESILIENCE)

In each case I have described, the harms of solitary are reduced from intensive exacerbation of interlocking oppressions to clinically mediated mental health problems. Correspondingly, at the remedial stage, this has given rise to three worries.

Screening as Net-Widening

The first worry relates to mental health screening. Screening prisoners for mental health conditions is central to the *Jahn* settlement as well as the federal government's (ongoing) responses to the recent *Charter* challenges. Screening is

---

[38] *R v Capay*, 2019 ONSC 535.
[39] Ibid, para 472.

also implicit in the Mandela Rules' exempting from solitary those whose mental health conditions are likely to be exacerbated.[40]

Why worry about screening? After all, it is potentially a mechanism of reasonable accommodation; disability must be identified before it can be accommodated. The problem is that mental health screening is likely, in prison environments if not in general, to translate trauma and underlying social–structural oppression into individualised pathology and risk. In turn, this may be predicted to have a net-widening effect,[41] justifying an increasingly stratified array of enhanced restrictions across prison spaces and so a shift from solitary as state of exception to solitary (or multiple varieties of 'seg-lite') as rule.

The question for those promoting mental health screening as a throughway to prisoner mental health is: what will prevent it from simply becoming a justification for intensified security? Kelly Hannah-Moffat has shown how correctional knowledge has adapted actuarial risk/need assessment in ways that reconfigure complex and overlapping oppressions as reasons for intensified control.[42] As Chris Cunneen observes, risk assessment substitutes for race/Indigeneity a set of ostensibly neutral markers (eg, family instability, involvement in the justice system, low education and employment attainment) with the effect of tracking inelastic patterns of material inequity while simultaneously performing race/Indigeneity against an implicit normative whiteness.[43] I suggest that mental health screening is likely to be conscripted into the same carceral project of reconfiguring oppression as rationalised risk containment.

Two terms of Canada's correctional laws support the point. Section 17(e) of the *Corrections and Conditional Release Regulations* lists 'any physical or mental illness or disorder suffered by the inmate' as one of a set of factors to be taken into account in security classification (alongside, *inter alia*, 'outstanding charges', 'potential for violent behaviour', and 'continued involvement in criminal activities'). Such association of mental health conditions with risk and dangerousness is arguably inevitable in an environment oriented to order and control. Relatedly, section 18 mandates consideration of the 'degree of supervision and control' a person requires. This assessment, too, is likely to be informed by mandated mental health screening – indeed, this would seem to be a, if not the, fundamental point of screening.

---

[40] UN General Assembly, *United Nations Standard Minimum Rules for the Treatment of Prisoners* (2015).

[41] S Cohen, *Visions of Social Control: Crime, Punishment and Classification* (Cambridge, Polity Press, 1985) 41–42.

[42] K Hannah-Moffat, 'Sacrosanct or Flawed: Risk, Accountability and Gender-Responsive Penal Politics' (2010) 22(2) *Current Issues in Criminal Justice* 193.

[43] See, eg, C Cunneen, 'Youth Justice and Racialization: Comparative Reflections' (2019) 1 *Theoretical Criminology* 8.

In short, mental health screening, an integral part of the remedial responses provoked by the solitary confinement litigation, threatens to reify the sources of trauma and oppression while justifying the stratification of enhanced restrictions across prison spaces.

Out of the Frying Pan ...

A second worry in the wake of the solitary confinement litigation relates to alternatives; the 'out of the frying pan' problem. What sorts of alternatives are currently in place and what alternatives are likely to emerge as administrative segregation recedes?

In December 2018, the federal government reformed its policy on administrative segregation. Those reforms exempted three categories of person: those with 'serious mental illness with significant impairment'; those 'actively engaging in self-injury which is deemed likely to result in serious bodily harm'; and those 'at elevated or imminent risk for suicide'.[44] But where are these exempted people to go?

The most obvious place is mental health observation. Federal correctional policy reserves mental health observation for prisoners 'at elevated or imminent risk for suicide', 'actively engaged in self-injurious behaviour' or 'identified by a health care professional as having a serious mental illness with significant impairment'.[45] Yet as Canada's Correctional Investigator has confirmed, mental health observation is at least as bleak and distressing as administrative segregation.[46] Placement is preceded by strip search.[47] On 'high watch', one is not entitled to personal items; on 'modified watch', this is discretionary. One has a right to a daily change of security gown but no right to shower. One is under constant surveillance by security camera. One is entitled to a mattress unless deemed at risk of using it in a self-injurious manner, in which case one sleeps on a thin blanket on the concrete slab bed. Feminine hygiene products may be deemed unduly risky, in which case women do without.

The other key characteristic of this alternative is lack of basic procedural protections. Framed as a therapeutic rather than a punitive or even administrative space, placement attracts no formal hearing. Instead, one is given an opportunity to 'provide input' into one's placement plan. One is to be 'informed of the reason' for the placement and given 'reasonable access to relevant documentation'. However, there is no right to counsel or duty to facilitate access to counsel; instead, one is allowed 'an advocate' defined as 'a person who, in the

---

[44] CD 709 (last update 2017-08-01) s19 (a) & (b). Barring 'exceptional circumstances' pregnant prisoners, those with significant mobility impairment and those in palliative care, are also exempt.
[45] CD-843 (last update 2017-08-01) s 10.
[46] *Risky Business: An Investigation of the Treatment and Management of Chronic Self-Injury Among Federally Sentenced Women Final Report* (Ottawa, ON: OCI, 2013) 17–22.
[47] Ibid, 19.

opinion of the Institutional Head, is acting or will act in the best interest of the inmate'. A review process is started, gradually moving up the command chain of correctional mental health; however, neither the individual nor their advocate or counsel is directly engaged in that.[48]

There is no formal cap on time in mental health observation. However, in practice, difficult-to-manage prisoners are likely to be shifted among intensely restrictive regimes within the prison (eg, back and forth between administrative segregation – or simulacra thereof – and medical observation) and/or other closely supervised clinical–correctional spaces.[49]

Other Alternatives

Reports on mental health care in Canada's correctional systems routinely emphasise the insufficiency of resources, staffing, and facilities to meet the needs of prisoners.[50] Thus, alternatives to segregation and/or mental health observation are few. In the federal context, men deemed highest risk may be transferred to the Special Handling Unit[51] (a supermax prison in Quebec) or one of five Regional Treatment Centres.[52] Women may be placed in one of the Structured Living Units in the women's prisons or transferred to the Regional Psychiatric Centre in Saskatoon. Transfer to a provincial psychiatric hospital is possible if the prisoner (and hospital/province) is willing, or without the prisoner's consent should they meet provincial involuntary hospitalisation criteria.[53]

Each of these alternatives is, itself, a site of intensive confinement and control. In 2017, an independent review of the Regional Treatment Centres identified 'low staffing ratios to patient needs' which 'can result in the overuse of segregation and clinical seclusion practices'.[54] While advocates tend to view provincially run psychiatric hospitals as the best alternative,[55] these sites, too, commonly engage in restrictive practices, typically with few or no procedural protections.[56] Between 2006 and 2010, one in four psychiatric inpatients in

[48] CD-843, ss 11–15.

[49] See, eg, *Risky Business* at 10.

[50] See Office of the Correctional Investigator, *Priority: Access to Physical and Mental Health Care* (2016). Available at: www.oci-bec.gc.ca/cnt/priorities-priorites/health-sante-eng.aspx.

[51] CD-708 (Special Handling Unit) (last update 2018-09-10).

[52] CD-706 (Classification of Institutions) (last update 2018-11-07).

[53] Guidelines 710-2-3 (Inmate Transfer Process). Available at: www.csc-scc.gc.ca/acts-and-regulations/710-2-3-gl-en.shtml.

[54] OCI Report 2017–18 at 21–22.

[55] See, eg, West Coast Prison Justice Society/Prisoners Legal Services, *Damage/Control: Use of Force and the Cycle of Violence and Trauma in BC's Federal and Provincial Prisons (2019)*. Available at: www.prisonjustice.org/news-release-report-calls-use-of-force-practices-in-bc-and-federal-prisons-traumatic-and-harmful-and-makes-recommendations-for-change/.

[56] See L Johnson, *Operating in Darkness: BC's Mental Health Act Detention System* (Vancouver, CLAS, 2017); I Grant and P Carver, 'PS v Ontario: Rethinking The Role of the Charter in Civil Commitment' (2016) 53(3) *Osgoode Hall Law Journal* 999; CT Sheldon, K Spector and M Perez, 'Re-Centering Equality from the Inside: The Interplay Between Sections 7 and 15 of the Charter in Challenges to Psychiatric Detention' (2016) 35(2) *National Journal of Constitutional Law* 19.

Ontario were subject to physical or chemical restraints or seclusion.[57] Deaths precipitated by use of restraints in provincial psychiatric and forensic hospitals have attracted inquiry processes revealing systemic discrimination (including on intersecting race and disability grounds) in conditioning use of force.[58] Beyond these overt material forms of control is the further element of bio-psychological control, through psycho-pharmaceuticals or other mechanisms that have proven even less susceptible to liberal-legal rights protections than the material and spatial restrictions of solitary confinement.[59]

The Future?

Recently added (June 2019) to the above alternatives is a law reform measure through which Canada purports to have abolished solitary confinement.[60] The legislation introduces Structured Intervention Units (SIUs). Prisoners may be placed in SIUs on the same bases as administrative segregation: safety and security. They are entitled to four hours outside cell daily instead of two, including two hours of 'meaningful human contact'. However, discretionary exceptions exist, including on security grounds. Other factors distinguishing SIUs from administrative segregation are a more active role for health professionals in making recommendations about placement and a new (rather convoluted) system of administrative oversight.

Senator Kim Pate has observed that, in many institutions, SIUs are simply rebranded administrative segregation units.[61] Beyond this are concerns about continued broad discretion (eg, to deny time out of cell); the fact that oversight powers rest in non-judicial bodies (which may, moreover, deny prisoners an oral hearing); lack of a hard time limit for placement; and lack of a clear duty on authorities to facilitate access to counsel. In short, the new regime, like the old, is tilted toward intensive security and light-touch review, even as it takes cover behind enhanced mental health and behavioural monitoring.

Similar concerns arise around policy changes in Ontario. The Placement of Special Management Inmates policy creates four categories of placement for prisoners deemed unsuited for the general jail population: behavioural care,

[57] TM Mah et al, 'Use of Control Interventions in Adult In-Patient Mental Health Services' (2015) 28(4) *Healthcare Management Forum* 139–45.

[58] Ontario Human Rights Commission, 'OHRC Settlement with the Waypoint Centre for Mental Health Care: A Step Towards Respecting the Human Rights of Diverse Patients' (2017). Available at: www.ohrc.on.ca/en/news_centre/ohrc-settlement-waypoint-centre-mental-health-care-step-towards-respecting-human-rights-diverse. See also Ontario Coroner's Inquest into the Death of Jeffrey James. Available at: www.empowermentcouncil.ca/PDF/Jeffery%20James%20Inquest.pdf.

[59] See L Steele, 'Temporality, Disability and Institutional Violence: Revisiting In Re F' (2017) 26:3 *Griffith Law Review* 378.

[60] An Act to amend the Corrections and Conditional Release Act and another Act, S.C. 2019, c. 27.

[61] Teresa Wright, 'Senator Says Solitary-Confinement Bill Will Make some Conditions Worse, not Better' (2019) Canadian Broadcasting Corporation. Available at: www.cbc.ca/news/canada/kitchener-waterloo/senator-says-solitary-confinement-bill-will-make-some-conditions-worse-not-better-1.5124649.

managed clinical care, stabilisation, and supportive care.[62] According to Justice David Cole, one of two experts appointed to oversee Ontario's compliance with the *Jahn* settlement:

> Though it is hoped that these policy changes will bring about significant changes to the segregation regime, unfortunately it is entirely possible that inmates (mentally ill or not) who were previously housed for lengthy periods of time in either 'administrative' or 'disciplinary' segregation, may now be routinely housed in 'behavioural care', where they may cycle in and out of these two statuses, merely with time frames superficially adjusted, accompanied by reams of paperwork to justify maintenance of much of the status quo.[63]

Again, the worry is that these so-called alternatives are but repackaged versions of solitary confinement, now with the legitimising veneer of clinical knowledge.

The Remainder

A third and final worry takes us back to the imperative of disability non-discrimination: an imperative reflected in the Mandela Rules and in *Jahn*, in the BC solitary confinement litigation and in *Capay*. The anti-discrimination imperative underlies the international prohibition on *any* solitary confinement of prisoners with mental health conditions. Yet, while the worry above was that alternative sites for those deemed mental health affected may be as bad or worse, the present worry is for those left behind. For once an exceptional class uniquely vulnerable to the harms of solitary confinement is extracted, those who remain are in an important sense positioned as fit for it.

That is, just as there are complexities around defining disability, so is there complexity around construction of those who do not qualify for disability-based accommodations. Here one must be particularly attentive to the propensity for racialised identification of those fit for hard time. Michael Martin, in a study of mental health screening of federal prisoners in Canada, reports greater resistance to screening on the part of racialised and Indigenous prisoners.[64] One may speculate on the reasons for this (eg, cultural or socio-political differences in interpreting or valuing psychiatric knowledge, association of psychiatry with colonial power, concerns about appearing vulnerable). An Indigenous elder testifying in the BC litigation made the straightforward suggestion that

---

[62] Justice D Cole, Interim Report [Jahn Settlement] at 23, 39–42. Available at: www.ohrc.on.ca/sites/default/files/Interim%20Report%20-%20Compliance%20with%20Jahn.pdf.

[63] Ibid, 41. 'As one difficult remand prisoner awaiting trial in an institution where some of these changes have already been instituted recently said in my court: "all this is b.s.; it's just seg. lite"' (fn52).

[64] M Martin, *Detection and Treatment of Mental Illness Among Prison Inmates: A Validation of Mental Health Screening at Intake to Correctional Service of Canada* (Ottawa, University of Ottawa, 2017).

prisoners resist mental health diagnoses out of fear they will be sent to a treatment centre.[65]

These insights are deepened in the work of Jasbir Puar, who identifies a category constructed in the shadow of successful disability rights claims she calls debility. Debility is the remainder: 'bodies sustained in a perpetual state of debilitation precisely through foreclosing the social, cultural, and political translation to [legally recognized, materially resourced] disability'.[66] In this vein, a recent report on use of force in federal and provincial prisons in BC describes the case of 'Joey', an Indigenous man who lost his primary caregivers as a child and has spent much of his life in solitary. Joey describes an incident during his time in youth detention:

> I remember the staff taking me down, twisting me up, banging my head against the floor, and putting me in straps. They hit my head so hard on the ground that my mouth would bleed. The straps were kind of like a Pinel bed or a straitjacket, but my legs were strapped together tight and pulled up to my chest. They would leave me like that and put me in an observation cell for a long time while they sat and watched me.[67]

Joey has spent over 2,100 days in federal segregation (and further time in segregation in provincial custody). He has been subject to frequent use of force, typically precipitated by self-harm. He has been diagnosed with PTSD and major depressive disorder.[68] Yet, one of the deepest challenges in this and other cases is obtaining the requisite professional approval for transfer from a correctional to a clinical site. The potential is always there for prisoners to be classed as drug- or attention-seeking, or simply disruptive, violent or offensive rather than actually 'sick'. Louisa Smith and Leanne Dowse elaborate on this dynamic, which they argue particularly affects persons subject to oppression on intersecting bases across multiple institutional sites.[69] Their argument reminds us that the clinical and correctional knowledges giving shape to the carceral archipelago are, in a sense, mirror images, working together to reduce complexity to justifications for confinement and control.

The claims-making device of disability discrimination – at least, detached from analysis of the social–structural foundations of disability and other forms of oppression – may paradoxically reinforce this way of sorting prisoners/patients. The worry is in part that in remediating disability discrimination we deepen the oppression of those not qualifying as disabled. The further worry

[65] BCCLA (BCSC) para 233.
[66] J Puar, *The Right to Main: Debility, Capacity, Disability* (Durham NC, Duke University Press, 2017) xiv.
[67] West Coast Prison Justice Society/Prisoners Legal Services, *Damage/Control* (2019) 5.
[68] Ibid.
[69] L Smith and L Dowse, 'Complexity and Disability: Drawing from a Complexity Approach to Think Through Disability at the Intersections' in Katie Ellis et al (eds), *Interdisciplinary Approaches to Disability: Looking Towards the Future* (Abingdon, Routledge, 2019) 123.

is that surrendering the field of prison justice to a clinically mediated 'disability' masks the complexity of both the mental health affected and the class(es) deemed fit for segregation or other security-centric treatment.

CONCLUSION

I have argued that recent Canadian litigation intent on bringing solitary confinement under the sway of human rights has proven an unwitting means of strengthening carceral–institutional resilience. That is, this litigation has permitted reductive translation of the problem of solitary – a problem inextricably imbricated in histories of trauma and oppression, in colonialism, racism, patriarchy, ableism and interacting with all of these, capitalist classism – to a 'mental health' problem inviting a clinical (or correctional–clinical) fix. Such reductivism is apparent not simply in the way the courts have dealt with disability discrimination, but also breach of security of the person and cruel and unusual treatment. Common to all these human rights-based successes has been a relinquishing of the field of justice to individualised clinical knowledge.

Does this mean that law, or human rights litigation, is doomed to reproduce carceral logics – to be a mechanism of carceral control? Arguably, as with any institution, law can be a site of resistance. In closing I turn to Debra Parkes, from whose work I draw three imperatives of anti-carceral lawyering: expose institutional violence while establishing solidarity with those inside; surface intersectional oppression; and seek anti-carceral remedies.[70] Canada's solitary confinement litigation has contributed in important ways to the first of these imperatives. However, it has failed (so far) on counts two and three.

Anti-carceral lawyering requires that we work backwards from anti-carceral remedies – and that we do so in solidarity with prisoners and others across the carceral archipelago, united by a commitment to intersectional substantive equality. It expresses a radical lawyering ethic grounded in the aspirations and capacities of specific communities to resist incarceration and fashion radical alternatives. It requires a willingness to devise strategies in and beyond the courts and to seek remedies reaching beyond the material sites of incarceration.[71] At the same time, lawyers aspiring after an anti-carceral ethic should cultivate familiarity with the insights of both prison abolitionism and critical disability theory, in order to resist (and advise resistance to) strategies that obscure the justice claims of those located at one or the other side of the prison justice/disability justice divide.

[70] Parkes, 'Solitary Confinement' (2017).
[71] In Canada, this work may be informed by ss 81 and 84 of the CCRA. These provisions enable Indigenous communities to enter into agreements with Canada to develop community-based strategies for supervising persons under sentence or on parole/statutory release.

Last, pursuit of anti-carceral remedies requires challenging conceptions of disability, or mobilizations of this concept or identity category in law, which would isolate disability from social–structural injustice in ways that invite individualising and pathologising 'remedies'. This means busting disability out of solitary and situating disability-based justice claims within a broader account of intersectional substantive (transformative) equality. Ultimately, cracking the foundations of solitary confinement requires us to rethink disability, justice, and human rights in a way that is mindful of intersecting oppressions as well as liberations.

Part Two

Complicated Alliances
The Confluence of Ableist, Sanist, Gendered, Classed and Racialised Logics in Law, Policy and Practice

PART ONE OF the collection outlines some of the complex legacies of institutionalisation in the 'deinstitutionalised' community. In that part, contributors draw attention to the ways that ostensibly positive moves towards reasonable accommodation, 'empowerment' and reducing the barriers facing people with disabilities in law, policy and practice struggle to entirely free themselves from the legacies and logics of institutionalisation. In this next part of the collection, we situate this struggle within a broader context: within and among other longstanding practices of oppression and segregation in society.

The five chapters in Part Two attend to the intersections of ableist, sanist, gendered, classed and racialised logics (among others) within law, policy and practice. While each of these five chapters considers the intersecting legacies of oppression and segregation within the 'deinstitutionalised' community, together they tell a larger story. Read together, these chapters offer insight into three themes which are considered infrequently within contemporary accounts of the 'deinstitutionalised' community.

First, the chapters within Part Two reveal the obscured, often historic confluence of, and alliances between, ableist, sanist, gendered, classed and racialised logics within law, policy and practice. Although this theme runs throughout the chapters, it is most clearly articulated in Chapters 7 and 8.

In Chapter 7, Ameil Joseph analyses anti-immigration discourses in the context of Brexit and Trump's politics. Here Joseph shows how present-day resentment and hostility towards immigrants is fostered by invoking historically fashioned ideas of threat, risk, burden and lack. Joseph's chapter shows us how these historically fashioned ideas both rely upon and extend longstanding colonial, eugenic, racial, ableist, sanist tropes and the technologies of white nationalism.

In Chapter 8, Karen Soldatic offers an aligned but unique set of observations. In this chapter, Soldatic draws attention to the ways that contemporary poverty management regimes in Australia – in particular, disability income regimes such as the Disability Support Pension – appear to rely upon neutral eligibility criteria but, in practice, continue longstanding settler–colonial population management strategies. Ultimately, Soldatic's chapter shows how the neoliberalisation of disability income regimes within settler–colonial Australia works to fix Indigenous Australians in place, subjecting them to an ever-tightening regime of disciplinary power which forces them to contort their bodies and minds in highly gendered and gendering ways.

The second theme illuminated in Part Two is that of the role of law and the institutions charged with its enforcement and administration in the legitimation of social norms. Put differently, chapters in this part of the collection offer insight into legal responses to those whose behaviour is considered non-normative and the often perverse consequences thereof. While this insight appears in each of the chapters included in Part Two, it is most clearly articulated in Chapters 9 and 10.

In Chapter 9, Isabel Karpin and Karen O'Connell examine cases in which women with personality disorder have turned to workers compensation and family law to facilitate or remediate their interactions with the social institutions of work and family. Karpin and O'Connell's chapter shows how these women's encounters with law often work against them. They show how when these women appeal to law to facilitate their inclusion within social institutions such as the workplace or family, it responds by amplifying their exclusion because their behaviour sits outside gendered, ableist and sanist social norms.

Leanne Dowse picks up this thread of inclusion and exclusion through law and its institutions in a different way in Chapter 10. In this chapter, Dowse focuses on people with cognitive disability experiencing corrosive social disadvantage and, in particular, on those who are subject to systematic and patterned regimes of incapacitation through institutions charged with law's enforcement and administration (ie, the prison). However, what Dowse illuminates in her chapter is not simply how this systematic and patterned regime of incapacitation emerges from the ways that people with cognitive disability are understood in relation to broader ableist, sanist, gendered, classed and racialised norms. Rather, Dowse shows us how this population is marginalised from a disability justice agenda and rights-based advancement because they further transgress accepted ways of 'being disabled' in a neoliberal biopolitical context. In this way, Dowse's chapter challenges us to consider what we valorise and normalise in our understandings of 'being disabled'. This challenge connects to the final insight offered by the chapters in Part Two.

The final theme illuminated in Part Two is that of resistance, protest and dissent, particularly in relation to the neoliberal, biopolitical frame. This theme appears in varying degrees and diverse forms within each of the chapters within Part Two, but it is brought to the foreground in Chapter 11, where Fleur Beaupert and Shelley Bielefeld analyse the emergence and operation of fixated persons units alongside counter-terrorism initiatives (ie, joint policing–mental health units developed to respond to persons who have allegedly become 'fixated' on public figures or social causes and are presumed to pose a risk of harm to the community). Through their analysis, Beaupert and Bielefeld suggest that the ableist conception of 'fixation' that underpins these units may operate to stifle legitimate political dissent and pathologise structural and socio-economic disadvantage. Indeed, what Beaupert and Bielefeld's chapter – among the others in Part Two – ultimately reminds us to consider is the ease with which dissenting responses to political marginalisation and structural injustice by those existing at the interstices of raced, ableist and classed oppression can be both silenced and subverted through law, policy and practice.

7

Excavating Hostility and Rationalising Violence through Anti-immigrant Confluent Discourses of Racial Threat, Risk, Burden and Lack

AMEIL JOSEPH

ECENT NATIONALIST/NATIVIST ATTENTIONS exemplified through discussions about Brexit in the United Kingdom (UK) and Donald Trump in the United States (US) have highlighted the need to re-examine reactions of consternation to immigration.[1] Anti-immigration discourses are not new and have always been slippery or evasive.[2] They can be historically presented and perceived as seldom, sparse, extreme or held in abeyance, while depictions of and reactions to immigration are simultaneously articulated with adulation in public performance and abnegation in policy practice.[3] The latest varieties of advances in anti-immigration discourses have been powerfully, publicly productive for policy and influence on a global scale.[4] Theses discourses wield both the

---

[1] See M Goodwin and C Milazzo, 'Taking Back Control? Investigating the Role of Immigration in the 2016 Vote for Brexit' (2017) 3 *The British Journal of Politics and International Relations* 19; R Waldinger, 'Immigration and the Election of Donald Trump: Why the Sociology of Migration Left Us Unprepared ... and Why We Should Not Have Been Surprised' (2018) 1 *Ethnic and Racial Studies* 16.

[2] See A McLaren, *Our Own Master Race: Eugenics in Canada, 1885–1945* (Toronto, University of Toronto Press, 1997); R Ward, 'National Eugenics in Relation to Immigration' (1910) 192 *The North American Review* 656; J G Young, 'Making America 1920 Again? Nativism and US Immigration, Past and Present' (2017) 5 *Journal on Migration & Human Security* 217.

[3] See H Gusterson, 'From Brexit to Trump: Anthropology and the Rise of Nationalist Populism' (2017) 2 *American Ethnologist* 44; Waldinger, 'Immigration and the Election of Donald Trump' (2018); S Bjork-James and J Maskovsky, 'When White Nationalism Became Popular' (2017) 3 *Anthropology News* 58.

[4] See M Chishti and J Bolter, *The Trump Administration at Six Months: A Sea Change in Immigration Enforcement* (Washington DC, Migration Policy Institute, 2017). Available at: www.migrationpolicy.org/article/trump-administration-six-months-sea-change-immigration-enforcement; AM Mayda and G Peri, 'The Economic Impact of US in the Age of Trump' in CP Bown, *Economics and Policy in the Age of Trump* (London, CEPR Press, 2017).

insidious ideas that are carried from the past and the direct and brazen contemporary forms of racism and colonial hatred that work together to rationalise institutionalised, state-authorised dehumanisation and violence.[5]

These ideas produce and reproduce historically entrenched positions of institutionalised advantage and disadvantage, delineating the police (the authorities, surveillance, protectors and punishers) and the policed. They rationalise, authorise and legitimise violence, exploitation and subjugation.[6] The dangerousness of these discourses is also energised because they are fluid and mobile. As they are carried within ideas, they can be poisonous and transmissible; they can have an aftermath while and where they continue to operate and reside. Anti-immigration discourses can be sanitised, embedded in regular usage and carry out work that becomes divorced from its original design to maintain its products and accumulate widespread solidarity. In this way, it mobilises as does an *esprit de corps* – it depicts dominance as natural, collective and under undue hardship, threat or opposition. It does so by claiming a morale of a group while constituting the identities, positions and politics of the group itself as deserving, worthy and desirable.

Anti-immigration discourses are frequently presented and challenged in ways that circulate and legitimate concerns about national identity, threat to security and costs to the public.[7] These concerns often obscure the confluence of historical ideas that brandish ableism, sanism, alongside biological notions of criminality, burden, risk and threat within anti-immigration discourses.

In this chapter, I analyse recent public and media examples of political positions on anti-immigration for their historical use of colonial, eugenic, racial, ableist, sanist tropes and the technologies of white nationalism. These ideas collaborate to foster resentment of immigrants by invoking historically fashioned ideas of threat, risk, burden and lack. Tropes of criminality and incivility, racial extinction, parasitic exploitation and biological threat are wielded together to consolidate popular support for projects of dehumanisation, immigration refusal, detention and deportation. I then discuss the dangerous products of these ideas as they impact and affect the lives of those who have already been made worthy of violence.

ANTI-IMMIGRATION DISCOURSES WITHIN BREXIT AND TRUMP

Anti-immigration discourses in the current historical moment can be appreciated for their powerful and popular influence through the examples of Brexit

---

[5] See IR Dowbiggin, *Keeping America Sane: Psychiatry and Eugenics in the United States and Canada, 1880–1940.* (Cornell University Press, 1997); McLaren, *Our Own Master Race* (1997); AJ Joseph, *Deportation and the Confluence of Violence Within Forensic Mental Health and Immigration Systems* (Basingstoke, Palgrave Macmillan, 2015).

[6] Ibid.

[7] See Goodwin and Milazzo, 'Taking Back Control?' (2017).

and the 2016 US Presidential election and resulting administration through to 2018. In June 2016, the UK held a referendum on European Union (EU) membership. The result was a 51.9 per cent vote in favour of leaving the EU. A shock was felt immediately, as the British pound fell to a '31-year low against the dollar and over 2 trillion dollars were wiped off shares globally'.[8] Some of the reasons offered for the outcome are that there has been a longstanding Eurosceptic electorate in the UK since 1973 (the year the UK joined the EU) and an anti-establishment/anti-immigration message that had grown ever louder, issuing not just from the UK Independence Party but across Europe prior to the Brexit vote.[9] A media analysis and survey data demonstrated that 'Conservative politicians dominated media coverage on both sides of the campaign, account-ing for almost two-thirds of all referendum-related media appearances'.[10] This framed the discourse within conservative messages. The 'remain' side argued that the economy was at risk if Brexit were to occur and the 'leave' side took positions about borders, lawmaking and immigration restriction.

While immigration was a stark deciding factor for Brexit, arguments continue to position the leave vote as an economic issue relating to the winners and losers of globalisation: 'In a nutshell, the "winners" of globalization – the young, well-educated professionals in urban centres – favour more open borders, immigration and international co-operation, whereas the "left behind" – the working class, less educated and the older – oppose such openness.'[11] Analyses have tended to focus on the conservative lines of debate, the economy and immigration considered in neoliberal market rationalities of cost.[12] This often obscures how Euroscepticism is so impactfully, deeply and closely connected to fear, stoking nationalism and 'a general hostility towards other cultures, such as negative attitudes towards minority groups and immigrants'.[13] As Goodwin and Milazzo note:

> the Leave vote was driven by identity concerns. Those who feel more strongly attached to a European identity are significantly less likely to vote for Brexit while those who have a strong British or English identity are more likely to vote to leave the EU.[14]

This was connected to hostility; specifically, 'those who voted for Brexit were significantly more hostile towards immigration and anxious about its perceived effects on the economy, culture and the welfare state'.[15] Perception of the threat

[8] SB Hobolt, 'The Brexit Vote: A Divided Nation, a Divided Continent' (2016) 9 *Journal of European Public Policy* 23.

[9] Ibid.

[10] Ibid.

[11] Ibid.

[12] See J Wadsworth, S Dhingra, G Ottaviano and J Van Reenen, *Brexit and the Impact of Immigra-tion on the UK* (London, Centre for Economic Performance, 2016); MJ Goodwin and O Heath, 'The 2016 Referendum, Brexit and the Left Behind: An Aggregate-Level Analysis of the Result' (2016) 3 *The Political Quarterly* 87.

[13] See Hobolt, 'The Brexit Vote' (2016).

[14] See Goodwin and Milazzo, 'Taking Back Control?' (2017).

[15] Ibid.

of demographic change, threat to identity and rising immigration, alongside the idea that Brexit would provide some sort of control over these issues, helped to generate support.

While immigration is considered in these analyses, the (re)constituted fear of immigrants and immigration is not explored in sufficient detail.[16] Considerations of racism, anti-Muslim[17] ideas, worries about criminality and the concept of biological threat (risk of disease, contamination, genetic influences) which were widespread during Brexit have not been adequately considered for their historical provocations, effects and influences. As Burnett notes:

> Research by the Institute of Race Relations into over one hundred incidents of racial violence reported in the mass media in the month after the EU referendum indicates that the 'spike' in such attacks has to be understood in terms of the racist climate created not just during the clearly nativist referendum debate, but also in the divisive policies and programmes of successive governments preceding it.[18]

Understanding anti-immigrant, nationalist and racist incidents as incidents delimits the ways in which analyses across larger temporal historical periods can be perceived and named. Anti-Muslim sentiments have been also been (re) invigorated globally since 11 September 2001, the attacks on the World Trade Centre in New York City and the Iraq War in 2003 and its aftermath.[19] Scholars have also demonstrated that the Brexit campaign:

> was underscored by two contradictory but inter-locking visions. The first was a deep nostalgia for empire, but one secured through an occlusion of the underside of the British imperial project: the corrosive legacies of colonialism and racism, past and present. The second was a more insular, Powellite narrative of retreating from a globalizing world that is no longer recognizably "British".[20]

These ideas worked together because they 'activated long-standing racialised structures of feeling about immigration and national belonging'.[21] One of the complicating features within the discourse was the appropriation of 'feminist and gay discourses of liberation – suitably de-fanged and shorn of their eman-cipatory potential'.[22] The liberation discourses appropriated from activism and critiques of dominance and subjugation were used to legitimise anti-immigrant

---

[16] See J Wadsworth et al, *Brexit and the Impact of Immigration on the UK* (2016); Goodwin and Heath, 'The 2016 Referendum, Brexit and the Left Behind' (2016); Hobolt, 'The Brexit Vote' (2016); Goodwin and Milazzo, 'Taking Back Control?' (2017).

[17] I do not rely on words like xenophobia and Islamophobia because they mobilise individualised levels of analysis and implications of ableist and sanist psychopathology to describe social, systemic and structural form of historical racialised violence.

[18] J Burnett, 'Racial Violence and the Brexit State' (2017) 4 *Race & Class* 58.

[19] A Kundnani, *The End of Tolerance: Racism in 21st Century Britain* (London, Pluto Press, 2007).

[20] S Virdee and B McGeever, 'Racism, Crisis, Brexit' (2017) 41(10) *Ethnic and Racial Studies*, 1802–19.

[21] Ibid.

[22] Ibid.

and specifically anti-Muslim sentiments, principally notions that British values of tolerance and diversity were superior to and under threat from Muslim culture (depicted in essentialised ways, with overt portrayals evoking imagery of incivility as anti-LGBTQI or oppressive to women). As Virdee and McGeever describe:

> As a result, femonationalist and homonationalist ways of thinking aided the consolidation of a new consensus on race and difference … in which anti-Muslim racism formed an intrinsic justification for the Labour and subsequently Conservative elite turn away from multiculturalism and towards an assimilatory nationalism.[23]

Many of the Brexit examples of anti-immigration discourse have taken a collaborating yet tangential turn in the US. Through some of the more brazen examples of racism and anti-immigration discourses, the necessity of considering the confluence of historical ideas that brandish ableism, sanism, alongside biological notions of criminality, burden and risk and threat within anti-immigration discourses becomes more ostensive.

During the 2016 US presidential election, Donald Trump promised uncompromising immigration restrictions. Some of the most widely discussed and protested examples include a ban on Muslim people, escalating deportations and building a wall along the Mexican border.[24] After Trump won the election, he signed a series of executive orders following through with those very promises, as well as ending the Deferred Action for Childhood Arrivals programme which allowed the children of 'illegal' immigrants a renewable two-year period free from threat of deportation and making them eligible for a work permit.[25] Trump was quite vocal about all of this, often taking pride in his executive ordering and defence of white supremacist nationalism to 'make American great again'. He has used social media and information 'leaked' from the White House, to publicly disseminate numerous examples of blatant racism: public incitements of anti-Muslim hate, attacks on the mayor of Puerto Rico, describing people from Mexico as bringing drugs, crime and stating that 'they're rapists'. In addition, insiders report Trump describing African countries as 'shitholes' and

---

[23] Ibid.

[24] See T Berenson, 'Donald Trump Wants "Complete Shutdown" of Muslim Entry to US' (2015) *Time*. Available at: www.time.com/4139476/donald-trump-shutdown-muslim-/; JC Timm, 'Trump Vows Humane "Deportation Force"' (2015) *MSNBC*. Available at: www.msnbc.com/msnbc/trump-vows-humane-deportation-force; M Pengelly, 'Donald Trump Backlash: "I Love Mexico" but Promises Border Wall if Elected' (2015) *The Guardian*. Available at: www.theguardian.com/us-news/2015/jun/28/donald-trump-mexico-immigration-presidential-campaign.

[25] See Anon, 'Trump's Executive Order: Who Does Travel Ban Affect?' (2017) *BBC News*. Available at: www.bbc.com/news/world-us-canada-38781302; J Pace, V Salama and R Zoll, 'Trump Signs Executive Order to Build His Mexico Border Wall' (2017) *The Washington Times*. Available at: www.washingtontimes.com/news/2017/jan/24/trump-sign-executive-order-border-wall-plans-immig/; DJ Trump, 'Executive Order: Enhancing Public Safety in the Interior of the United States'. Available at: www.whitehouse.gov/presidential-actions/executive-order-enhancing-public-safety-interior-united-states/; T Kopan, 'DACA Decision Appears to Shift to Congress' (2017) *CNN*. Available at: www.edition.cnn.com/2017/09/04/politics/daca-congress-trump-decision/index.html.

that Haitians 'all have AIDS' and should go back to their 'huts'.[26] He has also generally referred to some 'undocumented' Immigrants as 'animals'.[27] Donald Trump's examples of anti-Indigenous racism rely on casual dehumanisation and humiliation, referencing criminality and mocking indigenous identity.[28]

Donald Trump has also given senior positions to, campaigned for and openly supported white supremacists and white nationalists. Three prominent examples are:

- Steve Bannon, the former *Breitbart News* board member and founder, who advanced 'racist, sexist, xenophobic and anti-Semitic material'[29] for the alt-right, chief executive of Donald Trump's presidential campaign and chief strategist;

- Jeff Sessions, Attorney General of the United States from 2017–2018, whose nomination to be a judge for the US District Court in Alabama failed due to opposition from the National Association for the Advancement of Coloured People (NAACP) after multiple reports of Sessions' racist comments and support for the Ku Klux Klan. Four Department of Justice lawyers testified to the Senate Judiciary Committee about his racist remarks;[30] and

- Roy Moore, who Trump supported in a special election for a senate seat in 2017. Moore openly shared his ideas of a great America as being one in which slavery persisted.[31]

[26] See M Weaver, R Booth and B Jacobs, 'Theresa May Condemns Trump's Retweets of UK Far-Right Leader's Anti-Muslim Videos' (2017) *The Guardian*. Available at: www.theguardian.com/us-news/2017/nov/29/trump-account-retweets-anti-muslim-videos-of-british-far-right-leader; D Nakamura and J Wagner, 'Trump Attacks Mayor of San Juan, Ratcheting Up Tensions Over Crisis in Puerto Rico' (2017) *The Washington Post*. Available at: www.washingtonpost.com/politics/trump-attacks-mayor-of-san-juan-ratcheting-up-tensions-over-crisis-in-puerto-rico/2017/09/30/c9ce821c-a5fd-11e7-ade1-76d061d56efa_story.html.
K Reilly, 'Here Are All the Times Donald Trump Insulted Mexico' (2016) *Time*. Available at: www.time.com/4473972/donald-trump-mexico-meeting-insult/; JH Davis, SG Stolberg and T Kaplan, 'Trump Alarms Lawmakers with Disparaging Words for Haiti and Africa' (2018) *New York Times*. Available at: www.nytimes.com/2018/01/11/us/politics/trump-shithole-countries.html.
[27] See JH Davis, 'Trump Calls Some Unauthorized Immigrants "Animals" in Rant' (2018) *New York Times*. Available at: www.nytimes.com/2018/05/16/us/politics/trump-undocumented-immigrants.html.
[28] See D Leonhardt and IP Philbrick, 'Donald Trump's Racism: The Definitive List' (2018) *New York Times*. Available at: www.nytimes.com/interactive/2018/01/15/opinion/leonhardt-trump-racist.html?mtrref=www.google.com&gwh=7BDC834E08CBBD298440A321F008800D&gwt=pay&assetType=REGIWALL.
[29] See 'The Group Behind Steve Bannon's Toronto Event Also Funds Canada's Biggest Right-Wing Think Tanks' (2018) *Press Progress*. Available at: https://pressprogress.ca/the-group-behind-steve-bannons-toronto-event-also-funds-canadas-biggest-right-wing-think-tanks/.
[30] P Elliott and ZJ Miller, 'Inside Donald Trump's Chaotic Transition' (2016) *Time*. Available at: www.time.com/4574493/donald-trump-chaotic-transition/; NAACP, *NAACP Calls on Senate to Block Sessions for Attorney General* (2016). Available at: www.naacp.org/latest/naacp-calls-senate-block-sessions-attorney-general.
[31] LATimes.com, 'Video: Listen to Roy Moore Comments on Family, Slavery and When America was Great' (2017). Available at: www.latimes.com/95396983-132.html.

Trump has repeatedly and disproportionately spoken out against those he deems to be un-American and unpatriotic, mostly racialised people, often Black athletes.[32] His attacks on Barack Obama as lazy and questioning where he was born provoke historical racist tropes while stoking historically imbricated fears of some sort of coup by 'immigrants'.[33] His attacks on black women from military families and the news media and black female political representatives and celebrities, constitute state-supported misogynoir.[34] While unnerving, it has been difficult to find common threads in these positions beyond describing their inherent anti-Muslim hatred, misogyny, racism, or under a broader banner of nationalism or white supremacy.

Much of the anti-immigration discourse exemplified in Brexit and Trump has been presented as a result of real or perceived economic hardship, as a phenomenon that is emerging recently, or as a perceived '"rise" in "nationalist populism"'.[35] This concept of nationalist populism is both nebulous and contested. As Gusterson describes:

> This is the same broad phenomenon that Stuart Hall (1980) and Nicolette Makovicky (2013) call 'authoritarian populism,' Salih Can Aciksoz and Umut Yıldırım (2016) call 'right-wing populisms,' Gillian Evans (2017) calls 'cultural nationalism,' Ana Carolina Balthazar (2017) calls 'nostalgic nationalism,' Andre Gingrich and Marcus Banks (2006) call 'neo-nationalisms,' and Douglas Holmes (2016) calls 'Fascism 2.' Nationalist populism is quite different from the leftist populism of, say, US senator

[32] A Serwer, 'Trump's War of Words with Black Athletes' (2017) *The Atlantic*. Available at: www.scribd.com/article/359696036/Trump-s-War-Of-Words-With-Black-Athletes; A Jenkins 'This is Everything Donald Trump Said in His NFL Speech' (2017) *Time*. Available at: www.time.com/4954684/donald-trump-nfl-speech-anthem-protests/.

[33] Krieg, G, 14 of Trump's Most Outrageous 'Birther' Claims – Half from After 2011(2016) CNN. Available at: www.cnn.com/2016/09/09/politics/donald-trump-birther/index.html; A Tsoukala, 'Turning Immigrants into Security Threats: A Multi-Faceted Process' in G Lazaridis *Security, Insecurity and Migration in Europe* (Abingdon, Routledge, 2016); L Lucassen, *The Immigrant Threat: The Integration of Old and New Migrants in Western Europe Since 1850* (Champaign, University of Illinois Press, 2005).

[34] T Porter, 'Trump Attacked Oprah Winfrey as "Insecure" Amid Rumors the TV Star Will Run for President' (2018) *Newsweek*. Available at: www.newsweek.com/trump-attacks-oprah-rumors-810650; A Phillip, 'Trump Attacks ESPN's Jemele Hill, Calls for End to NFL Tax Breaks' (2017) *Washington Post*. Available at: www.washingtonpost.com/news/post-politics/wp/2017/10/10/trump-attacks-espns-jemele-hill-calls-for-end-to-nfl-tax-breaks/; J Diamond, 'Trump Keeps Up Attack on "Wacky" Congresswoman over Gold Star Call' (2017) CNN. Available at: www.cnn.com/2017/10/21/politics/trump-tweets-wilson-gold-star/index.html; R Shapiro, 'Maxine Waters on Trump's Latest Attack: I Am Not Intimidated By "Don the Con Man"' (2018) *Huffington Post*. Available at: www.huffingtonpost.com.au/entry/maxine-waters-trump-insult-don-the-con-man_n_5aa71383e4b009b705d56f35?ri18n=true.

[35] See H Gusterson, 'From Brexit to Trump: Anthropology and the Rise of Nationalist Populism' (2017) 2 *American Ethnologist* 44; Waldinger, 'Immigration and the Election of Donald Trump' (2018); LP Huber, 'Make America Great Again: Donald Trump, Racist Nativism and the Virulent Adherence to White Supremacy Amid US Demographic Change' (2016) *Charleston Law Review* 10; JK White, 'Donald Trump and the Scourge of Populism' (2016) 3 *The Forum* 14; DC Mutz, 'Status Threat, Not Economic Hardship, Explains the 2016 Presidential Vote' (2018) 115(19) *Proceedings of the National Academy of Sciences* doi.org/10.1073/pnas.1718155115.

and former presidential candidate Bernie Sanders, who refuses to scapegoat immigrants and favors income redistribution and deeper government intervention in the economy.[36]

What the populism discourse evades or constricts is a deeper analysis of what we are talking about and how we talk about it. The examples of Brexit, the 2016 presidential election of Donald Trump and Trump's work since, the National Front in France and the white supremacists who rioted in Charlottesville in August of 2017 (described as a 'Unite the Right Rally') have common and converging logics. The idea of populism implies the existence of some sort of collective or 'the people', appealed to as antagonistic to an existing structure of power and or dominant values or ideas. Populism carries within it a critique of modern Western democracies as not reflecting popular representations of people, voices or ideas.

Almost 20 years ago, Margaret Canovan published an influential paper on populism and democracy in the journal *Political Studies*.[37] In it, Canovan notes, 'we can identify three different senses that figure in populist discourse, though they tend in practice to be blended together'.[38] One is the discourse of a 'united people', another the idea of 'our people' and the third is that of 'ordinary people'. The first often rallies ideas of nation or country, the second of 'ethnic kith and kin' and the third ideas of normalcy. Canovan also identifies that: 'Populists in established democracies claim that they speak for the "silent majority" of "ordinary, decent people", whose interests and opinion are (they claim) regularly overridden by arrogant elites, corrupt politician and strident minorities.'[39]

Modern Western democracies can position populism as dangerous, as reactionary and without structure or government infrastructure. Populist revolt can lead to referendums or uprisings that radically undermine, remove or transform democratic infrastructure. However, populism also carries with it methods and strategies that mobilise grassroots organising, give voice to those who are excluded and resist the bureaucracy, elitism and self-serving nature of established

[36] See H Gusterson, 'From Brexit to Trump: Anthropology and the Rise of Nationalist Populism' (2017) 2 *American Ethnologist* 44; S Hall (1980) 'Popular-Democratic versus Authoritarian Populism' in *Marxism and Democracy*, ed Alan Hunt (London: Laurence and Wishart) 157–87; Makovicky, Nicolette. 2013. '"Work Pays": Slovak Neoliberalism as Authoritarian Populism' *Focaal*, no 67 (December): 77–90; Aciksoz, Salih Can and Umut Yıldırım (2016) 'Beyond the "Lesser Evil": A Critical Engagement with Brexit' 24(4) *Social Anthropology* 487–88.; Evans, Gillian. 2012. '"The Aboriginal People of England": The Culture of Class Politics in Contemporary Britain' *Focaal*, no 62 (March): 17–29.; Balthazar, Ana Carolina. (2017) 'Made in Britain: Brexit, Teacups and the Materiality of the Nation' 44(2) *American Ethnologist* 220–24.; Gingrich Andre and Marcus Banks (2006) *Neo-nationalism in Europe and Beyond: Perspectives from Social Anthropology*. New York: Berghahn.; Holmes, Douglas R. 2016. "Fascism 2." *Anthropology Today* 32(2): 1–3.
[37] See M Canovan, 'Trust the People! Populism and the Two Faces of Democracy' (1999) 1 *Political Studies* 47.
[38] Ibid.
[39] Ibid.

government. Herein lies an incredible danger; as Canovan describes, 'populism is a shadow cast by democracy itself'.[40] Populism as a discourse can be wielded and weaponised to build by fracturing, to dominate through resistance, to rule via freedom. Populism as a discourse in this current moment is activating already planted, seeded, sometimes dormant and often contradictory positions under an elusive banner. The discourse of populism is being used pejoratively to undermine the grassroots activism and collectivising of marginalised and oppressed groups, while reasserting technologies of racial (our people), national (united people) and biological (ordinary people) supremacy and dominance under the guide of anti-establishment/anti-elitism and transformation.

Often populism is confined within the discourses of socioeconomic class struggle. Diana Mutz has documented findings that support the argument that economic hardship was not what fostered populist support for Trump, rather preference for Trump was specifically related to 'issues that threaten white Americans' sense of dominant group status' which included American's perceived status of global dominance as well as a perceived internal threat of America losing its professed white identity as a result of the immigration of racialised people.[41] When we do not attend to the *how* and the *why* of anti-immigration sentiment beyond 'economic' concerns, we can avoid acknowledging the violence that is (re)produced as a result of the validation of racist, eugenic, colonial fears that are left unnamed. By exploring the historical confluence of discourses activated within conceptualisations and mobilisation of ideas of a 'united people' (nationhood), 'our people' (race, kith and kin) and 'ordinary people' (desirability/superiority), there exists potential for appreciating the ways in which contemporary anti-immigration discourses invoke historically fashioned racial, colonial and eugenic ideas of threat, risk, burden and lack by activating tropes of criminality and incivility, racial extinction, parasitic exploitation, as well as biological threat.

HISTORIOGRAPHIES OF POPULISM, NATIONALISM AND EUGENICS

Attention to the activation of racial, colonial eugenics and ableist and sanist logics within contemporary white nationalist populist discourses has been rather inadequate. Pamela Block and Michele Friedner note, through the experience of one class discussion, the importance of discussing eugenics in the class room in relation to the Trump presidency.[42] Also, the *LA Times* published an opinion/editorial on the eugenic history within Donald Trump's move to end the Deferred Action for Childhood Arrivals programme (DACA) that protected

---

[40] Ibid.

[41] See Mutz, 'Status Threat' (2018).

[42] See P Block and M Friedner, 'Teaching Disability Studies in the Era of Trump' (2017). Available at: www.somatosphere.net/2017/teaching-disability-studies-in-the-era-of-trump.html/.

the children of 'illegal' (undocumented) immigrants from deportation.[43] Beyond this, little attention has been given to the confluence of racist, sanist, ableist, eugenic, colonial logics that cohere and diverge within Brexit and Trump anti-immigration, populist discourses.

Trump has brazenly, publicly, commented that Black women have low IQs, are wacky, insecure and are a reason for low television ratings.[44] In addition, Trump has publicly mocked and insulted a reporter with a disability[45] and has also reversed policies developed to protect the human rights of trans people in schools and reinstated a military ban on transgender people.[46] Together with his comments that immigrants from Mexico, Haiti and Africa and predominantly Muslim countries bring drugs, crime, rape and terror and references to living in huts, AIDS as a biothreat and immigrants as animals, Trump summons a confluence of dehumanising discourses that render out continuing projects of racial, colonial eugenics, ableism and sanism.

The rise of eugenics in the later 1800s is often discussed in relation to Darwin's *Origin of Species* (1859)[47] which concretised attention to heredity, survival of the fittest and natural selection discourses. Such ideas influenced Darwin's cousin Francis Galton, who thought that the intentional manipulation of populations by restricting the birthrate or reproduction of those deemed 'unfit' while enhancing the fertility and reproductivity of those deemed 'fit' was a humane way of eliminating 'degeneracy' and 'feeblemindedness'.[48] Although 'The term *hérédité* was first used by French physicians in the late 1830s and in both Britain and the U.S. hereditary disease was a subject of study decades before the emergence of Darwinian theory',[49] 'the terms eugenics and racism have been used interchangeably'.[50] This practice often fails to capture the ways that belonging racially or ethnically did not protect one from being targeted for *feeblemindedness* or *degeneracy*. However, 'eugenics was never *not* about race'.[51]

[43] See M D'Antonio, 'Trump's Move to End DACA Has Roots in America's Long, Shameful History of Eugenics' (2017) *Los Angeles Times*. Available at: www.latimes.com/opinion/op-ed/la-oe-antonio-trump-eugenics-daca-20170914-story.html.

[44] Porter, 'Trump Attacked Oprah Winfrey' (2018); Phillip, 'Trump Attacks ESPN's Jemele Hill' (2017); Diamond, 'Trump Keeps Up Attack' (2018); Shapiro, 'Maxine Waters on Trump's Latest Attack' (2018).

[45] Anon, 'Donald Trump Under Fire for Mocking Disabled Reporter' (2015) *BBC News*. Available at: www.bbc.com/news/world-us-canada-34930042.

[46] CW Wong, 'LGBTQ Groups Slam Trump's Reversal of Transgender Bathroom Policies' (2017) *Huffington Post*. Available at: www.huffingtonpost.ca/entry/lgbtq-trump-transgender-policy_n_58af0bc6e4b05ca474a18b33?ri18n=true; J Diamond, 'Trump to Reinstate US Military Ban on Transgender People' (27 July 2017) *CNN*. Available at: www.edition.cnn.com/2017/07/26/politics/trump-military-transgender/index.html.

[47] See C Darwin *On the Origin of Species, 1859*. (London: Routledge, 2004).

[48] See A Bashford and P Levine (eds), *The Oxford Handbook of the History of Eugenics* (Oxford, Oxford University Press, 2010).

[49] Ibid.

[50] Ibid.

[51] Ibid.

Racial ideas gained a new kind of traction in Canada, the US, the UK and elsewhere when eugenic policies were implemented during the first two decades of the twentieth century. Eugenics catalysed and concretised colonial race fears and anti-immigration logics alongside notions of criminality, disease, lack and burden – commonly referred to as *undesirability*. Angus McLaren writes:

> Between 1896 and 1914 three million immigrants came to Canada. In the single decade between 1901 and 1911 the population jumped 43 percent in what had become the world's fastest growing country. In 1913 alone over 40000 immigrants arrived. What preoccupied their hosts was not so much the astonishing numbers as the fact that many (about 80000 in the first decade of the twentieth century) came from the non-Anglo-Saxon world.[52]

The idea that immigrants were carriers of hereditary defectiveness, criminality and disease led to public expressions of concern about 'race suicide', of 'our national burden of pauperism, vice, crime and insanity and racial degeneration'.[53] These notions of undesirability were consolidated as a confluence in Canada. Under section 3 of the Immigration Act of 1910, the 'prohibited classes' are identified in the following order: 'Persons mentally defective', 'Diseased persons', 'Persons physically defective', 'Criminals', 'Prostitutes or pimps', 'Procurers', 'Beggars and vagrants', 'Charity immigrants' and 'Persons not complying with regulations'. Notions of undesirability were used to justify who was worthy of immigration to Canada and of its public support and services.[54] These notions of undesirability also benefited from the established settler history that aimed to fabricate a history without Indigenous people. This generated a backdrop of ordered privilege based on who was perceived as being 'here first' and as the producers and claimants of Canadian wealth and resources – namely, Europeans.

In 2010, Howard W Odum published *Social and Mental Traits of the Negro*, based on his doctoral research at Columbia University.[55] This was one of many works by Odum pertaining to Black life in the US. As mentioned elsewhere:

> Professor Odum served as Assistant Director of Research for President Herbert Hoover's Research Committee on Social Trends and was President of the American Sociological Association in 1930 ... The subject of his research is described as having a tendency towards criminality, to addictions, to not wanting to work and 'mental defect oftener takes the form of idiocy and all acute psychoses like mania issue sooner in imbecility'.[56]

---

[52] McLaren, *Our Own Master Race* (1997).
[53] Ibid.
[54] See Joseph, *Deportation and the Confluence of Violence* (2015).
[55] See HW Odum, *Social and Mental Traits of the Negro: Research into the Conditions of the Negro Race in Southern Towns, A Study in Race Traits, Tendencies and Prospects* (New York, Columbia University, 1910).
Joseph, *Deportation and the Confluence of Violence* (2015).
[56] Ibid.

Odum founded the journal *Social Forces* and became a faculty member in the School of Public Welfare (which became the School of Social Work) and the Department of Sociology at the University of North Carolina at Chapel Hill. His son, Howard T Odum, was a widely respected ecologist who published influential works on general systems theory, theoretical orientation that has been foundational to social work for decades. Howard W Odum's influence carried a confluence of ideas that projected anti-Black racism via criminality, hereditary defectiveness, inferiority, indolence and sanism.

Also, in 1910, Robert De C Ward published an article in the *North American Review* advocating for eugenics in relation to immigration. Ward gives primacy to rallying people around a brazen nationalist racial threat to whiteness, rather than economic concerns:

> We in the United States have a very special interest in national eugenics, for we are here forming a new race of an extraordinarily heterogeneous character and we have a remarkably favorable opportunity for practising eugenic principles in the selection of the fathers and mothers of future American children through our power to regulate alien immigration. The United States, rather than England, should be the center of eugenic propaganda. Yet so far our people are practically silent on this question. Most of the discussions of the immigration problem in the past have been concerned with its economic side. The question is, however, a racial, perhaps even more than an economic one.[57]

These are death-dealing ideas that (re)produce tropes of the assailable while leaving open the door for the continuing rationalisation and legitimisation of colonial violence. Similarly, Canada's Department of Immigration and Colonization (est. 1917), was established to:

> ensure that Canada's colonial project was able to continue to monitor its regulation of immigrants and the colonization of Canada so that its racial composition and employment composition privileged British Canadians and restricted those who were identified as undesirable, of an inferior race, or an 'enemy'.[58]

As these brief examples make clear, the racism we see in the US and the UK that materialises in the present and reproduce historical colonial racist social relations exist in Canada's history and present.

Yet again, in 1910, the leading American eugenicist Charles B Davenport advocated for sterilisation for those identified 'with disabilities as subnormal, immoral and criminal as well as a burden to society and a threat to civilization'.[59] Eugenicists promoted immigration restriction and sterilisation in the UK.[60]

---

[57] R De C Ward, 'National Eugenics in Relation to Immigration' (1910) 192 *The North American Review* 656.

[58] See Joseph, *Deportation and the Confluence of Violence* (2015).

[59] See H Friedlander, 'The Exclusion and Murder of the Disabled' in R Gellately and N Stoltzfus (eds), *Social Outsiders in Nazi Germany* (Princeton, Princeton University Press, 2001).

[60] See L Bland and L Hall, 'Eugenics in Britain: The View from the Metropole' in A Bashford and P Levine (eds), *The Oxford Handbook of the History of Eugenics* (Oxford, Oxford University Press, 2010); R Hansen and D King, 'Eugenic Ideas, Political Interests and Policy Variance: Immigration and Sterilization Policy in Britain and the U.S.' (2001) 2 *World Politics* 53.

In Germany, prior to the First World War, Alfred Ploetz and Wilhelm Schallmayer 'studied family genealogies and the problem of degeneration, dividing population into superior (hochwertig) and inferior (minderwertig) individuals; they hoped to safeguard the nation's "genetic heritage" (erbgut) and viewed degeneration (entartung) as a threat'.[61] Karl Binding, a legal scholar and psychiatrist Alfred Hoche took things further in 1920 by advocating for the destruction of the disabled or 'mercy death'.[62] In 1933, sterilisation laws were promulgated in the German cabinet; soon after mass exterminations commenced, beginning with children with disabilities and then adults, later targeting Jews and gypsies. The murder and exclusion of the disabled and those deemed degenerate was founded upon ideas of hereditary defectiveness attached to immigration and protection of a national identity through the promotions of ideas that a better society would and could be produced.

Archival material has revealed that Davenport influenced eugenic laws significantly. The minutes of a meeting of the Committee on Immigration of the Eugenics Research Association, held at the Harvard Club, New York City, on 25 February 1920, demonstrates how passport and immigration documents were used to monitor and evaluate medical and behavioural inspections, specifically

> to afford adequate information concerning the early personal and the family history of each prospective immigrant before he leaves his own country, with the aim of admitting those of good personal and family history in their own country and rejecting those who, because of bad personal or family history, may be expected to bring with them not only undesirable personal qualities but also family tendencies of physical or mental defect or lack of self-control.[63]

Just as with the Canadian Immigration Act of 1910, here we see a confluence of ideas about good and bad family history (heredity), desirability, physical or mental defect and self-control. An archival letter from an influential eugenicist, CM Goethe, also demonstrates how eugenic interventions (including sterilisation and deportation) in France and Germany impressed him. He states that the US 'should (1st) pass a Quota Act against Latin America, (2nd) register all aliens (3rd) deport, like France, aliens to make jobs for the old American stock'.[64] Appreciation for eugenics-rationalised racism, sanism and ableism in ways that legitimated violence, yet – often in the same breath – eugenic nationalist colonial violence was deemed humane.[65] In 1934, the *New York Times* reported that Germany's sterilisation laws were being 'praised ... as the most important

---

[61] See Friedlander, 'The Exclusion and Murder of the Disabled' (2001).
[62] Ibid.
[63] See Immigration History Research Center, University of Minnesota, 'Eugenics, Race, & Immigration Restriction' (2015). Available at: www.cla.umn.edu/ihrc/news-events/other/eugenics-race-immigration-restriction.
[64] See 'Immigration History Research Center, 'Eugenics, Race, & Immigration Restriction' (2015).
[65] Ibid.

public-health measure since the discovery of bacteria'.[66] The article goes on to articulate that:

> All civilized races ... stand in imminent danger of degeneration because civilization has turned natural selection, which eliminated the sick and unfit automatically, into 'counterselection', which not only keeps the unfit alive but also enables them to breed more rapidly than the healthy and ambitious.[67]

Additionally, as Ann Stoler notes,

> colonial authorities and racial distinction were fundamentally structured in gendered terms ... the very categories of "colonizer" and "colonized" were secured through forms of sexual control which defined the domestic arrangements of Europeans and the cultural investments by which they identified themselves.[68]

These historical artifacts help to render out a continuity, a confluence of historical trajectories that implants, nests, cultivates and harvests racist, ablest, sanest and misogynistic ideas through the application of colonial eugenics thinking in ways that are craftily evasive of their project. The banners of populism, popular revolution, anti-establishment and economic rationale have been brandished to simultaneously wield deeply imbricated anti-immigrant racist sentiments inherently and historically connected to ideas of threat, risk, burden and lack. Tropes of criminality and incivility, racial extinction, parasitic exploitation and biological threat consolidate popular support for authorising and legitimating violent projects of dehumanisation, immigration refusal, detention and deportation. Confluently, notions of a 'united people' (nationhood), of 'our people' (race, kith and kin) and of 'ordinary people' (desirability/superiority) are (re)constituted and reproduced.

CONFLUENCES OF COLONIAL EUGENICS AND RACIST ABLEISM, AN EXCAVATED *ESPRIT DE CORPS*

As this edited collection aims to bring attention to the longstanding legacies of eugenics, racism and colonial logics within institutionalisation projects, it also queries how contemporary laws, practice and policies are complicit with these oppressive historiographies. Donald Trump and Brexit offer exemplary quotidian projections of these institutionalised racial, eugenic anti-immigration ideas and discourses. The language of free speech, populism and nationalism obscures the historical colonial racist discourses spoken through and for us for their political purpose.

---

[66] Ibid.
[67] Ibid.
[68] AL Stoler, 'Making Empire Respectable: The Politics of Race and Sexual Morality in 20th-Century Colonial Cultures' (1989) 4 *American Ethnologist* 16.

It should not surprise anyone that Trump openly insults people with disabilities, racialised groups and women and creates anti-LGBTQ policy. When Trump casually casts insults of inherent criminality, that Muslim people are dangerous, that immigrants carry disease, that Black women have low IQs, that black people are deserving of death, or that people from Mexico are bringing drugs crime and rape to the US, he participates in the continuance of a long historical colonial machinery, ideas embedded within the populace and much of policy and law in North America and in the UK. It is racist, eugenic and colonial in origin and design, wielding dehumanisation and authorising violence while re-making notions of white supremacy under threat.

Anti-immigrant, racist, nationalist, homophobic and misogynistic discourses are being and have always been met with resistance.[69] When people take to the streets to face those who continue to take black lives, when people stand idle no more, denounce and name the atrocities and violence within the projects of mass deportations, building giant walls and Muslim bans, we can learn to listen to the voices and perspectives of those affected – specifically because of how and what they contribute to analysis and for change. Resistance movements exemplify and operationalise experience in ways that expose these peculiar formations for their embodied affects. All too often, though, the voices of resistance and analysis of how ableism, sanism and racism, via colonial eugenics, are left unattended to historically. As we experience these complexities of race in the present, we also experience the inter-generational forms of violence and trauma that culminate in the now. We can and should heed the experiences and voices of resistance that have challenged racism throughout history. There are answers there. There are answers in the voices of experience. We often are handed the 'Other' to blame for the insecurities and exposure to violence that comes with colonial capitalism. Dehumanisation is needed for exploitation, conquest and appropriation to occur and to rationalise it in perpetuity. The uncivilised are said to require civilising, which is carried out via incivility and thereby we are the reification of colonial capitalism, the living embodiments of those made historically and presently worthy of violence, worthy of dominance and unworthy of basic safety, care and freedom. This is a lie that is bought and sold back to us, a lie we should denounce and boycott. An insidious and brazenly racist lie that should never be told nor heard again.

[69] S Roth (2018) 'Introduction: Contemporary Counter-Movements in the Age of Brexit and Trump' 23(2) *Sociological Research Online* 496–506.

8

Disability–Indigenous Gendered Relations in Settler–Colonial Australia
Continuities, Trajectories and Enmeshments

KAREN SOLDATIC

T HIS CHAPTER IS concerned with the ways in which the biopolitics of disability in settler–colonial Australia is harnessed to maintain racialised population management regimes that are both gendered and gendering. The racialisation of internal population mangement regimes across white settler–colonial societies is well-established. The work of postcolonial theorists such as Fanon,[1] Spivak[2] and Chibber,[3] alongside Indigenous scholars,[4] has revealed both the historicity of settler–colonial population management techniques of Indigenous populations and their enmeshment through bourgeoning settler–colonial regimes of population stratification across time. Povinelli remarks that even though white settler–colonial nation states and their more recent national narratives of inclusive nationalism appear to delink from their past trajectories, once examined in closer detail, the spectral presence of past regimes continue their haunting with their continual duplicity in biotechniques and practices of racialisation.[5] Nascent racialised discursive positions pivot around the historiography of settler–colonial eugenic imaginaries,

---

[1] F Fanon, *Black Skin, White Masks* (New York, Grove Press, 1967); F Fanon, *The Wretched of the Earth* (New York, Grove Weidenfeld, 1963).

[2] GC Spivak, 'Subaltern Studies: Deconstructing Historiography' in R Guha and GC Spivak (eds), *Selected Subaltern Studies* (Oxford, Oxford University Press, 1988).

[3] V Chibber, *Postcolonial Theory and the Specter of Capital* (New York, Verso, 2013).

[4] V Grieves, '"The Battlefields": Identity, Authenticity and Aboriginal Knowledges in Australia' in H Minde (ed), *Indigenous Peoples: Self-determination, Knowledge, Indigeneity* (Delft, Eburon Academic Publishers, 2008); V Hart, 'Teaching Black and Teaching Back' (2003) 22(3) *Social Alternatives* 5–22.

[5] EA Povinelli, *The Cunning of Recognition: Indigenous Alterities and the Making of Australian Multiculturalism* (Durham, Duke University Press, 2002).

albeit disguised under discourses of disparity, deprivation and dysfunction.[6] Indigenous scholar Maggie Walters argues that the continuity of settler–colonial rule is made invisible through the population foci of Indigenous inequality, disadvantage and deviance.[7] United States (US)-based disability scholars have argued, settler–colonial population management regimes in white settler societies are similarly grounded in white settler–colonial imaginaries of ablenationalism.[8] The spectrality of settler–colonial ablenationalism was also hinged against the biopolitical techniques of disability population management. Strategies of enclosure and containment for internal disability population management were developed in concert with the enclosure and containment of Indigenous populations within the settler–colonial state.[9] Moreover, eugenic genocidal practices of First Peoples and disabled peoples coincided with unique techniques of medicalisation, control and segregation.[10]

These dual, co-existing sites of population management came together around the gendering of internal population practices of settler–colonial biopolitics of reproductive control and were gendered and gendering through the pursuit of highly invasive medical regimes and practices of child removal. Reproductive controls, to forfeit disabled and Indigenous women's fecundity, proliferated across the Australian colony.[11] National strategies to promote the reproduction of the white settler–colonial polis through so-called positive eugenics strategies (pro-birthing strategies for white middle-class settler colonial women) through broad-scale maternal hygiene and social security regimes such as maternal payments and maternal health care, were coupled with strategies of 'negative' eugenics (sterilisation, withholding of maternal social security payments and health services and so forth). These eugenic practices were practices of white able-bodied settler colonial ontological securitisation, which not only aimed to erase the presence of Indigenous and disabled peoples but were premised upon making invisible the white settler–colonial anxieties of their own vulnerability and fragility. Negative reproductive controls on disabled women and Indigenous women's bodies thus pursued erasure, not only of highly racialised and disabled bodies, but also the haunting continuity of white settler–colonial vulnerability.

---

[6] A Haebich, 'Neoliberalism, Settler Colonialism and the History of Indigenous Child Removal in Australia' (2015) 19(1) *Australian Indigenous Law Review* 20–31.

[7] M Walters, 'Social Exclusion/Inclusion for Urban Aboriginal and Torres Strait Islander People' (2016) 4(1) *Social Inclusion*.

[8] SL Snyder and DT Mitchell (eds), *Cultural Locations of Disability* (Chicago, The University of Chicago Press, 2010).

[9] K Soldatic, '*Postcolonial Reproductions*: Disability, Indigeneity and the Formation of the White Masculine Settler State of Australia' (2015) 21(1) *Social Identities: Journal for the Study of Race, Nation and Culture*.

[10] Snyder and Mitchell *Cultural Locations of Disability*.

[11] H Meekosha and L Dowse, 'Distorting Images, Invisible Images: Gender, Disability and the Media' (1997) 57(1) *Feminist Review* 49–72.

While such gendered practices of reproductive controls have now been marked as discriminatory and illegal in most areas of Australia, as this chapter illustrates, with the onset of neoliberal biopolitics the settler–colonial state of Australia has developed a confluence of disability–Indigenous techniques and practices of governance via process of 'deep colonisation' where the 'colonising practices embedded … may conceal, naturalise, or marginalise, continuing colonising practices'.[12] These techniques occur via poverty management regimes, with tightened eligibility, prescriptive forms of payment conditionality and income sanctioning and penalisation. Through processes of making absent disability in the lifeworlds of Indigenous peoples, the white settler–colonial state is able to continue gendered disability–Indigenous biotechniques of population management. These neoliberal forms of poverty management techniques appear to not only naturalise Indigenous dispossessions of their lands, but their embodied subjectivities, because their experiences of living with disability are erased through white settler–colonial rule over their daily lives through neoliberal population management regimes. As Derrida asserts:

> A specter is both visible and invisible, both phenomenal and nonphenomenal: a trace that marks the present with its absence in advance. The spectral logic is de facto a deconstructive logic. It is in the element of haunting that deconstruction finds the place most hospitable to it, at the heart of the living present, in the quickest heartbeat of the philosophical. Like the work of mourning, in a sense, which produces spectrality and like all work produces spectrality.[13]

While Derrida unwittingly elucidates notions of spectrality through highly ableist discursive positionings of disability, as I suggest, his spectrality of invisible visibility as a witnessing device enables disability's (in)visibility. Disability's spectral presence, its polychronic biopolitical mobility, offers us an opportunity to see strategies of settler–colonial biopolitics of population management and the importance of understanding the gendered and gendering of settler–colonial population management strategies. Through engaging notions of spectrality via a critical disability lens, it becomes possible to reveal its pivotal function in maintaining settler–colonial structures of rule.

DISABILITY NEOLIBERAL POVERTY MANAGEMENT REGIMES: DISABILITY POVERTY MOBILITIES

The global intent of neoliberal welfare-to-work population management strategies to force bodies to move house and home to take up jobs in low-paid, precarious labour markets in urban centres, as Imrie illustrates, often keeps the

---

[12] DB Rose, 'Indigenous Ecologies and an Ethic of Connection' in N Low (ed), *Global Ethics and Environment* (London, Routledge, 1999) 176.

[13] J Derrida, 'Spectrographies' in J Derrida and B Stiegler (eds), *Echographies of Television: Filmed Interviews* (Cambridge, Polity Press, 2002), 121.

poor, the precariat and the disabled locked in place. A growing body of research suggests that this represents a form of 'stuckness'.[14] Those compelled into welfare-to-work programming with neoliberal reforms are 'stuck', with no real capacity for economic or social mobility. The continual churning through neoliberal poverty management programmes not only reinforces disabled people's position of economic marginality, but enmeshes them within deep structures of surplusisity that, despite their best efforts, scars them with the knowledge they are often surplus to neoliberal economic requirements.[15] Poverty mobilities of churning through welfare-to-work programming actually have disabled bodies and minds on the move, in a unique form of poverty mobility in which disabled people move and are moved through a range of time–space landscapes to manage their entrapment.[16] The logos of conditionality, a disciplinary regime, assumes that subordinating welfare recipients to this repetitive cycle will enforce positive behavioural development and assimilate them into the demands of the precarious labour market. Governed via the rationality of appointments, welfare-to-work participants are monitored with each temporal beat as they perform to the imposed rhythms of compliance.[17]

These temporal rhythms are not necessarily mapped from elite urban centres to regional landscapes in bureaucratic synchronicity. While it is technically no longer possible to compel Indigenous Australians to perform and behave for the benefit of the settler, Howitt and McLean argue that recent government policy suggests that there remains 'the persistent assimilationist assumptions that the only way "forward" for Indigenous Australians is to become indistinguishable ... from the total population'.[18] The neoliberalisation of Australian Indigenous policy exemplifies 'the spectacular failure of Australian politics to understand how geography matters in shaping Aboriginal experience'.[19] Technologies of compliance, conditionality and income management in regional landscapes have highly nuanced moral codings that contain Indigenous Australians under the panoptical gaze of white settler management in tightly bound places and spaces.[20] Controlling and containing Indigenous mobility is a highly racialised

---

[14] R Imrie, 'Space, Place and Policy Regimes: The Changing Contours of Disability and Citizenship' in K Soldatic, H Morgan and A Roulstone (eds), *Disability, Spaces and Places of Policy Exclusion* (Abingdon, Routledge, 2014).

[15] A Morris, S Wilson and K Soldatic, 'Hard Yakka: Disabled People's Experience of Living on Newstart' in C Grover and L Piggott (eds), *Work, Welfare and Disabled People: UK and International Perspectives* (Bristol, Policy Press, 2016).

[16] K Soldatic, 'Neoliberalising Disability Income Reform: What Does This Mean for Indigenous Australians Living in Regional Areas?' in D Howard-Wagner, M Bargh and I Altimarino-Jimenez (eds), *Indigenous Rights, Recognition and the State in the Neoliberal Age* (Canberra, ANU Press, 2018).

[17] K Soldatic, 'Appointment Time: Disability and Neoliberal Workfare Temporalities' (2013) 39(3) *Critical Sociology* 405–19.

[18] R Howitt and J McLean, 'Towards Closure? Coexistence, Remoteness and Righteousness in Indigenous Policy in Australia' (2015) 46(2) *Australian Geographer* 138.

[19] Ibid 140.

[20] S Bielefeld, 'Neoliberalism and the Return of the Guardian State: Micromanaging Indigenous Peoples in a New Chapter of Colonial Governance' in W Sanders (ed), *Engaging Indigenous Economy: Debating Diverse Approaches* (Canberra, ANU Press, 2016).

practice of colonial governance. The interstice of neoliberal Indigenous policy and disability income retraction results in a new form of Indigenous containment, fixing Aboriginal and Torres Strait Islander people with disabilities in a cyclical motion of poverty management.

MOBILITIES OF INDIGENOUS – DISABILITY POVERTY MANAGEMENT

For Aboriginal and Torres Strait Islander Australians living with disability who do not meet the threshold of Disability Support Pension (DSP) eligibility and are deemed, in socio-legal terms, to be partially disabled, their ongoing cyclical mobility through welfare-to-work spaces and places is a highly racialised process of stigmatisation. Often, this category of person has an illness or chronic condition that is coded with white settler narratives of suspect morality. Conditions such as kidney disease and diabetes are highly prevalent in Indigenous communities across Australia.[21] According to interviews conducted with a range of disability providers, these conditions were removed from the list of acceptable disabilities for pension eligibility in 2011. The removal of such conditions from the impairment scales may appear racially neutral, yet it is imbued with racialised moral signification, because these conditions are viewed as individual lifestyle choices, resulting from alcoholism, poor diet and poverty. With the neoliberalisation of disability income regimes, these measures are a form of penalisation for Aboriginal and Torres Strait Islander people living with such conditions.

The penalisation is twofold. First, the racialised individualisation of personal responsibility silences any recognition of the intergenerational effects of colonial management practices, the assertion of white settler power that moved Aboriginal Australians onto missions and outstations. Malnutrition was widespread in such settings.[22] Provisions were restricted to white settlers' rations of white flour and sugar and, at times, tobacco as a form of payment in lieu of wages.[23] Alcohol was also frequently used as a reward for Aboriginal workers on stations. Indigenous men were often under immense pressure to consume alcohol. Alcohol was not only an intoxicant, but was positioned by the coloniser as a highly valued symbol of status and esteem.[24] Second, penalisation denies the

[21] Department of Prime Minister and Cabinet, *Aboriginal and Torres Strait Islander Health Performance Framework 2014 Report: Employment* (Canberra, Australian Government, 2014). Available at: www.pmc.gov.au/sites/default/files/publications/indigenous/Health-Performance-Framework-2014/index.html.

[22] T Barta, 'Relations of Genocide: Land and Lives in the Colonization of Australia' in I Wallimann and MN Dobkowski (eds), *Genocide and the Modern Age: Etiology and Case Studies of Mass Death* (Westport, Greenwood Press, 1987).

[23] T Rowse, *White Flour, White Power: From Rations to Citizenship in Central Australia* (Cambridge, Cambridge University Press, 1998).

[24] E Hunter, *Aboriginal Health and History: Power and Prejudice in Remote Australia* (Cambridge, Cambridge University Press, 1993).

possibility that disability pension schemes work as a form of reparation for past colonial injustices marked upon Indigenous bodies and minds. It codifies in law long-held, stigmatising, white moral codes of so-called acceptable behaviour as well as punishing Indigenous Australians in their claims for redistributive justice to address the embodied outcomes of colonial rule. The removal of such chronic health conditions from DSP eligibility thus represents the material continuum of highly racialised colonial population management strategies.

Peter, an Aboriginal man from the north-west of Australia, best exemplifies this situation. Born before the 1967 referendum and now in his early 50s, Peter has worked for most of his life, beginning in his early teens, primarily as a stockman on a cattle station and later as a welder. Before the onset of his kidney condition, Peter also worked in a mosquito control programme in his local community. At the time of our discussion, Peter had been on dialysis for almost two years. He lives in an Aboriginal men's hostel within the town so that he can maintain access to his dialysis programme and attend the local men's homeless breakfast each Friday. Peter's medical report on file at the welfare-to-work agency clearly states he is on final-stage dialysis, requiring dialysis a minimum of three days per week for up to four hours at each session. Nonetheless, he is ineligible for a disability pension and has been assessed as having a work capacity of approximately 22 hours per week. Peter's employment officer, Janice, a local Aboriginal woman working as a disability employment case worker under welfare-to-work programming, outlined his situation:

> And I explained to [researcher] that you have dialysis three days a week and that [Peter], you know, because he's on Newstart, he has to look for work and do work. So um, you know, we're looking for some suitable work that on those days off, which is Monday and ah, Wednesday.[25]

Peter is also required to report to his employment office each fortnight as well as to the Australian Government welfare office, Centrelink, even with his ongoing dialysis treatment, to maintain his unemployment payment. Even though Centrelink has moved to online reporting with a purpose-built app, many of the Aboriginal participants in this age group (late 40s and older) have had little exposure to computers and, therefore, lack the information technology (IT) literacy required for them to feel safe and secure in reporting online. Peter undertook IT training at the local technical and further education (TAFE) institution to enable him to report online, lessening the frequency of forced travel between his welfare appointments. Yet he still travels to the Centrelink office, because he lives in a hostel and does not have ready access to a computer to go online to report as required.

> Yeah she [Janice] showed me how to move everything around. I got used to it. I didn't used to be used to it. So when I went over there to TAFE, I get used to it a little bit.

---

[25] Interview with Janice, July 2017.

But I'm slow on pressing A – B – whatever. Yeah …. When I go in there [Centrelink] to use the computer. I go up there and I ask them, do I have any appointments yet and yeah you've got an appointment yeah.[26]

For Newstart recipients, not adhering to stipulated reporting requirements will mean the loss or delay of their fortnightly welfare payment, as described earlier. New debilitating hardships, both financial and personal, are experienced by individuals who are not able to meet these forms of conditionality, either online or face to face. Jacob, who underwent forced medical retirement after a work-place accident yet was denied a DSP after extensive medical assessment, explains his recent purchase of a touchscreen mobile phone to enable him to report:

Jacob: Well it cost eighty-one dollars. And that wasn't buying it from […]. They reckon it's more dearer from […]. I bought it from [supermarket].

Karen: OK.

Jacob: Because I needed one of those ones where you … it's got no number on it, you just pressed something. [Centrelink are] going to show me tomorrow how to do it. They're going to put this app on there and show me how to do it. And I think it'll be no problem, but it's just if you ask me to do it on my own, I'll have no idea about it.[27]

To maintain access to Newstart, individuals are required to invest extensive personal energy and resources, purchasing mobile technologies and paying for private transport to/from the Centrelink office or the (often remote) employ-ment service to which they are required to report. Jacob, an Aboriginal man of 64 years, lives outside the main centre and cannot afford the petrol required to travel into the local Centrelink offices each fortnight. He resides in a caravan park which costs $275 per fortnight, leaving little left over for food and other expenses, such as petrol and vehicle maintenance. Jacob has been 'breached' in the past due to non-reporting and borrowed extensive funds from family and friends during these periods. He has drawn on his life savings, including from his accumulated aged pension fund, to cope with the ongoing financial stress.

Despite being hubs of economic activity to sustain rural and remote commu-nities, regional centres lack readily accessible public transport and it is also highly infrequent, particularly services to the fringes of town. Jerry, a young Aboriginal man with dyslexia residing in a small town on the southern seaboard of the state of New South Wales, explains:

I have been breached quite a lot. Because I have dyslexia I find the forms and letters really hard. I ask [his partner] to help me, but all it does is just increase her anxiety and depression. I just can't get to all of those appointments all the time. I don't have any money and I don't have a car.[28]

---

[26] Interview with Peter, July 2017.
[27] Interview with Jacob, July 2018.
[28] Interview with Jerry, March 2017.

The lack of transport is particularly debilitating for Indigenous Australians living on the fringes of regional communities, often in Indigenous social housing cooperatives, as Jerry does. The spatial dynamics of Indigenous struggles for land rights under native title claims frequently sees the state agree to the release of land in areas that have few public facilities, on the fringes of regional towns. Indigenous Newstart recipients with disability are required to plan their journeys to the welfare office with great precision. Welfare appointments are not coordinated with public transport options so that travel for reporting requirements can coincide with the transport available. For people with disabilities, this results in a debilitating process that can cause physical harm and injury, because they are left to navigate the streetscape, or find rest and shade waiting for the bus to return home, sometimes for hours due to the infrequency of its schedule. As Mary reveals, the real toll is on one's subjective wellbeing:

> It's frustrating and depressed, distressed, I cry sometimes at home. And I can't talk to anybody about it. It builds up.[29]

Mary's distress is generated through the nexus of neoliberal welfare conditionality and the dynamics of longstanding Indigenous dispossession and the deep processes of white stigmatisation of black Indigenous bodies and minds. Mary described herself as a proud Aboriginal woman, that she had done everything 'right', according to the coloniser's codes of moral behaviour. Throughout the interview, she was often extremely perplexed in thinking through her situation of being denied a DSP. Born in 1963, Mary was well trained in the settler's moralising codes of 'work' for Aboriginal Australia and, contradictorily, also understood that her employment in the open labour market could generate enough earnings to enable some freedom from the coloniser's control. She left home when she was 19 years old and worked consistently until the recent onset of her impairment. Mary had to return to her own country, top end Australia, to be close to family when she was forced into early medical retirement from the labour market. As she reveals, despite her 35 years of working as a cleaner, which took a debilitating toll on her body, reporting for Newstart costs those who live in regional Australia. The cost is not only in terms of increased financial insecurity with paying for travel to and from the welfare office, but the mental anguish of searching for ways to guarantee that they will make it to the appointment on time.

> Now how am I going to get there? I have to borrow some money from our next-door neighbour, you know? To get in here and do another report and then the next day I get paid, do I have to, when I'm home I have to borrow this money to go into town to make sure that money is in there, in the bank, you know?[30]

In Mary's narrative of the severe levels of deprivation and material insecurity she experienced so that she could meet the reporting requirements as 'the good

---

[29] Interview with Mary, July 2017.
[30] Ibid.

Aboriginal subject', the moral codings in neoliberal welfare to work reinforce coloniser narratives of the Indigenous 'humbugger'. The term, with its origins in eighteenthth-century England, was explicitly used by the coloniser to describe the everyday forms of Indigenous resistance to the structural violence of colonialism. In Australia it was and remains, a racialised pejorative term, used by the coloniser to articulate what they see as Indigenous resistance to take on the Protestant work ethic, as they refuse to be corralled into designated zones.

Australian Government narratives to justify racialised intervention into Indigenous Australia have relied on the racialised mythology of the Aboriginal humbugger. It was explicitly harnessed to describe Indigenous intra-relations among family, kin and community and to morally invalidate cultural collective modes of managing their economies under colonial invasion. Imbued with the religious rhetoric of the mission and coupled with the colonial imaginings of the slothful and lazy Aboriginal worker on the outstation, the term 'humbug' in Australia symbolises the continual historical meshing of the settler's racialised slurs to describe Indigenous Australia. As Billings illustrates, the trialling and testing of the harshest neoliberal welfare-to-work measures under the framework of the Northern Territory Intervention has been justified with explicit state rhetoric and imagery of the deceitful, lying, slothful Indigenous humbugger.[31] Often, the mythical character is gendered – the unruly Aboriginal man who is unemployed and living on welfare.[32] Jacob has worked since he was 13 years of age in a range of labouring jobs, from the mines as a young man through to his final job as a school yardhand. Jacob knows well the racism of Indigenous non-urban masculinities situated in neoliberal welfare to work. As he elucidates, the moral inscription of black Indigenous bodies is normalised under welfare-to-work population management strategies. The repetitive coloniser discourse of gendered Indigenous intra-relational mobility, ideologically positioned through narratives of male humbugging, saturates the process of reporting, inscribing Indigenous bodies -and minds with suspect value:

> It's like I'm another bludger that just walked in, sort of thing. And I said, I tell them, 'excuse me, I've been working since I was thirteen years old'. Foreman in mines, supervisors on railways and I've had my own business. I'm not a bludger. But that's … that's the impression you get that you know … Probably never worked in his life.[33]

The unruly Aboriginal man, the humbugger, was the primary bearer of responsibility for the government Intervention. In turn, the government was required to contain the wandering, black, dangerous, slothful Aboriginal man who moved from home to home across his familial and kinship networks. Core components

---

[31] P Billings, 'Social Welfare Experiments in Australia: More Trials for Aboriginal Families?' 2010 17(3) *Journal of Social Security Law* 164–97.
[32] A Moreton-Robinson, 'The White Man's Burden: Patriarchal White Epistemic Violence and Aboriginal Women, (2011) 26(70) *Australian Feminist Studies* 413–31.
[33] Interview with Jacob, July 2017.

of Aboriginal people's cultural expression, maintenance and connection were both gendered and gendering, particularly those patterns of mobility that did not conform to European patriarchal relations of power.[34] Colonial narratives of rescuing Indigenous women and children gave colonial authorities 'the validation they required to govern the most intimate spaces of Indigenous women and their families'.[35] Indeed, Indigenous women and children were in need of rescuing with the neoliberalisation of Indigenous welfare reform.[36] Accordingly, highly explicit political rhetoric sought to directly undermine longstanding practices of cultural mobility necessary to maintain Indigenous kinship relational networks and connections. The conceptual device of 'the Aboriginal humbugger' suggested that Indigenous masculine mobilities were motivated by the desire to extract money from vulnerable Indigenous women and mothers.[37] As Bielefield illustrates, the neoliberalisation of Indigenous social policy pivots on the white coloniser's need to reinstate their patriarchal authority as the protector of Indigenous women and children.[38]

Yet, as Mary reveals, neoliberal disability welfare to work creates its own contradictions through its repetitive grind of surveillance and conditionality, where its racialised presence becomes naturalised in ideological constructions of the Indigenous humbugger, particularly for Aboriginal people living with disability who have acquired adult-onset physical impairments through participating in the capitalist labour market. Mary, once a proud Aboriginal woman who was self-supporting, is left with few options but to reproduce the moral imaginary of the Aboriginal humbugger in fulfilling her welfare obligations. Her physical impairment of ongoing leg and back pain restricts her mobility and, with the lack of reliable, frequent and accessible public transport in her town, she is has to use privatised systems of transport. Rather than protecting Mary, the neoliberal retraction of disability income eligibility increases her vulnerability to forms of harm because she is often required to negotiate with strangers to get to and from the local Centrelink office. Given the level of economic insecurity of many of her family members and her desire to minimise financial requests to neighbours, she is often left to negotiate delayed payments with taxi drivers to ensure she gets to the welfare office on time:

> Or I try to look for some silvers, so I can pay something of the taxi and ask them if I can leave my key card [bank account card] with them until I get paid.[39]

---

[34] MD Jacob, *White Mother to a Dark Race: Settler Colonialism, Maternalism, and the Removal of Indigenous Children in the American West and Australia, 1880 –1940* (Lincoln, University of Nebraska Press, 2009).

[35] Ibid, xxxi.

[36] A Moreton-Robinson, 'Imagining the Good Indigenous Citizen: Race War and the Pathology of Patriarchal White Sovereignty' (2009) 15(2) *Cultural Studies Review* 61–79.

[37] Billings, 'Social Welfare Experiments in Australia' (2010).

[38] S Bielefeld, 'Income Management and Indigenous Women – A New Chapter of Patriarchal Colonial Governance?' (2016) 29(2) *University of New South Wales Law Journal* 843–78.

[39] Interview with Mary, July 2017.

Mary's sense of vulnerability and humiliation at having to rely on family members, friendship networks and neighbours alongside her negotiations with local taxi drivers to continually meet the demands of welfare-to-work reporting has come at a high cost to her own sense of dignity and self-respect. Further, Mary is acutely aware of the racialised aspect of welfare reform and has integrated the continuum of coloniser control over her embodied subjectivity as a recently disabled person – who acquired her impairment through years of low-waged, demanding physical labour – denied a disability pension:

> Yeah, I only have bread and tea. And that's the food we used to have when we were kids, when my parents were alive. Tea and bread for breakfast and our supper. Those days in the sixties and seventies, you know? And now I'm still having tea and bread, you know? But it fills me up.[40]

Mary's historical integration reaffirms Ann Laura Stoler's observations that 'colonising bodies and minds was a sustained, systemic, incomplete political project',[41] which continues with the new frontiers of neoliberal disability income management of Aboriginal Australia.[42]

GENDERING INDIGENOUS–DISABILITY NEOLIBERAL MOBILITIES

The governing of Indigenous Australia in the neoliberal age has seen a plethora of highly racialised policies. Howard-Wagner argues that it has been a distinctive political process to build a narrative of historical continuity, that is, intermeshing the paternalism and protectionism of twentieth-century Australia and its formation as a white settler–colonial consitutional state with the emergence, entrenchment and mobilisation of neoliberal welfare-to-work authoritarian governance.[43] As Irene Watson has illustrated, this historical enmeshment has been highly effective in extending white colonial management of Indigenous bodies and minds to explicitly contain Aboriginal and Torres Strait Islander movements across their lands, networks and communities.[44]

While paternalistic and protectionist white settler–colonial narratives have long constructed Aboriginal women as 'promiscuous' and 'nomads',[45] the repetitive reproduction of racialised discourses of Indigenous mobilities in

---

[40] Ibid.
[41] AL Stoler, *Carnal Knowledge and Imperial Power: Race and the Intimate in Colonial Rule* (Berkeley, University of California Press, 2010) 10.
[42] Soldatic, 'Neoliberalising Disability Income Reform' (2018).
[43] D Howard-Wagner, 'Governance of Indigenous Policy in the Neo-Liberal Age: Indigenous Disadvantage and the Intersecting of Paternalism and Neo-liberalism as a Racial Project' (2017) 41(7), *Ethnic and Racial Studies* 1132–51.
[44] I Watson, 'The Future is Our Past: We Once Were Sovereign and We Still Are' (2012) 8(3) *Indigenous Law Bulletin* 12–14.
[45] L Cutcher and T Milroy, 'Mispresenting Indigenous Mothers: Maternity Allowance and the Media' in S Goodwin and K Huppatz (eds), *The Good Mother: Contemporary Motherhoods in Australia* (Sydney, University of Sydney Press, 2010) 156.

neoliberal welfare to work is also explicitly gendered. Indigenous masculinities are particularly targeted, with the single aim to contain them in place. No longer contained within the mission or on the outstation, neoliberal policies cycle Indigenous bodies and minds through a range of welfare-to-work spaces and places, which all fix Indigenous people in mobilities of poverty management. The coloniser's self-referential techniques of gender performativities historically 'assumed that notions of family and motherhood were tenuous and shortlived for Aboriginal women'[46] because they were mobile. Yet nascent patternings of white colonial management under neoliberalism are gendered and gendering in the ways they juxtapose heteronormative positionalities of Indigenous masculine mobilities and, conversely, portray Indigenous mothers and children as the vulnerable victims of these masculine mobilities. Neoliberal narratives are thus both gendered and gendering. Gendered patterning to contain Indigenous mobilities, as Lake recognises, becomes heightened in public discussions surrounding Indigenous mothering and welfare entitlements.[47]

The neoliberalisation of disability income regimes for Indigenous Australians is a continuum of this political project. The inscription of Indigenous disabled bodies and minds as only partially disabled with the retraction of disability income regimes appears to be a structure of what Rose has articulated as a 'deep colonisation', where the 'colonising practices embedded … may conceal, naturalise, or marginalise, continuing colonising practices'.[48] While disability eligibility assessments present as racially neutral, the interstices, where Indigenous people living with a range of impairments, debilitating conditions and chronic diseases, are embedded and emplaced within disability technologies of inscription, revealing a highly racialised process. Indigenous people living with disability are forced into a highly gendered performance of contortment, to maneouvre their bodies and minds through tightly regulated and diminishing disability technologies of measurement. The neoliberalisation of disability income regimes thus offers the white settler–colonial state new disciplinary regimes of power to contain Indigenous people in place, fixing their bodies and minds in cyclical mobilities of disability poverty management.

ACKNOWLEDGEMENTS

This paper was funded by Karen Soldatic's DECRA project. I would also like to thank Niro Kandasamy for proofreading the paper. Parts of this chapter are reproduced by permission Routledge © from elements of Chapter 5 K Soldatic *Disability and Neoliberal State Formations: The Case of Australia* 2019.

[46] Ibid, 158.

[47] M Lake, 'The Politics of Respectability' in G Whitlock and D Carter (eds), *Images of Australia* (Brisbane: University of Queensland Press, 1992); Cutcher and Milroy 'Mispresenting Indigenous Mothers' (2018).

[48] Rose 'Indigenous Ecologies and an Ethic of Connection' (1999) 176.

9

Disability, Gender and Institutions
An Examination of Australian Cases
Involving Personality Disorders

ISABEL KARPIN AND KAREN O'CONNELL

T HE DEINSTITUTIONALISATION OF people with mental health issues from
psychiatric hospitals and mental health facilities in Australia from
the 1970s through to the 1990s[1] had the potential to be a liberalising
policy that ended harmful and dehumanising practices of isolation and abuse.
In fact, deinsitutionalisation as a process is ongoing and has had mixed success. Demands for compensation for those who suffered abuse in these 'total
institutions'[2] and punishment of the perpetrators continue.[3] By way of understanding the limited success of deinstitutionalisation, this chapter turns to what
initially might be considered an opposing desire: institutional inclusion. We
argue that the exclusionary practices of 'social institutions'[4] are a co-related

---

[1] A Rosen, 'The Australian Experience of Deinstitutionalization: Interaction of Australian Culture
with the Development and Reform of its Mental Health Services' (2006) 429 *Acta Psychiatrica
Scandinavica* 81, 83.

[2] 'Total institution' was coined by the American sociologist Erving Goffman and refers to a place
where a group of people is isolated from the community and under the control of others; E Goffman,
Asylums: Essays on the Social Situation of Mental Patients and Other Inmates (New York, Anchor
Books, 1961).

[3] See, eg, Senate Standing Committees on Community Affairs, *Violence, Abuse and Neglect
Against People with Disability in Institutional and Residential Settings Including Gender and Age
Related Dimensions and the Particular Situation of Aboriginal and Torres Strait Islander People with
Disability and Culturally and Linguistically Diverse People with Disability* (2015). Available at: www.
aph.gov.au/Parliamentary_Business/Committees/Senate/Community_Affairs/Violence_abuse_
neglect; Senate Standing Committees on Community Affairs, *Indefinite Detention of People
with Cognitive and Psychiatric Impairment in Australia* (2016). Available at: www.aph.gov.au/
Parliamentary_Business/Committees/Senate/Community_Affairs/Indefinite_Detention; Commonwealth of Australia, Royal Commission into Violence, Abuse, Neglect and Exploitation of People
with Disability. Available at: www.disability.royalcommission.gov.au/Pages/default.aspx.

[4] Jonathon Turner defines social institutions as 'a complex of positions, roles, norms and values
lodged in particular types of social structures and organising relatively stable patterns of human

problem. In order to make this argument, we consider the role for law in responding to situations where people with mental illness are denied access to, or rejected from, social institutions such as the workplace because they do not fit within the norms and values lodged in those institutions.[5] Douglas argues that '[t]he most profound decisions about justice are not made by individuals as such, but by individuals thinking within and on behalf of institutions'.[6] If social institutions structure our way of thinking and the abstract principles for regulating behaviour,[7] then it is easy to see how social institutions can, in practice, diminish the expected successes of the 'deinstitutionalisation' project by continuing to shut people with disabilities out of public life in ways that have largely escaped the degree of scrutiny imposed on total institutions. Law then, in its inadequate remedies, sometimes amplifies the exclusion of those whose behaviour sits outside social norms.[8]

Any discussion of deinstitutionalisation from 'total institutions' then, must occur in conjunction with consideration of exclusion from the 'social institutions' that play a crucial complementary role as gatekeepers to full public participation, offering community and access to social and financial resources. These benefits can be particularly elusive for people diagnosed with personality disorders whose behaviour (by definition) falls outside the norms and codes of conventional social institutional expectations. Under the definition in the *Diagnostic and Statistical Manual of Mental Disorders* (DSM-5) published by the American Psychiatric Association (APA),[9] a personality disorder is constituted by 'an enduring pattern of inner experience and behavior that deviates markedly from the expectations of the individual's culture'.[10] The current volume of the DSM also states that in relation to a personality disorder: 'Only when personality traits are inflexible and maladaptive and cause significant functional impairment or subjective distress do they constitute personality disorders.'[11]

People with personality disorders, then, are subject to a form of institutional exclusivism. This has limited the capacity of people who struggle to meet the

---

activity with respect to fundamental problems in producing life-sustaining resources, in reproducing individuals and in sustaining viable societal structures within a given environment'; J Turner, *The Institutional Order* (New York, Longman, 1997) 6.

[5] See also R Mykitiuk 'Accommodation in the Academy: Working with Episodic Disabilities and Living Inbetween', Chapter 5, this collection.

[6] M Douglas, *How Institutions Think* (Syracuse, Syracuse University Press, 1986) 124.

[7] Ibid, 120.

[8] See also R Mykitiuk 'Accommodation in the Academy'.

[9] American Psychiatric Association, *Diagnostic and Statistical Manual of Mental Disorders* (Arlington, APA, 2013). See also World Health Organization (WHO), *International Classification of Diseases and Related Health Problems 10th Revision* (ICD-10) (Geneva, WHO, 2016).

[10] Ibid.

[11] Ibid, 647; of the 455 cases that we identified over the three-year period from 2015 to 2017 which made some reference to personality disorders or personality traits, 52 referred to the DSM. When we narrowed the class down to those cases in which a diagnosis of a personality disorder was noted, the number of cases referring to the DSM was 36 (of 242).

stringent standards of 'normality' to gain access to social institutions. They do not fit easily within the institution's integral norms and values. Law is one of the primary mechanisms for ensuring access to institutional benefits and providing remedies where they are unfairly withheld. However, it, too, is a social institution and, as we will show in this chapter, a failure to acknowledge the socially constructed and contextual nature of behavioural disabilities such as personality disorders can feed into legal regulation and remedies that facilitate exclusion rather than inclusion. The law does this by defining the hurdle to full institutional access as disability in the individual (or accepting diagnoses to the same effect) rather than challenging the way that social institutions themselves are constructed.[12] This creates a seemingly beneficial regulatory system that nevertheless only measures harms against norms and values that do not include disability as intrinsic to the institution or, at most, include disability to the extent that accommodation requires only minor efforts. The economic profitability of the institution and its capacity to continue to function largely without disruption are paramount. In other words, while accommodation of disability is perceived as appropriate, it stops being appropriate when the institution is called upon to change fundamentally.

In this chapter we focus on how the law responds when women with personality disorders turn to the law to facilitate or remediate their interaction with the social institutions of work and family.[13] We examine, in the work context, the situation of women with personality disorders who, having been the subject of gendered violence such as sexual or physical abuse, have nevertheless managed to function as effective workers until they are subject to a work environment they experience as hostile, at which point their capacity to operate within the workplace is compromised. This is to highlight a central problem for law when

---

[12] K O'Connell, 'Should We Take the "Disability" Out of Discrimination Laws?: Students with Challenging Behaviour and the Definition of Disability' (2017) 35 *Law in Context* 108.

[13] The research for this chapter comes from a larger study of Australian civil law cases involving people whose behaviour has been described as abnormal and understood as stemming from a disability or disorder: Australian Research Council Discovery Project 'The Legal Regulation of Behaviour as a Disability' (DP150102935). In the larger study, we gathered and are analysing cases from 2015–17 that deal with autism spectrum disorder, attention deficit hyperactivity disorder, fetal alcohol spectrum disorder and personality disorders. Our sample of cases was obtained by searching and cross-checking three Australian case law databases: Austlii (austlii.com.au), LexisNexis Australia (lexisnexis.com.au) and WestLaw (www.westlaw.com.au) using relevant search terms. For the material discussed in this chapter, the sample included 455 cases with personality disorder relevant to one of the parties or to an individual affected by the legal dispute in some way. We analysed them to determine how the legal system constructs, understands and negotiates the role of personality disorders. Of the 149 cases involving borderline personality disorder, 100 (67%) involved women only, 39 (26%) involved men only, eight (0.05%) involved both men and women and one involved a person with non-binary gender (0.007%) We also conducted 29 interviews with advocates for people with challenging behaviour, psychiatrists and psychologists working with people with challenging behaviour and people or carers of people with disabilities involving challenging behaviour. Additionally, we surveyed people with disabilities or their carers or relatives about challenging behaviour; we received 122 responses. These results have not yet been published.

relying on psychiatric diagnoses that measure disorder against dominant cultural and institutional norms. The culture that forms a component of the diagnosis is itself laden with gender and other biases that are part of a long history of privileging and excluding certain groups within law and other social institutions. So, to be 'maladaptive', as in the diagnostic criteria of a personality disorder found in the DSM 5, one is not measured against some objective standard but a norm that is developed within a cultural and institutional context. This cultural environment includes, for example, some degree of acceptance of deep patterns of gendered violence and abuse. That acceptance then makes it possible to frame the maladaption as the woman's failure to adapt to an environment that others without a disability may dislike but may deal with more 'robustly'.

Andrea Nicki writes, for example, that where a woman has escaped a traumatic home environment, or – we would add – a 'total' institution:

> She is still living in a society riddled with sexism and inequality. If, for example, a woman has been verbally, physically, or sexually traumatized by her father and feels extremely anxious with sexist male work supervisors, on a psychiatric view, her strong response can be attributed to the original trauma and she may have trouble retaining employment because of it.[14]

An alternative view would see the response to sexist supervisors as rational and adaptive – a reaction to a genuine harm, given the actual cumulative impact of such behaviours, layered over time – rather than maladaptive and institutionally unacceptable.

As we shall see below, in some cases, when law takes up the language of personality disorders, a background of (gendered) abuse may be acknowledged but is typically framed as an individual harm that is disconnected from broader, systemic problems. Yet the ubiquity of gendered violence across societies and institutions in Australia and other Western democracies such as the United States and the United Kingdom means that abuse is inevitably and deeply embedded in culture. At the point where law most needs to be addressing the harms of gendered violence systemically, it provides only individual redress. Further, it accepts and is itself part of the culture that forms the measure of whether women who have experienced abuse are 'maladaptive'. Given this, it is significant that there is an accepted correlation between abuse and personality disorders, particularly in the case of borderline personality disorder (BPD), which has a much higher prevalence in women than men.[15] There is also a broad critique of

---

[14] A Nicki, 'Borderline Personality Disorder, Discrimination and Survivors of Chronic Childhood Trauma' (2016) 9 *International Journal of Feminist Approaches to Bioethics* 218, 236.
[15] APA, *Diagnostic and Statistical Manual of Mental Disorders* (2013); DM Johnson et al, 'Gender Differences in Borderline Personality Disorder: Findings from the Collaborative Longitudinal Personality Disorders Study' (2003) 44 *Comprehensive Psychiatry* 284; A Silberschmidt et al, 'Gender Differences in Borderline Personality Disorder: Results From a Multinational, Clinical Trial Sample' (2015) 29 *Journal Of Personality Disorders* 828.

the DSM for its failure to 'give us information about how gender, interacting with such phenomena as race, class or experience, can account for large percentages of what is observed and defined as "pathology"'.[16] Despite this, as we will show, in the case law we examined, responsibility for these types of harm is still attributed to the individual and the ongoing condition and vulnerability is seen as a problem internal to the 'disordered' person.

This attribution of responsibility is important because personality disorders are distinguished from trauma and stress exposure disorders such as post-traumatic stress disorder (PTSD) and so are understood as conditions of the inner self, rather than produced by external forces.[17] The distinction, however, is unsustainable even within the DSM itself, where it is noted that the trauma and the stress of abuse are indicators for a personality disorder.[18] Furthermore, PTSD sometimes co-occurs with personality disorders, so the distinctions between the two are blurred even further.[19] In our case law study, for example, 60 of the 455 personality disorder cases also involved PTSD. From a feminist and disability informed point of view, a 'disordered' response to institutional threats may therefore be a rational 'attunement to genuine danger'.[20] Yet, in some of the cases that we have examined dealing with women with personality disorders, it is clear that the law struggles to understand the perception of gendered danger by those who are the victims of gendered harm. Instead, it retreats to a psychiatric explanation of consequential behaviours that treats the underpinning trauma as a personal scar precipitating a maladaptive but internal (personality) response.

---

[16] LS Brown, 'A Feminist Critique of the Personality Disorders' in LS Brown and M Ballou (eds), *Personality and Psychopathology: Feminist Reappraisals* (New York, The Guildford Press, 1992), 115. See also LS Brown, *Feminist Therapy* (Washington DC, APA, 2018).

[17] D Becker and S Lamb, 'Sex Bias in the Diagnosis of Borderline Personality Disorder and Post-traumatic Stress Disorder' (1994) 25 *Professional Psychology: Research and Practice* 55; TE Galovski et al, 'Gender Differences in the Clinical Presentation of PTSD and Its Concomitants in Survivors of Interpersonal Assault' (2011) 26 *Journal of Interpersonal Violence* 789; EM Scheiderer, PK Wood and TJ Trull, 'The Comorbidity of Borderline Personality Disorder and Posttraumatic Stress Disorder: Revisiting the Prevalence and Associations in a General Population Sample' (2015) 2 *Borderline Personality Disorder and Emotion Dysregulation*; APA, *Diagnostic and Statistical Manual of Mental Disorders* (2013) 647.

[18] APA, *Diagnostic and Statistical Manual of Mental Disorders* (2013).

[19] A Ferguson, 'Borderline Personality Disorder and Access to Services: A Crucial Social Justice Issue' (2016) 69 *Australian Social Work* 206; Nicki, 'Borderline Personality Disorder' (2016) 218; J Briere, *Psychological Assessment of Adult Posttraumatic States: Phenomenology, Diagnosis and Measurement* (Arlington, APA, 2004); C Ross, *The Trauma Model: A Solution to the Problem of Comorbidity in Psychiatry* (Richardson, Manitou Communications, 2007); L Wall and A Quadara, 'Acknowledging Complexity in the Impacts of Sexual Victimization Trauma' (2014) *Australian Centre for the Study of Sexual Assault Issues* 16; JA Chu 'The Revictimisation of Adult Women with Histories of Childhood Abuse' (1992) 1(3) *Journal of Psychotherapy Practice and Research* 259; K Lewis and B Grenyer, 'Borderline Personality or Complex Posttraumatic Stress Disorder? An Update on the Controversy' (2009) 17(5) *Harvard Review of Psychiatry* 322.

[20] Nicki, 'Borderline Personality Disorder' (2016) 218, 236 quoting B Burstow, 'A Critique of Post-traumatic Stress Disorder and the DSM' (2005) 45(4) *Journal of Humanistic Psychology* 429, 436.

PERSONALITY DISORDERS IN AUSTRALIAN CASE LAW

Two workers compensation cases involving people with personality disorders, from our review of Australian civil law cases from 2015 to 2017,[21] illustrate this point. In both of these cases, compensation payments to claimants working at the Australian Taxation Office (ATO) ceased when Comcare (the federal body charged with administering the Commonwealth workers compensation scheme) determined that the psychological condition of the women who had been compensated previously was no longer caused by the workplace bullying that had precipitated their original complaints. In both cases, *de Leon*[22] and *LYHH*,[23] a crucial factor is that when the compensation was initially awarded, the individual was not compensated on the basis that she was a competent worker who was harmed by workplace bullying or harassment but rather that she was an 'already disordered individual' whose internal instability was aggravated by workplace bullying and or sexual harassment.[24] In the relevant section, an injury is defined to include:

> an aggravation of a physical or mental injury (other than a disease) suffered by an employee (whether or not that injury arose out of, or in the course of, the employee's employment) that is an aggravation of that injury that arose out of or in the course of that employment.[25]

In both cases, Comcare initially agreed to compensate the applicants for a workplace-induced aggravation of a pre-existing condition that, again in both cases, was variously diagnosed as a major depressive disorder or a personality disorder. While acknowledging prior trauma might seem important in understanding the nature of a claimant's vulnerability, as we show, this can later be applied in ways that reduce responsibility for the institutional harm.

These cases illustrate, not simply – or not only – a legal determination about when institutional responsibility ends for the further-harmed individual, but a set of institutional norms and values that function to render participants in the workplace primarily responsible for their own harm. Further, we argue that, in these cases, the workplace, the medical diagnosis and the law all interact in ways that do not recognise the uniquely gendered aspects of the series of harms that these women have suffered, because they are dispersed amongst and outside multiple social institutions and have no recognisable connection other than through the disordered personality of the person harmed. These cases illustrate a form of institutional engagement with disability where harm is pre-defined as individual and each institutional assault is temporary so that institutional responsibility is contained. All the damage accrues in the body of

---

[21] Nicki, 'Borderline Personality Disorder' (2016) 218, 236.
[22] *de Leon and Comcare (Compensation)* [2017] AATA 563.
[23] *LYHH and Comcare (Compensation)* [2017] AATA 1586.
[24] See also R Mykitiuk 'Accommodation in the Academy'.
[25] Section 14((1)(c) of the Safety Rehabilitation and Compensation Act 1988 (Cth) (Aus).

the purportedly disordered individual. However many incidents might occur at the site of the institution, the institution is not rendered 'disordered', only the woman. The individual is seen as permanently and irredeemably sensitive in a disordered way, while the institution, whatever it does, recovers and is redeemed.

That other responses, such as institutional acceptance of the ubiquity of gendered harm and ongoing responsibility for the many ways it might be amplified, seems unimaginable illustrates Douglas' point that 'all the classifications that we have for thinking with are provided ready-made along with our social life.'[26]

Comcare argued, successfully in both cases, that the pre-existing condition which had been latent but was triggered by the workplace bullying/harassment at the ATO was, at the time of these later claims, no longer caused by the incidents that occurred at the ATO but had now been triggered by subsequent events. The effect was to relieve Comcare of their continued responsibility to compensate the women despite the fact that neither was able to return to meaningful work. These cases sit inside a larger framework of compensation laws and the jurisprudence of causation for tortious injury that we cannot address here in their full complexity. Our interest is not in whether, according to the law, the decision was correct, but rather with the way in which the behavioural disabilities (the personality disorders) that may be attributable to gendered harms[27] are constructed as conditions located within the woman as personal damage that reverts back to her, intact.

In *De Leon*, one of the psychiatrists on whom the tribunal relied, Dr Synott, described De Leon as having a 'whole person impairment' and stated that given that nine years had passed since she worked at the ATO that there was 'no significant connection between her current psychological difficulties and the previous employment with the ATO'.[28] While the original harm is perceived as having no end date and is carried by the women in perpetuity, the intervening aggravating harm ends and any responsibility for care and compensation ends with it.

Dr Hong, one of the other experts the Administrative Appeals Tribunal found persuasive, diagnosed De Leon with BPD, which he stated was a disorder 'that often resulted from childhood abuse and manifested itself with periods of paranoia and psychosis-like symptoms'.[29] The Tribunal described De Leon as having 'an unfortunate, unhappy life' and listed a series of life events that had affected her, including:

> the separation of her parents, the fact that she was to be put up for adoption but then sent to live with relatives, that she suffered sexual abuse when she was nine and that she was, on occasions, beaten (although not apparently severely) by family members including her mother.[30]

---

[26] Douglas, *How Institutions Think* (1986) 99.
[27] Above n 11.
[28] *de Leon and Comcare (Compensation)* [2017] AATA 563 208.
[29] Ibid, 243.
[30] Ibid, 306.

Despite finding that De Leon had been subjected to ongoing and multiple life stressors, including bullying and mistreatment at the ATO and despite accepting that 'each traumatic event in her life, including the ATO incident, remains part of her psyche'[31] the Tribunal also found that the aggravation of her disorder by the ATO had 'for all intents and purposes ... ceased to be an issue'[32] in 2010–13 and that the other traumatic events took over as major current stressors after that time. Notably, Dr Teoh, another expert whose opinion was not as well received, said that 'because of the applicant's personality disorder, it was hard for her to deal with traumatic events and ... though the more recent episode was significant it really is cumulative.'[33]

Treating the incidents as disconnected from each other, even if permissible at law and as a finding of fact, means that the social institution of the workplace can extricate itself from a causal chain and therefore from responsibility. The workplace becomes a social institution that Ms De Leon will be permanently excluded from and there is a complete severing of any responsibility to make the institution accessible to her:

> Dr Synott felt that the applicant was not fit to work and nothing will change his view on this. He said 'she will never work again, she is a most unfortunate woman – she had a passive demeanour and a sense of helplessness. A most unfortunate life'.[34]

It is indeed 'unfortunate' that De Leon will be permanently excluded from work, from any compensation for that exclusion and that the legal system can offer her no remedy for the harm that she has been subjected to at so many stages of her life.

In *LYHH*, some of the intervening harms that were said to break the chain of causation in relation to her claim against the ATO, triggering her latent condition after 2004, were stresses that could be directly linked to the ongoing legal battle with Comcare and the financial instability that followed the cessation in compensation payments. Despite this, the Tribunal found 'LYHH's employment with the ATO as having ceased to be a material contributor to LYHH's current psychological symptoms/condition by 5 January 2015'.[35]

The two cases are illustrations of the way that law, in acknowledging prior trauma, treats it as abiding and part of the woman herself, while institutional stress and trauma can be severed. There are no acknowledged and continuing 'connectors' between incidents in the past, present and future, such as gendered harms, that might require responsibility and redress. And finally, by institutional harms being disconnected from other harms and ending, the institution has no ongoing responsibility, so that De Leon and LYHH are left as 'most unfortunate' – subjected

---

[31] Ibid, 322.
[32] Ibid.
[33] Ibid, 181.
[34] Ibid, 223.
[35] Ibid.

to institutional exclusivism and left to fend for themselves despite being harmed in a multitude of ways.

We now turn to four family law cases concerning people with personality disorders who were seeking parenting orders in the family court and who are identified as having a pre-existing history of abuse or assault. In these cases, a diagnosis of BPD in the mother of the child was contingent on finding that her allegations of physical or sexual abuse by the father were not true.[36] In *Viney v Riley*,[37] for example, the mother was assessed as having BPD during a psychiatric assessment, which presented a real 'reason to be concerned that the mother would lack the ability to protect the child from her feelings in relation to the father'.[38] However, it was then noted that the mother's allegations of the father's sexual violence were significant, particularly because they had:

> the capacity to amend the diagnosis made of the mother by Dr. F. In the event that these allegations are true, he says there is an impact upon his diagnosis of a Borderline Personality Disorder and the potential need to introduce a diagnosis of post-traumatic stress disorder.[39]

One diagnosis is framed as an internally driven maladaption that is highly stigmatised, the other – PTSD – is understood as a reaction to an external traumatic event. The decision to diagnose as one disorder or the other will likely have significant impact on the legal and other institutional responses that the woman receives from that point.

In *Shireman v Katsaros*,[40] the mother alleged a long history of violence from her former partner. In relation to alleged sexual violence, she claimed that she was forced to have sex throughout their relationship and that the sexual assaults were rough and caused her to bleed. The Court found that this violence could neither be proven nor disproven. At the same time, the Court saw the woman's close, extended family as 'enmeshed' and that the interdependent relationship put her child at risk of psychological harm. Whether there are any cultural differences in the way that particular families relate and what degree of closeness or distance is 'normal' was not at issue. In speculating as to whether the mother had borderline or histrionic personality 'disturbance', an expert report noted:

> If the mother's account of intimate partner violence can be relied upon then the major issue effecting (sic) her mental health is likely to be post traumatic; if that history cannot be relied upon then it is more likely that personality disturbance is the major issue.[41]

---

[36] *Viney v Riley* [2016] FamCA 742; *Shireman v Katsaros* [2015] FamCA 896; *Masri & Masri (No 2)* [2017] FamCA 898; *Heston & Norton & Ors* [2017] FamCA 154.
[37] *Viney v Riley* [2016] FamCA 742.
[38] Ibid at [94].
[39] Ibid at [17].
[40] *Shireman v Katsaros* [2015] FamCA 896.
[41] Ibid at [408].

While there was no determination on the allegations of sexual violence, the Court seemed to attach less weight to the risk of the father's violence than to the risk of the mother polarising or 'enmeshing' the child in her overly close relationships and custody of the child was transferred from the mother to father.

In *Masri v Masri* there was a similar contention about whether the mother's 'personality vulnerabilities' including 'eating behaviour and self-concept and … recurrent deliberate self-harm' arose from external abuse or her own personality.[42] Not all of the health professionals treating the mother agreed that she had a disorder 'and those who did not make the diagnosis of personality disorder had raised the possibility that her vulnerabilities may be a response to domestic violence'.[43]

The construction of a personality disorder as an internal (and individualised) problem separable from a context of abuse means that there is no appropriate legal accounting for the possible relationship between trauma and disability. In these four cases, the court speculates about whether the person has a personality disorder or whether their behaviour is a response to abuse or the threat of abuse as if the two cannot be connected.

First, this overlooks the fact that domestic violence is intertwined with trauma. Professor Kelsey Hegarty, in a witness statement to the Victorian Royal Commission into Family Violence, made the point that the trauma of domestic violence can be mistaken by courts for disability, since it manifests similarly:

> A woman who has experienced trauma might present poorly, particularly in stressful situations such as court or court-ordered assessments. She may present as 'difficult', be highly stressed and agitated and will find it difficult to present her evidence in a calm and coherent way. Her fear of what her ex-partner may be saying about her, of having to stand up and give evidence against her ex-partner and of the threat of losing her children cannot be divorced from the trauma of her past experience of his belittling, controlling or violent behaviour.[44]

This puts a different light on some of the certainty with which judges might accept evidence of personality disorder in the context of trauma and the stress of court. For example, in *Dylan v Bilson*, the judge seems to find the mother's lack of emotional regularity persuasive of a personality disorder, despite the highly stressful context:

> From what I saw of the mother in the witness box during the trial, I have no doubt that Dr R was correct in that assessment of the mother. She did not regulate her emotional state very well at all in the witness box and presented in an unregulated, relatively histrionic state for much of the time that she was giving evidence. She demonstrated, in my view, a distinct lack of judgment as to what was appropriate

[42] *Masri & Masri (No 2)* [2017] FamCA 898 at [49].
[43] Ibid.
[44] Victorian Royal Commission into Family Violence, *Witness Statement of Kelsey Lee Hegarty* (WIT.0098.003.0001, 5 August 2015) para 14.

behaviour and language to use in the Court setting. As an example of this, I note her repeated use of the expression 'my brain is fried' when attempting to explain her difficulty in answering questions.[45]

Second, if the Court accepts that the mother has a personality disorder, that is somehow treated as if it is not also gendered harm, despite the fact that personality disorder is itself highly correlated with abuse. In these cases, the 'truth' of the situation is presented as if it must be one or the other – domestic violence or a personality disorder – when it is also highly possible that it is both. A kind of severing of gendered harm from disability is taking place in these cases, instead of acknowledging that one may well underpin the other.

The discussion of personality disorder alongside traumatic violence is not only disturbing because the two are erroneously severed, it stigmatises the person who may already have been subject to trauma. The stigma of being diagnosed with BPD, for example, has significant material consequences. Sheehan et al argue that BPD is 'among the most stigmatized of all personality disorders, possibly because they are perceived to be purposeful rather than involuntary'.[46] They note that people with BPD 'are often seen as annoying and undeserving'.[47] Nicki cites Moore's finding that clinicians themselves have a bias against people with BPD and are reluctant to accept them as clients;[48] Lester also makes this claim, stating: 'Clinicians generally detest working with borderline patients.'[49] Our interviews[50] with psychiatrists and advocates reinforced this, with one interviewee stating that '… we know from health professionals but also from people with mental illness, that as soon as you've got a label of BPD it's very difficult to get any sort of service'.[51] Moreover, the label seems not only to restrict access to mental health services, but all health services. One interviewee in our study recounted the case of a young woman with a long history of an eating disorder and BPD who went to an emergency department with medical issues. The hospital wanted to discharge the woman. 'When her advocate came to find out what was going on, the response they got was: 'it's because of her condition'. Her advocate asked, 'What the eating disorder?' 'No, no, the borderline'.[52]

A diagnosis of any disability can carry unwelcome social stigma, but may be necessary to access appropriate medical services. With BPD, the medical diagnosis triggers stigma from health providers themselves – the very group

---

[45] *Dylan v Bilson* [2015] FamCA 573 at [207].

[46] L Sheehan, K Nieweglowski and P Corrigan, 'The Stigma of Personality Disorders' (2016) 18 *Current Psychiatry Reports* 11.

[47] Ibid.

[48] Nicki, 'Borderline Personality Disorder, Discrimination and Survivors of Chronic Childhood Trauma' (2016) 219.

[49] RJ Lester, 'Lessons from the Borderline: Anthropology, Psychiatry and the Risks of Being Human' (2013) 23 *Feminism & Psychology* 70.

[50] See n 11.

[51] I Karpin, interview with Michelle Blanchard, Deputy CEO SANE Australia (21 March 2018).

[52] Ibid.

responsible for allocating and responding to the diagnosis – potentially meaning reduced access to services as well as greater stigma. One of the psychologists we interviewed in our study put it like this:

> There's a huge stigma around borderline personality disorder … they're always diffi-cult to treat; they don't respect boundaries … But the reason for the stigma is really typically around recurrence of harm, recurrence of substance abuse. Recurrent over-doses … [and] the problems in maintaining and containing therapeutic alliance.[53]

This contrasts with people suffering from PTSD, who are viewed more sympa-thetically as victims of an external source of stress, particularly as the disorder is most keenly associated with soldiers returning from war. There is far less stigma attached to a diagnosis of PTSD than a diagnosis of BPD,[54] yet there is also significant overlap with many shared symptoms. Of 149 cases dealing with BPD in our study, 29 also mention PTSD as a potential diagnosis. BPD also has significant overlaps with what is termed 'complex PTSD', a form of the illness that has additional symptoms of difficulty with emotional regula-tion, self-regard and relationships.[55] In the early 1990s, Brown,[56] drawing on the work of Walker (who developed the concept of battered women's syndrome)[57] suggested an alternative diagnostic category of 'abuse and oppression artefact disorders', which – unlike PTSD – would take into account the repetitive nature of exposure to trauma that occurs in experiences of interpersonal violence and the adaption that results from exposure to its presence in everyday life. These have not been taken up in the DSM.[58]

When it comes to decision making, this shift to treating personality disor-ders as a response to exposure to trauma, but also to interpersonal, everyday traumas that are built into the fabric of oppressive institutional norms, is not a small matter. It fundamentally adjusts our conceptualisation of these kinds of personality disorders as 'enduring patterns of inner experience' to disorders resulting from exposure to external threats or traumas that may be systemic and

---

[53] I Karpin, interview with Psychologist A, (11 November 2018).

[54] Karpin, interview with Michelle Blanchard, Deputy CEO SANE Australia (21 March 2018); N Nehls, 'Borderline Personality Disorder: Gender Stereotypes, Stigma and Limited System of Care' (1998) 19 *Issues in Mental Health Nursing* 97.

[55] M Cloitre et al, 'Distinguishing PTSD, Complex PTSD and Borderline Personality Disorder: A Latent Class Analysis' (2014) 5 *European Journal of Psychotraumatology* doi: 10.3402/ejpt. v5.25097; R Frost, P Hyland, M Shevlin and J Murphy, 'Distinguishing Complex PTSD from Border-line Personality Disorder Among Individuals with a History of Sexual Trauma: A Latent Class Analysis' (2018) *European Journal of Trauma & Dissociation* doi: 10.1016/j.ejtd.2018.08.004.

[56] LS Brown, 'Toward a Feminist Perspective on Severe Psychopathology' in LS Brown and M Ballou (eds), *Personality and Psychopathology: Feminist Reappraisals* (New York, Guildford Press, 1992).

[57] LA Walker, 'Battered Women, Psychology and Public Policy' (1984) 39(10) *American Psycholo-gist* 1178.

[58] A very short section in the DSM-5 relating to personality disorder and PTSD states that when a person has experienced extreme stress, PTSD should be considered: APA, *Diagnostic and Statistical Manual of Mental Disorders* (2013) 649. Other references to trauma are littered throughout.

ubiquitous forms of gendered violence deeply embedded in our culture. It shifts our response from one of individualising responsibility to choosing to address the underlying inequality.

CONCLUSION

The definition of personality disorder presumes a potentially hostile culture for the individual being diagnosed when it uses, as a measure of disorder, deviation from the 'expectations of the individual's culture'. This includes the expectations of workplace cultures in which they participate. The presumption in the DSM definition is that cultural expectations are somehow benign and that the person who is unable to effectively adapt to them is disordered. However, this fails to take account of the reality and impact of hostile or oppressive cultures on individuals responding rationally – if sensitively – to the threat of harm, particularly if they have histories of gendered abuse.

The Australian workplace, though required under the federal Disability Discrimination Act 1992 (Aus) and equivalent state legislation to provide reasonable accommodations for people with disabilities, such as wheelchair ramps and hearing loops, has core values that work to exclude or stigmatise individuals whose interpersonal functioning is non-normative. Equality laws that have required people with disability to fight, mostly on an individual basis and often unsuccessfully, for access to the benefits of these institutions are piecemeal and inadequate. Douglas states:

> When individuals disagree on elementary justice, their most insoluble conflict is between institutions based on incompatible principles. The more severe the conflict, the more useful to understand the institutions that are doing most of the thinking. Exhortations will not help. Passing laws against discrimination will not help ... Only changing institutions can help. We should address them, not individuals and address them continuously, not only in crises.[59]

The exclusionary practices of the past and the correlated segregation and 'total' institutionalisation of people with mental illness has meant that people with disability have been historically separated from the social institutions that have shaped the modern workplace. Without their direct influence and participation, social institutions have developed cultures which are too narrow to properly include different kinds of social functioning. Law, which has a key role in defining when harms will be recognised and redressed, has a particular role to play in determining the extent to which the institutions of work and family include people with disability, a role that is underpinned by gendered harms. In the cases we examined in this chapter, law sees the relationship of personality disorders

---

[59] Douglas, *How Institutions Think* (1986) 125–6.

to trauma or abuse in problematic ways that have material consequences for institutional responsibility. The workers compensation cases, for example, show that treating personality disorders as contained within the individual can overlook systemic causes of harm, making it easier for social institutions to be absolved of any responsibility for a more radical inclusiveness. The family law cases we examined similarly show that individualising personality disorder and severing it from domestic violence and gendered abuse overlooks their systemic entanglement.

A legal and cultural transformation is needed to sufficiently broaden the current narrowly circumscribed idea of 'normal' behaviours within social institutions of work and family. For this to happen, law also needs to change. Rather than determining the rights and duties of institutions based on what constitutes an appropriate range of accommodations of non-normative individuals, the law needs to reimagine the non-normative individual as a fully rights-bearing citizen with presumptive access to all social institutions. For this to happen, alongside an acknowledgement of the harms of total institutions, we need to critique how law functions to perpetuate institutional harms through gendered and ableist definitions of disorders within work and family structures. When the law treats personality disorder as an inherently mitigating, neutralising or de-legitimating characteristic, it inflicts a secondary wrong.

ACKNOWLEDGEMENTS

We would like to thank Lamya Rahman, Ruby Lew and Ruby Wawn for their invaluable research assistance and the editors of this volume for their helpful and insightful comments on a draft of this chapter. This work was supported by Australian Research Council grant [DP150102935] Regulating Behaviour as a Disability.

10

Reconciling Cognitive Disability and Corrosive Social Disadvantage
Identity, Transgression and Debility

LEANNE DOWSE

T HIS CHAPTER FOCUSES on people with cognitive disability who are in contact with the criminal justice system. Many such people cluster around the edges of mutable and inconsistent categories of impairment and disability in the context of significant social disadvantage. For this group, individualised impairment may manifest in behaviour that challenges and in difficulties with communication, understanding, memory, attention, thinking or judgment. These difficulties are very often overshadowed or obscured by the social and material relations of disadvantage. Importantly, these disabling experiences do not simply co-occur with poverty and social exclusion, but rather exist in a corrosive interaction in which 'several dimensions of risk and disadvantage cluster together and compound one other'.[1] In recent years, scholars have turned to intersectional frameworks as a way to explain and make sense of the interdependence of major social divisions such as race, class, gender, sexuality and increasingly disability[2] and the ways these interact in different ways to oppress or construct identities.[3] While intersectional frameworks may have *prima facie* usefulness in explaining how the organisation of power affects disability as an identity category, one criticism of the approach concerns the overuse of personal identity as a category of analysis and the consequent

[1] J Wolff and A de-Shalit, *Disadvantage* (Oxford, Oxford University Press, 2007) 9.
[2] See, eg, L Dowse, C Frohmader and H Meekosha, 'Intersectionality: Disabled Women' in P Easteal (ed), *Women and the Law in Australia* (Chatswood, LexisNexis Butterworths, 2010); N Erevelles and A Minear, 'Unspeakable Offenses: Untangling Race and Disability in Discourses of Intersectionality' (2010) 4 *Journal of Literary and Cultural Disability Studies* 127–46; R Garland-Thomson, 'Feminist Disability Studies' (2005) 30 *Signs* 1557–87; M Pisani and S Grech, 'Disability and Forced Migration: Critical Intersectionalities' (2012) 2 *Disability and the Global South* 421–41.
[3] L McCall, 'The Complexity of Intersectionality' (2005) 30 *Signs* 1771–800.

under-emphasis on structural and particularly material conditions.[4] Erevelles, for example, argues for a focus on 'the actual social and economic conditions that impact disabled people's lives, and that are concurrently mediated by the politics of race, ethnicity, gender, sexuality and nation'.[5] That there is a need for terms of abstraction such as gender, class, race, age, sexuality for scholars, policymakers and practitioners to draw on in their attempts to conceptualise, analyse and describe multiple interconnected registers of inequity is unquestionable, but little scrutiny has been applied to the specific ways that 'disability' works as a key signifier in the complex intersectional domain of disability in/justice. In relation to the overarching theme of this volume, this chapter draws explicit attention to the ways that 'disability', in the context of these various registers, is drawn into and draws on legacies of institutionalisation in ways which ambivalently and simultaneously foreground and obscure its presence in the lived experience of those who may be considered behaviourally or socially non-normative, and whose impairments fall outside the bounds of more tangibly recognisable markers of disability, be they material, embodied or as identity.

Disability studies as a discipline has debated the relative importance of key concepts such as impairment and disability, identity, gender, geopolitical positioning and the relations between them for an overarching conceptual model of disability.[6] Early ascendant social models emerged in response to traditional medicalisation and tragedy views and positioned disability as a socially constructed category shaped by differential responses to non-normative bodies and minds.[7] Critiques of this somewhat simplistic position have emerged in more recent times to challenge thinking about the role of impairment, identity and of the intersectional operations of social inequality, in part as a response to the legacies of psycho/medical thinking about disability which characterised the so-called 'institutional' era and against which contemporary critical disability studies emerged as a 'post-institutional' emancipatory project. The focus of the current volume poses several questions for this binary or sequential institutional/post-institutional distinction, capturing contemporary concerns and observations of the enduring but metamorphosing project of institutionalisation, most particularly in the 'treatment' and 'management' of criminalised, materially, socially and/or culturally disadvantaged people with cognitive impairment. This questioning of what might be more productively conceptualised as 'institutionality', a more actively relational and individualising project which embeds new carceralities driven by changing practices of power beyond traditional spatial segregation, opens new horizons of inquiry. Among these – and the focus of

[4] P Hill Collins and S Bilge, *Intersectionality* (Malden, Polity Press, 2016).
[5] N Erevelles, *Disability and Difference in Global Contexts: Enabling a Transformative Body Politics* (New York, Palgrave Macmillan, 2011) 26.
[6] D Goodley, *Disability Studies: An Interdisciplinary Introduction* (London, Sage, 2011).
[7] M Corker and S French, 'Reclaiming Discourse in Disability Studies' in M Corker and S French (eds), *Disability Discourse* (Buckingham, Open University Press, 1999).

this chapter – is the abled/disabled binary and the porosity and fluidity of its boundaries. The chapter draws on an area of critique associated with contemporary philosophical and cultural studies scholarship, the emerging theme of biopolitics and applies its analytic framing of neoliberal biocapitalism to new forms of institutional and post-institutional readings of dis/ability. Primarily, the argument made here challenges disability activists and scholars to rethink the significance given to disability itself as an oppressed identity and to, instead, consider disability as part of a larger neoliberal biopolitical frame that implicates *all* embodied subjects.[8]

The promise of this new framing, premised on the non-binarised recognition that we are all a part of the 'dis/ability complex',[9] in turn prompts an interrogation of the ways in which a disability rights framework, advocating for social accommodation, acceptance, pride and empowerment, can account for 'transgressive' forms of disability. For people with cognitive impairment in contact with the criminal justice system, corrosive disadvantage may intersect with individual traits deemed transgressive to accepted forms of disability in ways that cannot be reconciled with contemporary claims that disability is an oppressed – yet normal and desirable – identity.[10] Here questions emerge as to how and why non-normative ways of 'being disabled' become both materially criminalised and conceptually marginalised from a disability justice agenda which valorises particular forms of disability for recognition and rights-based advancement. Moreover, a more explicit framing of transgressive disability associated with entrenched and intertwined intergenerational, geographic and/or circumstantial privation, overlaying more widely recognised forms of intersecting oppressions associated with race, class and gender, is formed under new alliances which give rise to contemporary transcarceral logics in the 'post-institutional' era. This more intersectional analysis allows a focus on the formation and understanding of multiple axes of power/domination and the ways that these alliances rely on new logics of segregation, facilitated separation, coercive 'care' and eugenics, which the editors of this volume identify in Chapter 1. A further and perhaps more important aspect of intersectionality for this chapter is how power works relationally in the formation and understanding of social identities and categories of difference.[11] These new transcarceral alliances and logics legitimate more nuanced and complex identities and less explicit or recognisable forms of dis/ability difference.

---

[8] K Fritsch, 'Gradations of Debility and Capacity: Biocapitalism and the Neoliberalization of Disability Relations' (2015) 4 *Canadian Journal of Disability Studies* 12–48.

[9] D Goodley, 'The Dis/ability Complex' (2018) 5 *DiGeSt. Journal of Diversity and Gender Studies* 5–22.

[10] D Mitchell and S Snyder, *The Biopolitics of Disability: Neoliberalism, Ablenationalism, and Peripheral Embodiment* (Ann Arbour, University of Michigan Press, 2015).

[11] R Bunn, 'Intersectional Needs and Re-Entry: Re-Conceptualising "Multiple and Complex Needs" Post-Release' (2019) 19 *Criminology & Criminal Justice* 328–45. See also HY Choo and MM Ferree, 'Practicing Intersectionality in Sociological Research: A Critical Analysis of Inclusions, Interactions, and Institutions in the Study of Inequalities' (2010) 28 *Sociological Theory* 129–49.

My motivation for this project emerges from my own intellectual struggle with the disciplinary ambivalence that characterises the intersection of disability and criminological studies, which is perhaps best summed up in two recurring questions: *Do we want our institutional spaces of criminal justice – carceral and virtual – to be inclusive of disability? If so, in what ways?* Two paradigmatic challenges are implicated in these questions: firstly a 'disability' framing in which traditional models fall short in allowing explanatory space for disabled bodies or identities that cannot always be celebrated with pride, such as those associated with criminality, and secondly, the 'criminological' framing in which disability or impairment cannot simply be relegated to an individual criminogenic risk factor. The challenges here are threefold. First to find a palatable inter/disciplinary positioning for the critical interrogation of the differential inclusions of transgressive forms of embodiment commonly identified in people with cognitive impairment in contact with the justice system. Second, to account for the dynamics of responses to these embodiments as simultaneously *individualising, criminalising* and *systemically purposeful*. Third, to ensure a connection between theory and practice that allows an explanatory account of the multiplicity and complexity of the lived experience of cognitive disability and corrosive disadvantage we see in the lives of Jack and Casey.[12]

JACK

A young man with diagnostic labels including Neurodevelopmental Disorder, Autism Spectrum Disorder, Attention Deficit Hyperactivity Disorder, Tourette's Syndrome and Attachment Disorder, Jack first comes to the attention of police when he is 10 years old and comes to school with a black eye. This precipitates a police investigation which results in the uncovering of systemic violence and abuse in his home, where his father and his father's de facto partner are identified as drug users and his father is diagnosed with schizophrenia. This begins a period of multiple short foster care placements. Just before his 11th birthday, Jack is removed into care permanently and comes under the 'parental responsibility of the Minister'. He is placed in a residential care setting with a group of young people who are all at least three years older than him. Police are regularly called to his school to 'discipline' him as a result of offences such as stealing and ringing the school bell and are also regularly called to his residential setting as a result of the behaviour of all four residents; Jack is reported to be damaging

[12] Case studies of Jack and Casey (pseudonyms) are drawn from the longitudinal administrative linked dataset compiled from the Australian Research Council Linkage project 'People With Mental Health Disorders and Cognitive Disabilities in the Criminal Justice System in NSW', University of NSW – Chief Investigators E. Baldry, L. Dowse and I Webster. Available at: www.mhdcd.unsw.edu.au. Ethics approval was obtained from all relevant ethics bodies, including from the University of New South Wales Human Research Ethics Committee.

property and sometimes biting workers. During his time in this placement, Jack regularly absconds from the residence and is reported to police as a missing person. Police note that Jack has 'issues managing his anger' in the group home setting. In both the school and residential setting, staff/house managers/school principal do not proceed with charges; instead they all indicate to police that their goal is to escalate the issues they are experiencing to a higher authority in an effort to force more secure and appropriate accommodation for Jack. Jack is subsequently placed in a foster home and has no police contact for several years. On breakdown of this placement at 14, Jack's contact with the Youth Justice system begins with multiple motor vehicle theft and related offences, for which he is often bailed then placed on community orders which he breaches and which result in periods in youth custody. He is also identified in police records as being a drug user. He is placed in a disability group home with 24-hour support but, at age 20, two incidents involving other residents lead to apprehended domestic violence orders. He is then moved from the group home to a caravan park, where support workers visit twice weekly. After this move Jack becomes destructive, smashes up his caravan, overdoses on medication and is disruptive in public places, frequently coming to the attention of police. His adult records show subsequent serial incarceration for violence, theft and justice offences.

CASEY

A young Indigenous woman, Casey, is labelled with intellectual disability, attention deficit hyperactivity disorder and other behavioural, emotional and mental health diagnoses. She has a long history of self-harm, physical abuse and trauma as a young person, with problematic alcohol and drug use from childhood and very poor school attendance, ceasing school entirely at age 13. At this age, Casey begins frequent calls to the police emergency number when 'no service is required' and on multiple occasions is found walking the streets at night, 'highly agitated' and threatening suicide. Police are also called to attend incidents where Casey is found damaging property and climbing on the roofs of various buildings, including the local school, hospital and the offices of the child protection agency, refusing to come down. This continues for some months; on the eighth occasion, she is picked up by police and, after her mother informs police that she is 'unable to have the child at home', she is taken to the local hospital, admitted under the state's Mental Health Act, restrained, sedated and released the following morning. On the ninth occasion, a doctor from the hospital informs the police that 'it was his professional opinion that the young person was not in need of medical or mental intervention' and Casey is refused admission to the hospital. The police and doctor concur that 'the young person just enjoyed the attention her behaviour generated' and Casey is taken into police custody, charged and given bail. The next day, police are called again, Casey is arrested, bail is refused and she is charged by police. She subsequently enters youth justice custody. Throughout her teenage years, Casey has multiple episodes of out-of-home care then disability residential placements, where she frequently damages property, assaults staff and absconds, resulting in police being called and charges being laid. As an adult she moves between prison (mainly as a result of breaches of bail conditions), disability accommodation settings and mental health facilities; in one of these she is sexually assaulted by another resident. Casey is frequently restrained or held in solitary confinement in these institutions and she very often self-harms.

DISABILITY AS VOLATILITY

Jack and Casey have multiple diagnostic labels that give them entry to an axiomatic conceptual category of 'disability' yet, as Fritsch observes, 'within disability studies, the everyday conceptualization of disability is typically characterized as an oppressed disabled person working against structural ableism and the medical–industrial complex that seeks to cure, alter, and rehabilitate a body that is abnormal or lacking'.[13] For Jack and Casey, we see few such attempts at recuperation or the instatement of the kind of citizenship privilege argued for in disability politics over the past half century. Rather, when set amongst multiple forms of disadvantage, their non-normative performance of 'disability' is deemed transgressive in ways that cannot be reconciled with independence, cure or consumption in a neoliberal economic context. As troublemakers and offenders, they are materially and conceptually abandoned to the vicissitudes of privation, marginality and criminality – dispatched on a road to 'slow death'.[14] As the central argument of this volume suggests, the laws, policies and practices which characterise efforts toward enhanced social and political participation in the community for disabled people are suspended for Jack and Casey. Instead, prevailing individual and systemic responses to their complex trauma, deprivation and distress serve to reinstate older forms and practices of segregation. At the same time, Jack and Casey's realities are marked by newer, multiple and contiguous forms and practices precipitated by their intersecting forms of disadvantage, such as movement from one institution to another and various medical or pharma interventions. Here, we observe the entrenchment of emergent 'transinstitutional' and 'transdisciplinary' forms of restraint and coercion, informed by, but also legitimated beyond, the logics of institutionalisation, uniquely applied to criminalised disadvantaged disabled people.

In interrogating 'disability' for Jack and Casey there is a pernicious pluralism at work – seen in the absence of disability *claims* by them or even on their behalf, but rather the *ascription* of disability – ostensibly evident in the multiple

---

[13] Fritsch 'Gradations of Debility and Capacity' (2015) 26.
[14] L Berlant, 'Slow Death (Sovereignty, Obesity, Lateral Agency)' (2007) 4 *Critical Inquiry* 33.

diagnostic labels both have accrued over their relatively short lives. Ostensive definitions of disability, particularly those deployed in the psy-complex, rest on observable evidence of impairment in functioning according to regimes of assessment that define a phenomenon by direct demonstration (achievement of a particular IQ score), or the observable presence/absence of human cognitive or emotional 'functions'. Such definitions, importantly, do not attempt to explain the nature of 'disability', and are even less likely to interrogate the ways that particular non-normative embodiments of 'disability' are bound up with life experiences of adversity, precarity and deprivation. Close attention to the boundaries of 'disability' in this context cause them to 'fray under close scrutiny' in the same way as the boundaries of race[15] and point to the inconsistencies associated with attempts to technically, legally and socially fix the able/disabled binary.

For Jack and Casey, disability identity is categorically ascribed and re/ produced in their everyday encounters and magnified through systemic responses which, rather than responding to their complex support needs or reading their volatility as resistance, rest primarily on the criminalisation of their transgressive behaviour. Drawing on Foucault, Tremain reminds us that the body can never be analysed or experienced apart from the historically contingent practices that bring it into being such that 'differences are always already signified and formed by discursive and institutional practices'.[16] Jack and Casey's disability is discursively encapsulated as 'challenging behaviour' which is encoded as individual, ahistorical and asocial. Attempts at definition typically identify such behaviour as anomalous inward (including self-harm) or outward (damage to property or violence against others) actions which are seen to have negative consequences for the individual and those around them. Institutionally, the diagnostic frameworks and classification mechanisms associated with conceptualisation, identification and intervention in challenging behaviour enable the generation of an ideological conception of the abnormal mind/body[17] which enables transgressive behaviour to be made to appear as part of disability and inherent to the person themselves.

Nunkoosing and Haydon-Laurelut provide an alternative reading of challenging behaviour as both excess and absence: too much anxiety, too much agitation, too much answering back, too much noise, too much aggression, too much seeking isolation, too much unwanted emotion, too much anger, too much love; not enough obedience, not enough talk, not enough sociability.[18]

---

[15] Havis, quoted in S Tremain, 'Dialogues on Disability: Shelley Tremain with Devonya Havis and Audrey Yap' (2018) *Disability and Disadvantage Blog*. Available at: www.philosophycommons.typepad.com/disability_and_disadvanta/2018/04/dialogues-on-disability-shelley-tremain-with-devonya-havis-and-audrey-yap.html.

[16] S Tremain, 'On the Government of Disability' (2001) 27 *Social Theory and Practice* 627.

[17] R Mickalko, 'The Excessive Appearance of Disability' (2009) 1 *International Journal of Qualitative Studies in Education* 22.

[18] K Nunkoosing and M Haydon-Laurelut, 'Intellectual Disability Trouble: Foucault and Goffman on "Challenging Behaviour"' in D Goodley, B Hughes and L Davis (eds), *Disability and Social Theory: New Developments and Directions* (Basingstoke, Palgrave Macmillan, 2012) 198.

Challenging behaviour and the spaces, places and scales at which it occurs are a 'product of relationships and of people who do not want to subject themselves, their identities, their bodies to the disciplinary regimes of care'.[19] In the examples of Jack and Casey, these excesses and absences can be understood as an embodied affective response that is multi-causal, multi-factorial and historically contingent, which positions them as at risk for a range of further negative responses. Here, processes of criminalisation can be explained as

> the exercise of bio-power over the non-docile body, and through the application of the pathological gaze to those whose behaviour challenges are constructed as in need of surveillance as a result of their defective biology or/and mind rather than the disabling social arrangements.[20]

These disabling social arrangements include both individual and systemic responses to behavioural transgressions. While others have called attention to the importance of, for example, police and social care agency responses to such individuals in the community,[21] less attention has been directed at systemic institutional responses, which associated with criminalisation, surveillance and multiple forms of confinement. These processes do not follow the accepted logics of institutionalisation in social care or criminal justice contexts. Administrative rather than physical segregation can also occur via the ascription of categorical identities of 'disabled' or 'offender' which, when bound up with complex social disadvantage, may not be associated with any one defined space or place. Rather, individuals so labelled often occupy liminal spaces in which they are subject to new and shifting forms and logics of exclusion and inclusion which emerge across the multiple systems in which they are engaged. By their nature, these experiences of intervention are often transient, clustering, and contingent on service eligibilities, policy cycles and system reforms rather than on an individual's need for support. These fluctuating inclusions and exclusions can be in and of themselves disabling in the sense that liminality and vulnerability to harm often go hand in hand.

Whether as acts of resistance, as responses to existential trauma or to material and social privation, Jack and Casey's rage against themselves and others does not simply signal that they have troubles, but, rather mark them as trouble.[22] The negative valence ascribed to their non-normative and transgressive embodiments of 'disability' become blended with racialised, classed, gendered and other registers of disadvantage to mark them as socially excludable[23] and

[19] Ibid, 203.
[20] Ibid, 204.
[21] E Baldry and L Dowse, 'Compounding Mental and Cognitive Disability and Disadvantage: Police as Care Managers' in D Chappell (ed) *Policing and the Mentally Ill: International Perspectives*. (Boca Raton, CRC Press, 2013).
[22] L Dowse, 'Disruptive, Dangerous and Disturbing: The "Challenge" of Behaviour in the Construction of Normalcy and Vulnerability' (2017) 3 *Continuum* 31.
[23] E Emerson, *Challenging Behaviour: Analysis and Intervention in People with Intellectual Disabilities* (Cambridge, Cambridge University Press, 1995).

dependent. In their movement through child safety, youth justice, psychiatric, disability and criminal interventions, we observe them becoming what Starr Sered and Norton-Hawke term 'institutional captives', where experiences of the welfare/penal/medical/disability 'support' system act as one interlocking metasystem[24] which cumulatively and inexorably leads to their incapacitation via protective, biomedical (physical and chemical), disability and carceral institutionalisation. In the context of contemporary neoliberalism, Berlant identifies this as marking them out for 'slow death'[25] via the debilitating ongoing-ness of structural inequality and suffering.[26]

DEBILITY: A BIOPOLITICAL ACCOUNT OF DISABILITY AND DISADVANTAGE?

In seeking resonant theorisations of the 'disability' experience for Jack and Casey, I am drawn to theorists working broadly under the umbrella of biopolitics who are seeking to redraw the boundaries of disability conceptualisation – and therefore disability politics – into a space which provides for accounts of those who Shildrick denotes as 'debilitated bodies that are beyond reinvigoration for neoliberalism';[27] which observe 'the compounding of disability and poverty as a field of debilitation'[28] and which 'trouble the assumption that disability is a uniformly oppressed category of being'.[29] Here, I do not offer an in-depth explication or critique of the notion of 'debility', which is available elsewhere;[30] instead, I propose to examine the utility of the specific deployment of the meanings of 'debility' as an explanatory framing for the volatility and mutability of 'disability' as it applies to people who experience cognitive disability in intersection with corrosive disadvantage.

   First, I turn to the work of Jasbir Puar, a queer theorist at the forefront of the deployment of debility as an analytic tool for disability scholarship. In coming to her current intellectual project of the biopolitics of debilitation, Puar recounts standing on a street corner in New York City equidistant from, on one side, a Disability Pride Parade with its increasingly visible disability empowerment discourse and, on the other, a 'Black Lives Matter' protest in which she observed the divestment of narratives of pride. Her position 'in the middle, perplexed'

[24] S Starr Sered and M Norton-Hawk, *Can't Catch a Break: Gender, Jail, Drugs, and the Limits of Personal Responsibility* (Berkeley, University of California Press, 2014) 13.

[25] Berlant, 'Slow Death' (2007) 33.

[26] JK Puar, 'Coda: The Cost of Getting Better: Suicide, Sensation, Switchpoints' (2012) 1, *GLQ: A Journal of Lesbian and Gay Studies* 149.

[27] M Shildrick, 'Living On; Not Getting Better' (2015) *Feminist Review* 13.

[28] JK Puar, *The Right to Maim: Debility, Capacity, Disability* (London, Duke University Press, 2017) 13.

[29] Fritsch, 'Gradations of Debility and Capacity' (2015) 15.

[30] See, eg, K Inckle, 'Debilitating Times: Compulsory Ablebodiedness and White Privilege in Theory and Practice' (2015) 111 *Feminist Review*, 42; R Garland-Thompson, 'The Story of My Work: How I Became Disabled' (2014) 2 *Disability Studies Quarterly* 34.

captures my own ambivalence as a scholar at the interstices of disability studies and criminology. I share Puar's sense of discord between 'disability empowerment and pride and the targeted debilitation of an entire racialised population'[31] – a discord echoed in the lives of Casey and Jack as simultaneously racialised, gendered, classed and ultimately criminalised, but where discourses of disability identity and empowerment are absent.

Puar argues for a differentiation of debilitation from disablement because it 'foregrounds the slow wearing down of populations instead of the event of becoming disabled' and contends that 'disability is not a fixed state or attribute but exists in relation to assemblages of capacity and debility, modulated across historical time, geopolitical space, institutional mandates, and discursive regimes'.[32]

In seeking an explanatory frame for the systematic violence and criminalisation endemic for people with cognitive disability and corrosive disadvantage, I am drawn to the particular proposition in Puar's work that troubles 'the binarised production of disabled versus nondisabled bodies that drives both disability studies and disability rights activism'.[33] Most usefully, Puar cautions that 'attachments to the difference of disabled bodies may reify an exceptionalism that only certain privileged disabled bodies can occupy' and points to disability justice activists' recognition that 'slow death is constitutive to debility, and disability must be rethought in terms of precarious populations'.[34] In her most recent work, Puar clarifies the relationship between the two in that:

> disability and debility are not at odds with each other. Rather they are necessary supplements to an economy of injury that claims and promotes disability empowerment at the same time that it maintains the precarity of certain bodies and populations precisely through making them available for maiming.[35]

As we see in their experiences above, Jack and Casey are drawn into 'disability' by institutional diagnostic designation, while at the same time both remain beyond the reach of an emancipatory politics of disability. Instead, they are subject to a systematic and patterned regime of incapacitation linked to their transgressive behaviour and social disadvantage, which draws them into discrete sites of debilitation that extend from child protection residential care, to the school, the psychiatric hospital, the disability group home and, ultimately, the prison. As Erevelles asks:

> how can acquiring a disability be celebrated as 'the most universal of human conditions' if it is acquired under the oppressive conditions of poverty, economic

---

[31] Puar, *The Right to Maim* (2017) 14.
[32] Ibid, 19.
[33] Puar, 'Coda' (2012) 153.
[34] Ibid, 154.
[35] Puar, *The Right to Maim* (2017) 23.

exploitation, police brutality, neocolonial violence, and lack of access to adequate health care and education?[36]

Margaret Shildrick also makes a contribution to this project via her reflections on 'exclusionary inclusion' which she previously observed through practices of rehabilitation, whereby 'certain people – and usually those with physical as opposed to cognitive disabilities – were relatively easily assimilated into the mainstream norms of society'.[37] In the context of the United Kingdom's austerity agenda and neoliberalism more generally, Shildrick furthers this analysis within a biopolitical frame through her assertion that 'debility may be the universal default under the conditions of contemporary capitalism but the slow death to which it assigns individuals and populations is unevenly distributed'.[38]

Taken together with her previous arguments for the inherent vulnerability of all bodies and analysis of the operation of abjection in relation to embodied vulnerability, Shildrick's work[39] leads us to understand the ways in which the non-normative and transgressive embodiments characteristic of people with cognitive disability who experience corrosive disadvantage become depoliticised and individualised in ways that would not apply to those whose biosocial disability identity is centred on working towards independence and productivity. Her understanding of the ways widespread economic insecurity 'creates the perfect storm of antagonism towards people with disabilities' and at the same time 'demands its scapegoats' points with some clarity to Jack and Casey's construction as 'debilitated bodies that are beyond reinvigoration for neoliberalism'.[40] Jack and Casey become 'excluded inclusions', whereby they are institutionally categorised, regulated and disciplined as 'disabled' via labelling of their observable impairments in 'cognition' or 'function'. Simultaneously, through the systemic management of their disruptive, dangerous and disturbing behaviour via institutionalisation and criminalisation,[41] their bodies are 'sustained in a perpetual state of debilitation precisely through foreclosing the social, cultural and political translation to disability'.[42]

CONCLUSION

People with cognitive disability who also experience corrosive social disadvantage are largely understood to fall outside neoliberal normative expectations of

[36] Erevelles, *Disability and Difference in Global Contexts* (2011) 119.
[37] Shildrick, 'Living On; Not Getting Better' (2015) 11.
[38] Ibid, 16.
[39] See M Shildrick, *Embodying the Monster: Encounters with the Vulnerable Self* (London, Sage, 2002); M Shildrick, *Dangerous Discourses: Subjectivity, Sexuality and Disability* (Basingstoke, Palgrave Macmillan, 2009).
[40] Shildrick, 'Living On; Not Getting Better' (2015) 19.
[41] Dowse, 'Disruptive, Dangerous and Disturbing' (2017).
[42] Puar, *The Right to Maim* (2017) 14.

self-management and self-reliance. This perceived failure lays the foundations for a well-trodden path to the liminal spaces of social marginalisation and affective dislocation via enmeshment in institutionalised regimes of material impoverishment, bodily surveillance, serial incarceration and systemic violence. In seeking to move beyond the currently limited capability offered in disability studies to conceptualise such processes, this chapter offers a partial and selective account of emerging notions of 'debility' identified with the work of Puar and expanded by Shildrick. The argument broadly made is that currently deployed conceptual tools in disability studies are anchored in a valourised notion of disability associated with empowerment and which privileges rational, articulate and agential forms of identity. In attempting to reconcile the more irrational, transgressive and non-normative embodiments of disability often associated with people who have cognitive impairment and corrosive social disadvantage, the notion of debility emerges as a promising interrogatory frame. This concept, with its foundations in critiques of neoliberal biocapitalism, questions the ways in which the binary of disabled/non-disabled is produced and offers a more variegated account of the intersection of bodily difference and disadvantage. This potentially opens up new understandings of the ways the individual and the social are directly connected to processes of de-authorisation in the academy and in policy and practice.

Contemporary approaches to the regulation and discipline of criminalised disadvantaged people with cognitive impairment clearly draw on prevailing historical logics of institutionalisation. In this chapter, however, I argue that these logics and legacies are increasingly diversified and augmented for people, such as Jack and Casey, whose transgressive social identities and embodied differences are characterised by volatility and marked out by debility. In responding to this group, new alliances have formed, which I argue are transinstitutional and transdisciplinary and which pose intersectional and compounding forms of injustice beyond the spatial and disciplinary segregations of the institutional era. These new forms pose challenges to theorists, researchers, policymakers and practitioners, in that they are more difficult to isolate, untangle, recognise and redress. Lessons which arise from this interrogation also highlight that disability is more than a biological, immutable and pathological abnormality that is apolitical, asocial and ahistorical.[43] Rather, giving prominence to disability also necessarily implicates ability, and similarly, underscoring disadvantage brings advantage into focus. This refocusing importantly grants the insight that 'neoliberal ableism – the elision of national economic independence with an individual and cultural celebration of autonomy'[44] shapes all our lives. The new logics of debility, transgression and identity now being built beyond our traditional framing therefore implicate all embodied subjects in post-institutional emancipatory projects.

---

[43] Dowse, 'Disruptive, Dangerous and Disturbing' (2017).

[44] D Goodley, *Dis/ability Studies: Theorising Disablism and Ableism* (New York, Routledge, 2014).

11

Fixated Persons Units

A Disability Studies and Critical Race Theory (DisCrit) Analysis

FLEUR BEAUPERT AND SHELLEY BIELEFELD

T HIS CHAPTER UNDERTAKES analysis of a joint policing–mental health model developed to respond to 'fixated persons' and 'lone actor violence' from the perspective of DisCrit, a framework that simultaneously engages Disability Studies and Critical Race Theory.[1] The assumption underlying this model is that people who come to police attention because of apparent 'fixation' on public figures or social causes are likely to 'have a serious mental illness'[2] or be otherwise 'disordered'.[3] 'Fixated persons units' or 'fixated threat assessment centres', referred to as 'FPUs' in this chapter, have been positioned from the outset alongside or within counter-terrorism measures. This model thus forms part of and extends legal and policy frameworks characterised by racist underpinnings and erosion of rights protections which have affected 'real or perceived' Muslims in particular.[4]

---

[1] S Annamma, D Connor and B Ferri, 'Dis/ability Critical Race Studies (DisCrit): Theorizing at the Intersections of Race and Disability' in D Connor, B Ferri and S Annamma (eds), *DisCrit: Disability Studies and Critical Race Theory in Education* (Teachers College Press, Columbia University, 2016) 13–15.

[2] MT Pathé, DJ Haworth and TJ Lowry, 'Mitigating the Risk Posed by Fixated Persons at Major Events: A Joint Police-Mental Health Intelligence Approach' (2016) 11 *Journal of Policing, Intelligence and Counter Terrorism* 63, 63–64.

[3] The term 'disordered' is used throughout this chapter to denote the amalgam of behaviours attributed to people labelled with 'fixation'. We use inverted commas around this word to indicate that this is a constructed category rather than an actual pathological mental state.

[4] TG Patel, 'It's Not About Security, it's About Racism: Counter-Terror Strategies, Civilizing Processes and the Post-Race Fiction' (2017) *Palgrave Communications* doi: 10.1057/palcomms.2017.31. See also V Sentas, 'Counter Terrorism Policing – Investing in the Racial State' (2006) 2 *ACRAWSA e-journal* 1, 6, 10–11; KP Sian, 'Surveillance, Islamophobia and Sikh Bodies in the War on Terror' (2017) 4 *Islamophobia Studies Journal* 38, 48.

Our analysis is centred on the operation of FPUs in Australian jurisdictions. The chapter begins with an overview of the emergence of FPUs, followed by an explanation of the DisCrit framework. We then apply this framework to develop three interconnected arguments regarding systemic impacts. First, we demonstrate how the ideologies and practices of FPUs construct race and disability in tandem to marginalise individuals and communities across and at the borders of, the criminal justice and mental health systems. Second, we argue that FPUs embody a 'pre-diagnosis' mechanism in the mental health context, mirroring and extending the increasingly 'pre-crime'[5] logic of counter-terrorism measures. Third, we suggest that the concept of 'fixation' underpinning FPUs operates to stifle legitimate political dissent by 'persons of interest' ('POIs')[6] and pathologise structural and socio-economic disadvantage by 'diagnosing' individual racialised and disabled bodies.

The chapter highlights how FPUs continue historical practices associated with the institutionalisation of people deemed mad and/or disabled. They are buttressed by segregationist logics and their outcomes encompass intensive and coercive interventions in the lives of people experiencing intersections of racial and ableist oppression. Our concern is that the legacies of institutionalisation embodied within this model may result in the disproportionate pathologisation, criminalisation, surveillance, silencing and exclusion of people existing at these intersections.

BACKGROUND TO FIXATED PERSONS UNITS

Fixated Persons Units emerged in the 2000s, incorporating mental health professionals and the 'psy' disciplines[7] into investigations about the threat of violence posed by 'fixated persons' and 'lone actors', as well as 'grievance-fuelled violence.'[8] Britain's Fixated Threat Assessment Centre, established in 2006,

[5] On the notion of 'pre-crime', see generally J McCulloch and D Wilson, *Pre-crime: Pre-emption, Precaution and the Future* (Abingdon, Routledge, 2015) 1.

[6] The term 'person of interest' – abbreviated to 'POI' – is used throughout this chapter to refer to individuals who are referred to a FPU because it approximates the status of this group as subjects of law enforcement. It also appears to be the term used by the Queensland Police Service: MT Pathé et al, 'Establishing a Joint Agency Response to the Threat of Lone-Actor Grievance-Fuelled Violence' (2018) 29 *The Journal of Forensic Psychiatry & Psychology* 37, 43. We use inverted commas around this term to reflect the tenuous nature of 'POIs'' connection to criminal acts.

[7] Rose contends that the 'psy' sciences (psychology, psychiatry and other disciplines designating themselves with this prefix) constitute techniques for the disciplining of human difference: N Rose, *Inventing Our Selves: Psychology, Power and Personhood* (Cambridge, Cambridge University Press, 1998).

[8] K Buggy, *Under the Radar: How Might Australia Enhance its Policies to Prevent 'Lone Wolf' and 'Fixated Person' Violent Attacks?* (Centre for Defence and Strategic Studies, Commonwealth of Australia, 2016) 2–5, 10; Pathé et al, 'Establishing a Joint Agency Response' (2018) 38–41; D James et al, 'The Fixated Threat Assessment Centre: Preventing Harm and Facilitating Care' (2010) 21 *Journal of Forensic Psychiatry & Psychology* 521, 521–22.

was based on findings of the Fixated Research Group, a United Kingdom (UK) Home Office initiative set up to research the harassment of prominent people,[9] which concluded that 'fixated' individuals rather than organised terrorists pose the greatest risk of harm to public officeholders.[10] This research characterises 'fixations' as involving 'warning behaviours,' such as 'problematic communications' to public office holders and proposes that intervention by mental health services is often an appropriate response.[11] Mullen and colleagues state that '[t]he majority of the fixated are driven by delusional beliefs based in potentially treatable mental disorders'.[12]

The Queensland Fixated Threat Assessment Centre (QFTAC), the first FPU established in Australia within the state of Queensland, involves 'a collaboration between the Security Operations Unit of the Queensland Police Service and Queensland Health's Forensic Mental Health Service'.[13] The QFTAC aims to identify 'fixated' people 'through their aberrant contacts with public office holders' and evaluates their 'concern levels (low, moderate or high)' using a 'risk matrix'.[14] Cases with a moderate or high concern rating may be assigned for further intervention with a view to reducing the risk considered to be posed to the person and the community.[15] Interventions include 'mental health treatment, conventional policing strategies and engagement with community-based programmes'.[16] QFTAC has expanded to include an arm called 'Project Solus' to deal with cases triggering the interest of security agencies.[17]

Fixated Persons Units were most recently established in the Australian states of NSW in May 2017[18] and Victoria in February 2018.[19] In March 2017, the Centre for Defence and Strategic Studies released a report recommending the creation of a National Fixated Threat Assessment Centre within the Australian Federal Police Service.[20] The stated intention was to provide a policy response to 'so-called "lone wolf" and "fixated person" violent attacks' and, in particular, to prevent violent extremism in light of the raising of Australia's terrorism

---

[9] Fixated Research Group. See www.fixatedthreat.com.

[10] Pathé, Haworth and Lowry, 'Mitigating the Risk' (2016) 64.

[11] Pathé et al, 'Establishing a Joint Agency Response' (2018) 41–42.

[12] PE Mullen et al, 'The Fixated and the Pursuit of Public Figures' (2009) 20(1) *The Journal of Forensic Psychiatry & Psychology* 33, 44.

[13] Pathé, Haworth and Lowry, 'Mitigating the Risk' (2016) at 63.

[14] Ibid, 64.

[15] Ibid.

[16] Pathé et al, 'Establishing a Joint Agency Response' (2018) 42.

[17] Ibid, 43.

[18] *Western Advocate*, 'NSW Police Introduce Fixated Persons Investigation Unit' (2017) *Western Advocate*. Available at: www.westernadvocate.com.au/story/4627585/new-police-unit-deals-with-obsessed-individuals-video/.

[19] T Mills, 'Extreme Threat: New Centre Aims to Thwart Lone-wolf Attacks' (2018) *The Age*. Available at: www.theage.com.au/national/victoria/extreme-threat-new-centre-aims-to-thwart-lone-wolf-attacks-20180228-p4z249.html.

[20] Buggy, *Under the Radar* (2016), 15, 21.

threat to 'high' in September 2014.[21] To lay the foundation for our analysis of how FPUs can operate along racialised and ableist contours, we next conceptualise DisCrit.

SIMULTANEOUSLY ENGAGING DISABILITY STUDIES AND CRITICAL RACE THEORY (DISCRIT)

Subini Annamma, David Connor and Beth Ferri pioneer 'DisCrit' as 'a new theoretical framework incorporating a dual analysis of race and disability' that combines aspects of Critical Race Theory (CRT) and Disability Studies (DS).[22] This approach aims to move beyond traditional approaches within CRT and DS which have tended to hinder collaboration between these fields.[23] DisCrit explores the mutual interdependence of material processes which construct subjects as raced and disabled. DisCrit's founders explain that '[R]acism and ableism are normalizing processes that are interconnected and collusive ... racism and ableism often work in ways that are unspoken, yet racism validates and reinforces ableism and ableism validates and reinforces racism'.[24]

Governing narratives of incapacity, deficiency and deviancy have been key rationalisations for slavery, colonialism, policy responses to asylum seekers, discriminatory disability-orientated interventions such as residential segregation and discrimination in the sphere of employment.[25] For example, in the context of Australian colonialism, Indigenous peoples were portrayed using pathologising discourses of disability, as occupying an inferior place in the human hierarchy, with child-like capabilities and minds stuck in a stage of partial development.[26] This portrayal 'had economic and other benefits for colonists intent on land acquisition and profits from slave labour'.[27] Nirmala Erevelles and Andrea Minear explain that there is a 'continued association of race and disability in debilitating ways' which is embedded in such historical contexts.[28]

In this chapter we apply a DisCrit lens to explore how attributions of disability and 'disorder' intersect with racial logics to 'shape recognition of whose body,

---

[21] Ibid, 1.

[22] Annamma, Connor and Ferri, 'Dis/ability Critical Race Studies' (DisCrit) (2016) 13–15.

[23] Ibid, 14.

[24] Ibid.

[25] DL Adams and N Erevelles, 'Shadow Play: DisCrit, Dis/respectability and Carceral Logics' in Connor, Ferri and Annamma (eds), *DisCrit* (2016) 131, 134; S Bielefeld, 'Income Management and Indigenous Women – A New Chapter of Patriarchal Colonial Governance?' (2016) 39 *University of New South Wales Law Journal* 843, 849, 875.

[26] D Hollinsworth, *Race and Racism in Australia* (South Melbourne, Social Science Press, 2006) 100.

[27] S Bielefeld and F Beaupert, 'Income Management and Intersectionality: Analysing Compulsory Income Management through the Lenses of Critical Race Theory and Disability Studies ('Discrit') (2019) 41(3) *Sydney Law Review* 327.

[28] N Erevelles and A Minear, 'Unspeakable Offenses: Untangling Race and Disability in Discourses of Intersectionality' (2010) 4 *Journal of Literary and Cultural Disability Studies* 127, 133.

mind, language and\or behaviour is acceptable and whose is deserving of incarceration, exclusion, silencing and\or punishment'[29] within and through FPUs.

OVERT AND COVERT COLLUSIONS: PATHOLOGISATION, RACIALISATION AND CRIMINALISATION

Ableism and racism can operate interdependently through FPUs to construct disabled and raced subjects across and at the borders of, the criminal justice and mental health systems. These collusions overtly deploy pathologising, ableist discourses of disability, positing psychosocial disability, cognitive disability and 'disorder' as the likely cause of violence that may be perpetrated by 'POIs'. While FPUs are also covertly sustained by racism, their racially neutral façade may operate to obscure their adverse impacts on racialised individuals and communities.

Disability studies scholarship has demonstrated that the pathologisation of disability and its association with dangerousness and deviancy has been used to justify discriminatory and violent practices which control, segregate, institutionalise, incarcerate, or indeed exterminate people with disabilities.[30] FPUs represent a concerning reformulation of such historical practices because they apply a distinct criminal justice response to alleged risk revolving around problematic assessments focused on disability-related criteria. They are premised on the understanding that a joint policing–mental health approach is needed in response to 'fixated people' because they are likely to have a 'serious mental illness';[31] the goal is to identify 'fixated' people who are 'seriously disabled as a result of mental illness' and to provide them with needed care.[32]

The negative and stigmatising association of dangerousness and psychosocial disability or 'disorder' produced through the policy discourses surrounding the FPU is clear. For example, research supporting the FPU model deploys ableist discourses of disability which construct 'POIs' as deviant and dangerous in the extreme. The relevant 'fixations' are asserted to be 'irrational', 'abnormally intense', 'pathological', potentially 'rooted in delusional beliefs'[33] and, crucially, unable to be accommodated by conventional law enforcement measures.[34] This characterisation produces a narrative of an abnormally dangerous and uncontrollable group. The posited 'fixations' are said to be abnormal on the basis that

---

[29] K Collins, 'A DisCrit Perspective on *The State of Florida v. George Zimmerman*: Racism, Ableism and Youth Out of Place in Community School' in D Connor, B Ferri and S Annamma (eds), *DisCrit* (2016) 183, 189.

[30] See, generally, SL Snyder and DT Mitchell, *Cultural Locations of Disability* (Chicago, The University of Chicago Press, 2006).

[31] Pathé, Haworth and Lowry, 'Mitigating the Risk' (2016) at 64.

[32] Mullen et al, 'The Fixated and the Pursuit of Public Figures' (2009) 46.

[33] Ibid, 34–35, 41–43.

[34] Pathé, Haworth and Lowry, 'Mitigating the Risk' (2016) 63–64.

individuals have spent 'much of their waking lives thinking about the object of their concern,' possibly with 'months or years of dedicated preoccupation'.[35] They have been represented as embodying a state of being that 'typically' leaves individuals 'isolated and destitute' and also in expressly ableist terms as involving an 'autistic engagement with the other'.[36] This collective attribution of uncontrollable dangerousness, deviancy and incapacity to 'POIs' has been deployed to justify resort to special measures to avert violence.[37]

Whilst these ableist underpinnings of FPUs are evident from their immediate policy framework, this model is covertly sustained by racist and racialised logics[38] due to its close connection with counter-terrorism measures. The positioning of FPUs alongside or within counter-terrorism units[39] manifests them as a security/policing measure geared towards preventing dangerous and potentially lethal criminal acts. Counter-terrorism regulation, such as laws providing for the proscription of declared 'terrorist organisations', has led to policing approaches that have disproportionately targeted certain racialised communities, rendering them the 'collective subjects of security policing'.[40] Associated national security rhetoric has been a way of 'keeping [the nation's] ideological borders as "morally clean" as possible'[41] constructing binary cultural constructions of in/civility which cast 'real or perceived' Muslims in particular in the role of the terrorist.[42]

The policy discourse immediately surrounding FPUs rarely explicitly mentions race and is not intended to target only those whose 'fixations' are linked to 'Islamic extremism'.[43] Such absence of express discriminatory language, however, cannot subvert the racial logics permeating the FPU model by virtue of its structural alignment with counter-terrorism policing units. As Vicki Sentas explains, the increasing tendency for regulatory discourses which have racialised implications to be presented in facially neutral terms does not diminish their ability to 'contribute to social relationships saturated in differential, racialised or racist outcomes'.[44] We argue that FPUs are likely to perpetuate the racial

[35] Mullen et al, 'The Fixated and the Pursuit of Public Figures' (2009) 34–35.
[36] Ibid, 35.
[37] We note, however, that this group is actually asserted to pose a relatively low risk of violence that cannot be accurately assessed, raising questions about the FPU's proportionality considering the coercive interventions it encompasses: see ibid, 42–44; Pathé et al, 'Establishing a Joint Agency Response' (2018) 40.
[38] In the sense described by DT Goldberg, *The Racial State* (Malden, Blackwell Publishers, 2002) 104.
[39] *Western Advocate*, 'NSW Police Introduce Fixated Persons Investigation Unit' (2017); Queensland Police Service, *2013–14 Annual Report* (2014) 36.
[40] V Sentas, 'Policing the Diaspora: Kurdish Londoners, MI5 and the Proscription of Terrorist Organizations in the United Kingdom' (2016) 1 *British Journal of Criminology* 898, 898, 904.
[41] S Patel, 'The Anti-terrorism Act and National Security: Safeguarding the Nation against Uncivilized Muslims' in J Zine (ed), *Islam in the Hinterlands: Exploring Muslim Cultural Politics in Canada* (Toronto, UBC Press, 2012), 272, 291.
[42] Patel, 'It's Not About Security' (2017) 4.
[43] Buggy, *Under the Radar* (2016) 2.
[44] V Sentas, 'Beyond Media Discourses: Locating Race and Racism in Criminal Justice Systems' in M Bhatia, S Poynting and W Tufail (eds), *Media, Crime and Racism* (London, Palgrave Macmillan, 2018) 359, 370.

othering of real and perceived Muslim individuals and communities because the persistent stereotype of the Muslim terrorist saturates the surrounding criminal justice structures.[45] In fact, the manner in which FPUs have been structurally and symbolically aligned with counter-terrorism, as reflected in regular media reports,[46] trades in 'an economy of fear'[47] and has arguably played a significant role in allowing this pre-emptive intervention mechanism to flourish without much public concern or debate.

Our analysis in this section suggests a circular relationship between racism and ableism in the context of the FPU model, whereby narratives associating disability with deviancy and dangerousness overtly support the pathologising of racialised bodies, whilst racialised logics covertly support the (further) pathologising of disability. In addition, since people who are investigated and targeted are, in the first instance, being ushered into the criminal justice apparatus in a systematic manner, these collusions may amplify the criminalisation of disabled[48] and racialised individuals[49] and people experiencing intersections of these oppressions.[50]

FROM 'PRE-CRIME' TO 'PRE-DIAGNOSIS' BY THE CRIMINAL JUSTICE AND MENTAL HEALTH SYSTEMS

The FPU model embodies a shift from the notion of 'pre-crime' to what we term 'pre-diagnosis'.[51] 'Pre-diagnosis' via FPUs pre-emptively and collectively labels 'POIs' as 'disordered' based largely on behavioural criteria, thereby relying on different standards for intervention than apply in both the criminal justice and mental health systems. The Fixated Research Group proposed that systematic attention to people identified as being 'fixated' on a public officeholder or cause through law enforcement can detect people in need of mental health treatment

---

[45] Patel, 'It's Not About Security' (2017) 4.

[46] Ibid; AAP, 'Melbourne Terror Attack: Radical Islam Greatest National Security Threat, says Prime Minister Scott Morrision [sic]' (2018) *Perth Now*. Available at: www.perthnow.com.au/news/terrorism/melbourne-terror-attack-radical-islam-greatest-national-security-threat-says-prime-minister-scott-morrision-ng-b881017869z; P Karp, 'Morrison Urges Muslim Community to be More "Proactive" in Tackling Terrorism' (2018) *The Guardian*. Available at: www.theguardian.com/australia-news/2018/nov/12/morrison-urges-muslim-community-to-be-more-proactive-in-tackling-terrorism.

[47] S Ahmed, *The Cultural Politics of Emotion* (New York, Routledge, 2015) 15. See, eg, P Maley, 'Police Focus on "Fixated" Persons and Lone Wolf Attacks' (2018) *The Australian*. Available at: www.theaustralian.com.au/national-affairs/national-security/police-focus-on-fixated-persons-and-lone-wolf-attacks/news-story/dd65f1027684dbd54daddfeea9530f5b.

[48] E Baldry, L Dowse and M Clarence, *People with Intellectual and Other Cognitive Disability in the Criminal Justice System*' (Sydney, University of New South Wales, 2012).

[49] C Spivakovsky, *Racialized Correctional Governance: The Mutual Constructions of Race and Criminal Justice* (Ashford, Ashgate, 2013).

[50] L Ben-Moshe, C Chapman and A Carey (eds), *Disability Incarcerated: Imprisonment and Disability in the United States and Canada* (New York, Palgrave Macmillan, 2014).

[51] On the notion of 'pre-crime', see generally J McCulloch and D Wilson, *Pre-Crime: Pre-Emption, Precaution and the Future* (Abingdon, Routledge, 2015) 1.

or disability support.[52] This is an altogether new (pseudo-)diagnostic method or route via and by the criminal justice system. 'Pre-diagnosis' operates in the mental health and disability contexts similarly to 'pre-crime' in the criminal justice system,[53] by preceding conventional methods of referral to services. Further, given the embedding of FPUs within security policing, 'pre-diagnosis' simultaneously *extends* 'pre-crime', bringing individuals pre-emptively within the criminal justice sphere without evidence of wrongdoing.

The concept of 'fixation' grounding FPUs does not fall within a diagnostic category in the DSM or ICD.[54] It is rather a pseudo-clinical category posited as an indicator of probable 'mental illness' or 'disorder', although some 'POIs' will have been diagnosed with a mental illness. To identify 'POIs', referrers and assessors apply behavioural criteria extending far beyond so-called 'serious mental illness'; these criteria cover autism, personality disorder, drug-induced psychosis and other non-categorised 'fixated' behaviour considered to be pathological.[55] 'Pre-diagnosis' thus appears to have a net-widening effect when it comes to who may come to be referred to mental health or disability services or be absorbed into the criminal justice apparatus. This represents a gross expansion of the 'pre-emptive turn' in counter-terrorism regulation, which has criminalised real and perceived Muslim individuals and communities 'due to their collective status', based on their religious and ethnic identity and political ideology rather than prior putative criminal acts.[56] Such regulation results in 'an obsessive monitoring of "suspicious" brown bodies'.[57]

In addition to referrals to GPs, inpatient and outpatient mental health services or alternate support services, FPU police may conduct home visits[58] and access a person's medical records.[59] The standard approach is to continue monitoring individuals until their 'concern level' has been reduced to low.[60] Involuntary hospitalisation or outpatient treatment is another possible route;[61]

---

[52] Mullen et al, 'The Fixated and the Pursuit of Public Figures' (2009) 42.

[53] 'Pre-crime intervenes to punish, disrupt, incapacitate or restrict those deemed to embody future crime threats': McCulloch and Wilson, *Pre-Crime* (2015) 1.

[54] American Psychiatric Association, *Diagnostic and Statistical Manual of Mental Disorders, DSM-5* (Arlington, VA, American Psychiatric Association Publishing, 2013); World Health Organization, *International Classification of Diseases*, 11th Revision (ICD-11) (Geneva, WHO, 2018). Available at: www.icd.who.int/browse10/2016/en.

[55] Pathé et al, 'Establishing a Joint Agency Response' (2018) 42–43.

[56] Sentas, 'Policing the Diaspora' (2016) 900.

[57] Sian, 'Surveillance, Islamophobia and Sikh Bodies' (2017) 38.

[58] Pathé et al, 'Establishing a Joint Agency Response' (2018) 46; Pathé, Haworth and Lowry, 'Mitigating the Risk' (2016) 67–68.

[59] Maley, 'Police Focus on "Fixated" Persons and Lone Wolf Attacks' (2018); Holmes and Nedim, 'NSW Police to Target Potential Lone-Wolf Terrorists' (2018) *Sydney Criminal Lawyers*. Available at: www.sydneycriminallawyers.com.au/blog/nsw-police-to-target-potential-lone-wolf-terrorists/. While access to mental health records by police is permissible in particular circumstances, the FPU involves a more systematic flow of information.

[60] Pathé et al, 'Establishing a Joint Agency Response' (2018) 45.

[61] Pathé, Haworth and Lowry, 'Mitigating the Risk' (2016) 68–69.

in fact, Mullen and colleagues have stated that appropriate treatment 'will, in practice, require the use of compulsory power in many cases'.[62] In other words, the range of responses include coercive mental health measures, in addition to invasive forms of monitoring which some 'POIs' will not even be aware of,[63] triggered by a lower bar than the standard 'criteria for investigation by detectives' or the exercise of police powers.[64]

These interventions flowing from FPUs have been presented in surrounding policy discourses as benevolent responses that will successfully divert people from a law enforcement route and provide needed treatment.[65] On the one hand, this downplays the possible outcome of re-routing to conventional law enforcement. On the other hand, it demonstrates a lack of awareness about potential stigmatising, coercive and violent impacts of mental health and disability services and laws.[66]

Impacts of FPUs include the bare reinstatement of the historical practice of institutionalising people with disabilities when they result in a person being detained in a mental health facility. These impacts, however, also extend to 'virtual' forms of institutionalisation which may have long-lasting impacts, such as ongoing control and surveillance or community treatment orders which can effectively detain individuals in community settings including through 'chemical incarceration' (the forced administration of psychiatric drugs).[67] 'Psy' knowledge is thus harnessed to legitimate and cast as therapeutic coercive practices which can be understood as forms of violence.[68]

[62] Mullen et al, 'The Fixated and the Pursuit of Public Figures' (2009) 45.

[63] NSW Police Force, 'NSW Police launch of the Fixated Person Unit' (2017) *Facebook*. Available at: www.facebook.com/nswpoliceforce/videos/the-new-south-wales-police-force-has-announced-a-new-specialist-unit-to-deal-wit/10154760858511185/.

[64] Holmes and Nedim, 'NSW Police to Target Potential Lone-Wolf Terrorists' (2018); *news.com.au*, "Fixated' Sydney Man Charged Over Plot to Carry Out Lone Wolf-Style Terrorist Attack' (2018). Available at: www.news.com.au/national/nsw-act/crime/sydney-man-charged-over-terror-plot/news-story/5f7919787bf4a549525611b9621efd7f.

[65] See especially NSW Police Force, 'NSW Police Launch of the Fixated Person Unit' (2017).

[66] See eg L Ben-Moshe, 'Disabling Incarceration: Connecting Disability to Divergent Confinements in the USA' (2013) 3 *Critical Sociology* 385, 389–90; F Beaupert, 'Freedom of Opinion and Expression: From the Perspective of Psychosocial Disability and Madness' (2018) 7(1) *Laws* www.doi.org/10.3390/laws7010003; F Beaupert, 'Silencing Prote(x)t: Disrupting the Scripts of Mental Health Law' (2018) 41 *University of New South Wales Law Journal* 746; C Spivakovsky, 'The Impossibilities of 'Bearing Witness' to the Institutional Violence of Coercive Interventions in the Disability Sector' in C Spivakovsky, K Seear and A Carter (eds) *Critical Perspectives on Coercive Interventions: Law, Medicine and Society* (Abingdon, Routledge, 2018) 96.

[67] See E Fabris and K Aubrecht, 'Chemical Constraint: Experiences of Psychiatric Coercion, Restraint and Detention as Carceratory Techniques' in L Ben-Moshe, C Chapman and A Carey (eds) *Disability Incarcerated: Imprisonment and Disability in the United States and Canada* (New York, Palgrave Macmillan, 2014) 185, 187–88.

[68] On disability interventions as 'lawful violence', see L Steele, 'Disability, Abnormality and Criminal Law: Sterilisation as Lawful and Good Violence' (2014) 23 *Griffith Law Review* 467; L Steele 'Restrictive Practices in Australian Schools: Institutional Violence, Disability and Law' in R Dixon, K Trimmer and Y S Findlay (eds), *The Palgrave Handbook of Education Law for Schools* (New York, Palgrave Macmillan, 2018) 533.

POLICING AND 'DISORDERING' POLITICAL DISSENT
AND STRUCTURAL DISADVANTAGE

The impact of FPUs may include the suppression of legitimate political dissent and the containment of structural and socio-economic disadvantage within racialised and disabled bodies because the foundational concept of 'fixation' renders the socio-political motivations of 'POIs' inherently suspect. FPU assessment processes are intended to distinguish those with legitimate grievances, such as political campaigners and social activists, from 'fixated petitioners' who are asserted to be giving expression 'to their personal feeling rather than any wider public agenda', their 'aims ... losing any connection they may once have had to the ideas and aspirations of their fellow citizens'.[69] Michele Pathé and colleagues describe 'fixations' as involving preoccupations with a '*perceived* injustice' (emphasis added).[70] There is a risk – consistent with numerous historical and ongoing instances of the pathologisation of resistance and political dissent through psy-techniques[71] – that the FPU model could inadvertently pathologise political marginalisation and structural disadvantage due to neoliberal governance strategies and the heightened security climate in which it is being used.[72]

The racialised nature of citizenship at present is such that people of colour, migrants and refugees are more likely to be deemed as having politically suspect motivations and governments increasingly collect information about individuals' motives with a view to making such assessments.[73] The 'civilizing narratives' associated with counter-terrorism measures have operated to render collectively suspect the political claims of Muslims.[74] We suggest that the FPU model, embedded within counter-terrorism measures and relying upon psy-assessments of the legitimacy of a person's asserted grievances, is likely to produce outcomes reflecting the prejudices characteristic of this wider socio-political climate.[75] The forms of suppression that may follow include criminalisation, but also exclusion and silencing through the use of coercive mental health measures, psychological therapy and drugs operating to treat and reframe a person's concerns as 'disorder' and massage or coerce them into a 'normal' state of being in which they are no longer able or motivated to pursue complaints or redress mechanisms.

---

[69] Mullen et al 'The Fixated and the Pursuit of Public Figures' (2009) 33, 41.

[70] Pathé et al, 'Establishing a Joint Agency Response' (2018) 39–40, 48; Pathé, Haworth and Lowry, 'Mitigating the Risk' (2016) 64.

[71] Fabris and Aubrecht, 'Chemical Constraint' (2014) 187–8; J Metzl, *The Protest Psychosis: How Schizophrenia Became a Black Disease* (Boston, Beacon Press, 2009) ix; Beaupert, 'Silencing Prote(x)t' (2018) 766–71.

[72] E Klein, *Developing Minds: Psychology, Neoliberalism and Power* (Abingdon, Routledge, 2017) 51–54; I Tyler, *Revolting Subjects: Social Abjection and Resistance in Neoliberal Britain* (London, Zed Books, 2013) 3–9.

[73] Patel, 'The Anti-terrorism Act and National Security' (2012) 286.

[74] Patel, 'It's Not About Security' (2017) 2–6.

[75] E Tseris, 'Biomedicine, Neoliberalism and the Pharmaceuticalisation of Society' in BMZ Cohen (ed), *Routledge International Handbook of Critical Mental Health* (Abingdon, Routledge, 2018) 283–94, 386.

Given the depth of socio-economic injustice replicating under neoliberal forms of governance,[76] it is disturbing that the Fixated Research Group claims that: 'Those fixated on a personal cause or quest for justice are of particular concern.'[77] Questionably, this framing locates the problem in the mind and/or behaviour of the individual fixated on righting injustice rather than on 'structural violence'[78] in society that may have produced such injustice – to which persistent resistance may be a reasonable response.

Despite its ostensibly benevolent aims, the unintended use or subtle manipulation of FPUs for anti-democratic and political ends is not a far-fetched possibility given the specific focus on contacts with public officeholders and public events such as the G20 Summit, which naturally attract protesters. Just over half of the 530 referrals made to the QFTAC from 1 June 2013 to 31 December 2017 were from State Electoral and Ministerial Offices.[79] As Emma Tseris has explained, psychiatry provides a viable means for the identification and 'pharmaceutical regulation' of 'individuals who are non-compliant with the increasingly narrow possibilities for citizenship available within neoliberal societies' including where they actively resist social norms but also where 'distress [relates] … to unachievable social expectations'.[80] FPUs may operate to intensify this effect, since they provide a dedicated psychocentric[81] avenue for public officeholders to divert citizens who are considered to be making unwanted communications. This could potentially have a chilling effect on legitimate democratic debate. The alleged detention and forced drugging of former Origin Energy employee and whistleblower Fiona Wilson, following an FPU referral because of attempts to contact a Queensland Minister with evidence regarding the coal seam gas industry, is a case in point.[82]

A critical factor requiring consideration in this respect is the relationship between class or socio-economic disadvantage and other sites of identity and oppression. We draw here on China Mills' recent analysis of how suicides in the UK connected to welfare reform and austerity measures have been depoliticised through processes of 'psychologisation' attributing them to individual mental health issues, rather than being framed within a 'wider pattern of such deaths' which indicates that 'austerity kills'.[83] Mills builds on scholarship offering psycho-political readings of what the psy disciplines frame as 'symptoms',

---

[76] Tyler, *Revolting Subjects* (2013) 3–9.

[77] Buggy, *Under the Radar* (2016) 11.

[78] J Galtung, 'Violence, Peace and Peace Research' (1969) 6(3) *Journal of Peace Research* 167, 171.

[79] Queensland Police Service, RTI/23636 (Response to Freedom of Information Request) (2019). Available at: www.police.qld.gov.au/rti/disclog/2018/Documents/RTI%2023636%20Final.pdf.

[80] Tseris, 'Biomedicine, Neoliberalism and the Pharmaceuticalisation of Society' (2018) 286.

[81] C Mills, '"Dead People Don't Claim": A Psychopolitical Autopsy of UK Austerity Suicides' (2018) 38 *Critical Social Policy* 302, 302, 304, 309.

[82] E Farrelly, 'Gender Equality: It Takes a Troubled Woman to Change a Troubled World' *The Sydney Morning Herald* (2018). Available at: www.smh.com.au/opinion/gender-equality-it-takes-a-troubled-woman-to-change-a-troubled-world-20180125-h0oip9.html.

[83] Mills, 'Dead People Don't Claim' (2018) 304–6.

172 Fleur Beaupert and Shelley Bielefeld

emphasising how seemingly 'disordered' behaviour may be a rational response to socially unjust and oppressive environments, including the 'maladaptive socio-economic politics of austerity'.[84] One question raised by this approach is whether some individuals and communities are more likely to be driven to resort to seemingly pathological, repetitive attempts to communicate with public officeholders about a grievance. People who do not have the necessary financial or other material resources to initiate legal or complaints mechanisms may instead use ongoing informal means of drawing attention to their claim. For instance, a person with literacy issues may be more likely to make repeated phone calls instead of lodging a single written complaint. This could bring them to the attention of an FPU.

In our view, there is a need for the operation of FPUs to be closely scrutinised applying an intersectional lens that takes into account its classed implications, particularly since people experiencing class-based discrimination are more likely to be referred to public mental health services with expansive coercive powers due to an inability to afford private services. Analytical attention should also be directed to the nexus between the expansion of control of marginalised populations within welfare law and policy[85] and the expanded policing–mental health monitoring powers that FPUs exercise. These mechanisms form part of a wider trend of increasing oversight that have specific impacts on people with disability,[86] and encompass net-widening, preventative, surveillance and control mechanisms which have been deployed in the counter-terrorism context as an exercise of state racial power.[87] This has been contributed to by a 'terror-panic climate.'[88]

CONCLUSION

The analysis in this chapter indicates that the FPU is premised upon an ableist conception of a hyper-dangerous and 'disordered' individual, superimposed over the racialised figure of the terrorist that derives from mythologies of 'a white, civilized and benevolent nation'.[89] FPUs harness this complex alliance between racism and ableism to reify profiling and surveillance practices that are increasingly common under the banner of counter-terrorism, in addition to expanding mental health and disability interventions in unprecedented ways.

---

[84] Ibid, 306.

[85] S Bielefeld, 'Cashless Welfare Transfers for "Vulnerable" Welfare Recipients – Law, Ethics and Vulnerability' (2018) 26 Feminist Legal Studies 1–23.

[86] Ibid, Mitchell and Snyder.

[87] Sentas, 'Counter Terrorism Policing' (2006) 1–13; Patel, 'The Anti-Terrorism Act and National Security' (2012) 280.

[88] TG Patel, 'Surveillance, Suspicion and Stigma: Brown Bodies in a Terror-Panic Climate' (2012) 10(3/4) Surveillance & Society 215.

[89] Patel, 'The Anti-Terrorism Act and National Security' (2012) 275.

Given the covert nature of the racist discourses sustaining FPUs, careful scrutiny is needed to determine the extent to which this model may replicate the historical construction of racialised and Indigenous peoples as inferior through ableist associations with disability.[90] For instance, Indigenous protestors in Australia have been constructed through state discourse as 'lacking self-control and reason', 'being out-of-control and not reasonably responding to … injustice',[91] characterisations resonating with the concept of 'fixation' within this model.

This chapter, secondly, demonstrates that FPUs constitute a problematic 'pre-diagnosis' mechanism, triggered by the labelling of 'POIs' as 'disordered' and in need of treatment. This process is pre-emptive when compared to other methods of entering the mental health and criminal justice systems. By emphasising 'care' and 'treatment' as the model's primary goal, the surrounding policy discourse masks the manner in which FPUs in fact reinstate coercive and segregationist logics and practices associated with the institutionalisation of people deemed mad and/or disabled. The representation of certain FPU interventions as therapeutic simultaneously facilitates the continuation of racialised and colonial practices of control,[92] in this case effected through counter-terrorism measures. Race and disability are thus (re)constructed as an interdependent set of practices with material and violent impacts upon people's lives.

Finally, we have drawn attention to the risk that FPUs may silence and subvert political dissent because of the pseudo-clinical conception of 'fixation' they are premised upon. While FPUs may lead to positive outcomes in particular individual cases, our analysis exploring impacts at the systemic level has raised questions about wider failures to address social and political marginalisation.[93] FPU methods pre-emptively invalidate 'POIs'' stated socio-political motivations by characterising them as the product of 'disordered' minds, thereby containing them within disabled and racialised bodies. The potential for this collective attribution of 'fixation' to reorientate political marginalisation and structural injustice as individual pathology for people existing at the interstices of raced, ableist and classed oppression, and other dimensions of social difference, warrants deeper consideration by policymakers and commentators than has been shown to date.

---

[90] See, eg, Bielefeld and Beaupert, 'Income Management and Intersectionality' (2019).

[91] T Anthony, *Indigenous People, Crime and Punishment* (London, Routledge, 2013) 165, 168.

[92] Examining the deportation of racialised people from Canada, Joseph shows how colonial, eugenic and racial rationales are reinstated through institutions and practices at the confluence of mental health and criminal justice systems: AJ Joseph, *Deportation and the Confluence of Violence within Forensic Mental Health and Immigration Systems* (London, Palgrave Macmillan, 2015).

[93] Similar questions have been raised in relation to criminal law diversion: L Steele, L Dowse and J Trofimovs, 'Who is Diverted?: Moving Beyond Diagnosed Impairment Towards a Social and Political Analysis of Diversion' (2016) 38 *Sydney Law Review* 179.

Part Three

Institutionalisation and Human Rights
The Role of the CRPD in the Emancipation of People with Disabilities

P ART ONE OF this collection is concerned with the complex legacies of
institutionalisation in policy and practice. Part Two considers how
the legacies of institutionalisation often form complicated alliances
with other longstanding practices of oppression and segregation in society.
Part Three is concerned with the role that the United Nations Convention on
the Rights of Persons with Disabilities (CRPD) may play in the emancipation of
people with disabilities (PWD) from the various legacies of institutionalisation
identified in the first two parts of the collection. It considers current tensions
and contradictions in law and policy surrounding implementation of the CRPD.
There are six chapters included in this final part of the collection.

The purpose of the CRPD is not to create new human rights for PWD, but
to articulate existing human rights in the context of disability. The result is a
ground-breaking international convention with a fresh approach to understanding the concept of human rights, coupled with innovative guidance on how to
realise human rights for PWD. The radical new framework offers an opportunity for States Parties to create fresh approaches and strategies that could enable
PWD to move beyond the legacies of the past.

Questions have been raised about the extent to which the CRPD is affecting change and the pace of that change. The CRPD explicitly focuses on the
social, political and economic marginalisation of PWD in contemporary society. It offers participation, self-determination and empowerment as the solution
to these problems. The new approach was developed precisely because previous human rights-based approaches had failed. Given the ambitious agenda of
the CRPD, it is perhaps unsurprising to find that CRPD-based frameworks and
innovations do not sit neatly with existing law and policy.

The chapters in Part Three consider the implementation of the CRPD over
a decade after it came into force internationally in 2008. On the one hand,
the chapters show how contemporary laws, policies and practices in the post-
deinstitutionalisation era continue or legitimate historical practices associated
with this population's institutionalisation. On the other hand, they point to an
ongoing struggle to bring the CRPD to fruition, showing how easily progress

can be compromised if the human rights objectives that animate legal and policy reform are not recognised.

In the first chapter of Part Three, Peter Bartlett considers the international submissions to the Committee on the Rights of Persons with Disabilities regarding a draft version of General Comment 1 on Article 12 – Equal recognition before the law. The submissions illustrate the emergence of a polarised debate about the scope of CRPD obligations. In light of interpretive conventions in international law, Bartlett ultimately rejects the argument that States Parties were somehow unaware of the possibility that the CRPD Committee would adopt a strong reading of the CRPD.

In her chapter, Lucy Series discusses recent litigation on the meaning of 'deprivation of liberty' in community care settings in England and Wales. She frames her discussion about the UK Supreme Court's controversial decision in *Cheshire West*[1] – which significantly expanded current interpretations of 'deprivation of liberty' by the courts – with reference to the ideology of freedom associated with community living in the post-carceral era.[2] Series notes that that the court's attempt to steer a path between the law as it is articulated by the European Court of Human Rights and the human rights principles expressed in the CRPD resulted in a legal analysis that emphasised the objective conditions of deprivation of liberty standards but neglected recognition of its subjective dimensions.

The two chapters about Spain provide examples of the contradictory effects of laws that purport to implement the CRPD but are poorly conceived and implemented. Melania Moscoso Pérez and R Lucas Platero show how the new disability laws in Spain subvert CRPD objectives, particularly in the context of economic crisis. Their analysis of the disability support schemes in Spain shows that only a very small percentage of people with disabilities receive professional assistance. Others rely on funding for personal assistance. These poorly paid care tasks are usually undertaken by female relatives or low-skilled women and immigrants. The authors argue that the scheme not only reinforces traditional gender-based caregiving roles but produces more disability in the long term through the exploitation of (mostly) female carers who are regarded as expendable.

In her chapter, Elvira Pértega Andía analyses the interaction of CRPD-based laws introduced in Spain with laws that regulate the practice of physical restraint for children and young people. She notes first that Spanish laws regulating physical restraint stand at odds with the CRPD, especially when those who are authorised to impose restraint are regarded as the guardians of the children in question. She

---

[1] *P v Cheshire West and Chester Council and another; P and Q v Surrey County Council* [2014] UKSC 19.

[2] C Unsworth, 'Mental Disorder and the Tutelary Relationship: From Pre- to Post-Carceral Legal Order' (1991) 18 *Journal of Law and Society* 2, 254.

then analyses the dynamics that encourage overuse of restraint, arguing that the law requires health professionals to ensure safety and maintain control over their patients. Health professionals are held responsible for harm in situations where harm has occurred and there was no evidence of action or intervention by the health professional. This encourages the use and overuse of physical restraint, despite the recognised harm that is associated with restrictive practices.

The final two chapters in the section point to the possibility of a more positive future. In her chapter, Jill Stavert describes Scotland's anticipated approach to CRPD-based law reform. She argues against a law reform approach that would merely 'update' existing law. Rather, she sees the task as one of embracing the paradigm shift that the CRPD requires. In particular, she points to the challenge of recognising and engaging with the principle that different treatment based on disability is no longer acceptable.

Finally, in his analysis of the implementation of CRPD-based laws in Indonesia, Dio Ashar Wicaksana describes how local civil society organisations in the province of Yogyakarta actively encouraged and assisted officials to understand and recognise the social model of disability as the basis for implementing a new disability laws in the Indonesian criminal justice system. The author argues that the open dialogue process was critical to the success of this strategy. By improving the officials' appreciation of 'diffability' issues, the new laws were given real substance in the province. This chapter is a testament to the importance of civil society involvement in all aspects of disability reform.

12

A Matter of Engagement

Analysing the Submissions to the CRPD Committee on General Comment #1

PETER BARLETT

I N THE AUTUMN of 2013, the United Nations Committee on the Rights of Person with Disabilities (hereinafter the 'Committee') engaged in a consultation exercise on a draft version of what would become its first General Comment. This concerned the scope and implementation of Convention on the Rights of Person with Disabilities (CRPD)[1] Article 12 on the right to equal recognition before the law. The draft General Comment included all the key elements that were eventually contained in the final General Comment. These included:

- the prohibition of a link between legal and mental capacity and the affirmation of the right of all persons to both, without discrimination based on disability;

- the requirement of an overall shift from substituted decision-making systems to supported decision-making and the consequent shift from decision-making based on the perceived best interests of the individual to the primacy of the individual's will and preferences;

- the demise of systems of guardianship as they have existed in most legal systems, including both systems of plenary guardianship and systems based on decision-specific assessments of capacity; and

---

[1] United Nations, General Assembly, A/61/611, 6 December 2006.

- consideration of how equality before the law engages with other rights of the CRPD, most notably calling for the abolition of compulsory detention and treatment based on disability (eg, as provided for under mental health legislation).[2]

These are significant proposals for change and, perhaps unsurprisingly, the General Comment has proven highly controversial. In this chapter, I analyse and reflect on the submissions to the Committee in that consultation exercise.

OVERVIEW OF THE SUBMISSIONS

There were 78 submissions.[3] Of these, six were relevant only to the consultation on accessibility that was occurring at the same time and were therefore rejected from my analysis, leaving 72 submissions that were coded. The geographic origin of the submissions is presented in Figure 1.

Figure 1 Origin of submissions

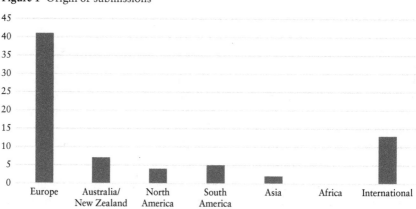

■ I: Location of Submissions

Notable is the strong bias towards the global north, the complete absence of submissions from Africa and the very few submissions from Asia. Some of the international organisations were active in the global south and commented on the situation there, but none were based there. The nature of the organisations or individuals making the submissions is presented in Figure 2.

---

[2] For draft general comment, see United Nations Committee on the Rights of Persons with Disability, Draft General comment on Article 12 of the Convention-Equal Recognition before the Law, adopted at session of 2–11 September 2013; for final general comment, see CRPD/C/GC/1, adopted 19 May 2014.

[3] The submissions are available at: www.ohchr.org/EN/HRBodies/CRPD/Pages/DGCArticles12 And9.aspx.

Figure 2 Persons and organisations making submissions

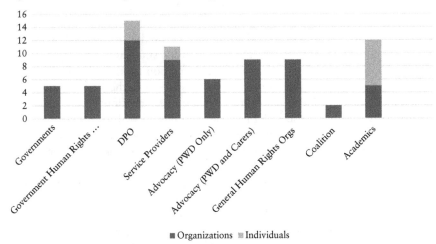

■ Organizations   ▧ Individuals

All the submissions from governments and government-based human rights organisations are from the global north, Australia and New Zealand. Indeed, all the government submissions come from the European Union (EU) plus Norway. Submissions from disabled people's organisations (DPOs) and people with disabilities (PWD) are, by comparison, much more extensive and geographically diverse. The service provider category is heterogeneous, including five guardianship organisations or providers of care services, an organisation of psychologists, a law society, a social worker and a psychiatrist.

There are few submissions from psychiatrists – one from an individual and one from a university unit of psychiatry and learning disability, both from the United Kingdom. Some psychiatrists or other medical professionals may have had some input into submissions from other service provider organisations, advocacy organisations or human rights organisations, but their overall involvement appears to be very limited. This is surprising. The overall direction of the Committee was known among psychiatrists involved in international work well before the consultation occurred and, at least in countries with developed professions, organisations of psychiatrists are politically astute and active in lobbying. As noted, the content of the General Comment has been controversial among medical professionals.[4] It is not clear why they chose not to engage with the consultation process.

---

[4] See, eg, MF Freeman et al, 'Reversing Hard Won Victories in the Name of Human Rights' (2015) 2 *Lancet Psychiatry* 844.

THE FUNDAMENTAL DIVIDE: FOR OR AGAINST
A STRONG READING OF THE CRPD

As noted above, the draft General Comment adopted a strong reading of the CRPD's right to equality before the law: guardianship should be replaced by supported decision-making and substituted decision-making should be abolished. This position was given overwhelming support in the submissions from DPOs and individuals with disabilities. Of the 15 submissions in this category, 11 expressly supported these changes and an additional three said nothing to contradict them. Only one DPO submission contemplated any continuing role for substitute decision-making. Instead, these submissions provided comments on how the strong reading could be reinforced in some circumstances and some suggestions were taken up in the version of the General Comment eventually adopted.

Some organisations provided justifications for their support of the strong position. Sometimes these included moving accounts of the discriminatory effects of the capacity system, such as the following from Autistic Minority International:

> Our very existence is in danger as long as autism, without regard to severity, continues to be viewed as something to be eradicated. Violence against us takes the form of behaviour modification, institutionalization and abusive medical and therapeutic practices, such as electric shocks. Instead, we should be taught self-esteem, self-confidence and how to advocate for ourselves. The autistic minority also includes those of us who hide their condition for fear of discrimination. This is no longer tenable at a time when millions of children diagnosed with autism come of age and many more get diagnosed as adults. Autism awareness must lead to acceptance, recognition and respect for autistics. Only autism acceptance will ensure our full and equal participation in all areas of public, economic and social life.

Others made more technical arguments, linking Article 12 with other human rights conventions. These are discussed in more detail below.

Either way, in both academic and human terms, these submissions reflect considered and remarkably consistent support for the strong interpretation of the CRPD from DPOs and PWD. The DPOs were not alone in this approach. Eight other submissions, from a variety of types of organisation, expressly supported the Committee's strong reading of the CRPD.

At the other extreme, some submissions support the status quo ante, sometimes rather vehemently. Most notable among these are the submissions from four of the five governments.[5] These make it clear that the governments in question see nothing wrong with the existing systems of guardianship and do not

---

[5] The brief from the Government of Hungary is the exception. Hungary reformed its guardianship laws following the introduction of the CRPD. The brief states that Hungary, as part of those reforms, has provided systems of supported decision-making and that restrictions on legal agency are now a thing of the past.

propose to change them significantly. If these submissions represent the views of governments more broadly, we can expect to see very little change on what the DPOs appear to view as a fundamental question of disability rights.

That is startling. The content of the government submissions will be discussed in more detail below, but what is notable here is the failure to engage with the issues raised by the DPOs. This failure is not lost on them. The Bundesverband Psychiatrie-Erfahrener eV, the largest psychiatric DPO in Germany, stated in its submission:

> We are appalled and indignant about the arrogant response of the Federal Republic of Germany. If this point of view gains acceptance, the UN Convention on the Rights of Persons with Disabilities will become a caricature. Its spirit and words will be perverted into the exact opposite. During the ratification process in Germany it became clear that the German government wants to exhibit human rights while it allows torture in psychiatries and retirement homes. Our demand not to ratify the UN Convention on the Rights of Persons with Disabilities when it is not implemented anyway was ignored.[6]

Other submissions shared the governments' uncompromising approach. Some of these came from service providers, but that category was by no means as united in its condemnation of the draft General Comment as were the governments: some service providers were quite supportive of the overall approach of the General Comment. The submission from the Bundesverband der Berufsbetreuer/innen, a German association of 6,400 professional guardians, is fierce in its support of the strong reading of the CRPD Committee:

> As guardians we try to support our clients to organize the needed assistance according to their preferences and to manage other personal affairs in the bureaucratized German society. Unfortunately, this kind of support is only accessible through a legal proceeding which regularly violates the human rights of the people concerned: It is the guardianship court and not the user themselves who appoints the support person. Furthermore, the appointment of the guardian automatically results in the transfer of the right to representation.
>
> [* * *]
>
> We very much welcome the draft General Comment on Article 12, because it gives strong counter-arguments to the conservative position of leading experts and politicians in Germany who claim that the German guardianship law fulfills the obligations of States Parties under Article 12 CRPD.

Many submissions fall between these extremes. Governmental human rights agencies, for example, were often hesitant or critical of the strong reading, but did, by and large, engage with some of the problems that the strong reading was trying to address. Many of the submissions, including those from some of

---

[6] The reference to 'torture' in this quote includes a citation to the UN Special Rapporteur on Torture and his comments on forced psychiatric treatment: see United Nations General Assembly A/HRC/22/53, para 64.

the DPOs and others supporting a fairly strong reading of the CRPD, pressed for detail on how 'hard cases' were to be dealt with and for more detail on what form supported decision-making should take. These submissions leave considerable scope for what international law is meant to produce: constructive dialogue.

At the core of the submissions, however, remains a fairly fierce divide between the strong reading with its call for fundamental reform, as opposed to a continuation of the status quo. It is this divide that is at the core of the remainder of this chapter, along with an exploration of what it tells us about the interpretation of the CRPD, possible ways forward and about human rights more generally.

THE GOVERNMENTS' VIEW OF INTERNATIONAL HUMAN RIGHTS LAW

At the core of the governments' position is a defensive view of the nature of international human rights law. The essential argument here, reflected in all five government submissions, is that General Comments cannot change the terms of the CRPD as actually agreed by the States Parties; they are advisory only. The strong interpretation is not what States Parties thought they were signing up to and the CRPD Committee has no business or authority to tell states otherwise.

This is convincing up to a point. Certainly, a General Comment cannot change the terms of a Convention: the words are the words. Interpretations of the terms of Conventions can and must develop over time, but the General Comment follows swiftly on from the development of the CRPD, so changed circumstances are not a factor here.

What is much less clear is what was agreed by governments during the negotiation and ratification of the CRPD. This has been discussed by others.[7] Suffice it to say that the strong interpretation of the CRPD was within the field of debate during its negotiation and was fervently supported by the DPOs involved in those negotiations at that time. Some of these negotiators, who had supported the strong reading of Article 12, were elected by the States Parties to the CRPD Committee. It is unsurprising that their views on the meaning of the Article had not changed and if the States Parties did not like it, they should presumably not have elected them.

The presence of the strong reading in the negotiations is reflected in the fact that 13 States either reserved on the question of continuation of substituted decision-making, or issued interpretive declarations stating that they interpreted Article 12 to continue to allow substitute decision-making in some circumstances. The perceived need for such reservations and declarations makes it clear that it was understood that Article 12 might well be given its strong interpretation.[8]

---

[7] See, eg, AM Lawson, 'The United Nations Convention on the Rights of Persons with Disabilities: New Era or False Dawn?' (2007) 34 *Syracuse Journal of International Law and Commerce* 563.

[8] See, eg, the Canadian reservation, which explicitly envisages this reading.

The formal effect of General Comments is a more complex question. The UN Human Rights Committee took the view in its General Comment 33 (2008) that States Parties that have signed up to optional protocols allowing individual complaints to be made to the Committee have thereby 'recognized the competence of the Committee to determine whether there has been a violation of the Covenant or not'. Assuming those decisions will be based, at least in part, on the Committee's General Comments, that suggests that, for those States Parties, the General Comments are very close to binding. That has been controversial among some States Parties and, in their defence, it might be noted that General Comment 33 was, of course, promulgated by that Committee and can, therefore, be no more binding than any other General Comment – leaving the whole business in something of an epistemic loop. The logic of the argument that General Comments are authoritative would further, of course, only apply to States Parties that have signed the optional protocol. According to the UN Treaties Collection website, 92 of the 161 signatories to the CRPD have done so but, rather awkwardly, these include Denmark, France, Germany and Hungary, all of whose submissions protested that General Comments were advisory only.

Lurking at the back of all this is the overarching question of how treaties ought to be interpreted. Clearly, the overarching duty is to interpret the text of the Convention in good faith. Certainly, the subjective interpretation of the States Parties is one approach to the interpretation of the text. If the meaning of the text is 'ambiguous and obscure' or 'manifestly absurd and unreasonable', regard may be had to the *travaux preperatoire* – the records of the negotiation of the Convention. These may give a sense of the intent of the parties to the negotiation, although in the present case they seem more to confuse than elucidate.

However, the subjective interpretation of the parties is only one of the canons of interpretation of the language of international treaties. The words can also be interpreted using a 'teleological' interpretation, allowing the purpose of the treaty to be taken into account as an aid to interpretation. That is arguably a more convincing approach to human rights treaties. Human rights treaties are intended to change the world for the better. There is ample evidence across the negotiation that this was the intent here. To ignore that the whole CRPD project was about creating an impetus for change – itself suggesting a teleological framework – in assessing its terms seems to miss the point.

EXISTING HUMAN RIGHTS

Existing human rights are discussed by submissions both in support of and in opposition to the strong reading of Article 12 and again the different treatments of this theme are telling. Submissions in support of the strong reading emphasise how Article 12 has grown organically from other human rights conventions, most notably the International Convention on Civil and Political Rights (ICCPR) and the Convention on the Elimination of all forms of Discrimination Against

Women (CEDAW). The CRPD is presented as the next stage in an ongoing project of human liberation through human rights.[9] Indeed, some submissions look to international human rights law to provide positive models that the Committee could make more of in pressing for its vision of Article 12 implementation, as in the following quotation from the Latin American Organizations' Alliance:[10]

> We consider it important for the Comment to make express reference to some IHRL constructions which could serve as guidance for States as regards the scope of safeguards in various settings, such as standards regarding due process guarantees and specific documents like the Report of the Special Rapporteur on Torture and Other Cruel, Inhuman or Degrading Treatment, without disregard for the progressive evolution proper of the human rights field.

Submissions opposing the strong interpretation of Article 12 similarly emphasised continuity with existing human rights instruments. Rather than pointing to their transformative potential in the area of disability rights, however, these submissions highlighted the restrictive interpretations accorded to rights in the context of disability.[11] Some of these submissions catalogue previous treaties, human rights conventions and other international instruments that have been interpreted to allow restrictions on the exercise of legal capacity, implicitly or expressly. The submission of the Government of France, for example, takes the view that 'the interpretation of the provisions of Article 12 of the Convention must of necessity be made coherent with other international instruments', going on to cite the Convention on the International Protection of Adults (2000),[12] the United Nations Declaration on the Rights of Mentally Retarded Persons (1971),[13] the United Nations Mental Illness Principles (1991),[14] the Committee of Ministers of the Council of Europe Principles concerning the Legal Protection of Incapable Adults (1999),[15] and the European Convention on Human Rights and Fundamental Freedoms (ECHR)[16] and its jurisprudence, before concluding:

> In these circumstances, the scope that the States Parties have intended to give to the provisions of Article 12 of the Convention are not, as stated by the Committee in the General Comment, the result of a 'misunderstanding', but translate instead into a

---

[9] See, eg, the briefs of the World Network of Users and Survivors of Psychiatry, the Austrian Monitoring Committee, the Australian Human Rights Committee, and Women with Disabilities Australia (WWDA).

[10] This was an alliance of 20 academic, human rights, DPO and advocacy organisations from six South American countries.

[11] See, eg, the briefs of the Essex Autonomy Project, FUTUPEMA, and the Manantial Foundation.

[12] Hague Conference on Private International Law, Convention 35 (13 January 2000).

[13] General Assembly Resolution 2856 (XXVI), 26 UN GAOR Supp (No 29) at 93, UN Doc A/8429 (1971).

[14] Principles for the Protection of Persons with Mental Illness, adopted by General Assembly Resolution 46/119 of 17 December 1991.

[15] Recommendation R(99)4, adopted by the Committee of Ministers 23 February 1999.

[16] Council of Europe, European Convention for the Protection of Human Rights and Fundamental Freedoms, as amended by Protocols Nos. 11 and 14, 4 November 1950, ETS 5.

desire for coherence and compatibility between the provisions of Article 12 and those contained in other relevant international instruments, notably those relating to the legal protection of adults.

These views of international human rights law must be viewed with some circumspection. Certainly, leading commentators on the ICCPR and similar conventions interpret them as allowing differential treatment for people with mental disabilities. While these submissions accurately reflect the standard interpretations of these conventions, the relevant commentators are not generally experts in disability law. The general human rights conventions were not themselves drafted with people with mental disabilities in mind and, generally, PWD had no involvement in their development. It is, therefore, questionable as to how far they should be read as limiting the interpretation of the CRPD. This point is made by the submission from a coalition of Australian organisations – People with Disability Australia, the Australian Centre for Disability Law and the Australian Human Rights Centre – regarding the prevalent interpretations of both the ICCPR and CEDAW:

> The authors of this submission believe that in light of the contemporary understanding of international law provided by the CRPD, the interpretation of legal capacity has moved on significantly from these positions. In doing so the authors concur with the universal recognition of capacity for all people with disability as articulated in Article 12.

A number of submissions refer to European conventions and instruments in this regard, particularly the ECHR. Their general argument is that the long-established legal framework developed within Europe regarding mental capacity is preferable to the one proposed in the draft General Comment.

Certainly, it is appropriate to ask how regional human rights systems will integrate into the system proposed by the draft General Comment and certainly, years of experience among human rights practitioners should not simply be consigned to the scrap heap. Some synergies may certainly exist. The ECHR is, for example, particularly strong on procedural safeguards, matters which also arise in the CRPD, including in Article 12(4).

Lurking at the back of these arguments, however, is a slightly different question: do the previous human rights instruments create a floor or a ceiling? How do international human rights cope with change? The Declaration on the Rights of Mentally Retarded Persons (UN, 1971), cited as authoritative in four submissions, was no doubt a profoundly progressive document for its time; but it is now almost half-a-century old. There must be a tacit acknowledgement of this in even the most conservative submissions, since it is difficult to believe that any of their authors would agree with the attitudes to the detention of 'persons of unsound mind' that prevailed when the text of the ECHR was finalised in 1950. At the same time, the submissions' reliance on status quo ante does raise the question of whether these instruments are a support or a limitation to human rights development. While it is certainly fair to say that we should not throw the baby out with the bathwater, it must also be the case that, at some point, we are allowed to say that the baby has grown up and we need to run a new bath.

A second set of considerations about the use of existing human rights instruments needs to be addressed. The submissions critical of the strong reading tended to view issues surrounding guardianship as a discrete human rights question. The submissions sympathetic to the Committee approach instead, like the draft General Comment itself, view it as the gateway to a full range of human rights. These submissions cited a wide array of human rights affected by the right to legal equality, including rights to community living, family life, free expression, housing, independent living and community integration, health, privacy, life, voting and freedom from poverty. Mentions of these were almost entirely absent from the submissions challenging the strong reading of the Convention.

The one additional right discussed in submissions both for and against the strong reading was the right to be free from violence, exploitation and abuse (Article 16). The differences in the ways this right was discussed further clarify the differences in the way the overall issues surrounding the draft General Comment were perceived. Submissions adopting a holistic approach to human rights in the draft General Comment tended to articulate the right to be free from exploitation and abuse as a right for the person with disability to be taken seriously by the police and a right of access to appropriate policing and similar protective services in the community.[17] Submissions adopting the view that guardianship issues were discrete human rights questions tended instead to view guardianship regimes as key mechanisms to provide protection from violence, exploitation and abuse of people with mental disabilities, often characterised in terms of their extreme vulnerability.[18]

This appears to be a significant divide in the understanding of Article 12 and the role of equality before the law. The submissions broadly supportive of the draft General Comment understand such equality as being integrated into one complex set of issues, rather than a discrete human rights topic. In this sense, the draft General Comment is about access to a wide array of rights, not simply a specific civil and political right.

If that is a coherent approach, the language of the critical submissions starts to appear somewhat threadbare. If the context of the draft General Comment is bound up with access to a full array of rights – political, civil, economic and social – it seems incumbent on the forces critical of the General Comment to address how this is to occur in their alternative conception. Their failure to do so may reflect and respect the traditional lines of human rights

[17] See, eg, the brief of FUB (the Swedish National Association for Persons with Intellectual Disability).
[18] See, eg, the submission of the Law Society of Scotland.

theory, where equality before the law is its own separate right, but it does not seem convincing in building the sort of world that the CRPD is meant to envisage for PWD.

OPINIO JURIS, DOMESTIC LAW AND INERTIA

The inactivity of governments is based not merely on their reading of international human rights law, but also on long-established domestic law and practice. This is reflected, for example, in the following quotation from the submission of the German Government:

> This is particularly relevant when the Committee itself concedes that its understanding of Article 12 diverges from the understanding common to the Contracting States, as evidenced by all the initial reports of State Parties so far. [...] It is, in the view of the German government, also obvious that the provision of an adequate network of support for decision-making will present many difficulties, not least financial, for many States Parties. It seems therefore that the Committee's interpretation is not shared by the State Parties in general; not even by a substantial minority. Germany doubts that it is appropriate to call an understanding of Article 12 common to the States Parties a 'misunderstanding'.

Essentially, the argument here is that nobody is complying with what the draft General Comment seems to say Article 12 means; therefore, the interpretation must be wrong. This returns the argument to the question of what an international human rights treaty is meant to do. If it is understood as codifying good practice that is already occurring in the world, then the submission's point has some force; but for a human rights treaty that must be an unjustifiably limited vision. Many of the human rights treaties are not about buttressing the status quo, but about affecting change; CEDAW,[19] the Convention on the Rights of the Child[20] and the International Convention for the Elimination of all forms of Racial Discrimination[21] are obvious examples.

The argument for a more transformative view is particularly strong regarding the CRPD. The impetus for the CRPD was the widespread acknowledgement that the existing human rights approaches had not provided PWD with the rights the rest of society took for granted.[22] A so-called 'new paradigm' was required and was meant to be embodied in the new convention. If that is the case, the approach of the States Parties, effectively limiting the operation of the treaty to reflect current practice, misses the point. It is at best doubtful how far the

[19] United Nations General Assembly, A/RES/34/180, 18 December 1979.
[20] United Nations General Assembly, A/RES/44/25, 20 November 1989.
[21] United Nations General Assembly, resolution 2106 (XX) of 21 December 1965.
[22] See, eg, D Mackay, 'The United Nations Convention on the Rights of Persons with Disabilities' (2007) 34 *Syracuse Journal of International Law and Commerce* 323.

'new paradigm' has been articulated. One of the telling discoveries is that most submissions that refer to a 'new paradigm' articulate it specifically in terms of a shift from substituted to supported decision-making, not in terms of an over-all conceptual shift regarding the CRPD more broadly (eg, from a 'medical' or 'welfarist' paradigm towards a 'human rights' or 'autonomy' paradigm). Quite what the new paradigm means, how it should be articulated and what effects on the law it may have may, therefore, remain open questions, but it seems reasona-ble to insist that the full range of stakeholders, including the governments of the States Parties, engage with that question, lest the CRPD become, in the words of the Bundesverband Psychiatrie-Erfahrener eV noted above, a 'caricature' whose 'spirit and words will be perverted into the exact opposite'.

CONCLUSION

On the face of it, the evidence is not encouraging that the General Comment and, indeed, Article 12 of the CRPD will usher in significant change. Insofar as the submissions are representative, they suggest that the governments of the States Parties are simply not interested in engaging with the CRPD project or, at least, not the elements of it that concern equality before the law. Instead, there is little evidence that they see a problem that requires correction. In itself, that is a matter of considerable concern for anyone who believes in a human rights approach to mental disability and takes the problems of the current systems seriously. The CRPD is likely to represent the best opportunity for a generation at least to see significant impetus for beneficial change to the lives of PWD. It would be tragic for that chance to be passed up.

There may be opportunities for research here. Governments are not, of course, monolithic and static entities. Presumably, the people on the negotiating teams knew full well, for example, that the strong reading had been very much part of the negotiations; why is this not reflected in the government submissions? There may be a variety of reasons. First, the government submissions occurred nine years after the negotiations of the CRPD. Particularly if the negotiators were people of relative seniority, it may well be that few of them remained in their posts at the time the submissions were written; the collective memory may well have been lost. It may also be the case that the systems of government do not favour a coherent approach: the negotiation team may have been entirely different from the implementation team – indeed, it may not even have been in the same ministry. Ensuring a seamless transition towards implementation may be problematic, when those in charge of implementation do not have the relevant experience of the negotiations and a consequent depth of understand-ing of what the CRPD was designed to achieve. For countries within the EU, there is an additional level of complexity, since the EU members negotiated as a bloc. Whatever the merits of that approach (and there may well have been some), it does suggest that the negotiations of the overall Convention have a second level of complexity within the bloc, a history that may also not be understood by the domestic implementation team. Research exploring how understanding of the CRPD worked its way through government bureaucratic processes might be instructive.

Whatever the reason, however, the absence of fundamental change flowing from the CRPD is likely to mean severe disappointment and frustration for PWD. They – as individuals and through their representative organisations – worked long and hard in the processes of negotiation of the CRPD. Notable by its absence in the government submissions is any suggestion of consultation with the community or civil society organisations of PWD in the development of strategies for implementation of Article 12 (or anything else, for that matter). That is blatantly inconsistent with the terms of the CRPD and, insofar as this represents the practices of the governments in question, PWD and their civil society organisations would be forgiven for questioning the good faith of the governments in the negotiation of the convention and its implementation. They are likely to be, quite properly, extremely frustrated.

If one wished to compound the pessimism, one might note that this is not all that dissimilar from so much of international human rights law. Politicians tend to be great at showing up for the photo ops, but not great at actually implementing significant change, particularly among marginalised groups; this is by no means a problem unique to the communities of PWD. Only five of the 161 States Parties that had ratified the Convention responded to the consultation. For the rest, it is fair to wonder whether international human rights law impacts their list of priorities.

It might, perhaps, be possible to argue that by adopting a less robust reading of the CRPD, greater traction with government policymakers might be possible. This is a doubtful strategy. The problem is not simply the content. The problem is that international human rights law itself has limited teeth and does not seem to figure large in governmental priorities. A similarly small number of governments made submissions to the CEDAW consultation on domestic violence (4): it would seem that this is not something that governments care about much and changing the message is not necessarily going to change that.

If that is the pessimistic vision, is there a more optimistic one? It is unclear who wrote the government submissions. They are mostly short and do not bear the hallmarks of people with a detailed knowledge of disability law and practice. Were they written by relatively low-level apparatchiks in ministries of foreign affairs? If that is the case, does it matter what they think? They are not the people who will be developing domestic policy, so their views are largely irrelevant. In that event, our focus would be better directed to the people in governments who are in charge of policy development and to a broader range of stakeholders who can influence policy. As noted above, the indications from the submissions are that this is a much more mixed bag. Certainly, many policy-makers are a long way from convinced by the strong interpretation of Article 12 represented in the draft (and final) General Comment. A number are contemptuous of the

Committee to the point of being crassly insulting, suggesting little possibility for productive dialogue. Some of the submissions from governmental organisations, however, show considerable awareness of the issues and, anecdotally, some have moved on considerably in the years since the consultation.

While that progress in some countries offers a glimmer of hope for PWD and their advocates, it should not be overstated. The number of submissions overall is very small and it is not obvious that the word is getting out to stakeholders about the problems that need solving, let alone the sorts of reform that are necessary, or the terms of any constructive dialogue that needs to happen.

13

Making Sense of Cheshire West

LUCY SERIES

IKE MANY WESTERN countries, the United Kingdom (UK) began its transition into what the socio-legal historian of mental health law, Clive Unsworth, terms the 'post-carceral era'[1] in the mid-twentieth century.[2] This era is characterised by policies and initiatives that seek to transplant populations of disabled people who might previously have been incarcerated in large institutions (long-stay hospitals, 'colonies', asylums and madhouses) into a mythical space called 'the community'.

The carceral era saw the proliferation of complex legal frameworks regulating institutional incarceration. Their function was to sort people into the locations where they 'correctly' belonged – institution, or community – and to command public legitimacy through regulation of the internal workings of institutions (albeit not conditions the public themselves wished to inhabit). Under carceral-era logic, detention was synonymous with institutionalisation and the community represented freedom. Accordingly, the legal status of populations now residing in the community changed: they were no longer 'detained'.

In the post-carceral era in England and Wales, a policy of 'informality' initially prevailed: the dismantling of complex carceral-era legislation, use of 'formal' detention apparatus only when hospital patients were actively resisting and very limited use of formal legal frameworks governing compulsory treatment, coercion or control in the community.[3] 'Informality' was necessary for the 'normalisation' of those being reintegrated into the community; 'legalism' hampered clinical discretion.[4] Supervisory mechanisms like guardianship existed but were little used and community treatment orders would not be implemented

---

[1] C Unsworth, 'Mental Disorder and the Tutelary Relationship: From Pre- to Post-Carceral Legal Order' (1991) 18 *Journal of Law and Society* 254.

[2] See especially Lord Percy, *Report of the Royal Commission on the Law Relating to Mental Illness and Mental Deficiency* (Cm 169, 1957).

[3] See especially Mental Health Act 1959.

[4] B Hale et al, *Mental Health Law* (London, Sweet and Maxwell, 2017).

until after the turn of the millennium.[5] However, by the late twentieth century 'legalism' was once again in the ascendant, resulting in significant reforms to mental health law[6] and a statutory framework underpinning acts of care and treatment (in hospital or community) in the 'best interests' of persons lacking the 'mental capacity' to give or refuse consent: the Mental Capacity Act 2005 (MCA).

Six decades into the post-carceral era, the identification of community as 'freedom' is increasingly in doubt. There is ample evidence of residential care homes and even settings espousing philosophies of 'independent living', failing to deliver on promises of choice and control, imposing restrictive regimes, coercion and sometimes abuse.[7] A recent report on independent living in Europe concluded that institutional care had not been eradicated but rather 're-imagined': 'we face a proliferation of "hidden" or "mini" institutions'.[8]

Twentieth-century de-carceration has been described as transincarceration,[9] population shifts from one carceral space to another. Ben-Moshe cautions against oversimplifying this claim and calls for a more nuanced account of what gets coded as incarceration, recognising 'a continuum of carceral edifices'.[10] The overlapping properties Goffman identified in 'total institutions' may surface in a variety of ways and places,[11] but this does not mean all carceral spaces are the same.

The question of what should be coded as incarceration has a legal analogue: what should we code as 'detention'? If 'community' is not synonymous with freedom and if some practices in the community are strongly reminiscent of carceral-era institutions, under what circumstances should these be regulated as a form of detention?

---

[5] P Fennell, 'Institutionalising the Community: The Codification of Clinical Authority and the Limits of Rights-Based Approaches' in B McSherry and P Weller (eds), *Rethinking Rights-Based Mental Health Laws* (Oxford, Hart Publishing, 2010).

[6] Mental Health Act 1983.

[7] See, eg, Care Quality Commission, *Learning Disability Services Inspection Programme: National Overview* (2012) Available at: www.cqc.org.uk/sites/default/files/documents/cqc_ld_review_national_overview.pdf; C Drinkwater, 'Supported Living and the Production of Individuals' in S Tremain (ed), *Foucault and the Government of Disability* (Ann Arbor, University of Michigan Press, 2005); R Fyson, B Tarleton and L War, *Support for Living?* (York, Joseph Rowntree Foundation, 2007); Commission for Social Care Inspection and Healthcare Commission, *Joint Investigation into the Provision of Services for People with Learning Disabilities at Cornwall Partnership NHS Trust* (London, Commission for Healthcare Audit and Inspection, 2006). Available at: www.webarchive.nationalarchives.gov.uk/20080609161229/http://www.healthcarecommission.org.uk/_db/_documents/cornwall_investigation_report.pdf.

[8] N Crowther, 'The Right to Live Independently and to be Included in the Community in European States' (2019) European Network of Academic Experts in the Field of Disability. Available at: www.disability-europe.net/theme/independent-living.

[9] See, eg, J Lowman, R Menzies and T Palys, *Transcarceration: Essays in the Sociology of Social Control* (Avebury 1987).

[10] L Ben-Moshe, 'Disabling Incarceration: Connecting Disability to Divergent Confinements in the USA' (2013) 39(3) *Critical Sociology* 385.

[11] E Goffman, *Asylums: Essays on the Social Situation of Mental Patients and Other Inmates* (New York, First Anchor, 1961).

CODING 'DEPRIVATION OF LIBERTY'

In England and Wales, we have been grappling with the meaning of 'deprivation of liberty' in post-carceral care settings for 15 years. Other countries and human rights bodies are also developing regulatory frameworks for detention in community settings.[12] However, there is no internationally agreed definition of 'deprivation of liberty'.[13]

The question arose in England and Wales following the ruling of the European Court of Human Rights (ECtHR) in *HL v UK*.[14] An autistic man 'informally' admitted to Bournewood Hospital in his 'best interests' was found to have been unlawfully detained, notwithstanding that (in the view of the treating clinicians) he was not 'objecting' to his admission and had not attempted to leave. The MCA was subsequently amended to include 'deprivation of liberty safeguards' (DoLS), which apply in hospitals and care homes.[15] The DoLS require, *inter alia*, independent assessments of a person's mental capacity and best interests, representation and independent advocacy and access to the Court of Protection to review deprivation of liberty authorisations. The DoLS have been heavily (and justly) criticised[16] and will soon be replaced by their successor – the Liberty Protection Safeguards.[17] However, they provided a basic framework for scrutinising and challenging restrictive practices that hitherto was largely absent in residential community settings.

The *Bournewood* case triggered 10 long years of litigation on the meaning of 'deprivation of liberty', culminating in the UK Supreme Court decision in

---

[12] See, eg, W Boente, 'Some Continental European Perspectives on Safeguards in the Case of Deprivation of Liberty in Health and Social Care Settings' (2017) 23 *International Journal of Mental Health and Capacity Law* www.dx.doi.org/10.19164/ijmhcl.v2017i23.632; E Fritze, J Chesterman and P Grano, *Designing a Deprivation of Liberty Authorisation and Regulation Framework* (Melbourne, Office of the Public Advocate, Victoria, Australia, 2017); Victorian Law Reform Commission (VLRC), *Guardianship Final Report Background Paper: Legislative Schemes Regulating Deprivation of Liberty in Residential Care Settings* (Melbourne, VLRC, 2012); UNHRC, *Report of the Special Rapporteur on the Rights of Persons with Disabilities, Catalina Devandas Aguilar* (2019) A/HRC/40/54. See also: Complaints to the CRPD Committee *DR v Australia* (14/2003) 19 May 2017, CRPD/C/17/D/14/2013 and Jurisprudence of the European Court of Human Rights, eg *Stanev v Bulgaria* [2012] ECHR 46; *DD v Lithuania* [2012] ECHR 254. For detention monitoring, see reports from National Preventive Mechanisms to the UN Subcommittee on the Prevention of Torture from New Zealand, Norway, Austria, Croatia, Serbia, France (2012), The Netherlands, Poland and Slovenia. Available at: www.ohchr.org/EN/HRBodies/OPCAT/Pages/Annualreportsreceivedfrom NPM.aspx.

[13] E Flynn, M Pinilla-Rocancio and M Gómez-Carrillo de Castro, 'Disability-Specific Forms of Deprivation of Liberty' (Centre for Disability Law and Policy and Institute for Lifecourse and Society, NUI Galway, 2019). Available at: www.nuigalway.ie/media/centrefordisabilitylawandpolicy/files/DoL-Report-Final.pdfs.

[14] *HL v UK* [2004] ECHR 720.

[15] MCA Schedule A1, inserted via the Mental Health Act 2007.

[16] House of Lords Select Committee on the Mental Capacity Act 2005, 'Mental Capacity Act 2005: Post-Legislative Scrutiny' (HL Paper 139); Law Commission, Mental Capacity and Deprivation of Liberty (Law Com No 372, 2017).

[17] New Schedule AA1, inserted into the MCA via the Mental Capacity (Amendment) Act 2019.

P v Cheshire West and Chester Council and another; P and Q v Surrey County Council[18] in 2014. The litigation concerned the ambit of Article 5 of the European Convention on Human Rights (ECHR), the right to liberty and security of the person. ECtHR jurisprudence identifies three limbs of deprivation of liberty: an 'objective' element of confinement in a 'certain limited space' for a non-negligible length of time; a 'subjective element' – the absence of valid consent to that confinement; and imputability to the state.[19] The litigation leading up to *Cheshire West* concerned only the 'objective element'; since 'mental capacity' was considered a necessary pre-requisite of valid consent it was taken to be missing in these cases.[20]

Several matters were at stake. The independent check required by Article 5 was increasingly attractive as confidence in other forms of care regulation collapsed.[21] DoLS secured access to essential tools such as legal aid and advocacy to challenge care and treatment decisions under the MCA.[22] A more expansive definition of deprivation of liberty captured growing recognition that restrictive practices occur widely in the community. However, there was (and is)[23] resistance to the idea that 'benevolently' intentioned care, provided in the community, could amount to a deprivation of liberty. It threatens the post-carceral ideology of community as freedom.

CHESHIRE WEST: THE FACTS

The Supreme Court heard two conjoined cases. The first concerned two sisters with intellectual disabilities, MIG (aged 18) and MEG (aged 17).[24] They were placed in foster care as teenagers because of a family background of sexual abuse and violence. MIG remained living with her foster mother. However, the placement with MEG's foster carer broke down and she was moved to 'an NHS [National Health Service] facility, not a care home, for learning disabled adolescents with complex needs'.[25]

---

[18] *P v Cheshire West and Chester Council and another; P and Q v Surrey County Council* [2014] UKSC 19.

[19] *Storck v Germany* [2005] ECHR 406, at 74, 89.

[20] *Cheshire West* (UKSC) 55, 68.

[21] See especially R Francis, Report of the Mid Staffordshire NHS Foundation Trust Public Inquiry (HC 947, 2012).

[22] L Series, P Fennell and J Doughty, 'Welfare Cases in the Court of Protection: A Statistical Overview' (Cardiff, Cardiff University, 2017). Available at: www.orca.cf.ac.uk/id/eprint/118054.

[23] E Flynn and M Gomez-Carrillo, 'Good Practices to Promote the Right to Liberty of Persons with Disabilities' (Galway, Centre for Disability Law and Policy and Institute for Lifecourse and Society, NUI Galway, 2019). Available at: www.nuigalway.ie/media/centrefordisabilitylawandpolicy/files/Good-practices-final-DoL.pdf.

[24] *Surrey County Council v MEG & MIG v Anor* [2010] EWHC 785 (Fam) (henceforth: *MIG and MEG* (HC)); *P & Q v Surrey County Council* [2011] EWCA Civ 190 (henceforth: *P & Q* (CoA)).

[25] *Cheshire West* (UKSC) 14.

The second case concerned a 38-year-old man with cerebral palsy and Down syndrome referred to as 'P'.[26] P lived with his mother until he was 37, when her health deteriorated. The council concluded she could no longer care for him and sought orders from the Court of Protection to move him into 'Z House'. Z House was not a care home, it was described as 'a spacious bungalow' with a 'pleasant atmosphere' near his family home and shared with two other residents.[27]

It is likely that Z House was 'supported living' accommodation. Under this service model, the resident is a tenant and receives 'domiciliary care'. As nominally private homes, these services are regulated differently to residential care[28] and can have more generous funding and charging arrangements. The philosophy behind supported living is avowedly post-carceral: 'every person has the right to lead their own life – determine how they live, with whom they live, who provides them with help and support and how they live their lives'.[29] It mirrors the concept of 'independent living' encoded in Article 19 of the UN Convention on the Rights of Persons with Disabilities (CRPD).[30] However, early pioneers of supported living later lamented that: 'Too much of what goes today as Supported Living is relabelled Residential Care.'[31] Investors attracted to new revenue streams built 'clusters' of 'units', separate from mainstream housing, but found that financial viability competes with meaningful choice and control.[32] Underlying supported living was a more fundamental problem: the reality was that often people were not making many critical decisions for themselves, others were making them on their behalf.[33] Substitute decision-making is hard to square with philosophies of supported living.

MIG, MEG and P all engaged in regular activities that took them outside their accommodation. P attended a day centre, hydrotherapy, saw his mother regularly and went out (with one-to-one support) for pub lunches, to parks and garden centres. MIG and MEG attended college during the week and were

---

[26] *Cheshire West and Chester Council v P & Anor* [2011] EWHC 1330 (Fam) (henceforth: *Cheshire West* (HC)); *Cheshire West and Chester Council v P* [2011] EWCA Civ 1257 (henceforth: *Cheshire West* (CoA)).

[27] *Cheshire West* (UKSC) 17.

[28] Care Quality Commission, 'A New System of Registration. Supported Living Schemes' (no date). Available at: www.cqc.org.uk/file/4861.

[29] P Kinsella, 'Supported Living: The Changing Paradigm – from Control to Freedom' (2001). Available at: www.family-advocacy.com/assets/Uploads/Downloadables/11288-Supported-Living-The-Changing-Paradigm.pdf.

[30] United Nations, Convention on the Rights of Persons with Disabilities (adopted 13 December 2006, entered into force 3 May 2008) 2515 UNTS 3 (CRPD).

[31] P Kinsella, 'Supported Living – Fact or Fiction?' (2008). No longer available online; copy archived by author.

[32] W Laing, *Homecare and Supported Living: UK Market Report* (Laing & Buisson, 2018); Voluntary Organisations' Disability Group and Anthony Collins Solicitors, 'When is a Care Home not a Care Home?' (2011). Available at: www.vodg.org.uk/wp-content/uploads/2011-VODG-When-is-a-care-home-not-a-care-home-briefing.pdf.

[33] J Mansell, 'The "Implementation Gap" in Supported Accommodation for People with Intellectual Disabilities' in T Clement and C Bigby (eds), *Group Homes for People with Intellectual Disabilities* (London, Jessica Kingsley, 2009).

described as having fairly active social lives. MIG also went on family holidays with her foster carer. Their lives did not fit the template of a person vanishing into a locked institution.

Yet, the reality was that each was subject to varying degrees of supervision and control by their caregivers. The judgments – and perhaps the reality – blur the line between 'support' and control exercised by caregivers. MIG was described as 'largely dependent on others', unable to 'go out on her own' and having 'no sense of safety and in particular no awareness of road safety'.[34] When not at the day centre she was 'under the control' of her foster mother or the council.[35] However, MIG was not restrained or locked in. If she tried to leave the house on her own 'she would be restrained for her own immediate safety', but she had never tried to leave or expressed any wish to do so.[36]

MEG and P's situations involved actual, rather than potential, restraint. Both received one-to-one or sometimes higher ratios of staff 'support' during their waking hours. MEG was described as having 'challenging behaviour' with 'outbursts' directed towards other residents, managed with restraint.[37] This was said to be 'stabilising' thanks to 'behavioural management techniques' and the administration of risperidone to control her 'anxiety'.[38] Despite growing concern about overmedication and restraint of people with intellectual disabilities,[39] neither the specific nature of the restraint nor the effects of risperidone on MEG were explored in detail in court.[40]

The local authority had a 'no restraint' policy and staff at Z House had no restraint training, yet P's arrangements involved a considerable degree of physical intervention. Like MEG, P was described as presenting 'challenging behaviour': stripping off his clothes, throwing things, self-harming, smearing faeces and occasionally 'pulling, pinching, grabbing and scratching' others. He also had continence problems. When living with his mother he had been 'allowed' to be naked, but in Z House he wore continence pads, which he would tear and sometimes put into his mouth. This choking risk had required hospital admissions.[41] Staff tried to reduce risk factors, for example through regular bathroom visits reducing the need for pads, verbal redirection and positive reinforcement, but 'sometimes had to resort to physical intervention' when P had 'stored' pieces of a pad or faecal material in his mouth. They would insert their fingers into his mouth to check for and remove material, hold P's hand to clean

---

[34] *MIG and MEG* (HC), 208, 210.
[35] Ibid, 211.
[36] Ibid, 210.
[37] Ibid, 215.
[38] Ibid, 215–16.
[39] See, eg, Care Quality Commission, 'Interim Report: Review of Restraint, Prolonged Seclusion and Segregation for People with a Mental Health Problem, a Learning Disability and or Autism' (2019). Available at: www.cqc.org.uk/publications/themed-work/interim-report-review-restraint-prolonged-seclusion-segregation-people.
[40] *MIG and MEG* (HC), 216.
[41] *Cheshire West* (HC) 8, 13.

it and change his pad and clothes. P would 'attempt to fight against staff during these interventions'.[42] A new approach of P wearing a 'bodysuit' prevented access to the pads.

Despite graphic descriptions of 'challenging behaviour' and caregivers' benevolent intentions, descriptions of claimants' subjective experiences of their living arrangements are scant and sometimes contradictory. None of the three chose their place of residence. MIG and MEG were described as not wishing to leave their homes, not wishing to live with their mother and having no 'capacity to conceptualise any alternative unfamiliar environment'.[43] Yet only MIG was described as having positive feelings about her situation: 'She does not wish to leave. She wants to stay with JW. She loves JW and regards JW as her "Mummy".'[44] At trial, MEG was described as wanting 'to remain living in her present environment',[45] but the Supreme Court judgment describes her as mourning the loss of the relationship with her foster carer and wishing she was still living with her.[46] The discrepancy between these accounts is not explored. Her 'outbursts' towards other residents suggest she may not have been happy living with them. The Court of Appeal acknowledged that 'antipsychotic drugs and other tranquillizers' might suppress potential objections, but nowhere analysed whether this was the case for MEG.[47]

We glean even less information about P's wishes and feelings from the judgments. An independent social worker flagged the need for a specialist communication profile and suggested his 'challenging behaviour' could be a method of communication.[48] He is described as 'sociable' with other residents and enjoying 'going out into the community'.[49] No force, threats or subterfuge were involved in his move into Z House.

WERE MIG, MEG OR P DEPRIVED OF LIBERTY?

The cases proceeded on separate but intersecting tracks through trial and appeals. Each of the claimants was represented by a litigation friend, the Official Solicitor, who argued they were deprived of their liberty.

Mrs Justice Parker found MIG and MEG had not been deprived of their liberty. Their situations were, she concluded, very far from the 'paradigm' of imprisonment.[50] She had not met MIG and MEG but concluded their 'wishes

---

[42] Ibid, 9.
[43] *MIG and MEG* (HC), 225.
[44] Ibid, 209.
[45] Ibid, 224.
[46] *Cheshire West* (UKSC), 14.
[47] *MIG and MEG* (CoA) 26.
[48] *Cheshire West* (HC) 7, 11.
[49] Ibid, 7, 11, 54.
[50] *MIG and MEG* (HC) 235.

and feelings are manifest and clearly expressed. They plainly have no subjective sense of confinement'. She suggested that: 'In a non-legal sense they have the capacity to consent to their placements.' She had not visited their placements but concluded no visitor 'would gain any sense of confinement or detention'.[51] Parker J placed considerable emphasis on the purpose (safety) and intentions (benevolent) of MIG and MEG's caregivers. She held that 'each lacks freedom and autonomy dictated by their own disability, rather than because it is imposed on them by their carers'.[52] The Official Solicitor appealed. In the Court of Appeal, Lord Justice Wilson concluded that any benevolent purpose was irrelevant to the objective analysis of whether a person was deprived of their liberty (but would be relevant to whether it was justified).[53] Wilson LJ identified two dimensions for the assessment of whether a person is 'objectively' deprived of their liberty: the 'relative normality' of their situation and whether or not they 'object'.[54] There was a 'wide spectrum' of how 'normal' a person's living arrangements could be. At one end was 'the most normal life possible' – a person living with their natural family; 'not much less normal' was life with a foster carer. At the other end of the spectrum were institutions designed for compulsory detention, like Bournewood Hospital, where HL was detained, with small children's homes or nursing homes falling in between.[55] The enquiry into 'normality' also considered activities and occupations such as attending college or a day centre and outside social contact.[56] However, Wilson LJ's enquiry into 'relative normality' did not consider other trappings of institutional life central to contemporary de-institutionalisation campaigns: restraint, regimes of supervision and control, choice over where and with whom one lives and from whom one receives support.

The second limb, objections, was relevant to the objective element of deprivation of liberty because it could lead to 'conflict', arguments, the stress of objections overruled, perhaps even 'tussles', restraint and forcible returns to confinement. Meanwhile, the absence of objections 'generates an absence of conflict and thus a peaceful life', pointing away from a deprivation of liberty.[57] Sedating or tranquillizing medication potentially suppressed objections and was thereby relevant to the enquiry.[58]

It was plain that MIG's situation did not satisfy either limb of this analysis but puzzling that MEG's situation was held not to either. MEG's life in an 'NHS facility' did involve 'tussles', with some suggestion of objections overruled or potentially suppressed via medication.

[51] Ibid, 234.
[52] Ibid, 233.
[53] *MIG and MEG* (CoA) 27.
[54] Ibid, 25, 28.
[55] Ibid, 28.
[56] Ibid, 29.
[57] Ibid, 25.
[58] Ibid, 26, 37.

P's case subsequently came to trial. Mr Justice Baker applied Wilson LJ's framework for 'relative normality'. He observed that the council and Z House 'have taken very great care to ensure that P's life is as normal as possible',[59] he did not live in accommodation designed for compulsory detention, had regular contact with his family, enjoyed a 'good social life' and went on outings. However, Baker J concluded that P was deprived of his liberty because

> his life is completely under the control of members of staff at Z House. He cannot go anywhere or do anything without their support and assistance. More specifically, his occasionally aggressive behaviour and his worrying habit of touching and eating his continence pads, require a range of measures, including at times physical restraint and, when necessary, the intrusive procedure of inserting fingers into his mouth whilst he is being restrained.[60]

The council appealed. On appeal, Lord Justice Munby revisited Wilson LJ's analysis of 'relative normality'. Baker J had applied the wrong test, he concluded, by comparing P's life to 'the life of the able-bodied man or woman on the Clapham omnibus'.[61] The correct comparator for the analysis of 'relative normality' was instead 'the kind of lives that people like X would normally expect to lead', an adult or child of similar age, similar 'capabilities' and affected by the same condition.[62] Applying this analysis, Munby LJ ruled that P was not deprived of his liberty. Further, Munby LJ resurrected Parker J's consideration of benevolent reasons for the restrictions as a factor pointing away from an objective deprivation of liberty.

Matters were, however, 'very different' if a person 'has somewhere else to go and wants to live there' but is prevented from doing so 'by a coercive exercise of public authority'.[63] This catered to situations like HL or, like Steven Neary – a man who was unlawfully deprived of his liberty in a 'positive behaviour unit', whom the court ruled could return to live in his own home with support from his father and a team of personal assistants.[64]

On Munby LJ's analysis, a person with 'nowhere else to go' would need to demonstrate that their life was abnormally more restrictive than others with a similar disability to qualify for detention safeguards. In *C v Blackburn and Darwen Borough Council*,[65] this approach meant that even a man who had broken down the door of a care home trying to escape was not deprived of his liberty because he had nowhere else to go. Meanwhile, in *CC v KK and STCC*,[66] a woman in a care home who wished to return to her own home was found not to be deprived of her liberty because although she was 'objecting' this no longer

---

[59] *Cheshire West* (HC), 58.
[60] Ibid, 59.
[61] *Cheshire West* (CoA) 87.
[62] Ibid, 97.
[63] Ibid, 58.
[64] *London Borough of Hillingdon v Neary* [2011] EWHC 1377 (COP).
[65] *C v Blackburn and Darwen Borough Council* [2011] EWHC 3321 (COP).
[66] *CC v KK* [2012] EWHC 2136 (COP).

led to a 'significant degree of conflict' and the care home was far removed from 'the type of institution associated with a deprivation of liberty' in Wilson LJ's spectrum.[67] She was not deprived of her liberty.

As commentators observed, the comparator approach rests on a medical model of disability that locates restrictions on liberty within the person, not their environment.[68] It imposed a discriminatory hurdle for disabled people to claim the protection of Article 5 ECHR. Together with consideration of the 'reasons' for any restrictions, it was hard to see how a person could both be deprived of their liberty and for it to be lawful under the DoLS.[69] The number of DoLS applications, already lower than government projections, fell for the first time.[70] The Official Solicitor appealed.

Seven justices heard the conjoined appeals to the Supreme Court. Lady Hale delivered the leading judgment. She prefaced her analysis by observing that if a person were not found to be deprived of their liberty then 'no independent check' is made on whether their care arrangements were in their best interests.[71] Munby LJ's 'comparator' approach was rejected by all seven justices, Lady Hale observing that 'the whole point about human rights is their universal character' and citing the UN CRPD.[72] Applying what she took to be the *ratio* in *HL* and subsequent cases before the ECtHR,[73] Lady Hale held that the 'acid test' of deprivation of liberty is whether a person is subject to continuous supervision and control and not free to leave.[74] That they are not objecting, that the arrangements are the least restrictive possible, that their living arrangements are as 'comfortable' or their life as 'enjoyable' as it could be, is irrelevant to the objective question of whether they are deprived of their liberty: 'A gilded cage is still a cage.'[75]

Three justices concurred with Lady Hale's analysis and three dissented; thus, by a slim majority, the 'acid test' remains the primary test of whether a person is deprived of their liberty by their care arrangements under UK law. Lords Carnwath and Hodge were concerned that this went further than the European Court of Human Rights: there was no precedent for a 'universal test',

[67] Ibid 99, 101.
[68] B Clough, '"People Like That": Realising the Social Model in Mental Capacity Jurisprudence' (2015) 23 *Medical Law Review* 1, 53.
[69] B Troke, 'The Death of Deprivation of Liberty Safeguards?' (2012) 3 *Social Care and Neurodisability* 2, 56.
[70] The judgment was handed down on 9 November 2011. See falling quarterly rates of DoLS applications after this point in Table 2 of Health and Social Care Information Centre, 'Mental Capacity Act 2005, Deprivation of Liberty Safeguards Assessments, England – 2012–13, Annual Report' (2013) 11. Available at: www.digital.nhs.uk/data-and-information/publications/statistical/mental-capacity-act-2005-deprivation-of-liberty-safeguards-assessments/mental-capacity-act-2005-deprivation-of-liberty-safeguards-assessments-england-2012-13-annual-report.
[71] *Cheshire West* (UKSC) 1.
[72] Ibid, 36.
[73] *Stanev v Bulgaria; DD v Lithuania; Kędzior v Poland* [2012] ECHR 1809; *Mihailovs v Latvia* [2013] ECHR 65.
[74] *Cheshire West* (UKSC) 48–49.
[75] Ibid 46.

however attractive.[76] They argued that 'nobody using ordinary language would describe people living happily in a domestic setting as being deprived of their liberty'.[77] They were concerned that such a test could now apply to HL, living at home with the carers who had fought to liberate him from Bournewood Hospital.[78]

DEPRIVATION OF LIBERTY IN THE POST-CARCERAL ERA

The *Cheshire West* 'acid test' shatters the institution/community binary underpinning both carceral and post-carceral-era ideologies of care, identifying that elements of supervision, control and loss of freedom exist outside of traditional institutions. This resonates with insights from critical disability studies.[79] A similar working model of deprivation of liberty was recently employed in a major study of disability-related detention.[80] The 'acid test' is attractive for those seeking to call out restrictive practices and coercion wherever they appear and challenge post-carceral mythology.

Whilst noting these attractions – and confirming that I too initially greeted the Supreme Court's judgment with enthusiasm – I must sound a note of caution on the *Cheshire West* model. The Supreme Court was, undoubtedly, right to reject analyses of deprivation of liberty that infantilised and discriminated against disabled people, which found that 'benevolent' purpose rendered coercion free of scrutiny, that attributed loss of autonomy to impairment, not environment, that was based on a fantasy life of freedom in the home and community. However, the consequences of *Cheshire West* have been very significant and not all are necessarily conducive to addressing legitimate concerns about carceral practices in post-carceral settings.

Following *Cheshire West*, an estimated 300,000 people are considered deprived of their liberty in connection with their care arrangements in England and Wales, including one in every 16 people aged over 85.[81] This exceeds the number of psychiatric detentions at the end of the carceral era. To cope with this increase in volume, the DoLS were replaced with more flexible but ultimately much weaker safeguards against arbitrary detention:[82] the trade-off with volume may be decreased protection of rights.

---

[76] Ibid 94.

[77] Ibid 99, see also Lord Clarke 108.

[78] Ibid 99. NB: As an adult, HL would not have 'foster parents'. His living arrangements resemble 'shared lives' schemes in which adults live in private homes with families who provide care and support.

[79] L Ben-Moshe, C Chapman and AC Carey (eds), *Disability Incarcerated: Imprisonment and Disability in the United States and America* (New York, Palgrave Macmillan, 2014).

[80] Pinilla-Rocancio Flynn, and Gómez-Carrillo de Castro, 'Disability-Specific Forms of Deprivation of Liberty' (2019).

[81] Department of Health and Social Care, 'Impact Assessment: Mental Capacity (Amendment) Bill' (2019). Available at: www.services.parliament.uk/Bills/2017-19/mentalcapacityamendment/documents.html.

[82] Mental Capacity (Amendment) Act 2019.

Cheshire West did not contest the legitimacy of the kinds of 'supervision and control' exercised over disabled people in post-carceral settings, it merely held that they must be regulated using the machinery of Article 5 ECHR. Neil Allen – an academic and barrister for Cheshire West and Chester Council in the litigation – argues that there is a risk that 'the law ends up cementing the care relationship to a prison paradigm'.[83]

One might respond that *Cheshire West* should act as a spur to *eradicate* such practices. The 'independent check' cited by Lady Hale may indeed address some restrictive practices on a case-by-case basis; however, this will operate within the menu of options available within an austerity-stricken and marketised landscape of adult social care. It will not make better options available. As Foucauldian scholars have observed, regulation can have paradoxical effects: 'by purporting to exercise its supervisory jurisdiction only over the more egregious aberrations, abuses and excesses of disciplinary power, law confirms the basic claim at the heart of disciplinary power.'[84]

The *Cheshire West* case is hard to reconcile to the CRPD. Doubtless, all disability human rights advocates agree that the definition of deprivation of liberty must not discriminate against disabled people. Article 14 CRPD confirms disabled people are entitled to equal due process guarantees, with reasonable accommodation, yet it also states that 'the existence of a disability shall in no case justify a deprivation of liberty'.[85] If indeed MIG, MEG and P are deprived of their liberty, we must ask whether there is any lawful justification for it under the CRPD.

In considering this question, we must take considerable care to ask what is being justified here. Is it measures to prevent, for example, MIG from wandering in front of road traffic or P from choking on an incontinence pad? I struggle to imagine any human rights advocate arguing that the CRPD prevents this. Yet we must be careful to distinguish interventions to prevent real, imminent and serious risks from their wider living arrangements. We might, for example, agree that interventions to prevent MEG attacking others could be justified (as they would be for any non-disabled person), but look at what is triggering this behaviour and explore other facets of her living arrangements, including behaviourism-inspired regimes and use of sedating medication. We might agree that P should not be left to choke but want to determine how he feels about the rest of his living arrangements.

One of the underlying problems with the 'acid test' is that it (deliberately) excludes consideration of the person's subjective experiences. This has the result of collapsing together the situation of someone like MIG, who appears to be positively happy with her living arrangements and someone like MEG, where there are reasonable grounds to suspect she may not be. Following *Cheshire West,*

---

[83] N Allen, 'The (Not So) Great Confinement' (2015) 5 *Elder Law Journal* 1, 45, 46.
[84] B Golder and P Fitzpatrick, *Foucault's Law* (London, Routledge-Cavendish, 2009) 66.
[85] Above fn 30.

the council that had unlawfully detained Steven Neary applied to the Court of Protection for authorisation of deprivation of liberty in his own home.[86] The processes to 'authorise' this was reportedly distressing for Neary. The council's assessors ultimately concluded that he was happy where he was (nonetheless, still detained).[87] The point is not only that in some cases the authorisation process itself may carry a cost for the person, but that by continuing to label a person as 'detained' when they are expressing a positive desire to live as they are, including the support they receive, this invalidates the person's own expressed wishes. It reinforces the very binary model of 'mental capacity' that the CRPD is said to repudiate.[88]

One option, therefore, is to deepen our consideration of the subjective element of deprivation of liberty and expand our horizons of what constitutes a valid consent to any element of 'supervision and control'. This was recently proposed by English barrister and academic Alex Ruck Keene[89] and endorsed by the Parliamentary Joint Committee on Human Rights.[90] An amendment to the MCA was tabled, proposing that a person should be considered to have given a 'valid consent' to a potential deprivation of liberty if they are 'capable of express-ing their wishes and feelings (verbally or otherwise)' they had expressed 'their persistent contentment' with the arrangements, there was 'no coercion involved' in their implementation and this was confirmed in writing by two profession-als (one independent of the person's care).[91] Despite potentially dramatically reducing the administrative difficulties posed by *Cheshire West*, this approach was rejected by the government on the basis that it conflicted with the position under the ECHR.[92] The idea that a 'mentally incapable' person could give a valid consent was unthinkable.

There are, undoubtedly, risks to the 'valid consent' approach. The judiciary in the *Cheshire West* litigation was content to describe even MEG as validly consenting in a 'non-legal sense' and as 'happy' in her accommodation, despite strong pointers to the contrary.[93] There is a risk that compliance by those who do not use conventional methods of communication, who are sedated, scared or institutionalised, may be constructed as 'consent'. There is equally a risk that

---

[86] Joint Committee on Human Rights, The Right to Freedom and Safety: Reform of the Depriva-tion of Liberty Safeguards (HC 890, HL paper 161, 2018) [38].

[87] M Neary, 'Silly DoLS Talking' *Love, Belief and Balls* (2018). Available at: www.markneary1dot-com1.wordpress.com/2018/06/09/silly-dols-talking/.

[88] CRPD Committee, 'General Comment No 1 (2014) Article 12: Equal Recognition Before the Law' (2014) UN Doc CRPD/C/GC/1, 2014.

[89] A Ruck Keene, 'Discussion Paper: Deprivation of Liberty, *Cheshire West* and the CRPD' (39 Essex Chambers, 2017). Available at: www.39essex.com/wp-content/uploads/2017/12/Valid-Consent-Discussion-Paper-December-2017.docx.pdf.

[90] Joint Committee on Human Rights, Legislative Scrutiny: Mental Capacity (Amendment) Bill (HC 1662 HL 208, 2018).

[91] Ibid, 12–13.

[92] HL Deb, 21 November 2018 vol 794 col 252 (Lord O'Shaughnessy).

[93] *MIG and MEG (HC)*, 24; *P & Q* (CoA) 24; *Cheshire West* (UKSC) 99, 108.

potential pointers that a person is unhappy may be pathologised and dismissed as 'challenging behaviour'. But surely the appropriate response is to engage with these risks head on through directly confronting these tropes and developing a better jurisprudential and cultural engagement with the subjective experiences of people with mental disabilities?

Based on the reported facts, the 'valid consent' approach would appear to identify MIG and Steven Neary as not detained, because they are expressing positive contentment (as opposed to not objecting) to their living arrangements and no direct coercion is used. MEG and P would still be considered detained, owing to uncertainty over their feelings and the use of coercion. This leaves us with the hard question of whether such measures can ever be justified under the CRPD, a question lying well beyond the scope of this chapter. The difficulty is that we are still trying to fit the binary machinery of detention regulation to a complex matrix of practices, which include intervention to protect against real, immediate and serious risks (eg, choking) but extend well beyond this. What appears to be required is an entirely new regulatory structure for the post-carceral age. It may well be that the CRPD is better placed to assist in its development than older paradigms still rooted in carceral ideology, but we have not found it yet.

14

The Production of 'Dependent Individuals' Within the Application of Spanish Law 39/2006 on Personal Autonomy and Dependent Care in Andalusia, Basque Country and Madrid

MELANIA MOSCOSO PÉREZ AND R LUCAS PLATERO

URING THE FIRST term of socialist president José Luis Rodríguez Zapatero (2004–07), many laws regarding the social rights of minority citizens were passed in Spain, taking the long-term demands of social movements into the mainstream political and policymaking agenda.[1] Some of these new laws referred State attention to disenfranchised groups, encompassing gender violence, gender equality, same-sex marriage, immigration regulation, support provisions for excluded citizens and sign language recognition, among others.[2] Subsequently, on 14 December 2006, the Spanish Congress approved the Ley de Promoción de la Autonomía Personal y Atención a las personas en situación de Depedencia (Law 39/2006 on Personal Autonomy and Dependent Care), providing services for the elderly and people with disabilities.[3]

Presented as an historical event that would 'expand the pillars of the Spanish Welfare State' Law 39/2006 added social care to the existing service provision

---

[1] C Kerman, 'Matrimonio Homosexual y Ciudadanía' (2005) *Claves de la Razón Práctica* 154.

[2] RL Platero, 'Outstanding Challenges in a Post-Equality Era: The Same-Sex Marriage and Gender Identity Laws in Spain' (2008) 21(1) *International Journal of Iberian Studies* 41–49.

[3] Spanish Government, *39/2006 Act on Personal Autonomy and Assistance of People with Dependency* OSG [BOE, Boletín Oficial del Estado] 299 14 December 2006.

of pensions, health care and education (known as the 'three pillars of the Welfare State').[4] Law 39/2006 is commonly known as the *ley de dependencia* ('dependence law') creating a new group of citizens labelled 'dependent people' – adults whose disabilities have been certified by the State, as well as the elderly (65 years and older).

Law 39/2006 was intended to fulfil Spain's commitments following its ratification of the Convention on the Rights of Persons with Disabilities (CRPD).[5] In order to further its commitment, the Spanish government passed Law 26/2011, which includes actions against intersectional discrimination, fosters local participation of people with disabilities (PWD), and describes a system of juridical protection which includes arbitration and intends to expand free legal assistance.

The implementation of Law 39/2006 has been problematic for several reasons. Firstly, Spain is a quasi-federal State, but the implementation of Law 39/2006 took place on a regional level, with disparate results which provided very different protection to citizens with dependency needs.[6] Secondly, the implementation of the law requires State funding, which has been severely affected by austerity cuts. Thirdly, even though Law 39/2006 was devised as an element to fulfil the requirements of the CRPD, its wording raises questions about the law's commitment to the social model of disability.[7] Fourthly, the law refers to care as a genderless action that nevertheless takes place within the family context.

On 2 September 2011, the Partido Popular, then in office, with the supporting votes of the other two major parties in Parliament, approved an amendment of Article 135 of the Spanish Constitution.[8] This restricts the capacity of the Spanish Government to issue public debt and to contract credit to 'the maximum structural deficit permitted for the State and for the Regional Governments in relation to the gross domestic product thereof' by the European Union.[9] This modification of the Constitution further aggravated inequalities among regions and we want to show how it has been put into practice in Madrid, Andalucía and

---

[4] IMSERSO, *Libro Blanco de Atención a las Personas en Situación de Dependencia en España* (Madrid, Ministerio de Trabajo y Asuntos Sociales, 2004).

[5] UN General Assembly, *Convention on the Rights of Persons with Disabilities*, 24 January 2007, A/RES/61/106.

[6] V Marbán-Gallego, 'Actores Sociales y Desarrollo de la Ley de Dependencia en España' (2012) 70(2) *Revista Internacional de Sociología* 375.

[7] F Guzmán-Castillo, M Moscoso-Pérez and M Toboso-Martín, 'Por Qué la Ley de Dependencia no Constituye un Instrumento para la Promoción de la Autonomía Personal' (2010) 48 *Zerbitzuan: Gizarte Zerbitzuetarako Aldizkaria. Revista de Servicios Sociales* 47.

[8] Spanish Constitution Art 135. Available at: www.lamoncloa.gob.es/lang/en/espana/leyfundamental/Paginas/titulo_septimo.aspx.

[9] Anon, 'El artículo 135 de la Constitución, Antes y Después de la Reforma de 2011' (2014) *El País*. Available at: www.elpais.com/politica/2014/11/24/actualidad/1416849910_452980.html.

the Basque Country. We have chosen these three regions because they show the heterogeneous reality of a quasi-federal Spain. The Basque Country pioneered an independent living programme (ILP) before Law 39/2006 came into force and it is by far the best developed programme in the country; Madrid is the administrative capital of the country, where the application of the law can be considered as average. Lastly, in the region of Andalucía, hardly any measures have been developed.

Therefore, in this chapter we analyse the implementation of Law 39/2006 across Spain and assess the concept of dependency which forms the basis of the Personal Autonomy and Dependence Law. Using a critical disability perspective, we show that the law reinforces dependency, with care being mainly provided by women or at the expense of a precarious third-sector workforce.

LEGISLATION AND ASSISTANCE FOR DEPENDENCY

According to the latest Spanish report, there are 3.84 million people in Spain with disabilities, representing 8.5 per cent of the population.[10] The average person with disability is 64.3 years old; 2.3 million are women and 1.55 million are men. According to data published by the *Consejo Superior de Investigaciones Científicas* (National Research Council) (CSIC), in 2017 there were 32.6 per cent more elderly women (4,995,737) than men (3,768,467) due to higher male mortality rates in all age groups.[11] In the same report, the CSIC shows that some regions in Spain have high rates of elderly people (21 per cent of the population), such as Asturias, Castilla y León, Galicia, the Basque Country, Aragón and Cantabria, while other regions like Murcia, Baleares and Canarias have low rates (below 16 per cent of the population). The proportion of the Spanish population that is elderly continues to grow due to two key factors: the continuous increase in the number of people aged 65 and over due to lengthening lifespans and the low birth rate (in 2018, Spain had its lowest birth rate since 1941).[12]

People with disabilities in Spain are categorised according to their level of dependency (see Table 14.1). Two thirds are women and one-third are men; more than 70 per cent are aged 65 years or older; and more than 50 per cent are aged 80 or older.

[10] VVAA, *Panorámica de la Discapacidad en España* (Madrid, National Statistics Institute, 2008). Available at: www.ine.es/revistas/cifraine/1009.pdf.

[11] A Abellán-García, J Ayala-García, A Pérez-Díaz and R Pujol-Rodríguez, 'Un Perfil de las Personas Mayores en España' in Informes Envejecimiento, *Indicadores Estadísticos Básicos* (Madrid, Informes Envejecimiento, 2018). Available at: www.envejecimiento.csic.es/documentos/documentos/enred-indicadoresbasicos18.pdf.

[12] Ibid.

Table 14.1 Number of people with disabilities in Spain over time by level of dependency

	2005	2010	2015	2020 (est.)
Stage III: Great Dependency	194,508	223,457	252,345	277,884
Stage II: Severe Dependency	370,603	420,336	472,461	521,065
Stage I: Moderate Dependency	560,080	602,636	648,442	697,277
Total	1,125,90	1,246,429	1,373,248	1,496,226

Source: *Libro Blanco de la Dependencia*, with data from the *Instituto Nacional de Estadística* (National Statistics Institute), 2004.[13]

What Services are Offered to Dependent Individuals?

As summarised in Table 14.2, the dependency law provides economic support for the provision of care services, including services aimed at preventing dependency situations and funding for personal assistance, which is intended to improve the living situation and personal autonomy of severely dependent adults.[14]

Table 14.2 Catalogue of services granted by Law 13/2006

1. Helpline services	Remote medical assistance Health services delivered to the home
2. Home care service	Household chores: cleaning, washing, cooking and others Personal care in carrying out activities of daily living
3. Day and night care centres	Day care centres for the elderly Day care centres for under-65s Special day care centres Night care centres
4. Nursing home care	Nursing homes for elderly dependent adults Care centres for dependent adults based on severe disability
5. Personal assistance	Household chores but also assistance to be able to work and study

Source: *Agencia Estatal de Evaluación de las Políticas Públicas y la Calidad de los Servicios* (Spanish Agency on Evaluation of Public Policies and Quality of Services) (AEVAL) 2008.[15]

Care can be provided either by professionals, hired by a company which is linked to the local social services or by non-professional individuals.[16] Caregivers are

---

[13] Libro Blanco de Atención a las Personas en Situación de Dependencia en España 2004.
[14] 39/2006, Art 19.
[15] AEVAL, *Evaluación sobre la participación de la Administración General del Estado en el sistema para la autonomía y atención a la dependencia* (Madrid, Ministerio de Administraciones Públicas, 2008) 19.
[16] 39/2006, Art 18.

often female relatives or immigrants, who are modestly paid for this work.[17] The precarious situation of caregivers has an impact on the quality of services dependent individuals receive and on the caregivers themselves.

The financial aid contributes to the hiring of personal assistants for a certain number of hours, enabling people to access education, work and basic activities of daily living. The funding received for personal assistance varies among regions. Funding is only offered to those individuals in the two higher degrees of dependency (see Table 14.1), with active lives that may include study or paid employment.[18]

The Spanish government currently funds 17 per cent of these expenses, regional administrations 63 per cent, and the remaining 20 per cent is paid for by citizens themselves.[19] In 2017, there was an increase of 89,267 in the number of recipients, but one in every four had to wait for funding to be granted.[20] Although the waiting list shrank to 38,189 by the end of 2017, it is likely to take eight years for the last person on the list to receive services. In 2016, more than 40,000 individuals died without accessing the services they needed.[21]

DEPENDENCY VS AUTONOMY

Although the term 'autonomy' is used in the legislation, the key concept in Law 39/2006 is dependency, defined as:

> (...) the permanent state of a person who, by reason of age, illness or disability and in connection with a lack or loss of physical, mental, intellectual or sensory autonomy, requires the care of one or more others, or significant aid, to carry out basic activities of daily living or, in the case of persons with intellectual disability or mental illness, other forms of support for his or her personal autonomy.[22]

Furthermore, the focus on adults clearly puts children and young people at risk, leaving families with total responsibility for coping with their difficulties. Dependency also raises a feminist debate concerning how all individuals are interdependent and interconnected, constructing care as a social issue rather than a personal problem.

The law's restrictive concept of dependency is focused on physical or psychological impairment that decreases the abilities of the person, the inability to perform the basic activities of daily living related to self-care or needing

---

[17] Ibid.

[18] INTERSOCIAL, *Análisis Econométrico: Estudio Comparativo de la Asistencia Personal y la Atención Residencial* (Madrid, OVI, ASPAYM, Comunidad de Madrid, 2014).

[19] IMSERSO, *Información Destacada de la Evolución de la Gestión del SAAD* (Madrid, Ministerio de Trabajo y Asuntos Sociales, 2019).

[20] Ibid.

[21] Ibid.

[22] 39/2006 Art 2.

a third-party's assistance.[23] Dependency is thus related to the ageing of the population and focuses solely on the most basic activities of daily living and self-care, which are the services funded by Law 39/2006.

Asís and Barranco see the definition of dependency in Law 39/2006 as coming entirely from the biomedical model, rather than from the social model of disability.[24] They note that 'dependent situations may originate or be aggravated ... from lack of social inclusion such as lack of accessible environments and adequate resources for elderly people'.[25] Law 39/2006 therefore, poses dependency as an individual problem.

As opposed to dependency, autonomy points to agency and the ability to live life on one's own terms. However, in Law 39/2006, autonomy is defined as being able to carry out one's own personal care and household chores and possessing essential mobility, as well as the ability to understand and perform basic orders. It focuses on not being a burden to others: 'It is the situation in which a person with a disability makes decisions on their own lives and actively takes part in community according to the right to the free development of one's own personality.'[26]

José Luis Rodríguez Zapatero's socialist government addressed dependency as a radical issue that could transform the basis of the welfare state but did not provide relevant funding nor include feminist perspectives in this policymaking. In addition, the austerity measures implemented by the conservative government of Mariano Rajoy Brey played a key role in putting PWD and their families at risk. In fact, the New General Law on Disability (2013), approved by Mariano Rajoy, restricts the provision of services even further, with increasing budgetary restrictions for familial caregivers, resulting in fewer hours of caregiving.[27]

THE 39/2006 LAW IN PRACTICE

As mentioned previously, Spain has a multilevel political system, in which national law is implemented at a regional and local level. The Spanish regions have different levels of economic development and, more importantly, different degrees of development of social services and the welfare state, ranging from excellent (Basque Country and Navarre) to well developed (Madrid) or struggling (Andalucía). In the following section we examine the development of ILPs in these regions and examine how they construct the notion of dependency as an identity.

---

[23] Ibid.

[24] RD Asís-Roig and MDC Barranco-Avilés, *El Impacto de la Convención Internacional Sobre los Derechos de las Personas con Discapacidad en la Ley 39/2006, de 14 de Diciembre* (Madrid, Colección Convención ONU, 2016).

[25] Ibid, 28.

[26] 39/2006 Art 2.

[27] Spanish Government, *Royal Decree 1/2013, Final Text of the General Law on the Rights of People with Disability and their Social Inclusion* OSG [BOE, Boletín Oficial del Estado] 289, 29 November 2013.

Etxean – An Independent Living Programme in the Basque Country

The first pilot programme in independent living took place in Gipuzkoa, one of the three Basque Country provinces. The pilot programme, called *Etxean* (At home), was started in February 2004, two years before the 39/2006 law was passed, based on Gipuzkoa Law 11/2004.[28] In order to be accepted into the programme, an adult was required to have been a legally registered resident for two or more years, have an accessible dwelling, a network of support and be willing to manage a *plan individual de atención* (PIA) (individual care programme). The PIA can include a moderate co-payment (never less than 70 per cent). Each participant in the programme must manage their own personal assistants, including recruitment (which excludes family members, since there is specific budget provision in Law 39/2006 for family caregivers), training and timetables. Because of the amount of paperwork this implied and the novelty of the programme, a cooperative was set up, called *Bikcovi*.[29]

Since 2008, ILPs spread throughout Gipuzkoa and, by 2011, *Etxean* covered 1,063 of 8,393 applicants.[30] The Basque Country province of Araba has run an ILP that offers funding for personal assistance since 2013. It involves a substantial co-payment (40–100 per cent), includes children over the age of three years and is extended to dependence Stage I in some circumstances. The applicant has to prepare a PIA, be a legal resident, be involved in educational pursuits or in the workforce and be able to manage their own personal assistants or, in the case of minors, have a registered person to help them. Another difference between the programmes in Gipuzkoa and Araba is that the Araba Act sets requirements for those working as personal assistants, which include being 18 years old or older, being a legal resident in Spain and holding a vocational training degree in socio-cultural services.[31]

Bizkaia also started its own programme of independent living in 2013, also with a substantial co-payment (never less than 70 per cent). Eligible applicants must have Stage I dependence or above and be aged between 16 (emancipated in the case of minors) and 65 years. It sets a minimum of 3–5 hours of personal assistance for each dependence stage. The Bizkaia programme excludes household chores and no more than 75 per cent of the hours can be used on basic

---

[28] Gipuzkoa Government, *Local Decree 11/2004, Regulating Individual Grants for People with Disability or a Dependency Situation* OSG [BOG, Boletín Oficial de Gipuzkoa] 39, 24 February 2004.

[29] X Urmeneta-Sanromá, 'La Vida Independiente en Gipuzkoa: Una Alternativa para las Personas con Discapacidad y Dependencia' (207) 42, *Zerbitzuan: Gizarte Zerbitzuetarako Aldizkaria. Revista de Servicios Sociales*, 87.

[30] X Urmeneta-Sanromá, 'Vida Independiente y Asistencia Personal' (2011). Available at: www. forovidaindependiente.org/wp-content/uploads/vi_ap_urmeneta.pdf.

[31] Álava Government, *Local Decree 39/2014, Regulating Economic Assistance for the Autonomy of Dependent People in Álava: Grants for Caregiving Within Families and Non-Professional Caregivers, Funding for Personal Assistance and Related Services* OSG [BOTHA, Boletín Oficial de Álava] 143, 23 July 2013.

activities of everyday life.[32] As in Gipuzkoa and Araba, the participants must prepare their own PIA.

As outlined above, the three provinces of the Basque Country implemented the guidelines of the Gipuzkoa pilot programme with some differences with respect to age, assistant requirements and stage of dependency. Assistance is always offered to those individuals pursuing further education or who are able to work and implies the management of assistance professionals. The Basque Country has 184,451 PWD, of whom 14,475 live in residential facilities and 169,400 in their homes.[33] Only 5,372 people have received personal assistance from the most developed programme of independent living in Spain.

Madrid and the ASPAYM Independent Life Programme

The *Parapléjicos y Personas con Gran Discapacidad Física de la Comunidad de Madrid* (ASPAYM) (Association of Paraplegics and People with Great Physical Disability in the Community of Madrid) set up a pilot ILP in Madrid in July 2006. Initially, the programme targeted 35 people and later offered personal assistance to 62 people, hiring 120 personal assistants between 2006 and 2008.[34] Over 2008–11, 63 people received personal assistance, of whom 52 per cent held a job, 35 per cent were studying and 13 per cent were both studying and working. Forty-two per cent of them were aged 18–30 years, and the remainder were older.[35]

Personal assistants provide people with support for the basic activities of daily living, according to each person's unique needs. The programme provides a maximum of 11 hours per day and is funded by the Local Government of Madrid. More than 113,280 PWD live in Madrid;[36] ASPAYM's eligibility criteria are active involvement in community life and/or studying/working, actively looking for a job, or having family-related duties. Accessible housing and a reliable network of support are also required. People with lower incomes are given priority.[37]

Andalusia

Andalusia is the most populous Spanish region, with 20 per cent of the national population, and has the largest number of people in a situation of dependency. At 9.1 per cent, the proportion of Andalusia's population with a disability is

---

[32] Bizkaia Government, Local Decree 103/2013, regulating individual grants for personal assistance, OSG [BOB, Boletín Oficial de Bizkaia] 143, 23 July 2013.

[33] Panorámica de la discapacidad en España 2008.

[34] Observatorio Estatal de la Discapacidad, *2006–2016: 10 años de la convención internacional sobre los derechos de las personas con discapacidad: Balance de su aplicación en España* (Madrid, 2017).

[35] Government of Madrid, *II Action Plan for People with Disabilities in Madrid 2005–2008* (2015) p. 10.

[36] Panorámica de la discapacidad en España 2008.

[37] Government of Madrid, *III Action Plan for people with disabilities in Madrid 2012–2015* (2016).

slightly above the Spanish average. Some 54 per cent of the population are aged 65 years or older, while 43.5 per cent are aged between 16 and 64. Andalusia has higher migration rates (both regular and irregular) than other areas. Many of these migrants come from the former Spanish colonies of Morocco and Western Sahara and end up working within the black economy, perpetuating the colonial exploitation of people in low-paid jobs.

The Andalusia Independent Living Programme was launched in 2008, led by Viandalucía. Despite an eligible population of 80,189, the programme was offered to a very small group of individuals. In 2013, 14 individuals were registered on the programme, the most since its launch.[38] As of 2018, nine individuals were receiving personal assistance.[39]

In 2016, the Committee on Equality, Health and Social Policy, along with the Spanish Left Party, urged the Andalusia Parliament to develop programmes and funding for personal assistance, in accordance with Article 19 of the CRPD. However, the 2019 elections brought a coalition of right-wing parties into office, reducing the prospects that the needs of people with dependency in Andalusia will be met.

Even though legislation addresses the uneven distribution of care, dependency remains a personal problem due to insufficient State-funded service provision.[40] Unemployment has led to many families in Andalucía taking their elders out of nursing homes. Familial caregivers contributed to the household economy through the familial care service allowance (€350 per month) and their retirement pensions.[41] The attempt to dignify caregiving, mainly performed by women through the familial care service allowance, was very short-lived, being offered only until 2013.[42] Since 2013, these women have provided services for free, with few to no options of returning to the labour market. Some families also apply for family caregiving, in an effort to alleviate their financial struggle in a situation of endemic unemployment, aggravated by the debt crisis.[43] The familial care allowance was revoked in Andalusia as part of austerity measures proclaimed in Royal Decrees 16/2012, 1050/2013, and 1051/2013.[44]

[38] Viandalucía, 'Un Paso Adelante para la Vida Independiente en Andalucía' (Sevilla, Federación Vida Independiente, 2013). Available at: www.federacionvi.org/un-paso-adelante-para-la-vida-independiente-en-andalucia/.
[39] The typical recipient is a 38-year-old man, with a university degree and stage III dependency. A Iáñez-Domínguez and JL Aranda-Chaves, *Impacto Económico y Social de la Asistencia Personal en Andalucía* (A Coruña, Diversitas Ediciones and Andalusia International University, 2017).
[40] Andalusia Government, *I Action Plan for the Promotion of Personal Autonomy and Prevention of Dependency in Andalusia (2016–2020)* (Sevilla, Andalusia Government, 2016) art 3. Andalusia Government, *I Action Plan for the Integral Assistance of Children Under 6 with a Dependency Situation* (Sevilla, Andalusia Government, 2017).
[41] I Zambrano-Álvarez, MT Martin-Palomo, JM Muñoz-Terrón and E Olid-González, 'Nuevos Interrogantes en el Modelo de Provisión de Cuidados en Andalucía' (2015) 60 *Zerbitzuan: Gizarte Zerbitzuetarako Aldizkaria. Revista de Servicios Sociales* 113.
[42] Ibid
[43] Ibid, 123.
[44] Spanish Government, *Royal Decree 16/2012, on Urgent Actions to Guarantee the Sustainability of the National Health Care System, and the Improvement of Quality and Security of*

CRITICAL ANALYSIS

Law 39/2006 on Personal Autonomy and Dependent Care can be framed within what Mitchell calls a 'bait and switch scheme'.[45] It enabled dependent people to live in their communities, with discrete State funding for familial caregivers between 2007 and 2011, after which point they found themselves back in their previous situation – dependent on the unsalaried female caregiving of a relative. As the case of Andalusia demonstrates, the bait and switch scheme has continued since the debt crisis onset in 2011, with women who were laid off or who have left the workforce to become a familial caregiver (under the €350 stipend) having few opportunities to return.

As noted previously, there are regional differences in budgets for social services and service provision for people with dependency in Spain. Between 2006 and 2012, the national budget for dependency was reduced to €0 in the Spanish General Budget, which transferred the costs to regional governments.[46] This situation was a result of Zapatero's amendment (2011) of Article 135 of the Spanish Constitution, which limits the level of State debt.[47] Since then, the national and regional budgets have been set by the European Union, so that Spain can meet the mandate concerning its debt.

Law 39/2006 creates, as Jasbir Puar would put it, 'objects of uncare' targeting certain groups of the population.[48] In the three regions we analysed, areas with stronger social services, lower debt and comparatively lower migration, such as the Basque Country, have the best ILPs. Meanwhile, Andalusia, hit hard by chronic unemployment and with less capability to offer social services, has only marginally implemented ILPs. The ILP in Madrid is somewhere in between, stable but with lower provision of services than in the Basque Country.

As Jasbir Puar has pointed out, disability is a 'rhetorical biopolitical positioning' enabling care and life.[49] Puar analyses how the concepts of disability in our liberal democracies define it as 'an exceptional accident or misfortune',[50] while leaving aside impairments due to imperial war or environmental hazard, thus disqualifying significant numbers of people from receiving any kind of

---

Assistance OSG [BOE, Boletín Oficial del Estado] 98, 20 April 2013; *Royal Decree 1050/2013, Regulating Minimum Protection Under 39/3006 Act on Personal Autonomy and Assistance of People with Dependency* OSG [BOE, Boletín Oficial del Estado] 313, 27 December 2013; *Royal Decree 1051/2013, Regulating the Service Provision for People's Independence and Autonomy for Dependent Individuals Established on the 39/3006 Act on Personal Autonomy and Assistance of People with Dependency* OSG [BOE, Boletín Oficial del Estado] 313, 27 December 2013.

[45] DT Mitchell, *The Biopolitics of Disability: Neoliberalism, Ablenationalism, and Peripheral Embodiment* (Ann Arbor, University of Michigan Press, 2015) 39–40.

[46] Anon, 2014.

[47] Ibid.

[48] JK Puar, *Terrorist Assemblages: Homonationalism in Queer Times* (Durham NC, Duke University Press, 2017) 92.

[49] Ibid, 104.

[50] Ibid, 66.

protection. Moreover, the category of disability often serves as an ideological tool to injure colonial populations, as we have suggested in the case of Andalusia.

Modern democracies are torn between two conflicting tendencies: 'embracing disability as a universal and inevitable condition'[51] which discredits the concept of disability as a personal tragedy and allows for the fight against the production of disability, on the one hand, and targeting one collective as recipients of benefits, services and care on the other. Regarding the latter, Puar states that:

> ... disabled people have shifted from modernity's exception (a line of defect to be isolated and eradicated) to postmodernist [neoliberal] exceptionality (failing bodies resuscitated by an increasingly medicalized state). In this latter state, the ontology of disability retrieves a formerly fallen object and makes it newly available for 'cultural rehabilitation', a euphemism for producing cultural docility. Mitchell and Snyder track this shift of people with disabilities located from 'a former era of economic burden' of paternalistic, institutional, and welfare regimes when disabled people were 'social pariahs,' to what they term 'objects of care' that impel the investment of service economies and neoliberal strategies of intervention and rehabilitation – a 'hot' ticket item for potential research and funding schemes.[52]

Analysis of Gender in Law 39/2006

Disability is presented in Law 39/2006 and its implementation as a singular misfortune and a private tragedy but at the same time, disability should not be conceptualised as a universal problem affecting everyone.[53] The numbers of people with dependency vary across regions of Spain. Class, age and gender are also relevant to the development of a disability. Dependency (aging and disability) is not a neutral event that can happen to anyone.

What is not so evident is that with the production of dependency comes an invisible production of debilitation as an active practice of exploitation of those who care for the dependent individuals.[54] Caregivers are mostly working-class women, who are close relatives of the dependent individuals and, when they are not available, migrants of both genders provide care. Therefore, Law 39/2006 reinforces the tradition of a female caregiving role, something deeply ingrained in Mediterranean culture.

The conditions in which care is provided produce more disability in the mid-to-long term, as a consequence of the exploitation practices that follow from Law 39/2006. As we have described, the provision of services to dependent individuals has fallen primarily to familial caregivers, with little impact on

---

[51] Ibid, 70.
[52] Ibid, 46.
[53] Ibid, 70.
[54] Ibid.

independent living in most Spanish regions. The Law enabled the incorporation into the workforce of women and migrants who had precarious jobs, many of whom were laid off as soon as austerity measures came into force.

The National Statistics Institute's Survey on the Use of Time in 2018–19 (yet to be published) estimates that the annual hours of caregiving in Spain amount to 28 million full-time jobs.[55] As we have shown, very little of this time counts as jobs, since even in the regions with the best-developed systems ILPs require a developed support network. According to sociologist María Ángeles Durán, the conditions in which these caregivers work would be deemed 'unacceptable by any collective agreement'.[56]

This divide between receivers of care and caregivers is already misleading, because many of the caregivers are middle-aged or elderly women, whose vulnerabilities have not been taken into account and are therefore considered an expendable population. In *Right to Maim*, Jasbir Puar argues that disability serves as an ideological tool which entwines the politics of disability (identifying populations as deserving of protection and citizenship), and the politics of deliberate exhaustion of the population targeted to be maimed.[57] The divide between people labelled as dependent under Law 39/2006 singles out a whole category of people as legitimate receivers of care, while it correlatively sets out a totalising category of caregivers as 'not needing care'. This targets women in precarious jobs and migrants for low salaries and extenuating jobs as a population to be worn out and debilitated.

CONCLUSION

With the dramatic political and social changes going on in Spain since the onset of the debt crisis, an in-depth analysis of the implementation of Law 39/2006 in the country was needed to evaluate its impact on the wellbeing of its target populations, what we have called 'dependent people', as well as on caregivers. Our analysis provides valuable insights for both policymakers and grassroots organisations that can be used to design future public services and policies.

In this chapter we have analysed how a new social category – the dependent individual – was created by Law 39/2006 and its implementation in three regions of Spain. Governmental practices targeting the elderly and PWD create a dichotomy between those who receive and those who provide care. This false dichotomy singles out those performing care services – overwhelmingly women and migrants. Often, women provide unpaid caregiving in their families. As a

[55] MA Durán, 'El Trabajo del Cuidado' (2019) *El País*. Available at: www.elpais.com/elpais/2019/03/06/opinion/1551891773_900685.html.

[56] Ibid.

[57] JK Puar, *Right to Maim: Debility, Capacity, Disability* (Durham, NC, Duke University Press, 2017).

result of austerity cuts, women and migrants have little to no chance of rejoining the workforce. They become an expendable population that will eventually fill up the ranks of dependent people themselves due to their precariousness.

At the same time, the CRPD prepares dependent people for what David Mitchell[58] has called a bait and switch scheme (ie, making a whole cohort of people legally eligible for benefits that are never implemented by regional and local institutions). The fact that, as of 2019, every day 80 people eligible for benefits under Law 39/2006 died before receiving those benefits[59] reveals the gap between what a person labelled as dependent is nominally entitled to demand under the provision of Law 39/2006 and the services he or she may actually receive.

In this scenario, national legislation, such as Law 39/2006, uses disability as a 'rhetorical biopolitical positioning' which singles out a collective in a positive way, enabling care and life to conceal colonial and patriarchal practices of debilitation and the wearing out of migrant and female populations.[60] In a similar fashion, Mitchell has pointed out that under the strictures of increasing scarcity due to the debt crisis, PWD have become the object of an exceptionalist discourse, thus making them symbols of civilisational aptitude at the expense of precarious female, often migrant, caregivers in what he calls 'ablenationalism'.[61] Therefore, we want to stress the importance of an intersectional policy analysis to disentangle the impact of implementing legislation aimed at fulfilling the commitments Spain accepted on signing the CRPD amidst a context of budgetary restrictions imposed by the EU. The fact that, after 2011, the funding of Law 39/2006 was left to regional and local authorities created gross inequalities across the country.

Lastly, we want to highlight the State's abandonment of many people with dependency on waiting lists, who must turn to their families or to charitable organisations for care. The Spanish population continues to age, with fewer and more debilitated social services, especially in those regions that have a larger debt and, in some of them, increasingly conservative governments willing to dismantle an already weakened welfare state.

---

[58] Mitchell, 'The Biopolitics of Disability' (2015).

[59] EFE, 'Cada día mueren en España 80 personas esperando recibir las ayudas de la dependencia' (2019) *Radio Televisión Española*. Available at: www.rtve.es/noticias/20190228/espana-mueren-80-personas-dia-esperando-recibir-ayudas-dependencia/1892124.shtml.

[60] Puar, 'Terrorist Assemblages' (2017) 104.

[61] Mitchell, 'The Biopolitics of Disability' (2015).

15

To Use or Not to Use Physical Restraints in Paediatric Psychiatric Care

Should Health Professionals as Guarantors Use Coercive Measures to Protect from Potential Harm?

ELVIRA PÉRTEGA ANDÍA

MENTAL HEALTH HAS been a neglected issue throughout human history, with a prevailing legacy of unacceptable human rights violations within mental health facilities.[1] In response to this, the 2030 Sustainable Development Agenda recognises mental health as a global imperative. The Convention on the Rights of Persons with Disabilities[2] (CRPD) established the international commitment for a paradigm shift from coercion and discrimination to dignity and trust. It brought about a new approach towards disability, moving from a medical model to a social model, recognising that disability is not a problem based on the person but rather a problem generated by societal barriers.[3] Importantly, the CRPD has become the universal standard for the human rights of persons with disabilities, taking precedence

---

[1] UN General Assembly (UNGA), *Report of the Special Rapporteur on the Right of Everyone to the Enjoyment of the Highest Attainable Standard of Physical and Mental Health* (28 March 2017) UN Doc A/HRC.

[2] UNGA, *Convention on the Rights of People with Disabilities* and *Optional Protocol* (13 December 2006) UN Doc A/RES/61/106.

[3] World Health Organization (WHO), *World Report on Disability* (Geneva, WHO, 2011). Available at: www.who.int/disabilities/world_report/2011/report/en/.

over previous instruments.[4] This means that the CRPD principles of non-discrimination, autonomy, equal treatment and inclusion should be embedded within the State Members' legislation affecting people with disabilities. CRPD principles challenge current legal frameworks that regulate involuntary treatment, involuntary placement and physical restraint. In Spain, although the CRPD has been signed and ratified, the legislation has not been modified to reflect its principles. Spain has not adopted an 'absolute ban'[5] on coercive practices towards persons with psychosocial disabilities in psychiatric facilities. Hence, there is an urgent need to re-examine the existing legislation that still allows the use of any form of coercion towards those with mental health problems in Spain.

Using physical restraints to control behaviour by confining a patient's bodily movements[6] continues to be a common and controversial practice.[7] Some view physical restraint as the oldest unsolved problem in institutional psychiatry today.[8] Particularly worrisome is the case of children and adolescents, whose unique vulnerability puts them at a much higher risk of experiencing physical restraint than adults[9] and of suffering more serious emotional and physical sequelae.[10] Protecting minors from the damage of physical restraint requires special attention and higher care standards.[11] Current laws and physical restraint guidelines refer to adult populations, disregarding the more profound consequences for children and adolescents, their legal and emotional dependency on adults, their developmental characteristics and the essential role of parents/tutors in their lives.[12] In order to pay the necessary attention to the use of physical restraint in children and adolescents, in this chapter I focus on the laws and guidelines that regulate the use of physical restraint with minors in psychiatric units.

My aim is to clarify whether health professionals, who act as patients' guarantors, are legally responsible for their use of coercive measures such as physical

---

[4] International Disability Alliance (IDA) *Position Paper on the Convention on the Rights of People with Disabilities and other Instruments* (Geneva, IDA, 2008). Available at: www.internationaldisabilityalliance.org/resources/position-paper-convention-rights-persons-disabilities-crpd-and-other-instruments.

[5] UNGA, *Report of the Special Rapporteur on Torture* (2013).

[6] E Sailas and M Fenton, 'Seclusion and Restraint for People with Serious Mental Illnesses' (2000) 2 *Cochrane Database Systematic Review* Doi10.1002/14651858.CD00163.

[7] DM Day, 'Examining the Therapeutic Utility of Restraints and Seclusion with Children and Youth: The Role of Theory and Research in Practice' (2002) 72 *American Journal of Orthopsychiatry* 266, 278.

[8] T Steinert and P Lepping, 'Legal Provisions and Practice in the Management of Violent Patients. A Case Vignette Study in 16 European Countries' (2008) 24 *European Psychiatry* 135, 141.

[9] A Furre et al, 'Characteristics of Adolescents Frequently Restrained in Acute Psychiatric Units in Norway: a Nationwide Study' (2017) 12 *Child and Adolescent Psychiatry Mental Health* 3.

[10] M De Hert et al, 'The Prevention of Deep Venous Thrombosis in Physically Restrained Patients with Schizophrenia' (2010) 68 *International Journal of Clinical Practice* 1109, 1115.

[11] UNGA, *Report of the Special Rapporteur on the Right of Everyone* (2017).

[12] E Pértega, *Health Professionals' Decision-Making Process About the Use of Physical Restraints in Inpatient Pediatric Psychiatric Units* (New York, DPhil Thesis, New York University, 2016).

restraint. As a starting point, I contrast the CRPD approach to the use of physical restraint with the approach in Spanish national legislation. Stemming from this legal discrepancy, I assess how health professionals' legal responsibility as patients' guarantors shapes their behaviour; on the one hand, the CRPD prohibits health professionals from using coercion (ie, physical restraint) on the basis of disability and argues that they should instead protect people with disabilities from violence, abuse and torture.[13] On the other hand, Spanish legislation assigns to health professionals the duty to protect from harm using coercive measures such as physical restraints, if necessary, as a last resort in emergency situations. I recommend changing current Spanish legislation that obliges health professionals to intervene using coercive measures (ie, physical restraint) if necessary to protect from imminent harm. As an alternative, I suggest that the law does not consider the lack of use of coercive measures, such as physical restraint, to protect from imminent harm to constitute negligence or malpractice, even if harm occurs.

CRPD AND SPANISH LEGISLATION – DIFFERENTIAL CONSIDERATIONS IN RELATION TO PHYSICAL RESTRAINT

While the CRPD does not mention physical restraint specifically, McSherry[14] concludes that physical restraint is incompatible with the CRPD because it is a form of inhuman and degrading treatment (Article 15) and substituted decision-making (Article 25). With respect to children, Article 7 of the CRPD emphasises that all actions (and so physical restraint) must be in 'the best interests of the child' who has the right to 'express his/her views freely giving due weight according to their age and maturity'.[15]

Spain ratified the CRPD and the Optional Protocol on 21 April 2008. From the moment the CRPD came into effect on 3 May 2008, it became part of internal legislation in accordance with Article 96 of the Spanish Constitution of 1978. In order to make the rights included in the CRPD effective, Law 26/2011 of 1 August of Normative Adaptation to the International Convention on the Rights of Persons with Disabilities was enacted. Nevertheless, despite Law 26/2011, the laws regulating physical restraint stand at odds with CRPD principles. The discrepancy comes from laws that permit the use of restrictive practices in certain contexts. For example, the Spanish Civil Procedure Act 2000, 2012 763 (1) and organic law 1/1996 of Judicial Protection of the Minor authorise the institutionalisation of minors on the grounds of disability. In this context, the

---

[13] UNGA, *Report of the Special Rapporteur on Torture* (2013).

[14] B McSherry, 'Regulating Seclusion and Restraint in Health Care Settings: The Promise of the Convention on the Rights of Persons with Disabilities' (2017) 53 *International Journal of Law and Psychiatry* 39, 44.

[15] UNGA, *Convention on the Rights of People with Disabilities* (2006).

General Act on Health 1986 and Act 41/2002, of 14 November, Basic Regulator of the Patient's Autonomy and Rights and Obligations regarding Information and Clinical Documentation allows physical restraint to be used without the patient's free and informed consent when s/he is not intellectually, emotionally or mentally capable of taking such decisions.

HEALTH PROFESSIONALS' LEGAL RESPONSIBILITY IN RELATION TO PHYSICAL RESTRAINT ACCORDING TO THE CRPD AND SPANISH LEGISLATION

In paediatric psychiatric settings, physical restraint is practiced within a milieu in which children and adolescents with mental health problems may lack legal capacity to make their own decisions both due to 'minority of age' and their mental status.[16] In effect, health professionals become the patients' guarantors. This influences the responsibility that health professionals must provide care and protect patients and others from harm. It is at this point that a conflict between care and coercion arises: physical restraint, although intrusive and stressful, is used as a protective measure.[17] This contradiction is key to the accountability of health professionals in relation to the use of physical restraint in paediatric psychiatric settings. Physical restraint in this context is described as an 'uneasy fit',[18] correlating with the 'moral stress'[19] and 'collective dissociation'[20] that health professionals feel when they use physical restraint. The controversy stems from the fact that physical restraint is used for safety reasons, while being a technique with questionable therapeutic benefits with proven harmful consequences, including interference with personal liberty.[21] In addition, empirical evidence shows that non-consensual measures are counterproductive – harmful, traumatic, a form of punishment and ineffective for ensuring safety.[22] What is more, there is no scientific evidence about the use of physical restraint.[23] Nevertheless,

---

[16] P Simón-Lorda, 'La Capacidad de los Pacientes para Tomar Decisiones: Una Tarea Todavía Pendiente' (2008) 28 *Revista de la Asociación Española de Neuropsiquiatría* 325, 348.

[17] M McCain and K Kornegay, 'Behavioral Health Restraint: The Experience and Beliefs of Seasoned Psychiatric Nurses' (2005) 21 *Journal for Nurses in Staff Development* 236, 242; S Bigwood and M Crowe, '"It's Part of the Job, but it Spoils the Job": A Phenomenological Study of Physical Restraint' (2008) 17 *International Journal of Mental Health Nursing* 215, 222.

[18] WK Mohr, 'Restraints and the Code of Ethics: An Uneasy Fit' (2010) 24 *Archives of Psychiatric Nursing* 3, 14.

[19] K Regan, 'Trauma Informed Care on an Inpatient Pediatric Psychiatric Unit and the Emergence of Ethical Dilemmas as Nurses Evolved Their Practice' (2010) 31 *Issues in Mental Health Nursing* 216, 222.

[20] SS Kennedy and WK Mohr, 'The Conundrum of Children in the US Health Care System' (2001) 8 *Nursing Ethics* 196, 210.

[21] M De Hert et al, 'Prevalence and Correlates of Seclusion and Restraint Use in Children and Adolescents: A Systematic Review' (2011) 20 *European Child Adolescent Psychiatry* 221, 230.

[22] PM Soininen et al, 'Secluded and Restrained Patients' Perceptions of Their Treatment' (2013) 22 *International Journal of Mental Health Nursing* 47, 55.

[23] Day, 'Examining the Therapeutic Utility of Restraints' (2002).

because health professionals perceive their role is to ensure safety[24] and maintain control,[25] they use physical restraint to protect from harm[26] even though it may actually cause harm. If the safety of a patient or others is at risk, physical restraint use may be regarded as necessary.[27] The use of legitimate physical restraint is regulated by clinical guidelines and laws that aim to clarify 'how and when'[28] physical restraint is appropriate. Nevertheless, it is unclear what 'appropriate' means and, in general, guidelines indicate that physical restraint should be used as a last resort and only where the risk of inaction outweighs its use. To be appropriate, physical restraint should be the least-restrictive alternative when other strategies have failed to protect the patient or others from imminent harm. Despite these attempts to provide clear indications for the use of physical restraints, ultimately it is up to the health professional to determine what 'last resort', 'least restrictive', 'no harm' and 'inappropriate' mean in each situation.

Regarding the CRPD perspective on health professionals' legal responsibility in relation to physical restraints, based on Articles 3, 12, 15, 17 and 25 we can infer that health professionals are responsible for avoiding the use of physical restraints and even for ensuring that other persons do not do so. As far as Spanish legislation is concerned, contractual obligations regulate health professionals' legal responsibility when accepting the duty of care in a healthcare institution. Such acceptance implies that health professionals provide treatment and care and build a relationship with the patient based on trust, thus acquiring the legal responsibility to act to protect the person from harm in case of danger. A health professional's obligation to intervene to protect is also regulated in Spanish legislation using the concept of 'guarantor', as stated in Article 11 of Organic Law, of 3 November of the Penal Code. According to this Article, health professionals have a normative duty to act if they have the capacity to do so to prevent a risky situation that might lead to harm; in other words, their 'legal status of guarantor' implies that their practice is regulated by the normative functions of control and safety so that 'no action' may involve the existence of 'commission by omission'. This means they will be held liable or responsible for harm in situations where harm occurs, but there has been inactivity or no action by the health professional. Given that physical restraint is typified as the action to limit the person's movements in case of a 'dangerous' behaviour when other less-restrictive measures have been ineffective to prevent harm, the duty to ensure a safe environment, coupled with the role of 'guarantor', imposes a responsibility to use physical restraint. In practical terms, if health professionals do not use physical restraint as a 'last resort' to control patients' behaviour, when this is assessed as dangerous, they could be accused of 'commission by omission'

[24] Bigwood and Crowe, '"It's Part of the Job, but it Spoils the Job"' (2008).
[25] E Perkins et al, 'Physical Restraint in a Therapeutic Setting; A Necessary Evil?' (2012) 35 *International Journal of Law & Psychiatry* 43, 49.
[26] S Goethals et al, 'Nurses' Decision-Making in Cases of Physical Restraint: A Synthesis of Qualitative Evidence' (2011) 68 *Journal of Advanced Nursing* 1198, 1210.
[27] Ibid.
[28] D Horsburgh, 'How, and When, Can I Restrain a Patient?' (2004) 80 *Postgrad Med Journal* 7, 12.

if harm occurs. Health professionals are obliged to act using 'protective' physical restraint as a last resort if no other less-restrictive alternatives are available, despite the risk of damage associated with physical restraint itself.

TWO CONFLICTING DUTIES: TO PROTECT FROM RISK OF HARM USING PHYSICAL RESTRAINT VERSUS TO PROTECT FROM PUNISHMENT, ILL-TREATMENT AND TORTURE BY NOT USING PHYSICAL RESTRAINT

According to the CRPD, health professionals should not use coercive measures (ie, physical restraint) as they may amount to punishment, ill-treatment and torture, but Spanish legislation obliges health professionals to use coercive measures (ie, physical restraint) to protect their patients from potential harm. This tension is manifested when facing a decision about using physical restraint, which generally occurs in emergency situations when health professionals assess that the patient's behaviour is putting him/herself or others at risk. Hypothetically, health professionals should give equal weight to rights and protection when facing physical restraint decisions. However, in this section I claim that the duty to protect from risk of harm using physical restraint always overrides the duty to avoid ill-treatment and torture, making health professionals more prone to use physical restraints. This claim is grounded in three main arguments.

First, Spanish national legislation directly regulates health professionals. Therefore, they tend to follow the Spanish legislation (rather than CRPD principles) opting to use coercive measures (ie, physical restraint) to protect patients or others from potential harm.

Second, the decision to act in an 'at risk situation' using physical restraint to protect from potential harm turns on an assessment of the risk of intervening compared to the risk of not intervening. Such estimation is impossible, since physical restraint decisions are not decisions made under conditions of risk but are decisions made under conditions of uncertainty.

Third, after taking the decision, health professionals assess the appropriateness of having used, versus not having used, physical restraints based on the observed outcome. For this assessment to be accurate, health professionals should be sure that harm would have occurred had they not used physical restraint to legitimise the coercive intervention. Nevertheless, this verification is impossible as physical restraint decisions are taken in 'split-brain institutions' (explained below), so only one side of the decision can be evaluated. According to Gigerenzer,[29] in institutions that require employees to perform a moral duty, health professionals can commit two types of failure: false alarms and misses. Both influence employees' behaviour, as Gigerenzer argues: '... if an institution

---

[29] G Gigerenzer 'Moral Intuition = Fast and Frugal Heuristics?' in W Sinnott-Armstrong (ed), *Moral Psychology, Vol. 2: The Cognitive Science of Morality: Intuition and Diversity* (Cambridge MA, MIT Press, 2008).

does not provide systematic feedback concerning false alarms and misses, but blames the employees when a miss occurs, it fosters employees' instinct for self-protection over the desire to protect their clients and support self-deception.'[30]

Gigerenzer[31] calls this environmental structure 'split-brain institutions' and claims that health professionals:

> … are likely to be sued for overlooking a disease but not for overtreatment and over-medication, which promotes doctors' self-protection over the protection of their patients and supports self-deception.

Importantly, the split-brain mechanism also operates in paediatric psychiatric settings for physical restraint decisions. In this case, 'false alarms' happen if health professionals use physical restraint when it is unnecessary and 'misses' happen if health professionals do not use physical restraint when necessary. This means that if a failure occurs because physical restraint was not used, it can be detected (ie, no physical restraint so a patient or others get hurt), but if a failure occurs because physical restraint was used it cannot be detected (ie, physical restraint was used when there would have been no harm without it). Thus, only one side of physical restraint decision-making consequence can be tested; the other result is always unknown. In a split-brain institution, health professionals do not receive any feedback about the appropriateness of the physical restraint decision, since it cannot be proved that no harm would not have occurred if physical restrain was not used. The likelihood of being sued for not using physical restraint, rather than for using physical restraint, suggests that health professionals are more prone to use physical restraint, doing so for self-protection rather than for protecting patients or others from harm.

LEGAL RECOMMENDATIONS

In this chapter I have argued that health professionals have a tendency to use physical restraint to legally protect themselves from being accused of malpractice if they did not use it. Consequently, to prevent the unnecessary use of physical restraint, it is advisable to enact a legal provision that specifically addresses this issue, stating that health professionals should intervene using other methods, such as removing environmental hazards or talking to the patient but, in any case, not applying physical restraint to the patient can be considered negligence, inaction or malpractice even if harm happens. In the particular case of the Spanish legislation, I recommend that Article 11 of the Penal Code should be modified by adding the provision that health professionals' role of guarantor excludes the possibility of using coercive measures as required interventions to protect persons with psychosocial disabilities from harm.

---

[30] G Gigerenzer, *Gut Feelings: Short Cuts to Better Decision Making* (London, Penguin Books, 2008).
[31] Gigerenzer, 'Moral Intuition' (2008).

16

Scottish Mental Health and Capacity Law

Replacing the Old with the New or the Old in Policy, Law and Practice?

JILL STAVERT

T HE MOTIVATING FACTOR behind the United Nations Convention on the Rights of Persons with Disabilities (CRPD)[1] was the view that previous human rights-based approaches were simply not delivering for persons with disabilities' equal and non-discriminatory enjoyment of human rights.[2] This was largely because existing approaches tended to view rights through the lens of medical models of disability[3] which simply defined the perimeters of protection and intervention rather than working to proactively empower persons with disabilities.[4] The protection and intervention approach was reinforced by the fact that different treatment of people with disabilities and lower levels of

---

[1] UN General Assembly, *Convention on the Rights of Persons with Disabilities* A/RES/61/106 24 January 2007.

[2] LO Gostin and L Gable, 'The Human Rights of Persons with Mental Disabilities: A Global Perspective on the Application of Human Rights Principles to Mental Health' (2004) 63 *Maryland Law Review* 20; R Kayess and P French, 'Out of Darkness into Light? Introducing the Convention on the Rights of Persons with Disabilities' (2008) 8(1) *Human Rights Law Review* 1.

[3] OM Arnardóttir, 'A Future of Mutidimensional Disadvantage Equality' in OM Arnardóttir and G Quinn (eds), *The UN Convention on the Rights of Persons with Disabilities: European and Scandinavian Perspectives* (Leiden and Boston, Martinus Nijhoff, 2009), 41–66; P Bartlett, 'Implementing a Paradigm Shift: Implementing the Convention on the Rights of Persons with Disabilities in the Context of Mental Disability Law' in *Torture in Healthcare Settings: Reflections on the Special Rapporteur on Torture's 2013 Thematic Report* (Washington DC, Centre for Human Rights and Humanitarian Law, American University Washington College of Law, 2014) 169.

[4] Gostin and Gable, 'The Human Rights of Persons with Mental Disabilities' (2004); Kayess and French, 'Out of Darkness into Light?' (2008).

rights enjoyment have traditionally been permitted where there is objective and reasonable justification for the limitation of rights.[5]

By reinforcing equality and non-discrimination and in integrating civil, political, social and economic rights and its principles of equality, non-discrimination, active inclusion, participation and autonomy, the CRPD disallows such differentiation in rights enjoyment.[6] Different treatment based on disability is seen as inherently discriminatory and therefore an obstacle to equal rights enjoyment. It is in discontinuing such an approach and putting in place the necessary societal and state support that the CRPD paradigm shift lies.

Effecting such a paradigm shift, however, requires serious reconsideration of the entire legal, policy and practice landscape within which persons with mental disabilities are able to enjoy their human rights.[7] The CRPD compels a refocus on what these rights are actually supposed to be achieving for persons with mental disabilities to live fulfilled lives. In this sense, it is very much akin to the capability approach as promoted by Sen and Nussbaum, which essentially recognises the primary moral importance of all individuals to be able to achieve wellbeing and the need, therefore, to provide the opportunities to do this.[8] It also requires the realisation that restricting individual autonomy to protect a person with a mental disability from abuse may amount to discrimination where the same standards are not applied to all persons.[9]

[5] A Nilsson, 'Objective and Reasonable? Scrutinising Compulsory Mental Health Interventions from a Non-Discrimination Perspective' (2014) 14 *Human Rights Law Review* 459; UN Human Rights Committee, *Gillot and others v France* (932/2000) A/57/40 at 270 (2002) 15 July 2002; 10 IHRR 22 (2003) paras 13.2 and 13.17; UN Human Rights Committee, *Guido Jacobs v Belgium* (943/2000), CCPR/C/81/D/943/2000 (2004) 17 August 2004 para 9.5; UN Committee on Economic, Social and Cultural Rights, *General Comment 20: Non-Discrimination in Economic, Social and Cultural Rights (Art 2(2))* E/C.12/GC/20 2 July 2009; 16 IHRR 925 (2009) para 13.

[6] UN Committee on the Rights of Persons with Disabilities, *General Comment No 6 (2018) on Equality and Non-Discrimination*, CRPD/C/GC/6 9 March 2018; JE Goldsmidt, 'New Perspectives on Equality: Towards Transformative Justice through the Disability Convention?' (2017) 35(1) *Nordic Journal of Human Rights* 1; J Stavert and R McGregor, 'Domestic Legislation and International Human Rights Standards: The Case of Mental Health and Incapacity' (2018) 22(1) *International Journal of Human Rights* 70.

[7] T Minkowitz, 'CRPD and Transformative Equality' (2017) 13(1) *International Journal of Law in Context* 77; BA Clough, 'New Legal Landscapes: (Re) Constructing the Boundaries of Mental Capacity Law' (2018) 26(2) *Medical Law Review* 246; J Stavert, 'Paradigm Shift or Paradigm Paralysis? National Mental Health and Capacity Law and Implementing the CRPD in Scotland' (2018) 7(3) *Laws* 26. Available at: www.mdpi.com/2075-471X/7/3/26.

[8] See, eg, MC Nussbaum, *Frontiers of Justice: Disability, Nationality, Species Membership* (Cambridge MA, Belknap Press, 2006); MC Nussbaum, *Creating Capabilities: The Human Development Approach* (Cambridge MA, Belknap Press, 2011); A Sen, *Why Health Equity?* Paper presented at the Global Health Equity Initiative; Public health, ethics and equity, Harvard University (1999, February); A Sen, *The Idea of Justice* (London, Allen Lane, 2009); S Venkatapuram, *Health Justice. An Argument from the Capabilities Approach* (Cambridge, Polity Press, 2011); S Venkatapuram, 'Mental Disability, Human Rights and the Capabilities Approach: Searching for the Foundations' (2014) 26(4) *International Review of Psychiatry* 408–14.

[9] A Keeling, 'Organising Objects: Adult Safeguarding Practice and Article 16 of the United Nations Convention on the Rights of Persons with Disabilities' (2017) 53 *International Journal of Law and Psychiatry* 77, 77–78; C McKay and J Stavert, *Scotland's Mental Health and Capacity*

This presents particular challenges for mental health and capacity law, policy and practices, most of which do indeed justify a loss of autonomy through substitute decision-making mechanisms[10] based on the existence of mental disability and/or related mental impairment and what is perceived to be in the individual's best interests. Articles 12 and 14 of the CRPD seek to address this, with the Committee emphasising that laws, policies and practices that discriminate on the basis of disability, in both institutional and community settings, are wholly unacceptable.[11] The nature and extent of such challenge is, however, best illustrated by putting it in context. The remainder of this chapter, therefore, will do this through the lens of existing mental health and capacity law in Scotland and its potential reform.

HUMAN RIGHTS AND SCOTLAND'S MENTAL HEALTH AND CAPACITY LAW

Legal and Policy Status of CRPD in Scotland

The United Kingdom (UK), of which Scotland is currently a devolved region, adopts a dualist approach to international law. Rights identified within international human rights treaties ratified by the UK can be nationally enforced only if they are specifically incorporated in national legislation. As such, incorporation occurs solely with regard to the European Convention on Human Rights (ECHR) rights and not CRPD rights, the latter carrying less legal weight than the former.

In Scotland, mental health and capacity law and policy is devolved to the Scottish Parliament and the Scottish Government. As a matter of law, devolved legislative provisions and actions of the Scottish Ministers that are incompatible with ECHR rights are invalid.[12] The Human Rights Act 1998 also requires all public bodies to be ECHR compliant,[13] thus allowing individuals to enforce their rights through Scottish courts and tribunals. The lack of similar legislative enshrinement of CRPD rights means they cannot be enforced in the same way. Moreover, at the time Scotland's current mental capacity and mental health legislation was enacted, the UK was already an ECHR state party but had not yet ratified

---

Law; The Case for Reform (Edinburgh, Mental Welfare Commission for Scotland/Centre for Mental Health and Capacity Law, 2017) 31. Available at: www.mwcscot.org.uk/media/371023/scotland_s_ mental_health_and_capacity_law.pdf.

[10] The Committee on the Rights of Persons with Disabilities clarified what it considers to constitute a substitute decision-making arrangement in January 2018. See UN Committee on the Rights of Persons with Disabilities, *General Comment No 1 (2014) Article 12: Equal Recognition Before the Law – Corrigendum* CRPC/C/GC/1/Corr.1 26 January 2018.

[11] UN Committee on the Rights of Persons with Disabilities, *General Comment No 1*; UN Committee on the Rights of Persons with Disabilities, *Guidelines on Article 14 of the Convention on the Rights of Persons with Disabilities: The Right to Liberty and Security of Persons with Disabilities* September 2015; UN Committee in the Rights of Persons with Disabilities, *General Comment No 5(2017) on Living Independently and Being Included in the Community* CRPD/C/GC/5 27 October 2017.

[12] Scotland Act 1998, ss 29(2)(d) and 57(2).

[13] Human Rights Act 1998, ss 2, 3 and 6.

the CRPD. Thus, whilst the Adults with Incapacity (Scotland) Act 2000 (AWIA) and Mental Health (Care and Treatment) (Scotland) Act 2003 (MHA) were both lauded as good examples of human rights-informed legislation governing non-consensual interventions, it was the ECHR rights framework that was most influential.[14] However, subsequent developments in ECHR jurisprudence and the UK's ratification of the CRPD and its Optional Protocol in 2009 has resulted in calls for relevant legislation and related policy and practice to be revisited.

The CRPD may have less legal purchase than ECHR rights in Scotland, but its impact should not be underestimated. Devolved legislation and actions of the Scottish Ministers can now be prevented on the basis of non-compliance with the UK's CRPD State Party international obligations.[15] Moreover, CRPD influence is very evident in recent Scottish Government consultations on AWIA reform and responses to these[16] and its announcement of a MHA review.[17] It is also reflected in the Scottish Government's 2016 CRPD Delivery Plan[18] and in its Mental Health Strategy 2017–27.[19] The Article 12 CRPD support paradigm has been advanced through the Scottish Government's proposed Supported Decision-Making Strategy, and some sheriffdoms have issued directions relating to AWIA applications requiring evidence of real efforts to support the exercise of legal capacity before sheriff courts will consider guardianship applications.[20] In 2016, the Mental Welfare Commission also published supported decision-making guidance.[21]

Calls for Reform of Mental Health and Capacity Law

Recommendations for adaptation of the AWIA to ensure Article 12 CRPD compliance were made in the Essex Autonomy Project *Three Jurisdictions* report,[22] which has influenced the Scottish Government AWIA reform process.

---

[14] Fischer, 'A Comparative Look' (2006).

[15] Scotland Act 1998, ss 35(1)(a) and 58(1).

[16] Scottish Government, *Responses to the Scottish Government's Consultation on the Scottish Law Commission's Review of Adults with Incapacity* (Edinburgh, Scottish Government, 2016). Available at: www.gov.scot/Resource/0050/00502699.pdf; *Adults with Incapacity (Scotland) Act 2000 Proposals for Reform* (Consultation Paper) (Edinburgh, Scottish Government, 2018). Available at: www.gov.scot/Publications/2018/01/4350/downloads#res530800.

[17] 'Review of the Mental Health Act' (Edinburgh, Scottish Government, 2019). Available at: www.gov.scot/news/review-of-the-mental-health-act.

[18] *A Fairer Scotland for Disabled People – Our Delivery Plan to 2021 for the United Nations Convention on the Rights of Persons with Disabilities* (Edinburgh, Scottish Government, 2016). Available at: www.gov.scot/Resource/0051/00510948.pdf.

[19] *Mental Health Strategy: 2017–2027*. Available at: www.gov.scot/Resource/0051/00516047.pdf.

[20] Sheriffdom of Lothian and Borders, *Practice Note No 1 of 2016, Applications Under the Adults with Incapacity (Scotland) Act 2000* (2016). Available at: www.scotcourts.gov.uk/rules-and-practice/practice-notes/sheriff-court-practice-notes-(civil).

[21] *Good Practice Guide: Supported Decision-Making* (Edinburgh, Mental Welfare Commission for Scotland, 2016). Available at: www.mwcscot.org.uk/media/348023/mwc_sdm_draft_gp_guide_10__post_board__jw_final.pdf.

[22] W Martin et al, *The Essex Autonomy Project Three Jurisdictions Report: Towards Compliance with CRPD Art. 12 in Capacity/Incapacity Legislation across the UK* (Colchester,

However, a much broader call for change came in the form of the Mental Welfare Commission and Centre for Mental Health and Capacity Law 2017 joint report *Scotland's Mental Health and Capacity Law: The Case for Reform.*[23] The report was based on a mental health and capacity law reform scoping exercise which collected the views of professional and academic stakeholders on the implementation of the three Acts and considered relevant literature. The objective of the exercise was to gain greater insight into any operational and human rights compliance issues, as well as how ready the system is to embrace structural changes and human rights developments going forward. It particularly considered the basis for intervention under the AWIA and MHA and whether or how unified mental health and capacity – similar to that recently enacted in Northern Ireland – and a 'graded guardianship' system might help address operational and compliance issues. Its findings were supplemented by a parallel Mental Welfare Commission consultation exercise canvassing the views of persons with lived experience of mental illness of involuntary interventions.[24]

Scotland's Mental Health and Capacity Law: The Case for Reform – Findings and Recommendations

The *Case for Reform* report by the Mental Welfare Commission and Centre for Mental Health and Capacity Law identified two significant concerns based on more than a minority opinion and are of particular significance in CRPD terms reflecting the concerns articulated in the CRPD Committee's General Comment No 1 on Article 12 CRPD.[25] These were:

- the problem of using existing capacity or decision-making thresholds as the basis, even partially, for involuntary interventions. Adults deemed to be 'incapable'[26] fall within the remit of the AWIA and persons with 'significantly

University of Essex, 2016). Available at: www.autonomy.essex.ac.uk/wp-content/uploads/2017/01/EAP-3J-Final-Report-2016.pdf.

[23] McKay and Stavert, *Scotland's Mental Health and Capacity Law* (2017).

[24] *Capacity, Detention, Supported Decision Making and Mental Ill Health* (Edinburgh, Mental Welfare Commission for Scotland, 2017). Available at: www.mwcscot.org.uk/media/371015/capacity__detention__supported_decision_making_and_mental_ill_health.pdf.

[25] UN Committee on the Rights of Persons with Disabilities, *General Comment No 1 (2014) Article 12.*

[26] AWIA, s 1(6). "Incapable" is defined as being incapable of:

'(a) acting; or
(b) making decisions; or
(c) communicating decisions; or
(d) understanding decisions; or
(e) retaining the memory of decisions,

as mentioned in any provision of this Act, by reason of mental disorder or of inability to communicate because of physical disability; but a person shall not fall within this definition by reason only of a lack or deficiency in a faculty of communication if that lack or deficiency can be made good by human or mechanical aid (whether of an interpretative nature or otherwise) ...'

impaired decision-making ability'[27] because of their mental disorder within the MHA's remit, subject to both Acts' other principles and criteria for non-consensual intervention; and

- the feeling that the reality is that the MHA and AWIA, rather than enhancing and protecting the autonomy of people with cognitive, intellectual and psychosocial disabilities, merely articulate more clearly when involuntary interventions are permissible.[28]

In light of these two significant concerns, the *Case for Reform* report made eight recommendations, the first calling for widescale reform as follows:

> Recommendation 1: There should be a long-term programme of law reform, covering all forms of non-consensual decision making affecting people with mental disorders. This should work towards a coherent and non-discriminatory legislative framework which reflects UNCRPD and ECHR requirements and gives effect to the rights, will and preferences of the individual. Further, in accordance with Article 4(3) UNCRPD, persons with lived experience of mental disorder must be actively consulted in any reform process.[29]

Other recommendations include the increased convergence of the legislation over time, particularly with respect to the criteria justifying intervention[30] and that there should be a single judicial forum to oversee non-consensual interventions.[31] In terms of this single forum, the majority view during the information gathering exercise was in favour of the new Mental Health Chamber (currently

---

[27] MHA ss 36(4)(b), 44(4)(b) and 64(5)(d). 'Significantly impaired decision-making ability' is not defined in the MHA. However, its Code of Practice (Scottish Government, 2005) states that whilst it is a concept that is separate to the AWIA definition of 'incapacity', factors similar to those which are taken into account in its assessment will in practice be considered. That being said, it is potentially a broader concept than the more decision-specific capacity test under the AWIA and allows for someone to be subject to MHA compulsion whilst at the same time retaining the ability to consent to specific treatments.

[28] People First (Scotland), *'Citizens' Grand Jury Report: Care, Protection and Human Rights or Danger, Neglect and Human Wrongs?'* (Edinburgh, People First (Scotland) 2011). Available at: www.peoplefirstscotland.org/files/2012/10/citizensgrandjuryreportweb.pdf; Mental Welfare Commission for Scotland, *Visit and Monitoring Report: Updated Survey of Recorded Matters* (Edinburgh, Mental Welfare Commission for Scotland, 2014). Available at: www.mwcscot.org.uk/media/203366/updated_survey_of_recorded_matters__2_.pdf; *Visit and Monitoring Report: Suspension of Detention Visits (May–Dec 2014)* (Edinburgh, Mental Welfare Commission for Scotland, 2015). Available at: www.mwcscot.org.uk/media/233726/suspension_of_detention_report_final_1.pdf; Mental Welfare Commission for Scotland, *Visit and Monitoring Report: Visits to People on Longer Term Community-Based Compulsory Treatment Orders* (Edinburgh, Mental Welfare Commission for Scotland, 2015). Available at: www.mwcscot.org.uk/media/243429/ccto_visit_report.pdf; Mental Welfare Commission for Scotland, *Visit and Monitoring Report – Intensive Psychiatric Care in Scotland 2015* (Edinburgh, Mental Welfare Commission for Scotland 2016). Available at: www.mwcscot.org.uk/media/315618/intensive_psychiatric_case_in_scotland_report_final.pdf; Mental Welfare Commission for Scotland, *Adults with Incapacity Act Monitoring Report 2016–17* (Edinburgh, Mental Welfare Commission for Scotland, 2017). Available at: www.mwcscot.org.uk/media/389068/awi_monitoring_report_2016–17.pdf.

[29] McKay and Stavert, *Scotland's Mental Health and Capacity Law* (2017).

[30] Ibid, recommendation 2.

[31] Ibid, recommendation 3.

the Mental Health Tribunal for Scotland) of the devolved Scottish tribunals system. However, the report envisages that the use of 'capacity thresholds' for intervention, albeit improved, would still be on the agenda. It contains a recommendation to replace the MHA 'capacity' test with one more akin to the AWIA capacity test.[32] That being said, recognising some of the problems associated with capacity assessments, it is also recommended that priority should first be given: '(a) to improve practice and develop consistent standards across medicine, psychology and the law on the assessment of capacity and (b) to identify and implement practical steps to enhance decision making autonomy whenever non-consensual interventions are being considered.'[33] Moreover, in proposing 'graded guardianship', there is no suggestion that guardianship be abolished, although the suggested design allows for support for the exercise of legal capacity. It also only permits full guardianship in cases where it was impossible to ascertain an individual's will and preferences.

The broad thrust of the report's recommendations can be discerned in the ministerial March 2019 MHA review announcement,[34] although at the time of writing it is impossible to assess the extent to which they will ultimately be adopted in any legislative reform. The report's recommendations are pragmatic in accepting that the current appetite for the CRPD at state level does not necessarily extend to the more radical implications of effecting the CRPD paradigm shift, notably the CRPD Committee injunction of completely replacing existing non-consensual psychiatric treatment and guardianship regimes. It nonetheless advocates a real drive forward towards CRPD compliance. However, this begs the question of whether any concrete steps towards it can realistically be achieved in this way, in turn raising several issues that I will consider now.

Adapting Existing Frameworks for Non-Consensual Intervention

At present, whilst the AWIA and MHA require that the present and past wishes and feelings of the individual must be taken into account, the principle is not paramount and is only one of several considerations. Indeed, whilst neither Act allows for 'best interests' decisions to be made, and both only permit interventions that provide a benefit to the individual not otherwise attainable, evidence suggests that opinions of what may 'benefit' an individual can override such wishes and feelings.[35] In addition, support for the exercise of legal capacity may be implied and, to a limited degree, identified in both Acts. For example,

---

[32] Ibid, recommendation 8.

[33] Ibid.

[34] See Scottish Government, 'Review of the Mental Health Act' (2019); J Stavert, 'Mental Health Act Review in Scotland: Some Initial Observations' (2019) 93 *Mental Capacity Report: Scotland* 3, 3–10.

[35] A Ward and A Ruck Keene, 'With or Without Best Interests: The Mental Capacity Act 2005, the Adults with Incapacity (Scotland) Act 2000 and Constructing Decisions' (2016) 22 *International Journal of Mental Health and Capacity Law* 17.

psychiatric advance statements are recognised and there is a right to local authority services for care and to promote wellbeing and a specific right to independent advocacy identified in the MHA.[36] Provisions relating to the regulation of powers of attorney (as forms of advance planning) and the requirement to encourage skills development are contained within the AWIA[37] and it specifically recognises the role of independent advocacy to a limited degree.[38] However, the purpose and operation of such support requires clarification and expansion and is currently very much envisaged in the context of, rather than in terms of avoiding, interventions.[39]

It has been suggested that CRPD compliance can be achieved in Scotland by reframing and reordering the MHA and AWIA principles that underpin decisions to intervene during the implementation of interventions. Importantly, this would include adding a presumption in favour of the rights, will and preferences of the individual, articulating support for the exercise of legal capacity more clearly and permitting non-consensual interventions only when it is genuinely impossible to ascertain a person's will and preferences and/or there is a risk of harm, such risk being assessed on a non-discriminatory basis.[40]

In such an environment the primary focus would be on providing adequate and appropriate support for the exercise of legal capacity for persons with mental disabilities rather than considering the efficacy of involuntary interventions. Moreover, non-consensual interventions would arguably only be permissible in situations akin to those envisaged by the CRPD Committee when it acknowledges that when after making 'significant efforts' it has not been practicable to determine an individual's will and preferences then a 'best interpretation of will and preferences' (as opposed to a best interest's decision) may be adopted[41] and in emergencies.[42]

This might work but, at the same time, there are potential stumbling blocks such as the continued use of capacity and risk assessment as thresholds for intervention and the role of judicial bodies in protecting individual rights and of supported decision-making in the context of such interventions.

Maintaining Capacity and Risk Assessments as Thresholds for Intervention

The first potential obstacle lies in retaining capacity assessments as the threshold for non-consensual interventions. While there is some scope for arguing that

[36] MHA, ss 25–27, 259 and 275–276.
[37] AWIA, ss 1(5) and 15–24.
[38] Ibid, s 3(5A).
[39] Martin et al, *The Essex Autonomy Project Three Jurisdictions Report* (2016); McKay and Stavert, *Scotland's Mental Health and Capacity Law* (2017).
[40] Ibid.
[41] UN Committee on the Rights of Persons with Disabilities *General Comment No 1 (2014) Article 12.*
[42] E Flynn and A Arstein-Kerslake, 'State Intervention in the Lives of People with Disabilities: The Case for a Disability-Neutral Framework' (2017) 13(1) *International Journal of Law in Context* 39, 49–52.

such assessments allow for parity of treatment between persons with physical and mental disorder,[43] it became clear during the law reform scoping exercise that Scotland does not possess the answer to non-discriminatory capacity (or decision-making) assessments. Indeed, these were found to be unreliable in terms of lacking uniformity, depth and perceptions about the impact of mental disability, including those surrounding risk.[44] Perceptions of risk were also often considered to be the driving force in capacity assessments.[45] This view echoes concerns expressed elsewhere.[46]

In short, capacity assessments, in practice, have the potential to deny real personhood and allow for a potentially discriminatory means of justifying non-consensual interventions for persons with mental disabilities. In this respect, the *Case for Reform*'s recommendation on revisiting how capacity assessments are made is correct. This must, however, be accompanied by a real consideration of how existing perceptions and presumptions about capabilities of and risks concerning persons with mental disabilities may lead to discriminatory outcomes. This leads to a second issue about the role of judicial bodies, such as mental health tribunals, in reinforcing and protecting the rights of persons with mental disabilities against non-consensual interventions justified on discriminatory grounds.

The Role of the Mental Health Tribunal for Scotland (or Mental Health Chamber)

The UN Special Rapporteur on the right of everyone to the enjoyment of the highest attainable standard of physical and mental health has stated that accountability for the enjoyment of the right to mental health depends upon, amongst other things, independent review provided by judicial bodies. However, at the

---

[43] J Dawson and G Szmukler, 'Fusion of Mental Health and Incapacity Legislation' (2006) 188 *British Journal of Psychiatry* 504; C Harper et al, 'No Longer "Anomalous, Confusing and Unjust": The Mental Capacity Act (Northern Ireland) 2016' (2016) 22 *International Journal of Mental Health and Capacity Law* 57; G Szmukler et al, 'A Model Law Fusing Incapacity and Mental Health Legislation' (2010) 20 *Journal of Mental Health Law* 9.

[44] Mental Welfare Commission for Scotland, *Consultation Report: Capacity, Detention, Supported Decision Making and Mental Ill Health* (2017); McKay and Stavert, *Scotland's Mental Health and Capacity Law* (2017).

[45] McKay and Stavert, *Scotland's Mental Health and Capacity Law* (2017).

[46] House of Lords Select Committee on the Mental Capacity Act, *Report of Session 2013–14: Mental Capacity Act 2005: Post-legislative Scrutiny* (2014) HL 139; A Kampf, 'Involuntary Treatment Decisions: Using Negotiated Silence to Facilitate Change?' in B McSherry and P Weller (eds) *Rethinking Rights-Based Mental Health Laws* (Oxford, Hart Publishing, 2010); P Gooding, 'Supported Decision-Making: A Rights-Based Disability Concept and its Implications for Mental Health Law' (2013) 20 *Psychiatry, Psychology and Law* 431; E Flynn and A Arstein-Kerslake, 'Legislating Personhood: Realising the Right to Support in Exercising Legal Capacity' (2014) 10(1) *International Journal of Law in Context* 81; G Quinn, 'Concept Paper – Personhood and Legal Capacity – Perspectives on the Paradigm Shift of Article 12 CRPD' (HPOD Conference, Harvard Law School, Cambridge, MA, USA, 20 February 2010).

same time, he notes an increase in mental health tribunals that legitimise coercion and isolate people within mental health systems from access to justice.[47]

It is not clear whether the Mental Health Tribunal for Scotland is considered to fall within this category. Certainly, it must adhere to MHA principles in its decision-making and an absence of successful challenges indicates that this is occurring. However, psychiatric compulsion and guardianship is currently increasing, not decreasing, in Scotland.[48] Moreover, studies conducted to date, albeit limited,[49] on the operation of the tribunal have tended to indicate that its decision-making is heavily influenced by its medical panel members.[50] Whilst this tends to reflect perceptions of mental health tribunals elsewhere,[51] if they adhere to the potentially discriminatory perceptions of capacity and risk, this is a cause for concern. However, a Chamber with a widened jurisdiction, as recommended by the *Case for Reform* report, and commitment to ensuring the equal enjoyment of human rights would be a positive step.

Support for the Exercise of Legal Capacity/Supported Decision-Making

Another issue is that if the focus is to be on supporting the exercise of legal capacity and not on intervention, it is necessary to consider whether available support meets Article 12(4) of the CRPD requirements. While studies and evaluations are currently taking place across the globe, we do not yet have a comprehensive evidence base for what works.[52]

Moreover, there remains a lack of terminological clarity surrounding the terms 'support for the exercise of legal capacity' and 'supported decision-making' and

[47] UN High Commissioner for Human Rights, *Mental Health and Human Rights* (Human Rights Council 34th session, 27 February–24 March 2017 A/HRC/34/32 31 January 2017) paras 30–34.

[48] Mental Welfare Commission for Scotland, *Adults with Incapacity Act Monitoring Report 2016–17* (2017); *Mental Health Act Monitoring Report 2016–17* (Edinburgh, Mental Welfare Commission for Scotland, 2018). Available at: www.mwcscot.org.uk/media/395255/mha_monitoring_report2016-17_feb2018.pdf.

[49] A much more extensive study is currently being undertaken ('The Mental Health Tribunal for Scotland: The Views and Experiences of Patients, Named Persons, Practitioners and Members' Oct 2017–Sept 2020, Centre for Mental Health and Capacity Law, Edinburgh Napier University, and Queen's University Belfast (funded by the Nuffield Foundation)).

[50] F Dobbie et al, *An Exploration of the Early Operation of the Mental Health Tribunal for Scotland* (Edinburgh, Scottish Government, 2009). Available at: www.gov.scot/Resource/Doc/263296/0078751.pdf; J Ridley and S Hunter, 'Subjective Experiences of Compulsory Treatment form a Qualitative Study of Early Implementation of the Mental Health (Care and Treatment) (Scotland) Act 2003' (2013) 21(5) *Health and Social Care in the Community* 509.

[51] A Macgregor et al, 'Are Mental Health Tribunals Operating in Accordance with International Human Rights Standards? A Systematic Review of the International Literature' (2019, July) 27(4) *Health and Social Care in the Community* e494–e513.

[52] T Carney, 'Clarifying, Operationalising and Evaluating Supported Decision-making Models' (2014) 1 *Research and Practice in Intellectual and Developmental Disabilities* 46; 'Supporting People with Cognitive Disability with Decision-Making: Any Australian Law Reform Contributions?' (2015) 2 *Research and Practice in Intellectual and Developmental Disabilities* 6.

what they are supposed to achieve in giving effect to an individual's rights, will and preferences.[53] In addition, whilst 'shared' and 'participatory' decision-making have been buzzwords for some time now, there must be a real appreciation – too often, it is suggested, missed – that there is a distinction between supporting someone to participate in decision-making processes where ultimately their autonomy can be overridden and/or to make 'the right decisions' and supporting someone to exercise their legal capacity. This is something that the Mental Welfare Commission's supported decision-making guidance attempts to stress but, because it was designed to work within existing legislative frameworks, it will be interesting to see how successful it is. For the CRPD paradigm shift to be made real, such support needs to be adequately resourced (as does research into and evaluations of effective forms of support for the exercise of legal capacity). Existing initiatives such as the previously mentioned Scottish Government's proposed Supported Decision-Making Strategy, sheriff court directions and Mental Welfare Commission guidance are laudable but, when accompanied by, for example, legal aid cuts and reduced resourcing for the already over-burdened independent advocacy provision in Scotland,[54] one must wonder how effective this will be.

Whilst all these difficulties should not prevent Scotland from pressing ahead, it is important to be alive to the fact that poor and ineffective supported decision-making and deficiencies in terms of supportive environments and removing obstacles to equal rights enjoyment might actually militate against such equal enjoyment. There is also a need to address the issue that the European Court of Human Rights, whose jurisprudence Scotland must follow, continues to consider that it is acceptable to limit or deny autonomy on the basis of existence of mental disability and/or related mental impairment, admittedly subject to strict safeguards.[55] That being said, it is certainly arguable that the closer to the CRPD paradigm Scotland is able to move, the more effectively and realistically it will be able to address issues such as those currently faced concerning compliance

---

[53] RD Dinerstein, 'Implementing Legal Capacity under Article 12 of the UN Convention on the Rights of Persons with Disabilities: The Difficult Road from Guardianship to Supported Decision-Making' (2012) 19 *Human Rights Brief* 8; M Browning et al, 'Supported Decision-Making: Understanding How its Conceptual Link to Legal Capacity is Influencing the Development of Practice' (2014) 34 *Research and Practice in Intellectual and Developmental Disabilities* 36; P Gooding, 'Navigating the "Flashing Amber Lights" of the Right to Legal Capacity in the United Nations Convention on the Rights of Persons with Disabilities: Responding to Major Concerns' (2015) 15(1) *Human Rights Law Review* 45.

[54] Scottish Independent Advocacy Alliance, *Map of Advocacy across Scotland 2015–2016* (Edinburgh, Scottish Independent Advocacy Alliance, 2016). Available at: www.siaa.org.uk/wp-content/uploads/2017/09/SIAA_Advocacy_Map_2015-16-1.pdf; Mental Welfare Commission for Scotland, *The Right to Advocacy – A Review of Advocacy Planning Across Scotland* (Edinburgh, Mental Welfare Commission for Scotland, 2018). Available at: www.mwcscot.org.uk/media/395529/the_right_to_advocacy_march_2018.pdf.

[55] This approach was very much reinforced in the recent *A-MV v Finland* ruling (*A-MV v Finland* App no 53251/13 (ECtHR, 23 March 2017).

with Article 5 ECHR (the right to liberty) for persons with mental disabilities following, amongst others, the *Bournewood* and *Cheshire West* rulings.[56]

CONCLUSION

Many jurisdictions – including Scotland – are considering CRPD compliance. To date, this has largely been through suggesting or implementing adaptations to existing legal, policy and practice frameworks by introducing or reinforcing legislative principles to give greater respect for the will and preferences of persons with mental disabilities and requiring accompanying supported decision-making mechanisms. However, it is unclear whether any come close to ensuring that an individual's will and preferences are genuinely reflected in all decisions that concern them on an equal basis with others. This is not something that has been lost on the UN Committee on the Rights of Persons with Disabilities.[57] Indeed, it is worth considering whether such adaptations might even be an impediment to achieving the CRPD paradigm shift.

To ensure genuine enjoyment of all human rights equally and without discrimination for persons with mental disabilities in Scotland, it is essential to avoid initiatives (such as those pursued by the Scottish Government) and recommendations (such as those contained in the *Case for Reform* report) becoming mere rhetoric, with no meaningful movement towards the required culture shift in terms of our law, policy and practice. This importantly still requires tackling some fundamental ideological and cultural issues.

Legislative changes take time. Although the CRPD Committee states that the right to equal recognition before the law identified in Article 12 CRPD is a civil right and, as such, must be implemented immediately, it does have to be accepted that fundamental legislative change at national level cannot occur immediately. However, whilst the law is an essential component in driving forward culture change – and, indeed, the required CRPD paradigm shift – significant steps towards achieving such change can be commenced immediately within existing legal frameworks through policy, practice and resource allocation that focus on ensuring the equal and non-discriminatory enjoyment of human rights by all and what can be done to ensure it.

[56] *HL v UK* (2005) 40 EHRR 32 ('Bournewood'); *P (by his litigation friend the Official Solicitor) (Appellant) v Cheshire West and Chester Council and another (Respondents); P and Q (by their litigation friend, the Official Solicitor) (Appellants) v Surrey County Council (Respondent)* [2014] UKSC 1 ('Cheshire West'). Both judgments emphasise that individuals who lack capacity to consent to a deprivation of liberty are entitled to the same legal and procedural safeguards as others.
[57] See, eg, UN Committee on the Rights of Persons with Disabilities, *Concluding Observations on the initial Report of Sweden*, CRPD/C/SWE/CO/1 12 May 2014; UN Committee on the Rights of Persons with Disabilities, *Concluding Observations on the Initial Report of the United Kingdom of Great Britain and Northern Ireland*, CRPD/C/GBR/CO/1 3 October 2017; UN Committee on the Rights of Persons with Disabilities, *Concluding Observations on the Initial Report of Latvia*, CRPD/C/LVA/CO/1 10 October 2017.

17

Diffabled People's Access to Indonesia's Criminal Justice System

DIO ASHAR WICAKSANA

I NDONESIA SUCCESSFULLY AMENDED Law 8/2016 regarding disabled people in early 2016, in compliance with its ratification of the Convention on the Rights of Persons with Disabilities (CRPD) in 2011.[1] The amendment recognises the fundamental rights of disabled people and groups to equality and opportunity in Indonesia. It also reconstructs the definition of disability, characterising people with disability as people with physical and mental limitations on their ability to communicate with other people as equals and participate effectively in the community.

Disabled people, alongside women, LGBTQI[2] and other minority groups, are commonly discriminated against in Indonesian society.[3] Disabled activists believe that being disabled is a natural part of human diversity – something that should be valued and respected, rather than pitied, feared and discriminated against. Disabled people are victimised at four to ten times the rate of 'other' people.[4] However, until 2016, there was inadequate protection for victims under Indonesian law, especially woman and disabled people.[5] In 2016, the Indonesian Judicial Monitoring Society studied all published Indonesian judicial decisions regarding disabled people who had experienced sexual and/or other violent crime during 2011–15. It found that disabled women face higher levels of discrimination and sexual and physical harassment.[6]

---

[1] Available at: www.bphn.go.id/data/documents/11uu019.pdf.

[2] Abbreviation for lesbian, gay, bisexual, transgender, questioning (or: queer), intersex.

[3] Available at: www.difabel.tempo.co/read/1164091/lgbt-penyandang-disabilitas-mengalami-diskriminasi-berkali-lipat/full&view=ok.

[4] D Sobsey, *Violence and Abuse in the Lives of People with Disabilities* in Supriyadi Widodo Eddyono and Ajeng Gandini Kamilah (eds), *Aspek-Aspek Criminal Justice bagi Penyandang Disabilitas (the Aspects of Criminal Justice for Disabled People)*, (Jakarta, Institute Criminal Justice Reform, 2015) 9.

[5] Available at: www.mappifhui.org/2017/02/28/peradilan-yang-adil-bagi-penyandang-difabel-oleh-dio-ashar-wicaksana/.

[6] Available at: http://mappifhui.org/2017/12/12/22-putusan-hakim-dari-tahun-2011-2015-terhadap-kekerasan-seksual-yang-dialami-oleh-difabel/.

Before 2016, the Indonesian legal system used the term 'impaired' to refer to people who have physical and mental limitations. This term was criticised, particularly by human rights activists, who claimed it led to discrimination.[7] Following the CRPD, Law 8/2016 replaced the terms 'impaired persons' with 'disabled persons'. Nonetheless, Indonesian activists prefer to use 'diffabled' rather than 'disabled' because 'diffabled' derives from 'differently abled', a term quite different to disabled, which relates to 'disabilities'. Use of this alternative term has struggled to change the social perspective from one where a diffabled person is incapable of 'normal' activities to recognising that the diffabled person is able to do something, with different abilities.[8] For instance, Nurul Saadah is a person who walks with a stick. It means that she can perform 'normal' activities like another person, but with a different ability; other people might walk using only their feet, but Nurul walks using her feet and a stick.[9] The concept of 'normal' activities is subject to considerable misunderstanding.

Indonesian scholars Mansour Fakih and Setia Adi Purwanta coined the term 'diffabled' to reconstruct the negative perspective of impairment.[10] In this chapter, I use 'diffability' to replace the normative term 'disability'. The term 'disabled' was originally developed as part of a medical model. This approach regards disabled people as weak, needy and dependent and assumes that disabled people are incapable of getting good jobs and living and participating fully in society.[11]

Diffabled people face barriers when accessing the legal system, just as they face barriers in other areas of their lives. The United Nations Development Programme (UNDP) identifies barriers to the justice system such as long delays, gender bias, lack of proper information, lack of legal aid support, limited public participation, an excessive number of laws, avoidance of the legal system for economic reasons, formalistic and expensive administrative legal procedures and severe limitations on existing remedies.[12] In some cases, law officers do not process the cases because they find it difficult to reconstruct cases which involve diffabled people, particularly where there is a deficiency in mental ability.[13] It may also be that cases involving diffabled people are not taken seriously due to discriminatory attitudes towards them. Muhammad Buchary Kurniata

---

[7] Voluntary Service Overseas (VSO), *A Handbook on Mainstreaming Disability* (London, VSO, 2006) 16 Available at: https://asksource.info/pdf/33903_vsomainstreamingdisability_2006.pdf.

[8] M Syafi'ie, Purwanti and M Ali, *Potret Difabel Berhadapan Dengan Hukum Negara (Portrait of Diffabled within National Law)* (Sleman, Sasana Integrasi dan Advokasi Difabel (SIGAB), 2014) 11.

[9] CR Ramadhan et al, *Analisis Konsistensi Putusan Difabel (Consistency Analysis of Diffabled Judicial Decisions)* (Depok, MaPPI-FHUI, 2016) 11.

[10] Suharto, 'Community-based Empowerment for Advocating Diffability Rights' (2011) 13 *DevISSues* 12.

[11] K Sullivan, 'The Prevalence of the Medical Model of Disability in Society' (2011) AHS Capstone Projects Paper 13, 2.

[12] UNDP (2004) *Executive Summary Access to Justice (Practice Note)*, 4.

[13] Syafi'ie, Purwanti and Ali, *Potret Difabel Berhadapan* (2014) 20.

Tampubolon (Kurniata), the Chief of Wonosari District Court, suggests that most law officers lack understanding about the diversity of diffabled people.[14] Kurniata believes the mindset of judges is insufficiently attuned to diffability issues; instead they apply the same mindset as for non-diffabled people. For example, in sexual violence cases, a judge will usually ask 'Why didn't you fight back?' or 'Why didn't you run away or scream?' A diffabled person, who may not be able to speak or walk, is therefore unable to run away, scream or fight back. Thus, the basic problem is that judges' lack the capacity to understand a diffabled person's perspective. Moreover, Indonesian legal policy lacks measures to compensate for the powerlessness of diffabled people, so many judges consider powerlessness as weakness in the face of aggression.

This chapter focuses on the experiences of diffabled people in Yogyakarta, a province in Indonesia in which the local civil society actively encourages and assists officials to implement the social model of disability in the Indonesian criminal justice system. The chapter incorporates the results of a study that used in-depth qualitative interviews to explore and understand how diffabled people perceive accessibility, especially in relation to their needs and rights within the Indonesian criminal justice system. A beneficial characteristic of qualitative research is the opportunity it presents for direct information and observation.[15] The research gathered information about the experiences of Indonesian civil society organisations (CSOs), legal officers and other experts in Yogyakarta. It focused on the real needs of participants and the obstacles that they experienced first-hand after Law 8/2016 was enacted.

In this chapter I discuss the social model approach for diffabled people, the barriers they face in the criminal justice process, the Indonesian criminal justice system and how CSOs are essential for the implementation of the social model in Yogyakarta.

THE MEDICAL AND SOCIAL MODELS OF DISABILITY

According to Kathryn Sullivan,[16] models of disability are conceptual frameworks for understanding diffability issues that can provide evidence of how diffabled people are viewed in society. There are two common models of disability – the medical model and the social model[17] – which provide different perspectives on and approaches to understanding diffabled people.

In the late nineteenth and early twentieth centuries, the medical model, which emphasizes the health condition of diffabled people, dominated views

---

[14] DA Wicaksana, interview with Kurniata (Yogyakarta, 13 July 2017).
[15] JW Creswell, *Research Design: Qualitative, Quantitative and Mixed Methods Approaches* (Thousand Oaks CA, SAGE Publishing, 2014).
[16] Sullivan, *The Prevalence of the Medical Model of Disability in Society* (2011).
[17] Ibid, 1.

of diffability.[18] (This model, also known as the individual model, identifies the underlying cause of the problems as the individual's medical condition or impairment.) In the medical model, society is not understood as having a responsibility to accept diffabled people: they are considered 'unhealthy' and should 'recover', through treatment or/and rehabilitation, so they can exist and participate in society. The medical model assumes that diffabled people's 'impaired' bodies and mental states are evidence of incapacity. Diffabled people generally reject this idea. They argue that this model leads to low self-esteem, undeveloped life skills, poor education and high unemployment levels.[19]

The social model was influenced by the Fundamental Principles of Disability developed by the Union of the Physically Impaired against Segregation. Under this model, diffabled people can make independent decisions about their own lives.[20] This approach focuses on removing disabling barriers and takes a human rights perspective that asserts that society is responsible for diffabled people's limited accessibility. Critics of the social model assert that it ignores the reality of impairment and the fact that there are some conditions for which diffabled people need medical treatment. However, it could be argued that the social model rejects the medicalisation of diffabled people, not medical intervention.[21] Medical personnel play a major role in determining the medical elements of the various disability standards[22] and should have primary responsibility for identifying and responding to the medical issues of diffabled persons.

Indonesia's Law 8/2016 is a new legal framework which blends aspects of the medical and social model of disabled people. The purpose of this law is to enable diffabled people to live independently, access all public facilities and be protected from discrimination. One of the sectors specifically regulated in Law 8/2016 is access to justice in law, including in the criminal justice sector.

THE BARRIERS FACING DIFFABLED PEOPLE IN THE INDONESIAN CRIMINAL JUSTICE SYSTEM

Diffabled people face accessibility barriers in relation to the legal system, just as they face accessibility barriers in other areas of their lives. Research has identified numerous barriers for diffabled people in the Indonesian criminal justice system.

---

[18] J Midgley, *The Handbook of Social Policy* (Thousand Oaks CA, SAGE Publishing, 2000), 2.
[19] D Crabtree, 'Models of Disability' (2013). Available at: www.englishagenda.britishcouncil.org/sites/default/files/attachments/models_of_disability.pdf.
[20] B Albert, 'The Social Model of Disability, Human Rights and Development' (2004), Disability KaR Research Project pdfs. Available at: semanticscholar.org/3ada/f481faab930f323658fd447e9a0ef71d0b68.pdf.
[21] Ibid, 5.
[22] FS Bloch, *Disability Determination: The Administrative Process and the Role of the Medical Professional* (London CT, Greenwood Press, 1992) 113.

These can be summarised as: physical facilitation, non-physical facilitation, the attitudes of law officers, procedural law and the effect of shame and stigma.

Physical and Non-Physical Facilitation

Physical facilitation encompasses the availability of ramps, guiding blocks, braille and video-audio resources. Non-physical facilitation encompasses the availability and accessibility of services such as translators, expert assistance and legal aid.

The Attitudes of Law Officers

Eko Riyadi identifies as barriers the knowledge and attitudes of law officers,[23] including those who handle investigation processes. As noted earlier, Kurniata suggests that most law officers lack understanding about the diversity of diffabled people.[24] In order to identify the barriers facing diffabled people, researchers analysed 22 Indonesian judicial decisions during 2011–15 which involved diffabled people as the victims in cases of sexual violence.[25] They found no information that guardians were involved during the trial process in 68 per cent of cases and, in 41 per cent of cases, the victims had no legal aid.

Most law officers in Indonesia think that diffabled people are better off being pitied and feared by society. Thus, their approach tends to exaggerate giving any help to them.[26]

Indonesian legal policy does not require that people participating in the criminal justice system should be assessed for diffability. Researchers suggest that many Indonesian policymakers assume that everyone is 'normal' with respect to their physical or intellectual condition.[27] Profile assessments would identify the needs and barriers for diffabled people, enabling law officers to create strategies to meet their needs.

Indonesian Criminal Procedure

Purwanti,[28] who provides legal assistance to diffabled people, sees a problem of substance in Indonesian criminal procedural law. She argues that law

---

[23] DA Wicaksana, interview with Eko Riyadi, Director of the Center for the Study of Human Rights at Indonesia Islamic University (Pusham UII) (Yogyakarta, 11 July 2017).

[24] DA Wicaksana, interview with Kurniata (Yogyakarta, 13 July 2017).

[25] CR Ramadhan et al, *Consistency Analysis of Diffabled Judicial Decisions* (2016).

[26] Eko Riyadi et al, *Aksesibilitas Peradilan bagi Penyandang Disabilitas (Judicial Accessibility for Diffabled People)* (Yogyakarta, Pusham UII, 2015) 96.

[27] Ibid, 111.

[28] DA Wicaksana, interview with Purwanti, Indonesian diffabled activist, SIGAB (Yogyakarta, 11 July 2017).

discriminates against diffabled people by not recognising their testimony as equal to that of others. Basically, there is an assumption that diffabled people are too confused to give testimony during criminal cases. Moreover, Purwanti argues that law officers actually misunderstand Indonesian criminal procedure law. The law states that a witness is a person who sees, hears and/or experiences the alleged crime that is the subject of the case; it does not suggest that diffabled people have reduced capacity to act as witnesses.[29] Nevertheless, in Indonesian law, mentally diffabled people are not usually recognised as having capacity. Accordingly, all the decisions which concern diffabled people are decided by their parents or guardians, even if the diffabled person has a different view.[30]

Law 8/2016 is limited by Indonesian Criminal Procedure Law (KUHAP),[31] which has no specific provisions regarding diffability. Law 8/2016 regulates the facilitation and protection for diffabled people, but not how the Indonesian law officers sentence offenders. Thus, the individual perspective of law officers remains paramount when they are handling diffabled people.

Shame and Stigma

Purwanti states that, when sexual violence has occurred, most diffabled people do not wish to disclose their situation and what has happened to them, due to shame they feel for themselves and their families. As Kurniata Tampubolon[32] explained, mentally diffabled people who are victims of sexual violence think the offender is not criminally liable and instead blame themselves. Therefore, some judges will be confused about how to deliver justice and sentence appropriately.

Purwanti also mentions that most diffabled people, especially those from poor families, have complicated psychological and social problems. They face difficulties in accessing information and communicating with their peers. Despite Law 8/2016 seeking to improve access to justice for diffabled people, it is not to the same standard as that enjoyed by 'able-bodied' people.[33]

THE ROLE OF CIVIL SOCIETY ORGANISATIONS IN IMPROVING ACCESS FOR DIFFABLED PEOPLE

Civil society encompasses actors and entities with a wide range of goals, structures, membership and geographical coverage. They include non-government organisations (NGOs), professional associations, charitable organisations,

---

[29] Indonesia, *Act Number 8/1981 regards Criminal Procedure Law Code* (KUHAP), Art 1 Point (26).
[30] DA Wicaksana, interview with Purwanti (Yogyakarta, 11 July 2017).
[31] Indonesia, *Act Number 8/1981 regards Criminal Procedure Law Code* (KUHAP).
[32] DA Wicaksana, interview with Kurniata (Yogyakarta, 13 July 2017).
[33] DA Wicaksana, interview with Purwanti (Yogyakarta, 11 July 2017).

indigenous groups, faith communities, labour unions and labour organisations, grassroots associations, as well as foundations.[34] In Indonesia, CSOs who focus on diffability issues include international and national NGOs and disabled persons' organisations (DPOs). DPOs follow a traditional model of advocacy, including making submissions about national disability strategy and are vulnerable to cooption by government officials.[35]

In Yogyakarta, local CSOs are seeking to use their influence to promote the implementation of the social model of disability in legal institutions. These include SIGAB, Pusham UII, Sentra Advokasi Perempuan Difabel dan Anak (SAPDA) and Rifka Annisa. However, Yogyakarta's CSOs have a specific role in policymaking and implementation, because formal institutions rarely take action to reform policy and increase the awareness of its officers. Eko Riyadi (2016), the director of Pusham UII, initiated discussions with Yogyakarta's legal institutions aimed at improving accessibility for diffabled people. This included a meeting with Kurniata, the chief of Wonosari District Court; it was reported that he was receptive to the idea.[36] They agreed to provide training in diffability issues to the judges in the Wonosari district court.[37]

Lack of knowledge about and capacity to deal with diffabled people is a serious problem, compounded by the inadequacy of the facilities of the Yogyakarta district court. During his meeting with Eko Riyadi, Kurniata acknowledged that court buildings are inaccessible for diffabled people;[38] they have no ramps, handrails, guiding blocks, special toilets or braille signage. However, Kurniata said that he had no authority to modify the building as this was under the control of the Supreme Court. Mr Eko, therefore, invited Kurniata and the leaders of the Supreme Court to participate in a focus group discussion about developing a curriculum training module regarding fair trials for diffabled people. During the discussion (in September 2016), Kurniata had a positive interaction with diffabled people, another district court judge, and several Supreme Court judges.[39]

This meeting was successful in improving Kurniata's perspective: he realised the level of commitment of the DPOs to this issue and its importance for diffabled people. In a follow-up meeting, Kurniata stated that he would work to improve accessibility for diffabled people in the Wonosari District Court. He also agreed to create a memorandum of understanding between the Court and Pusham UII, noting that the latter would provide advice regarding alterations to the structure of the building and work with the SIGAB and Center of Interpreter

---

[34] Ibid, 7.

[35] S Meyers, V Karr and V Pineda, 'Youth with Disabilities in Law and Civil Society: Exclusion and Inclusion in Public Policy and NGO Networks in Cambodia and Indonesia' (2014) 1(1) *Disability and the Global South* 5–28. Available at: www.dgsjournal.org/volume-1-number-1/.

[36] DA Wicaksana, interview with Eko Riyadi, Director of Pusham UII (Yogyakarta, 11 July 2017).

[37] Ibid.

[38] Ibid.

[39] Ibid.

Service (PLJ) to create and implement a sign language video and provide information in braille at the court's information desk.[40]

Civil society organisations are not only involved in policy making but also offer paralegal/legal assistance for diffabled people before and during criminal procedures, including finding lawyers, translators and medical experts and collecting evidence. In one case, Purwanti's organisation convinced judges to take the mental diffability of their client into consideration during sentencing.[41]

Another activist, Rini Rindawati,[42] spoke about her organisation's focus on giving legal assistance to diffabled women in the criminal process. She said the Yogyakarta police had given her office space so she could help to find translators and teachers for diffabled women, sometimes working in collaboration with the prosecutor. Rini argued that DPOs and other CSOs should strive to reconstruct the attitudes of law officers and improve their understanding of the barriers and needs of diffabled persons, rather than simply undertaking dialogue and discussion with legal institutions.[43]

CONCLUSION

In this chapter I have argued that diffabled people can be considered a minority group who have struggled for recognition of their equal rights. Diffabled activists reject medical intervention as the main approach to diffabled people within Indonesian legal policy, believing that this approach generates stereotypes of diffabled people as weak and incapable of participating equally in society. Therefore, activists promote the social model as the normative legal context for dealing with diffability issues. In response, the Indonesian Government reconstructed the terms of impairment for disability in Law 8/2016, enacted in early 2016. This was based on the substance of the CRPD, which the Indonesian Government ratified in 2011.

Despite this promising development, the main problems for diffabled people's in their interactions with the legal system relate to the content of law, the procedure of criminal process, accessibility, and the attitudes of law officers. Purwanti believed there has been no significant transformation since early 2016. Law 8/2016 is very new, but cultural perspectives on diffability have been institutionalised for many decades. More time is needed to implement this law; the Indonesian government should incorporate it into internal regulations within legal institutions. This would enable legal institutions to allocate budget, staff and programmes in accordance with the purpose of Law 8/2016.

[40] Ibid.
[41] Ibid.
[42] Rini Rindawati is a diffabled activist working for SAPDA, an Indonesian DPO based in Yogyakarta.
[43] DA Wicaksana, interview with Rini Rindawati, an activist working with SAPDA (Yogyakarta, 14 July 2017).

I mentioned the preliminary success of Yogyakarta's CSOs in establishing a human rights perspective and the social model in Yogyakarta's legal institutions. The interesting point is that this improvement and reform had to be initiated by CSOs; formal legal policy, such as the CRPD and Law 8/2016, does not, in itself, change the bureaucratic culture of legal institutions. However, local CSOs use the formal policy to apply pressure or provide assistance to legal institutions so they can improve facilitation and public service.

The success of the Yogyakarta CSOs has important lessons for implementing national policy at the local level. Dialogue is needed to share ideas; dialogue between Pusham UII and Kurniata increased his awareness of diffability issues and he began to understand the importance of equal interaction and accessibility for everyone. Rini Rindawati's experiences also show that increasing the understanding of law officers has a positive impact. However, the challenge is to continue to improve knowledge about diffability issues. In Indonesian legal institutions, law officers are usually promoted or move to another district after a few years, so local CSOs must continuously identify and 'train' new champions within judicial institutions. However, this initiative should be supported by the formal institutions. Local knowledge should be used to train judges in all provinces and areas. Therefore, the advance of progressive ideas about diffability issues will not depend on a few champions in the judicial institutions.

The next challenge for CSOs is to expand the diffability discourse to the national level, Although, Yogyakarta CSOs are fundamental for improving policy at the local level, central government support is still vital in the highly centralised bureaucracy of the Indonesian government.

Finally, I recommend that the Indonesian Government engage with DPOs to implement the social model approach and collaboratively evaluate the implementation of Law 8/2016. Sound evidence is the best basis for the development of more effective policy for implementing the social model of disability in the Indonesian criminal justice system.

Index

CPSIA information can be obtained
at www.ICGtesting.com
Printed in the USA
LVHW030224030523
745978LV00008B/164